THE BUDDHA NATURE

BUDDHIST TRADITION SERIES

VOLUME 11

THE BUDDHA NATURE

A study of the
Tathāgatagarbha and Ālayavijñāna

BRIAN EDWARD BROWN

MOTILAL BANARSIDASS PUBLISHERS
PRIVATE LIMITED • DELHI

Reprint : Delhi, 1994, 2004, 2010
First Edition: Delhi, 1991

ISBN: 978-81-208-0631-3

MOTILAL BANARSIDASS
41 U.A. Bungalow Road, Jawahar Nagar, Delhi 110 007
8 Mahalaxmi Chamber, 22 Bhulabhai Desai Road, Mumbai 400 026
203 Royapettah High Road, Mylapore, Chennai 600 004
236, 9th Main III Block, Jayanagar, Bangalore 560 011
Sanas Plaza, 1302 Baji Rao Road, Pune 411 002
8 Camac Street, Kolkata 700 017
Ashok Rajpath, Patna 800 004
Chowk, Varanasi 221 001

PRINTED IN INDIA

By Jainendra Prakash Jain at Shri Jainendra Press,
A-45 Naraina, Phase-I, New Delhi 110 028
and published by Narendra Prakash Jain for
Motilal Banarsidass Publishers Private Limited,
Bungalow Road, Delhi 110 007

FOREWORD

Brian Brown's treatise is a thematic-interpretative study of the textual sources of the *ālayavijñāna* and *tathāgatagarbha* doctrines of Mahāyāna Buddhism. He applies accute reasoning in ontological and experiential terms to certain prominent works in these special Buddhist topics. Among such works as have appeared in western translation and research are mainly the *Śrī-Mālādevīsiṃhanāda-sūtra*, *Ratnagotravibhāga* and *Laṅkā-vatāra-sūtra*. It is a credit to these particular Buddhist works that such a philosophical and semantic analysis is feasible. The author is correct in claiming that his work is the first to attempt this ambitious intellectual task. Brown appears to avoid the arbitrary use of western terminology. He proceeds with utmost carefulness and sensitivity with a remarkable consistency of approach.

Alex Wayman

To

my loving wife
AMARILYS

and

my esteemed teacher
THOMAS BERRY

CONTENTS

PART ONE

THE *TATHĀGATAGARBHA* IN THE *ŚRĪ-MĀLĀ SŪTRA* AND THE *RATNAGOTRAVIBHĀGA*

PART TWO

THE *ĀLAYAVIJÑĀNA* IN THE *LAṄKĀVATĀRA SŪTRA* AND THE *CH'ENG WEI-SHIH LUN*

Contents

PART THREE

[illegible] SUMMARY AND COMPARISON

INTRODUCTION

One of the fundamental tenets of Mahāyāna Buddhism, animating and grounding the doctrine and discipline of its spiritual path, is the inherent potentiality of all animate beings to attain the supreme and perfect enlightenment of Buddhahood. This book examines the ontological presuppositions and the corresponding soteriological—epistemological principles that sustain and define such a theory. Within the field of Buddhist studies such a work provides a comprehensive context in which to interpret the influence and major insights of the various Buddhist schools. Thus, the dynamics of the Buddha Nature, though non-thematic and implicit, is at the heart of Zen praxis, while it is a significant articulation in Kegon, Tendai, and Shingon thought. More specifically, the study seeks to establish a coherent metaphysic of Absolute Suchness (*Tathatā*), synthesizing the variant traditions of the Tathāgata-embryo (*Tathāgatagarbha*) and the Storehouse Consciousness (*Ālayavijñāna*).

The study's contribution to the broader field of the History of Religions rests in its presentation and analysis of the Buddhist enlightenment as the salvific-transformational moment in which *Tathatā* "awakens" to itself, comes to perfect self-realization as the Absolute Suchness of reality, in and through phenomenal human consciousness. It is an interpretation of the Buddhist Path as the spontaneous self-emergence of "embryonic" absolute knowledge as it comes to free itself from the concealments of adventitious defilements, and possess itself in fully self-explicated self-consciousness as the "Highest Truth" and unconditional nature of all existence; it does so only in the form of omniscient wisdom.

Aside from Ruegg's *La Théorie du Tathāgatagarbha et du Gotra*,[1] and Verdu's study of the *Ālayavijñāna* in *Dialectical Aspects in Buddhist Thought*,[2] Western scholarship treating of the subject is

1. David Seyfort Ruegg, *La Théorie du Tathāgatagarbha et du Gotra: Etudes sur la Sotériologie et la Gnoséologie du Buddhisme*, Publications de l'Ecole Francaise d' Extreme-Orient, vol. 70 (Paris: École Francaise d' Extreme-Orient, 1969).

2. Alfonso Verdu, *Dialectical Aspects in Buddhist Thought: Studies in Sino-Japanese Mahāyāna Idealism*, International Studies, East Asian Series, no. 8 (n.p.: Center For East Asian Studies, the University of Kansas, 1974).

negligible. And while both sources are excellent technical treatises, they fail to integrate in any detailed analysis the dual concepts as complementary modes of each other. Thus, the present work, while adopting the methodology of textual analysis, has as its emphasis a thematic-interpretative study of its sources.

Structurally, the work is divided into three major parts. The first part focuses on the *Tathāgatagarbha*, the second on the *Ālayavijñāna*, the third on their relation and deeper significance in the human thought tradition. The first two parts are sub-divided into seven and four chapters respectively. The former seven chapters establish the ontological identity of the Tathāgata-embryo (*Tathāgatagarbha*) through a critical examination of the major sūtral authority for the concept, i.e., the *Śrī-Mālā-Sūtra*, and the primary śāstral elaboration inspired by it, viz., the *Ratnagotra-vibhāga.*

Following the same pattern, the four chapters of part two note the role of the *Laṅkāvatāra Sūtra* as a principal scriptural advocate for the theory of the Storehouse Consciousness (*Ālayavijñāna*), while detailing the scholastic amplification of it in Hsüan Tsang's *Ch'eng Wei-Shih Lun*. Part three concludes the study by recapitulating the principal developments in the emergent complementarity of the two concepts, arguing that any adequate discussion of the Buddha Nature must be informed on the one hand by the theory of the *Tathāgatagarbha* which grounds and authenticates its ontological status, and on the other by the *Ālayavijñāna*, its noetic-cognitive determination. While the former tends to elucidate the process towards, and experience of enlightenment as a function of Absolute Suchness (*Tathatā*), the latter adopts the reciprocal perspective and examines the subject in the light and function of phenomenal consciousness. By way of comparison with Western thought, the chapter demonstrates the analogous dynamics in the bilateral theory of the *Tathāgatagarbha-Ālayavijñāna* and the Hegelian Absolute Spirit in-and-for-itself. Focusing upon *The Phenomenology of Spirit*, the chapter notes that the self-becoming process in and through which consciousness realizes its own plenitude, is strikingly homologous to the theory of Buddhist enlightenment presented through the concept of the *Tathāgatagarbha-Ālayavijñāna*. It suggests that these two representative thought systems mutually illumine each other, and together illustrate a correspondent framework within which the relationship of the Absolute and relative may gain a more universal conception and, therefore, a more comprehensive resolution. A more specific précis of each chapter is now made.

Part One

Chapter 2 conducts a detailed analysis into the structure of the *Śrī-Mālā Sūtra*, regarded as the primary scriptural advocate in India for the doctrine of a universal potentiality of Buddhahood. Its purpose is to delineate the ontological, soteriological, and epistemological foci assumed in its presentation of the Tathāgata-embryo (*Tathāgatagarbha*). Since the presupposition of the sūtra is the identity of the embryo with the Absolute Body (*Dharma-kāya*), the chapter relates its tripartite focus to an elucidation of that identity. To begin with, the ontological status of the embryo as the ground of *saṃsāra* and *nirvāṇa* is set forth, and a distinction between ontic substance and ontic subject is discussed. The chapter argues that the latter is the more exact definition of the Tathāgata-embryo in its processive advance to realize itself perfectly as Absolute Body. Because it is the necessary emergence of itself to itself, its movement from potential to actual Tathāgatahood, the embryo is then identified as the fundamental soteriological principle upon which the concept of the one vehicle (*ekayāna*) is founded. Its subsequent identification as the Great Vehicle (*Mahāyāna*) and Buddha Vehicle (*Buddhayāna*) is evaluated in the light of the various stages of the spiritual path belonging to the Arhat, Pratyekabuddha, and Bodhisattva. The main question to be answered concerns the relationship between an original, a priori enlightenment and the reality of the numerous stages towards its explicit realization. The reconciliation of the problem is advanced in the chapter's interpretation of the embryo as both end and means to its attainment.

The *Śrī-Mālā*'s epistemological critique of the Arhats and Pratyekabuddhas as attaining only a "fractional *nirvāṇa*" requires an examination of the "nescience entrenchment" as the fundamental nexus of ignorance and the ground of all defilements. It is presented as the main obstruction to the complete self-knowledge of the embryo as the Absolute Body. In this framework, the controversial role of the Buddha natures (*Buddhadharmas*) inherent to the embryo as modalities of wisdom and knowledge is discussed. Under the principle of self-liberation as self-explication, the chapter argues that they are both the cause and the effect in the removal of the nescience entrenchment. A similar critique of the ordinary persons, Disciples, Self-Enlightened Ones, and novice Bodhisattvas reveals the explanation of the four Noble Truths as the precise exponent of the Tathāgata-embryo (*Tathāgatagarbha*). The knowledge which perfects their meaning, penetrating to the source of all suffering and removing ignorance at its root, is the knowledge of the *Tathāgatagarbha* as empty (*śūnya*) of the adventitious defilements and not empty (*aśūnya*) of the innumerable Buddha natures intrinsic to it; such "inconceivable voidness knowledge", when perfected, signals the attainment of the Absolute Body.

The critical interpretative argument of the chapter is advanced at this point. The *Tathāgatagarbha* is not to be understood as the object of a knowledge external to it, existing formally and formerly outside it; it is rather, self-explicating knowledge itself. The embryo as realized Absolute Body is simultaneously comprehended and comprehending; it is the point where the embryo knows itself as it is inherently in itself, as empty (*śūnya*) of all the defilement stores, but not empty (*aśūnya*) of the innumerable Buddha natures. If it is originally understood as an object of faith, and therefore an object of consciousness, the *Tathāgatagarbha* must ultimately be considered as the movement towards its perfect self-realization and thus, as object of self-consciousness.

The chapter concludes by suggesting that the relationship between the *Tathāgatagarbha* and the *Dharmakāya* is that of a cycle that presupposes its beginning and reaches its beginning only at its end. If the Tathāgata-embryo is the beginning or cause, then the Absolute Body is essentially the result, the end where the Tathāgata-embryo becomes what it is in truth. The nature of the embryo is to be actual, that which becomes itself. For if it starts with itself, the *Tathāgatagarbha* reaches its consummation with itself as the Absolute Body (*Dharmakāya*) and in fact, the *Dharmakāya* is the *Tathāgatagarbha* when it has not yet freed itself from the adventitious defilements, i.e., when it has not yet attained full self-conscious awareness as being intrinsically and always free of them. The cyclic transformation then of the *Tathāgatagarbha* into the *Dharmakāya* is that of an original absolute becoming fully self-expressive, where the only transition is in the sphere of self-exposition from hiddenness to manifestation.

Chapters 3 to 8 offer a detailed exposition of the *Ratnagotravibhāga*, the major śāstral elaboration of the *Tathāgatagarbha* which synthesized the significant scriptural development of the idea, prior and subsequent to the *Śrī-Mālā*. Chapter 3 details that textual information and introduces the context within which the *Ratnagotra* amplifies the concept. While the *Śrī-Mālā* generally emphasized the *garbha* as process, the self-evolutive potentiality of the embryo to become itself as *Dharmakāya*, the śāstra discusses the identity of those two poles as ontological antecedent, i.e., though linguistically different *Tathāgatagarbha* and *Dharmakāya* are identical. The two terms simply reflect different modalities of Absolute Suchness (*Tathatā*). *Samalā Tathatā* represents Absolute Suchness under conditions of phenomenal defilement, and is thus synonymous with the *Tathāgatagarbha*, while *Nirmalā Tathatā* designates its actual freedom from all concealment, and is equivalent to the *Dharmakāya*. Through the threefold hermeneutic of *Dharmakāya* as universal penetration of wisdom, of *Tathatā* as the inherent purity of phenomena, and of *Gotra* as the germinal essence of Buddhahood, the chapter analyzes the axiom that "all living beings are possessed of the *Tathāgatagarbha*", i.e., are capable of attaining the omniscient wisdom of supreme enlightenment. While all three terms are the *Ratnagotra's* critical, simultaneous determinations of the *Tathāgatagarbha*, the chapter pays particular attention to the connotation of *gotra* in its technical role as soteriological principle within the variant traditions of the *Mādhyamika* and the *Vijñānavāda*.

Chapters 4 and 5 evaluate the tenfold characteristics through which the *Ratnagotra* articulates the *Tathāgatagarbha*. Its nature (*svabhāva*) as absolute purity as well as the cause (*hetu*) and result (*phala*) of its purification from the adventitious defilements receives the specific attention of chapter 4. Of central concern is the vindication of the *Tathāgatagarbha* theory and its attribution of supreme purity, unity, bliss, and eternity to the *Dharmakāya* against charges of advocating a hypostatic and substantial absolute, and of thus violating the fundamental Buddhist tenet of non-substantiality or emptiness (*Śūnyatā*). The chapter defends the *Ratnagotra's* use of those four attributes by stressing their pedagogical value as antidotes against delusive thinking. It discusses them within the context of the classical fourfold delusion (*viparyāsa*) which posits eternity, bliss, purity, and egohood to conditional phenomena. The necessary corrective is to see them as they are, viz., non-eternal, full of sufferings, of no substantial ego, and impure. However, this very inversion would itself be delusive and perverse if it were taken as unconditional and erroneously attributed to the Absolute Body of the *Tathāgata*, the *Dharmakāya*. Remedially applying its antidotal dialectic to such a mistaken notion, the *Ratnagotra* establishes the supreme eternity, bliss, unity, and purity of the *Dharmakāya*. The chapter relates the *Ratnagotra's* methodology to Nāgārjuna's validation of remedial statements as one of the four *siddhāntas*. In addition to that demonstrated similarity of method, it is shown that the *Ratnagotra* fully subscribes to the doctrine of *Śūnyatā* as the superior truth of a universal non-substantiality, the antidote counteracting the heretical stance of independent, self-subsistent individuals and entities.

Its basic orthodoxy emerges more clearly through the chapter's analysis of *ātma-pāramitā* as supreme unity, in which the *Ratnagotra* expressly opposes the heretical perception of multiple, independent, self-supsistent ego-natures. The apparent self-contradiction of non-substantiality (*Śūnyatā*) as the perfection of self (*ātma-pāramitā*) is related to the paradoxical inversions of the *Prajñāpāramitā* literature, as well as to specific references from the Vijñānavādin tradition. It is concluded that the śāstra's *ātma-pāramitā* as self-reference is nothing other than a reference to the real self, the real nature of one's being as universally co-relational, neither exclusive of other selves nor as anything ultimate and absolute in its empirical mundane reality. As the truth of non-substantiality (*Śūnyatā*), this perfection of self-clings neither to the specific individual, body-mind complex, nor to the idea that this determinate and conditional entity is absolutely so, i.e., unconditionally conditioned, and therefore cut off from the ultimate reality, the pure and absolute Suchness (*Tathatā*). On the one hand, it respects the concept of the ordinary empirical self which may be meaningfully (because non-clingingly) employed as that through which one works for the good and welfare of all sentient beings, because on the other hand, it knows the universal inclusiveness of just those beings in the truth of absolute non-substantiality. The *Ratna's* assertion of the supreme self as the highest unity derives from its intuition of the pure, non-dual essential nature of absolute Suchness (*Tathatā*) in all animate beings. And it is this Reality, conceived as the undifferentiated whole, that is the text's more accustomed expression for the truth of non-substantiality (*Śūnyatā*) as the universal selfhood of all beings.

Chapter 5 studies the remaining characteristics of the *Tathāgatagarbha*: its manifestation (*vṛtti*) in the three classes of beings (ordinary persons, saints and Buddhas); the different degrees of its apparent purity (*avasthāprabheda*); its universally pervasive presence within all beings (*sarvatraga*); its unchangeability (*avikāra*); and the non-differentiation (*asambheda*) of Buddhahood and *Nirvāṇa*. Attention is directed to the *Ratnagotra's* polemical insistence against the theory of the *Icchantikas* as those beings who are forever incapable of rejecting impurity and producing the proper remedies. That the *Icchantikas* are those who belong to the lineage of never attaining the perfect *nirvāṇa*, is a mere conventional expression. While it may be used to indicate the conditional period when a being may suffer from a delusive repulsion to the doctrine of the *Mahāyāna*, there will come a time when he is not so afflicted, and will be open to attain the ultimate self-purification, by nature of his endowment with the germinal essence of Buddhahood, i.e., the *Tathāgatagarbha*.

Under further analysis, the critical interpretation of Suchness (*Tathatā*) as ontic subjectivity is clearly reiterated by the śāstra's repeated use of the term *gotra* which defines *Tathatā* as self-emergent absolute wisdom, universally present in animate reality. In and through all beings, *Tathatā* arrives at varying degrees of self-witnessing self-possession; it does so as "the immaculate nature of the mind" (*Cittaprakṛti*). The chapter analyses the latter as the epistemic-noetic determination of *Tathāgatagarbha* and demonstrates its significance for an adequate resolution to the problem of ignorance and its defilements.

It is argued that *avidyā*, in its ultimate nautre, is not different from the immaculate nature of the mind. Ignorance is not any substantial entity, any ultimate element, but, as "the irrational action of mind", is itself dependent upon *Cittaprakṛti;* the latter is the condition for the possibility of the former which, while it may be manifested as an unwise discrimination or wrong conception, cannot take place without that fundamental substratum. If defilements exist, they do so as deluded modes of consciousness, assuming their appearance as forms (no matter how distorted) of one elemental reality, the innately pure mind.

The chapter addresses itself to the question of how Absolute Suchness as the undifferentiated universal reality, the unilateral "immaculateness" in all beings, can undergo a process which is said to perfect it; how can that which is unalterable as Reality without any specific character or nature, be subject to a transformation implying its imperfection? As demonstrated by the entire structure of the *Ratnagotra*, *Tathatā* moves from a condition of non-manifestation, where it is concealed by defilements, to total revelation of its innate purity. The process is one of conscious self-explication. Initially mistaken as ontic substance, *Tathatā* is quickly identified as the inherent movement of self-realization and thus, as ontic subjectivity. This takes place through and in the phenomenal consciousness of sentient beings where various stages along the spiritual path are interpreted as the germinal advance of *Tathatā* toward final and complete self-revelation. And it is in the person of the Buddha that Suchness, overcoming all duality "has come" (*Tathāgata*) to possess itself in total self-awareness; if it "has been perfected", it is through the self-maturation in consciousness of what it always is. As embryonic (the *garbha*), Suchness is essentially replete with the factors of its own purification, its own self-unfoldment. In its movement from implicit to explicit fullness nothing is super-added upon "*Tathatā* which, as reality in-itself, necessarily moves toward its own self-possession, i.e., as reality in-and-for-itself.

Chapter 6 examines the graphic illustrations found in the *Tathāgatagarbha Sūtra* which depict the concomitance of the adventitious defilements and the essentially pure innate mind. These nine symbolic representations complement and dramatize the formal philosophical orientation of the *Ratnagotra's* text. This brief iconographical study supports the interpretation of *garbha* as "embryo" and introduces the śāstra's final remarks on the threefold nature of the *Tathāgatagarbha* as *Dharmakāya*, *Tathatā*, and *Gotra*. That all animate beings are possessed of the *Tathāgatagarbha* testifies on the one hand to the universal extension of the Absolute Body of the Buddha, comprehensively pervading sentient reality as elemental omniscient wisdom. Next, it is explained that since *Tathāgata* is an alternate designation for *Tathatā* which is the unconditioned essence of phenomenal existence, *Tathatā* is the embryo (*garbha*) of all sentient beings, understood as their inner essence. Any distinction between *Tathāgata* and *Tathāgatagarbha* is said to be only apparent. The first represents *Tathatā* when it has perfected its purification, while the second is still *Tathatā*, only as yet hidden by the defilement-covering; *Tathāgata* and *Tathāgatagarbha* both signify Absolute Suchness in its respective conditions as *nirmalā* (undefiled) and *samalā* (defiled). As the final term of the threefold nature, *gotra* represents the immanent, processive movement of the Absolute toward the perfect realization of itself as the unconditioned Suchness of reality. As such, it is the unqualified assurance and validation of a universally attainable supreme enlightenment for all classes of sentient beings.

Chapter 7 evaluates the *Ratnagotra's* crucial axiom that the *Tathāgatagarbha* represents the true conception of non-substantiality (*Śūnyatā*) and its associated claim that the *Prajñāpāramitā* literature is an earlier, and thus incomplete codex of Buddhist teaching; the *Ratnagotra* reserves for itself alone, the title of "the ultimate doctrine" (*uttaratantra*).

The śāstra first reviews the various positions of the four classes of beings, and concludes that each entertains an erroneous conception of *Śūnyatā* which subsequently hinders their correct understanding of the *Tathāgatagarbha*. Those who maintain the existence of independent, self-subsistent individualities; those who conceive of *Śūnyatā* as the dependent and conditional nature of phenomena, while failing to perceive it as the unconditional, indeterminate and undivided real nature of the same phenomena; those who cling to *Śūnyatā* as the perfect *nirvāṇa*, misapprehending it as absolutely transcendent and separate from the realm of conditioned phenomena, thinking to "attain it" by a nihilistic disavowal of mundane reality; and those who similarly regard *Śūnyatā* as an eternal absolute, existing over against and opposed to the *skandhas* and the entire conditioned world that is coextensive with them; all are condemned by the *Ratnagotra.* Challenging all such errors of misplaced absoluteness, it implicity represents *Śūnyatā* as the authentic middle path. It refutes the tendency to seize the relative and determinate as ultimate and unconditioned, equally countering the alternate assertion as to the absolute relativity of all specific, particular entities. It rebukes the misapprehension that considers the distinction between the determinate and indeterminate as an absolute exclusion, the one from the other. The comprehensive non-duality of *Śūnyatā* is preserved and manifested in the *Ratnagotra's* opposition to an eternalism projected upon phenomena as well as that applied to *Śūnyatā* as an absolute thing-in-itself, or to any nihilistic devaluation of mundane reality in the name of an exclusively independent *Śūnyatā,* or an absolutely unqualified relativity of persons and things.

It is in this context, that the chapter examines the meaning of the formula,

> Here there is nothing to be removed and absolutely nothing to be added; the truth should be perceived as it is, and he who sees the Truth becomes liberated. The Essence of the Buddha is by nature devoid (*śūnya*) of the accidental pollutions which differ from it; but it is by no means devoid (*aśūnya*) of the highest properties which are, essentially, indivisible from it.[1]

Key passages from the *Abhisamayālankāra*, the *Pañcavimśatisāhasrikā* and the *Astasāhasrikā Prajñāpāramitā Sūtras* confirm the *Ratnagotra's* interpretation that as long as one regards any *dharma* (including the defiling passions) as an absolute fact, existing in and of itself, one intensifies the force of ignorance which is engendered precisely by the erroneous belief in the reality of things. In the very attempt to overcome the defilements, falsely conceived under the notion of realism, one aggravates through unconscious reinforcement the deeply rooted ignorance which will continue all

1. Jikido Takasaki, *A Study on the Ratnagotravibhāga* (*Uttaratantra*), Serie Orientale Roma, vol. 33 (Rome: Instituto Italiano per il Medio ed Estremo Oriente, 1966), pp. 300-301.

the more to obstruct the perfect manifestation of omniscient wisdom. Only when one perceives the essential original nature of all things as *svabhāvaśūnya*, as empty of any ultimately separate, particular own-being, can one traverse the path of practice and meditation free from error. Originally unborn and unproduced, no *dharma* can be extinguished; one cannot halt that which, from the beginning, remains essentially non-existent, i.e., as any particular thing-in-itself.

The chapter then proceeds to examine the suggestion that the *Ratnagotra* actually advances a mere relative emptiness (*itaretaraśūnyatā*), insinuating some hypostatic absolute entity, existing in reality as empty of all extrinsic and conditional factors, without however, itself being empty of an essential own-being (*svabhāva*). The chapter argues that such a claim of heterodoxy is tantamount to accusing the śāstra of a major self-contradiction which simply cannot be sustained by the bulk of evidence to the contrary. This is clear from several instances throughout the text where the idea of ultimate reality as an essentially separate reality, completely distinct from phenomena, was flatly rejected; any invidious polarization of *saṃsāra* and *nirvāṇa* had been clearly refuted. Further, the *Ratnagotra* censured all tendencies to view the five *skandhas*, the twelve sense-fields, and the eighteen elements as empty of a self while still persisting as real entities, possessing any number of precisely defined, real attributes. The *Ratnagotra* is thoroughly aware that the analytical factors exposing the relative conditionality of phenomena, can become in their turn, determinations of unconditional reality. It strongly opposed all such delusion.

As further indication that the śāstra repudiates any departures from the comprehensive nature and scope of *Śūnyatā*, which would amount to a relative emptiness, is its definition of the *Tathāgatagarbha* as "the embryo of the Absolute Essence". As such, it is said to be inaccessible to those who in any way, no matter how subtly, maintain the conception of separate individuality. As synonymous with *Tathatā* and *Śūnyatā*, *Dharmadhātu* is shown to represent the indeterminate, incomposite, real nature of all things and, as universal essence, it invalidates all assertions of ultimate distinctions among separate, individual entities. It is concluded that from several different perspectives the *Ratnagotra* resists all views that either neglect entirely or else significantly misapprehend the true intent of *Śūnyatā*. Whether it be the gross materialism of ordinary beings, the unqualified contingency of the Śrāvakas and Pratyekabuddhas, or the eternalistic and nihilistic extremities of novice Bodhisattvas, the śāstra testifies to a non-substantiality which, as revelatory of the universal, dependent correlativity among phenomena, is simultaneously the non-dual, unconditional, essential nature of the same.

But if the *Ratnagotra* is essentially free from any heretical misrepresentation of *Śūnyatā*, it nevertheless presents itself within the Buddhist tradition as the standard critique upon, and legitimate corrective for the abuses of the *Śūnyavāda*. Its claim to supersede the *Mādhyamika* and to style itself as the "treatise on the Ultimate Doctrine of the Great Vehicle" needs investigation. In doing so the chapter points out the strong practical and pastoral orientation, the important psychological and pedagogical significance that animates and inspires the *Ratnagotra's* formal ontology. To ignore the explicit prescriptive intention of its criticism, is to confuse its censure of the detrimental effects of the *Śūnyavāda* for an outright castigation of *Śūnyatā*. Thus said, it examines the śāstra's allegation that the *Śūnyavāda* has five serious defects: its focus on the unreality of the world easily engenders severe depression and despair on the part of the seeker; the resolve toward enlightenment can lead to a subtle pride and assume a judgmental superiority over others; there exists a tendency to cling to unrealities, since the very inferiority of those to whom he feels superior, is in fact, empty; an insistence not only upon the unreality of defects and defilements, but of all virtues as well, which are in fact real and pure by nature; because of that inability to appreciate the reality of their virtues, one never realizes genuine benevolence and compassion by which he regards all other living beings as equal to himself.

In evaluating these criticisms, the chapter reviews the *Prajñāpāramitā* literature, the sources of the Śūnyavādin tradition, and clearly demonstrates that they were themselves aware and addressed themselves to those very dangers which the *Ratnagotra* voiced. Thus, as to the unreality of the world, the perfection of wisdom (*prajñāpāramitā*) does not destroy the existence of anything, but is the very mode by which one investigates and truly perceives the essential nature of phenomenal reality as it is, a universal correlativity and mutual interdependence. As to the charge that the doctrine of *Śūnyatā* can cause depression in the mind of the individual, the wisdom texts readily assent. It is only by his endowment with the skillful means (*upāya*) and the assistance of good spiritual friends that enable the Bodhisattva to go forth to all-knowledge and reach the knowledge of all modes. And it is precisely through the *upāya* of comprehensive detachment that apprehends nothing and therefore leaves no opportunity to discriminate between things, that he resists the insidious self-pride alluded to by the *Ratnagotra*.

Similarly, it is shown that the practice of non-apprehension fends off the other criticism that the *Śūnyavāda* focuses upon the defects of beings rather than their virtues. Due to the perception of absolute emptiness, all things are unproduced, isolated, trackless, unseizable and noncognizable. Because no defiled person or thing is to be discriminated, any particular regard towards "the defects" of beings betrays a wisdom not yet perfect. Likewise, the *Prajñā* texts indicate how *Śūnyatā* leads not to the depreciation of reality, but to its exact perception and revelation. With a precision not found in the *Ratnagotra*, the *Prajñāpāramitā sūtras* elucidate *Śūnyatā* as the crucial medium which, far from degrading phenomena, preserves the essential integrity of their Absolute Suchness from the perversions of erroneous conceptions and false imagination. Chapter six concludes then, that the weakest and most fallible aspect of the *Ratnagotra* lies in the quality of its critique upon the *Śūnyavāda*. Its particular charges are not borne out against the scrutiny of the Wisdom texts which were the authoritative sources and the sustaining inspiration of the *Mādhyamika* philosophy. The *Prajñāpāramitā* literature was itself sensitive to the stated dangers, and with an acuity unsurpassed by the *Ratnagotra*, isolated, exposed and corrected the errors incipient within its fundamental tenets.

The chapter interprets the śāstra's censure of the *Śūnyavāda* not as a repudiation of it, but as a movement within the Buddhist tradition towards a more positive formulation of the Absolute. *Śūnyatā* is not only the animating principle of an exacting critique upon rational processes. As critical methodology, it is the very vehicle of its own manifestation as the non-conceptual, indeterminate, unconditioned Absolute Reality, the highest truth and ultimate nature of things; as such, *Śūnyatā* is a cognate expression, an alternate designation of *Tathatā*. The complaint of the *Ratnagotra* evidently lies in its estimation that *Śūnyatā* as logical critique lacked sufficient cohesion with *Śūnyatā* as unconditioned, transcendent ground. Undoubtedly, it was as a corrective to what it considered an excessively negative epistemological review that the *Ratnagotra* advanced its ontology of the *Tathāgatagarbha*. But that it did so as a development upon and integration of the *Śūnyavāda* is clearly obvious from its definition of the essence of the Buddha or Tathāgata-embryo as representing the genuine meaning of *Śūnyatā*.

Chapter 8 discusses the meaning of the properties of the Buddha, which are said to be intrinsic to the *Tathāgatagarbha*, that of which it is not devoid (*aśūnya*). Very briefly, their essence is nothing other than absolute wisdom; they are the self-expressive modes of its complete manifestation as the Body of the Highest Truth, the *Dharmakāya*. They are shown to be the intrinsic forms of wisdom's appearance and spontaneous activity. For if wisdom is the goal, it is at the same time the very vehicle of its own manifestation. The perfect disclosure of the Buddha-properties on the level of the *Dharmakāya* is possible only because they are already germinally present and indivisible from the *Tathāgatagarbha* which, as embryonic absolute knowledge, is the active emergence of an implicit to an explicit fullness.

The chapter next discusses the relationship between the *Rupakāya* and the *Dharmakāya* and concludes that in the former, *Tathatā* represents itself to itself in definite shape and specific appearance; the *Rupakāya* is an essential and necessary stage towards *Tathatā's* perfect self-comprehensive awareness. But as yet external form, *Tathatā* is not immediately present to itself; it still projects itself in the cast of an other than itself. As long as the experience of the Buddha-personality, in the multiple expressions of the *Rupakāya*, fails to be understood as the self-created reflections of the Innate Mind, *Tathatā* remains concealed by its own symbolizations, fails to know itself, to recognize itself perfectly as what it is in itself. In the perception of the visible features and marks, actions and teachings, qualities and virtues of the Rupakāya-Buddha, the Innate Mind of all sentient beings (i.e. *Tathatā*) projects self-reflective images for its own self-recognizacne. Should an individual fail to realize this true identity of the *Rupakāya*, fail to identify these external forms as symbolizations of the one Innate Mind common to himself and all animate beings, and thus as the interior dimensions of his own authenticity, *Tathatā* becomes fixated in a form that is not the adequate medium for, does not completely correspond to its essence; put otherwise, it is the failure of the *Tathāgatagarbha* to realize itself perfectly as *Dharmakāya*.

Chapter 8 draws to a close the formal treatment of the *Tathāgatagarbha* by remarking the implicit indications for a complementarity with the Vijñānavādin tradition of the *Ālayavijñāna*.

That *Tathatā* advances through various stages of unconcealment to its ultimate self-awareness as the Absolute Suchness of reality, specifies that both the goal (enlightenment) and the path towards it, are noetic determinations. Consciousness then, is directly implicated in the concept of the *Tathāgatagarbha* as the very locus and form of its processive self-transformation. This became explicit in the *Ratnagotra's* references to *Cittaprakṛti*. Human consciousness was interpreted as the vehicle through which the Absolute Body gains self-conscious recognition of its inherent nature. The all-prevading Innate Mind is the immanent mode by which the *Dharmakāya* becomes fully self-aware in and through phenomenal human consciousness.

The *Ratnagotra* thus implied that the planes of conceptual human awareness are, in fact, merely the self-reflective moments in which the Absolute Body affirms itself as the perfectly pure essence, the Suchness of all reality. It failed to directly address the problem of how finite, particular consciousness functions with and is transformed into the infinite, universal and absolute consciousness. What must the structure of consciousness be that would allow for the coherent dynamics of such a relationship? While the *Ratnagotra* clearly indicated that the Innate Mind is the fundamental noetic substratum common to ordinary beings and Buddhas alike, it sustained no detailed analysis of its active interplay with and upon the phenomenal mind. The latter is depicted as the vehicle of ignorance, with little appreciation for its positive contribution to the attainment of enlightenment. Further, the *Ratnagotra's* insistence upon the ontic character of *Cittaprakṛti* dissipated the uniqueness of the finite and particular consciousness.

The chapter concludes that the śāstra's psychological analysis is simply not adequate to the comprehensive scope of its metaphysics. Only the more refined nuances of the Vijñānavādin tradition would satisfactorily answer its ambiguities. In the *Ratnagotra, Cittaprakṛti* essentially remains a metaphysical construct, representing the primordial stratum of pure awareness in all animate beings. How precisely the phenomenal mind, individuated out of, but not separate from that fundamental Innate Mind, compromises and defiles the latter as it strays from its identity with it, demands a generic theory of consciousness. While the *Ratnagotra* succeeded in establishing the metaphysical context in which to interpret the transformational event of enlightenment, it lacked that adequate psychological detail necessary for the translation of that theory into the practical discipline of the spiritual path.

Part Two

Chapter 9 opens the second major section of the study with an analysis of the *Laṅkāvatāra Sūtra* which explicitly incorporates the *Tathāgatagarbha* into the psychological schema of the Vijñānavādin tradition of the *Ālayavijñāna*. It proceeds to identify the novel definition assumed by the *Tathāgatagarbha* and the *Ālayavijñāna* stemming from their dynamic union. If the nature of the *Ālaya* represents the formally noetic aspect of Absolute Suchness (*Tathatā*) through its identification with the *Tathāgatagarbha*, its function is to recognize itself as such in the multiplicity of phenomenal forms. It is this recognition that defines the transformative realization of the *Tathāgatas* which is the intent of the *Laṅkāvatāra* to disclose. And while it adopts the epistemology and psychology of the *Vijñānavāda* to identify the dynamics of that recognitive process, the sūtra grounds itself in the ontology of the *Tathāgatagarbha*, i.e., Absolute Suchness (*Tathatā*). While the Ratnagotra extended the precise delineation of *Tathatā* as the universal, immaculate essence of phenomenal existence, the *Laṅkāvatāra* explores the manner in which *Tathatā* (noetically conceived as absolute consciousness, i.e., the *Ālayavijñāna*) comes to perfect self-awareness as that comprehensive totality. In doing so, it nuances the ontological context defined by the śāstra and with which it implicitly agrees by its focus upon the epistemology proper to that context. This analysis in turn, demands a coherent structure of the phenomenal mind, an adequate psychology, which was lacking to the *Ratnagotra*.

The chapter briefly introduces the sevenfold structure of phenomenal consciousness, grounded upon and animated by the *Ālayavijñāna,* and then proceeds to explain the sūtra's interpretation of the three self-natures: *parikalpita, paratantra,* and *parinispanna.* The *Laṅkavatāra's* emphasis upon epistemology without a clearly articulated ontology critically compromises the status of phenomenal reality as perceived by consciousness. Because the text fails to adequately attest their dependent cooriginate nature (their proper *paratantrasvabhāva*), the human organism and its material environment tend to be incorporated into its criticisms of false imagination (*parikalpita*) as the forms intrinsic to its misrepresentations. The chapter argues that this reflects the *Laṅkavatāra's* uneasy integration and amplification of the metaphysics of the *Tathāgatagarbha* into its basic Vijñānavādin psychology. While the doctrine of the Buddha-embryo significantly nuanced the ontic status of the *Ālayavijñāna,* it failed to creatively inform and coherently ground the extensions of that Absolute Mind in the multiple forms of existence.

Nor is this neglect confined to the realm of objectivity. There is a correspondent ambiguity that similarly jeopardizes the integrity of the phenomenal subject, i.e., the five sensorial consciousnesses, the *manovijñāna,* and the *manas.* The sūtra fails to adequately delineate the ontic structure of the phenomenal psyche from the epistemological processes that define its function. While there is a difference between the form of human consciousness and the ignorant activities that may at times characterize it, such a distinction is absent in the *Laṅkāvatāra.* The sūtra therefore implies that phenomenal subjectivity is not only the product of ignorance, but also the condition for its continued influence, and that *nirvāṇa* would accordingly be attained only through its abandonment.

The chapter details the contradictions inherent in such a conclusion and notes that a transcendental illusion may indeed distort the interepretation with which the relative consciousness invests that which it apprehends and orders into unified forms of intelligibility. But this interpretative function of false imagination is more formally an epistemological process than an ontic reality; it is an activity peculiar to relative consciousness, but not exhaustively definitive of it. It is this failure to adequately distinguish between ontology and epistemology, between consciousness as a stratum of being and consciousness as an interpretative process, that is at the root of the *Laṅkāvatāra's* doctrinal ambiguities. It is for this reason that the study of the *Tathāgatagarbha-Ālayavijñāna* advances to its final phase with an investigation of the *Ch'eng Wei-Shih Lun* of Hsüan Tsang.

Chapter 10 pointedly stresses the well-defined ontology of *parikalpita*, *paratantra*, and *pariniṣpanna*, free of the ambiguities that hampered the *Laṅkāvatāra's* similar classification. It is shown how the principal tenet of consciousness-only (*vijñaptimātratā*) nuances the definition of those three *svabhāvas*. Thus, the universal interdependence of phenomena are *paratantra* primarily because they appear only as the result of numerous conditioning factors within consciousness itself, while false imagination (*parikalpita*) assumes that the images and forms constituting the perceived aspect of consciousness are self-subsistent particularities, autonomous not only from one another, but more fundamentally, from consciousness itself. As the genuine nature of consciousness only, Absolute Suchness is equivalent to ultimate reality (*pariniṣpanna*) The latter's emergence as primal consciousness (the presupposition of both knowledge and ignorance) whose essence is to know itself in the universality of its extension as the essential nature of all things, is indicated. Since the point of the Holy Path's culmination in the supreme wisdom of *Mahābodhi* is co-instantaneous with the perfect revelation of *Mahāparinirvāṇa*, it is the moment of *Tathatā's* absolute self-awareness, its immediate self-coincidence as subject and object.

The chapter proceeds to specify the radical idealism that crucially distinguishes the ontology of the *Ch'eng Wei-Shih Lun* from that of the *Ratnagotravibhāga*. Since there is but one reality, mere-consciousness, the self-transparency of *Tathatā* in the totality of phenomena is the self-recognition of consciousness in the multiplicity of its forms. *Tathatā* is the essential nature of consciousness and consciousness is the essential nature of phenomena. The sensible shapes and contours of the latter are the immanent developments and structured modalities of the former. *Tathatā* (*Parinispanna*) can know itself as the indeterminate, unconditional nature of all things (*Paratantra*) because they are the radically ideal manifestations or transformations from within itself, noetically conceived as absolute consciousness (*Ālayavijñāna*).

It is the principal contribution of the chapter that it details the dynamics of the *Ālaya's* self-manifestation through a precise study of the *bīja* theory. For, it is by virtue of its common or universal *bījas* that it develops into the manifold appearances of the physical universe, while it is its non-common or non-universal *bījas* that account for the unique formations of the individual physical bodies and accompanying sense faculties. The uniformity of the physical shapes and localities of the world system; the interpretation of spatio-temporal determinations; the process by which human consciousness transforms itself through every activity of body, voice, and mind; the dynamic energies that define the *Ālayavijñāna* in the unceasing self-propagation of the *bījas*; the creation and persistence of conscious states; the creation of new *bījas* through novel experiences of the empirical consciousness; and the manner in which the *Ālaya* is projected from one life cycle to the next, are all carefully delineated and explained.

The chapter concludes that the phenomenal universe and the empirical human consciousness are the radically ideal manifestations and transformations from within the *Ālayavijñāna*, the noetic determination of Absolute Suchness (*Tathatā*). It is only when they are falsely considered to be self-subsistent particularities, independent of consciousness, that they are designated as mere imaginations. Collectively, the forms of the phenomenal universe and human individuality are the images (*nimitta*) in and through which *Tathatā* appears to, and recognizes itself. Since the structure of the phenomenal consciousness evolves from immanent, archetypal self-patternings of the absolute consciousness, i.e., from the innate *bījas* of the *Ālayavijñāna*, and since that phenomenal consciousness exists as the differentiated identity of the absolute consciousness, the perception of the phenomenal consciousness are the perceptions of the *Ālaya*.

Chapter 11 isolates the problem of ignorance in its two fundamental forms: the tenacious belief in the reality of an independent, autonomous ego (*ātmagrāha*), and the even more radical adherence to the notion of discrete, self-subsistent particularities or things-in-themselves (*dharmagrāha*). The relationship of the former to "the barrier of vexing passions" (*kleśāvaraṇa*) and of the latter to "the barrier impeding supreme enlightenment and hindering absolute knowledge" (*jñeyāvaraṇa*) is explained through the metaphysics of consciousness-only (*vijñaptimātratā*).

The origin of *ātmagrāha* through the extrinsic influence of erroneous teachings upon the *manovijñāna*, the faculty of ideal conceptualization, as well as the innate "natural" belief in the reality of an autonomous ego and independent things-in-themselves, is fully chronicled. Particular attention is focused upon the fourfold ignorance that intrinsically accompanies the *manas*, which then appropriates the *Ālayavijñāna* as the determinate center of its own, discrete self-identity, the *ātman*, rather than recognizing it as the universal, absolute consciousness, the generic animating principle of all sentient beings. Under the sway of *manas*, defiled by ignorance, the *manovijñāna* instinctively imputes an ego identity to the constituents of the phenomenal personality. In addition, the objects of the physical universe constituted by it through the mediation of the sense consciousnesses, are invested by the *manovijñāna* with a similar degree of self-reality. Rather than perceiving the sense consciousnesses, sense organs, and sense objects as the self-manifested forms of the *Ālayavijñāna*, the *manovijñāna*, pervaded by the *manas*' appropriation of the *Ālaya* as an independent self-entity, becomes ensnared by the self-reality it in turn attributes to them. As long as this fundamental misapprehension remains the dominant mental horizon informing all acts of consciousness which prompt physical deeds, produce speech or elicit deliberation and judgment, those acts are rendered impure and defiled.

The chapter concludes by noting a subtle, though critical qualification on the nature of ignorance, representing a significant advance by the *Ch'eng Wei-Shih Lun* over the *Laṅkāvatāra Sūtra*. Though an inherent accompaniment of the *manas* and *manovijñāna*, ignorance is only an "associated mental activity" (*caitta*), not the essential nature (*svabhāva*) of those two constituents of human consciousness. While in the *Laṅkāvatāra* the cognitive processes of the *manas-manovijñāna* are radically compromised as originated by ignorance, the *Ch'eng Wei-Shih Lun* preserves their integrity as the innate self-determinations (the *bījas*) of the *Ālayavijñāna* through which it perceives itself in the universality of its self-manifested forms.

According to the text, ignorance develops from within the very ground of the *Ālayavijñāna* along with the seeds (*bījas*) of wisdom and virtue. The critical argument of the chapter is that human consciousness is a product neither of ignorance nor of wisdom; its natural condition is the very interplay of their mutual presence. That the *Ālaya* grounds and posits the phenomenal mind with seeds (*bījas*) of both ignorance and wisdom, specifies the mind's active self-emergence as the necessary opposition between the two. For it is only in the expansive illumination of wisdom, gradually dilating the restrictive vision of ignorance, that human consciousness attains the awareness of its own universality. So far from being the problematic dualism which the obscure ontology of the *Laṅkāvatāra* was incapable of avoiding, ignorance is integrated into the essential dynamic through which the mind realizes itself in the omniscience of Buddhahood.

Chapter 12 details that process in a step-by-step analysis of the Buddhist Path as found in Hsüan Tsang's treatise. The initial "stage of moral provisioning" is presented in relation to the problematic gulf separating the illusory independent subject (*grāhaka*) and the world of similarly independent (and thus, illusory) objects (*grāhya*) which it encounters and perceives. In the second "stage of intensified effort", through the influence of four meditative practices, human consciousness understands that error and begins to realize the mutual implication and interdependence of the perceiving subject and the perceived object. Yet those meditations are not capable of removing the primordial, inherent attachment of the *manas* and *manovijñāna* to the existence of individual selfhood and thinghood, and the subliminal impressions created by it and by the multiple passions arising from it.

It is the third "stage of unimpeded penetrating understanding" that accomplishes that end through the non-discriminating transcendental wisdom and the subsequent wisdom peculiar to it.

Thoroughly informed by and exercised in the truth of *pudgala śūnyatā* and *dharma śūnyatā*, the *manas* comprehends the identity of all things and the complete equality between itself and all other sentient beings; it perceives the universal, essential nature common to all of them, their Absolute Suchness. It is at this stage that *Tathatā* attains a radical self-presence, in which it knows itself directly as the ultimately real, self-subsistent absolute. However, that self-intuition is only temporary and interrupted by the emergence within the empirical consciousness of various forms of the primordial *ātmagrāha* and *dharmagrāha*, originating from residual impressions within the fundamental consciousness of the *Ālaya-vijñāna*.

In the fourth "stage of exercising cultivation", the text isolates ten singularly obstinate forms of innate ignorance, and defines the classical ten *bhūmis* through their active repudiation of them and removal of every trace of their subliminal impressions (*bījas*). In each *bhūmi* the tenacious influence of ignorance is increasingly weakened by the expansive exercise of wisdom in the tenfold form of the moral perfections (*pāramitās*) which are said to reveal in each "land", the particular modality of Absolute Suchness peculiar to it. In even its most subtle and latent forms, ignorance is now annulled as its psychic basis within the *Ālayavijñāna*, is progressively and consistently illumined by the perfections of wisdom.

In the reversal of their instinctive tendencies to fragment reality by positing a multiplicity of independent, self-subsistent persons and things, the *manas* and *manovijñāna* are respectively transformed in and by the Universal Equality and Profound Contemplation Wisdoms, modalities of *Mahābodhi*. Conjointly, they illumine the mind so that it may discern precisely the unique features and peculiar characteristics of all *dharmas*, while at the same time comprehending their complete equality as the thoroughly ideal forms of Absolute Suchness. Both wisdoms are exercised throughout the ten *bhūmis* of the fourth stage, and both are perfected by the complementary exercise of the ten *pāramitās*.

But the chapter interprets the *bhūmis* from a more fundamental level than simply the process in which human consciousness attains a more thorough and precise understanding of absolute reality. For essentially, they represent the various refinements in the self-explication of *Tathatā*. Suchness, in its noetic activity as *Ālayavijñāna*, having become fully self-conscious in and through the human mind's experience of the non-discriminating transcendental wisdom, delineates that immediate self-intuition in the more deliberate conceptions of that mind. Since the *Ālaya* contains the seeds (*bījas*) of perfect wisdom that assume the particular form of the *pāramitās* within the phenomenal consciousness which it grounds, the realizations of the ten *Tathatās* which "they attain" in the ten *bhūmis* are in fact the moments of its perfect, self-comprehensive elucidation.

With the tenth *bhūmi*, the chapter moves to the fifth and final stage of the holy path, the "stage of ultimate realization" and identifies the meaning and function of the Great Mirror Wisdom through which *Tathatā* knows the exact delineations of all phenomena simultaneously and without hindrance of spatial and temporal distinctions. For as *Ālayavijñāna* it is the univeral storehouse which contains them as its own immanent determinations, its *bījas*, and the Great Mirror Wisdom is the self-luminosity, the perfect self-comprehension of the *Ālaya* in the entirety of those ideal determinations. If the human consciousness in and through the combined Universal Equality and Profound Contemplation Wisdoms recognized the *bījas* in their temporal projections as the phenomenal forms of mere-consciousness, the absolute consciousness (*Ālayavijñāna*), in and through the Great Mirror Wisdom, recognizes them in their unmanifest, immediate inherence to itself. While the Universal Equality and Profound Contemplation Wisdoms represent the comprehensive knowledge of each particular thing in its sheer Suchness (*sarvajñatā*) as perceived by the phenomenal consciousness, the Great Mirror Wisdom is omniscience proper, the simultaneous and exhaustively detailed knowledge of all forms (*sarvākarajñāta*), including the Universal Equality, Profound Contemplation and all other modalities of wisdom itself. It is as the Great Mirror Wisdom then, that *Tathatā* attains its ultimate self-conscious form. Since it is to possess itself as its own object by knowing itself as the unconditional nature of all things, its knowledge must be adequate to its content. Through the Universal Equality and Profound Contemplation of Wisdoms, *Tathatā* clearly knows itself in the individual forms of the phenomenal universe. But it is only as the Great Mirror Wisdom, that *Tathatā* having realized itself as perfect wisdom, knows itself as perfect wisdom. If it is to know itself as that which it is, it is not enough that it recognize itself in the mere diversity of physical shapes and material contours. For, in that very recognition it determines itself ever more exactly in the form of the Universal Equality and Profound Contemplation Wisdoms, and its self-knowledge is only complete when it comprehends itself in that form. It does so through the Great Mirror Wisdom. It is with this final development that the emergent complementarity of the *Tathāgatagarbha* and *Ālayavijñāna* concludes.

Part Three

Chapter 13 reviews the significant developments of the preceding chapters, identifying the salient moments in the comprehensive metaphysics of Absolute Suchness which the union of the two notions defines. Having delineated the principle that the Buddhist Absolute is the dynamic self-emergence from latent, abstract universality to perfect self-explicit awareness of and as that integral wholeness of reality, the processive self-determination of substance to subject, the chapter specifies that principle as the dominant theme within Hegel's *Phenomenology of Spirit*.

Briefly reviewing the stages in the latter's self-evolution of consciousness, the chapter concludes noting several points of convergence between the Buddhist conception of the *Tathāgatagarbha-Ālayavijñāna* and the Hegelian Absolute Spirit in-and-for-itself. Both share a common interpretation of reality as a generic process of self-transformation, the conscious disclosure of itself to itself as integral totality. For both, the Absolute is its own becoming, both means and end of its self-actualization. It does so by virtue of its essential nature as knowledge: the inherent self-activity which modifies it from mere substance to subject, and defines both the process and the goal as self-consciousness. Likewise, both conceptions posit a dynamic union of infinite and finite consciousness in which the latter is transformed and perfected in the self-realization of the former, of which it (finite consciousness) is the very vehicle. Finally, both appropriate ignorance and finitude as the necessary conditions for the self-explication of the Absolute in and through human consciousness. The chapter concludes, noting the importance of these corollaries for the continued dialogue between Buddhist thought and Western philosophy.

At this point an important clarification must be made. As indicated above and will be detailed throughout, the present study focuses the convergence of the *Tathāgatagarbha* and *Ālayavijñāna* as the emergence of *Tathatā* "from ontic substance to ontic subject". It may be objected that such a formulation violates the Buddhist tradition by imposing upon it far too Western a category of thought, thus distorting the uniqueness of the Buddhist reality and forcing a conformity that does not exist. But such is not the case. Rather than an alien and superimposed philosophical principle, the axiom suggests itself from within the very texts themselves as a precise description of the Buddhist Absolute.

While there is no exact equivalent of "ontic" within the Buddhist texts, the sūtras and śāstras explicitly insist upon its implied significance, i.e., a distinction in the degree of entitative value or self-being assigned to any particular thing or things. The *Śrī-Mālā* sets the tone by clearly delineating a contrast between the unconditional, self-consistent stability of the *Tathāgatagarbha* as that of "ultimate existence without beginning or end", and the processes of death and re-birth that define conditioned phenomena. The *Tathāgatagarbha's* priority over saṃsāric reality is clearly "ontic" in nature; that which is permanent, steadfast, and eternal enjoys a degree of reality in and of itself not so accorded the transient contingency of all other existents.

The entitative value of the *Tathāgatagarbha* is even more clearly articulated by the *Ratnagotravibhāga* which, having identified it as the immanent modality of Absolute Suchness (*Tathatā*), characterises it variously as the fundamental nature (*dharmatā*), the basic substratum (*āśraya*), and the universal essence (*dhātu*) common to all things. To speak here of an ontic status is to do no more than to recognize the plenary reality of the *Tathāgatagarbha* on the one hand and the mutual, participatory dependence of phenomena on the other. Far from foreign imposition, this is the very context in which the *Ratnagotravibhāga* developes its comprehensive metaphysics of Absolute Suchness (*Tathatā*).

Finally, all residual claims against the appropriateness of references to the ontic nature of the Buddhist reality must reckon with the Vijñānavādin delineation of *parikalpita*, *paratantra*, and *parinispanna.* Nowhere within the tradition of the *Tathāgatagarbha-Ālayavijñāna* is there such vivid, incontrovertible testimony to varying degrees of entitative value or self-being than in this tripartite classification. The first represents that which is completely lacking ontic significance, utterly void of reality, a mere imaginary figment. The being of the *paratantra* on the other hand, is that of a mutual interdependence where the universe of phenomenal forms reciprocally contribute to and mutually inhere a common identity—a shared reality, sustained by and dependent upon *parinispanna*, the ultimately real self-subsistent absolute—genuine Suchness (*Bhūtatathatā*). Such a schema, critical to the Vijñānavādin system and within which the theory of the *Tathāgatagarbha-Ālayavijñāna* attains its final phase, so clearly articulating distinct levels of self-being (*svabhāva*), naturally accommodates and validates references to the "ontic" priority and nature of that reality. To speak of *Tathatā* as ontic subject is to do no more than indicate its absolute value as that which comes to perfect self-awareness as integral totality in and through human consciousness. That this is in strict fidelity to the Buddhist tradition itself, and not merely the convenient formula of a foreign hermeneutics will be sustained by the attentive textual analysis of the following chapters.

PART ONE

THE TATHĀGATAGARBHA IN THE ŚRĪ-MĀLĀ SŪTRA AND THE RATNAGOTRAVIBHĀGA

CHAPTER I

ANALYSIS OF THE ŚRĪ-MĀLĀ SŪTRA

FROM BOTH logical and historical perspectives the *Śrī-Mālā Sūtra* is of critical importance for the study of the *Tathāgatagarbha* theory. It became the primary scriptural authority for the *Ratnagotravibhāga*, which is the most comprehensive śāstral treatment of that subject within Mahāyāna Buddhism. Of equal significance is the claim that the *Śrī-Mālā* had a direct role upon the inspiration and composition of the *Laṅkāvatāra Sūtra*, itself a primary authority for the concept of the *Ālayavijñāna*.[1] But perhaps its most apparent and creative influence is reflected in the *Awakening of Faith*, where the *Śrī-Mālā*'s bipolar designation of the *garbha* as "empty-nonempty" (*śūnya-aśūnya*) has been preserved and developed as the categorical specification of Suchness (*Tathatā*).

That the *Śrī-Mālā* was considered the primary scriptural advocate in India for the doctrine of a universal potentiality of Buddhahood, undoubtedly contributed to its historical popularity as commentarial subject by Buddhist scholars in both China and Japan. Its composition has been determined as a third century product of the Mahāsāṅghika sect of southern India, and therefore post-dates the early texts of the *Prajñāpāramitā sūtras*, a fact to be considered against the *Śrī-Mālā's* warning concerning the doctrine of emptiness (*Śūnyatā*). But while the *Ratnagotravibhāga*, appearing some two hundred years later, explicitly presents the *Tathāgatagarbha* theory as a direct critique of the *Prajñāparamitā sūtras*, such a judgement remains only implicit in the earlier *Śrī-Mālā*.

1. While it is evident from the text of the *Laṅkāvatāra* that the author was aware of the *Tathāgatagarbha* theory which he equates with the *Ālayavijñāna* and that he directly quotes from the *Śrī-Mālā*, it is interesting that Wayman and Wayman attribute a most profound influence of the latter upon the *Laṅkāvatāra* and that in fact, perhaps the reason why the *Ratnagotravibhāga* fails to quote the *Laṅkāvatāra*, was its disagreement with the latter's interpretation of the *Śrī-Mālā*. See *The Lion's Roar of Queen Śrī-Mālā: A Buddhist Scripture on the Tathāgatagarbha Theory*, trans. Alex Wayman and Hideko Wayman (New York : Columbia University Press, 1974), pp. 6–7.

Before proceeding, it should be made clear as to the methodology in the following analysis of the *Śrī-Mālā* text. In their excellent philosophical-historical introductory section and footnoted material throughout, Wayman and Wayman elucidate the sūtra's presentation of the *Tathāgatagarbha* against the completed development of that theory as found in the *Ratnagotravibhāga* and its commentaries. The problem with that in terms of the present study, is that the *Ratnagotra*'s exegesis of the *Śrī-Mālā* has been somewhat modified and determined by the insights into and modes of presentation of the *garbha* theory provided by more than twenty other sūtras that serve as the *Ratnagotra*'s additional sources. It is the intention here however, to analyze the *Śrī-Mālā* in its own terms so as to illustrate the problems raised in this earlier expression of the *Tathāgatagarbha,* and thus to better appreciate the more comprehensive dimensions and refinements of the later *Ratnagotra*'s coherent synthesis. Despite its brevity, the sūtra succeeds in suggesting the outlines for the subsequent elaboration of the theory, with the later introduction of the Vijñānavādin concept of the *Ālayavijñāna* ("Storehouse Consciousness").

TATHĀGATAGARBHA AS ONTIC SUBJECTIVITY

To begin with, it is not immediately obvious that the *Śrī-Mālā*'s briskly didactic concluding section in which it finally deals with the nature of the *Tathāgatagarbha* itself, underlies the lengthier preceding sections treating of the Illustrious Doctrine, *nirvāṇa*, the noble truths and the knowledge modalities of the various classes of beings. What first appears then, to be a rather loosely connected series of statements on various topics, is actually the examination of one reality, the *Tathāgatagarbha,* taken from a soteriological, epistemological and ontological focus. But it is not until its ontic status has been established towards the very end of the sūtra that one becomes aware of the self-consistency of the *garbha* doctrine as presented in the earlier sections of the text.

In style more declarative than expository, the *Śrī-Mālā* defines the *Tathāgatagarbha* as the ground of phenomenal existence or *saṃsāra*, since it is possessed of an ultimate existence without beginning or end, and is of an undying and unborn nature. While "perished" and "born," are processes conventionally descriptive of the respective loss and renewal of the physical senses, the *Tathāgatagarbha* is beyond such mundane referents, beyond all that is caused, conditioned or compounded (*saṃskṛta*). Because it isn't born, nor does it perish, nor is it subject to transmigratory change; it rather, is designated as permanent (*nitya*), steadfast (*dharma*), and eternal (*śāsvata*). For this reason, the *garbha* alone can be the ground of the Buddha natures (*buddhadharmas*) which are stated as inseparable and indivisible from it, and are comprehended as liberated from the stores of defilement. And for the very same reason (i.e., its permanence and eternity), the *garbha* is simultaneously the base of those very defilement stores which are however, separate from, and extrinsic to it:

> But Lord, the Tathāgatagarbha is not born, does not die, does not pass away to become reborn. The Tathāgatagarbha excludes the realm with the characteristic of the constructed. The Tathāgatagarbha is permanent, steadfast, eternal. Therefore, the Tathāgatagarbha is the support, the holder, the base of constructed (Buddha natures) that are nondiscrete, not dissociated, and knowing as liberated from the stores (of defilement); and furthermore is the support, the holder, the base of external constructed natures that are discrete, dissociated and knowing as not liberated.[2]

While disavowing any misconceptions of the *garbha* as some elemental self, soul or personality, the *Śrī-Mālā* accords it an unmistakeable ontic status, emphasizing its ultimate and self-consistent stability. And yet, its unconditional nature is not that of an absolute substantiality, so much as of an absolute subjectivity. The *Tathāgatagarbha* is the support (*ādhāra*) of both *saṃsāra* and *nirvāṇa* not as any primordial objective entity, but rather as that which alone is capable of experiencing suffering, and thus manifests itself as reactivity against the pain of phenomenal existence, and a simultaneous intentionality toward the emancipation of *nirvāṇa*:

2. *Ibid.*, pp. 104–105.

> Lord, if there were no Tathāgatagarbha, there would be neither aversion towards suffering nor longing, eagerness, and aspiration towards Nirvāṇa. What is the reason? Whatever be these six perceptions, and whatever be this (other) perception, these seven natures are unfixed, momentary and lack experience of suffering; hence these natures are unfit for aversion towards suffering or for longing, eagerness, and aspiration towards Nirvāṇa.[3]

While the classical Chinese and Japanese commentaries on the *Śrī-Mālā*[4] themselves remain obscure as to the exact interpretation of the seventh perception referred to by the text, it is obvious that the first five refer to those consciousnesses (*vijñānas*) which distinguish by the senses the objects of the external world (i.e., sight, hearing, smell, taste, and touch consciousness). The sixth, is undoubtedly the sense center consciousness (*manovijñāna*) which unifies and coordinates the precepts derived from the first five sense consciousnesses. Whether the seventh perception or consciousness be the "root consciousness" (*mūlavijñāna*) common to the Mahāsāṅghikas, or the "defiled mind" (*kliṣṭa-manas*) of the later *Laṅkāvatāra sūtra*, the *Śrī-Mālā*'s indictment remains the same. Only the *Tathāgatagarbha* of "ultimate existence without beginning or end"[5] possesses an unconditional awareness and consciousness that is alone adequate to a definitive comprehension of phenomenal existence as suffering. What is profoundly significant here, is the *Śrī-Mālā*'s implicit identification of the *garbha* not so much as ontic substance, but rather as ontic subject. It is suggested that this insight is precisely the germ that would later initiate the *Laṅkāvatāra*'s explicit equation of the *Tathāgatagarbha* with the ultimate consciousness that is the *Ālayavijñāna*.

The *garbha's* condition as ontic subjectivity simultaneously demonstrates its dynamic role as primary soteriological principle.

3. *Ibid.*, p. 105.

4. See Junjirō Takakusu, gen. ed., *Taishō Shinshū Daizōkyō*, 85 vols. (Tokyo : n.p., 1914-22), vol. 39.1, no. 1744 : *Shêng-man ching pao-k'u* by Chi-Tsang. See also Jōin Saeki, *Shōmangyō Kōsan* (Osaka : n.p., 1939). Both commentators (Chi-Tsang and Saeki) are consistently cited throughout the Waymans' translation.

5. *Lion's Roar*, trans. Wayman and Wayman, p. 106.

Its mode of existence is not one of mere passive submission, but a concurrent movement towards *nirvāṇa*. And this conative function of the *garbha* is by no means an undefined aspiration, or indeterminate striving. Here, the *Śrī-Mālā*'s generic designation of the *garbha* as "embryo" assumes its critical significance. Once its ontic status as ground of phenomenal existence has been asserted, it follows logically that the embryonic potentiality which the *garbha* is, predestines all sentient beings not to a multiplicity of goals, but to one and the same "rightly completed enlightenment," the universal awakening of Tathāgatahood. Expanding upon this, the scripture affirms that there can only be one ultimate "*Nirvāṇa* realm" which is synonymous with the Absolute Body (*Dharmakāya*) of the Tathāgata, and the definition given to this latter effects a direct, if not coterminous equivalence with the Tathāgata-embryo (*Tathāgatagarbha*):

> The Dharmakāya of the Tathāgata is named 'cessation of suffering,' and it is beginningless, uncreate, unborn, undying, free from death; permanent, steadfast, calm, eternal; intrinsically pure, free from all the defilement store; and accompanied by Buddha natures more numerous than the sands of the Ganges, which are nondiscrete, knowing as liberated, and inconceivable. This Dharmakāya of the Tathāgata when not free from the store of defilement is referred to as the Tathāgatagarbha.[6]

While a technical distinction remains unresolved within the text between the Absolute Body (*Dharmakāya*) which is attributed with the perfections of permanence, pleasure, purity, and self, as against the warning that the Tathāgata-embryo (*Tathāgatagarbha*) is not a self, the discrepancy is never raised to a dogmatic issue by the *Śrī-Mālā*.[7] What is more apparent is that the affirmative epithets specifying the Absolute Body (*Dharmakāya*) in the

6. *Ibid.*, p. 98.

7. Wayman and Wayman are correct in pointing out, that it is for this very (though seemingly minute) discrepancy that the *Śrī-Mālā* can never be said to absolutely identify the *Tathāgatagarbha* with the *Dharmakāya*. It will only be through the refinement of the *Ratnagotravibhāga's Samalā Tathatā* and *Nirmalā Tathatā* that their identity will be exactly determined. See *ibid.*, n. 83, p. 98.

above citation are substantially identical with those earlier attributed to the Tathāgata-embryo (*Tathāgatagarbha*). Both are not born; do not die; have no beginning or end; are permanent; steadfast; eternal; and (most important) are inseparable from the intrinsic Buddha natures. Thus, the major thrust of the scripture is its insistence upon the bivalent character of the Absolute Body (*Dharmakāya*), on the one hand freed from the store of defilement and on the other, non-free and concealed by it; in this latter condition it is organically conceived as embryonic. Therefore, though never explicitated as such the *Śrī-Mālā's* terminological designation of "embryo" establishes a causal link between the *Tathāgatagarbha* and its resultant finalized state as Absolute Body (*Dharmakāya*).[8]

TATHĀGATAGARBHA AND SOTERIOLOGY

Having clarified the nature of the Tathāgata-embryo (*Tathāgatagarbha*) as the ontic ground of the totality of existence in both its saṃsāric and nirvāṇic modalities, its condition as fundamental soteriological principle should be more obvious, and the *Śrī-Mālā's* lengthy discourse on the "Illustrious Doctrine" (*Saddharma*) can be more cogently understood as integral to the embryo (*garbha*) theory. By the very fact that, as embryo, it alone is unconditional awareness of phenomenal existence as suffering, and it alone as realized Absolute Body (*Dharmakāya*) is synonymous with "cessation of suffering," itself equivalent with the highest nirvāṇa realm of the Tathāgata (as opposed to various "fractional" nirvāṇic states), the *Tathāgatagarbha* is the basis for the *Śrī-Mālā's* doctrine of the "one vehicle" (*ekayāna*) theory.

However, at this point within the *Śrī-Mālā*, confusion can easily arise, due to an apparent disjunction within the logical sequence of the text itself. This is compounded by the nebular terminological variation between "Illustrious Doctrine" (*Saddharma*) and "Great Vehicle" (*Mahāyāna*). The body of the sūtra

8. "En insistant sur le fait qu'il s'agit d'un *garbha*—c'est-á-dire d'une 'essence embryonnaire' (snin po)—ce passage fait ressortir la difference entre le *dharmakāya* résultant (*phala*) et le *Tathāgatagarbha* 'causal'." Ruegg, *La Théorie du Tathāgatagarbha et du Gotra*, p. 359.

begins when Queen Śrī-Mālā, having taken ten vows[9] in the presence of the Buddha, proceeds to elaborate upon the praises and meaning of the last vow, in which she binds herself to embrace and never forget the "Illustrious Doctrine." As will be more clearly indicated below, the remarks which then follow concerning the "Illustrious Doctrine" substantially demonstrate a distinction of superiority among classes of beings, not only between that of the Bodhisattva on the one hand, and the disciples and Pratyekabuddhas on the other, but even among the levels of Bodhisattvas themselves. The problem becomes focused when the sūtra, somewhat abruptly, makes a direct equation of the "Illustrious Doctrine" with the "Great Vehicle" which recognizes no distinctions between the vehicles of the Bodhisattva, the Disciple or the Pratyekabuddha. How does one explain the apparent inconsistency between the two terms?

At issue is the implicit congruence of the *Śrī-Mālā's* doctrine of the Tathāgata-embryo (*Tathāgatagarbha*) as fundamental soteriological factor. It is, in fact, the reality of the embryo that accounts for the equation of the terms "Illustrious Doctrine" and "Great Vehicle," though this is never articulated as such by the sūtra. It is here suggested that the discrepancy between the scripture's section on the "Illustrious Doctrine" with its recognition of various stages and levels, and its statements on the "Great Vehicle" which seemingly contradict such a position, is not ultimate but merely perspectival. It has already been noted that viewed from the aspect of finality, the Tathāgata-embryo is virtually synonymous with the Absolute Body (*Dharmakāya*), while from a causal vantage it is characterised as a processive movement toward that very self-actualization.

Now, the *Śrī-Mālā's* concept of the "Great Vehicle" (*Mahāyāna*) accommodates itself exactly, in ultimacy and finality, to the Absolute Body (*Dharmakāya*). Its "greatness" does not polemically oppose itself to any "lesser vehicle" (*Hīnayāna*), but rather ontically grounds and contains within itself all other vehicles however they be named, as well as all excellent qualities of knowledge and power. The *Śrī-Mālā's* choice of imagery is strikingly deliberate:

9. The ten vows are listed in appendix 1.

> For example, whatever seeds there are, and plants, shrubs, trees, all of them, based on the great earth and resting on the great earth, sprout and grow. In the same way, whatever vehicles there be of Disciples and of the Self-Enlightened and whatever mundane and supramundane virtuous nature there be, they are based on the Great Vehicle, sprout and grow. Hence, Lord, when one is based on the Great Vehicle, and embraces the Great Vehicle, he also has recourse to and embraces all the vehicles of Disciples and of the Self-Enlightened and all the mundane and supramundane virtuous natures.[10]

As the text advances its interpretation on the comprehensive nature of the "Great Vehicle", its concordance with the *Lotus Flower of the Wonderful Law* (*Ṣaddharmapuṇḍarīkā sūtra*) is evident. Like the *Śrī-Mālā,* the latter presents the "Great Vehicle" as inclusive of the vehicles belonging to the Disciples and Self-Enlightened not as a third path, but as the one and only genuine path. Like the *Śrī-Mālā*, its claim is based on the major premise that there is only one goal, one universally realizeable awakening, one ultimate, innate Buddha-knowledge. *The Lotus of the Wonderful Law* agrees then, with the *Śrī-Mālā*'s equivalence of the "Great Vehicle" as the "Buddha Vehicle," and this is unique.[11]

Turning to the text of the *Śrī-Mālā* itself then, a passage of critical significance demonstrates through a series of correlative terms the consummation of the "Great Vehicle" as the realized Absolute Body (*Dharmakāya*). Therefore, it amounts to an implicit definition of the Tathāgata-embryo (*Tathāgatagarbha*) conceived here from its perspective as ultimate soteriological principle, since it is the one vehicle (*ekayāna*) that is "Great" (*Mahāyāna*)

10. *Lion's Roar*, trans. Wayman and Wayman, p. 79.

11. "Because the buddhas, the world-honored ones, desire to cause all living beings to open (their eyes) to the Buddha-knowledge so that they may gain the pure (mind), (therefore) they appear in the world; because they desire to show all living beings the Buddha-knowledge,..; because they desire to cause all living beings to apprehend the Buddha-knowledge,..; because they desire to cause all living beings to enter the way of the Buddha-knowledge, they appear in the world... The Tathāgata, by means of the One Buddha-vehicle, preaches to all living beings the law; there is no other vehicle, neither a second nor a third... Such (teachings) all are in order to secure perfect knowledge of the One Buddha-vehicle, Sariputra'. In the whole universe there are not

precisely because of its inherent identity with the Absolute Body (*Dharmakāya*), and its universal presence within all beings, no matter how they be designated:

> The vehicles of the Disciples and the Self-Enlightened ones are included in the Great Vehicle. Lord, 'Great Vehicle' is an expression for Buddha Vehicle. In that way, the three vehicles are counted as one vehicle (*ekayāna*). By realizing the 'one vehicle' one attains the incomparable rightly completed enlightenment. Lord, 'incomparable rightly completed enlightenment' is an expression for the Nirvāṇa-realm. 'Nirvāṇa-realm' is an expression for the Dharmakāya of the Tathāgata. The ultimate realization of the Dharmakāya is the One Vehicle. Lord, the Tathāgata is not one thing, and the Dharmakāya something else, but the Tathāgata is himself the Dharmakāya. The ultimate realization of the Dharmakāya is the ultimate of the One Vehicle. Lord, 'ultimate of the One Vehicle' is an expression for the absoluteness of the One Vehicle.[12]

In terms of logical priority, it is only when this insight into the Tathāgata-embryo (*Tathāgatagarbha*) as "Great Vehicle" has been grasped, that one can reach a clarified interpretation of the sūtra's previous section on the "Illustrious Doctrine" which allows of different categories and stages among beings.

While the Tathāgata-embryo (*Tathāgatagarbha*) has been shown as implicitly identical to the Absolute Body (*Dharmakāya*) in terms of finality, it simultaneously identifies itself as the necessary emergence of itself to itself. Organically conceived as embryo (*garbha*), it is the inherent process of moving from a latent to an articulate ultimacy, the self-expressive development from potential to actual Tathāgatahood. And the dynamics of its self-explicitation by no means precludes but even implies, the factor of stages or degrees towards that fullness of self-realization. While all sentient beings

---

even two vehicles [those of the Śrāvaka and Pratyekabuddha], how much less a third [that of the bodhisattva]." *The Threefold Lotus Sūtra*: *Innumerable Meanings*, *The Lotus Flower of the Wonderful Law*, and *Meditation on the Bodhisattva Universal Virtue*, trans. Bunnō Kato, Yoshirō Tamura, and Kōjirō Miyasaka (New York: Weatherhill, 1975; Tokyo: Kosei, 1975), pp. 59–61.

12. *Lion's Roar*, trans. Wayman and Wayman, p. 92.

may have the potentiality of Buddhahood, may be tacitly considered as already enlightened, through the universal endowment with the Tathāgata-embryo, that doesn't necessarily presume its immediate and total actualization. It is the recognition of the implied stages within the Tathāgata-embryo's self-objectification, that reconciles the *Śrī-Mālā*'s remarks on the "Illustrious Doctrine" and its superficially conflicting identification of it with "Great Vehicle." The coherance of the Tathāgata-embryo as fundamental soteriological principle is preserved whether it be conceived as in process or as ultimately realized.

In highly laudatory terms, the *Śrī-Mālā* presents the "Illustrious Doctrine" initially as an object to be embraced, relied on, rejoiced in, and displayed by all sentient beings, because of its definitive salvific capacity to attain "the perfection of aim."[13] As such, it is variously described as a thing of enormous scope, having far ranging meaning, of great benefit, great fruit and possessing infinite merit. More specifically, it is thus credited because of its unequalled and singular ability to perfect all the innumerable Buddha natures; to counteract the 84,000 defilements; to pour down countless maturations of merit and infinite knowledge jewels. Depicted as an immeasurable womb, the embrace of the Illustrious Doctrine is said to give rise to all the magical deeds of the Bodhisattvas, and to provide the various entrances into the light of the Doctrine, and to all mundane perfection, mundane mastery, and supramundane bliss.[14]

Then, in a manner consistent with what has already been noted elsewhere in the text, the *Śrī-Mālā* effects a significant equation:

> Lord, the embrace of the Illustrious Doctrine is called 'embracer of the Illustrious Doctrine'. The Illustrious Doctrine is not one thing and the embracer of the Illustrious Doctrine something else. That embracer of the Illustrious Doctrine is himself the Illustrious Doctrine. Neither is he different from the Perfections, nor are those different from the embracer of the Illustrious Doctrine. Lord, that embracer of the Illustrious Doctrine himself is the Perfections.[15]

13. *Ibid.*, p. 66.
14. *Ibid.*, pp. 69–70.
15. *Ibid.*, p. 72.

No longer is the Illustrious Doctrine to be considered an object to be grasped but, as already indicated, something to be "displayed," to be realized and actualized, within the phenomenal consciousness of all beings. Within such a process of concretization, the *Śrī-Mālā* clearly recognizes degrees of success judging that, "even a little embrace of the Illustrious Doctrine of the Great Vehicle, because of its expanse, is superior to all virtuous doctrines of the Vehicles of the Disciples and the Self-Enlightened."[16] Recalling what the scripture has already declared concerning the all-comprehensive nature of the "Great Vehicle" as the "One Vehicle" (*Ekayāna*), while the Bodhisattva always remains superior to the Arhat and Pratyekabuddha because of his vow, the latter are not excluded from but rather incorporated into, the stages of Bodhisattva progress. Where exactly they fit into the traditional ten stages of the Bodhisattva, is never mentioned by the *Śrī-Mālā* itself, but has been garnered from the centuries of Chinese and Japanese exegetical commentaries on the sūtra. From such sources, Wayman and Wayman have concluded that the Bodhisattva shares his body made of mind with the Arhat on the sixth stage and with the Pratyekabuddha on the seventh.[17] The eighth, ninth, and tenth stages have been commentatively designated in the Queen's remarks descriptive of "the good son or good daughter of the family" who makes three renunciations for the sake of all beings. Here, the sūtra distinguishes a level of superiority among the class of Bodhisattva itself, delineating all those who have not yet renounced body (agreed by the majority of commentative material to be the 8th stage Bodhisattva), life force (the 9th stage Bodhisattva), and possessions (the 10th stage Bodhisattva), as "all those newly entered in the Great Vehicle who still care for body and life force."[18]

Since the *Śrī-Mālā*'s own remarks remain only suggestive as to any exact classification, what is significant for the present study is the peculiarly universal soteriological context in which the Illustrious Doctrine is presented. Certain salvific effects of the embrace of the Illustrious Doctrine have been noted above. It was there

16. *Ibid.*, p. 77.

17. For the technical details of their conclusion see the Introduction to *Lion's Roar*, pp. 29–33.

18. *Ibid.*, p. 77.

depicted as an ultimate maternal principle which, womb-like, is alone capable of bringing all sentient beings to the highest level of spiritual maturity. The same image is operative where the sūtra discusses those who embrace, display and actualize the Illustrious Doctrine within themselves, indeed become the Illustrious Doctrine as its phenomenal manifestation. Their mode of activity regardless of the level of their own development, is expressly maternal in their function of supporting and bearing four great burdens. Embodying the fructifying principle that the Illustrious Doctrine is, those who embrace it (to whatever degree) are themselves called "the world mother of the Dharma";[19] this, because they sustain like the earth (itself a maternal metaphor) the four tasks of helping beings to be virtuous; adding others to the vehicle of the Disciples; entering others into the vehicles of the Self-Enlightened; or leading still others into the Great Vehicle. In this process, while there is recognition of different stages of developmental maturity (expressed in the terminology of the particular vehicles) there is no sectarian polemic. This is because, as was demonstrated above, the Illustrious Doctrine is itself the Great Vehicle which is itself the One Vehicle, all inherent definitions of the Tathāgata-embryo (*garbha*) in its universal, causal and thus, soteriological aspect. In its explicitation of itself as what it implicitly is as Absolute Body (*Dharmakāya*), it is not only conceived as active potentiality and thus as embryonic, but also as nutritive maternal principle leading all sentient beings to their finalized maturity in Buddhahood. Hence, its implied designation as "womb."

This dual aspect of the *garbha* concept as both "embryo" and "womb" has remained somewhat problematic in the development of the theory, and especially among the various Chinese, Tibetan, and Western translators.[20] But as will be noted in the third chapter of the present work, the *Tathāgatagarbha* is susceptible of various terminological nuances, all of which depend upon the perspective

19. *Ibid.*, p. 72.

20. For the technical, comprehensive review and evaluation of those translations of *Tathāgatagarbha* see Ruegg, *La Théorie du Tathāgatagarbha et du Gotra*, pp. 499–513. See chap. 3, n. 4 below for a summary of those pages and Ruegg's argument sustaining this study's translation of *garbha* as "embryo."

from which it is considered. This has been the hermeneutical principle for the present interpretation of the *Śrī-Mālā sūtra*. While never directly referred to as such by the text, it appears certain that the *Tathāgatagarbha* is simultaneously an ontological, soteriological and epistemological principle and the present investigation is attempting to demonstrate the interdependent coherence of all three aspects. Thus, it has been argued that the scripture's remarks on both the Great Vehicle and the Illustrious Doctrine, represent the *Śrī-Mālā*'s understanding of the *Tathāgatagarbha's* significance as primordial salvific factor. Its implicit intention has not been to expose any contradictory ambivalence but rather, to expound the *garbha's* inherent richness as both active potentiality leading to its own inherent finality (and thus, as "embryo"), and its simultaneous status as universal maternal determinant (and thus, as "womb").

The Status of the Buddha

Now, if it is true that there are degrees of one's embrace of the Illustrious Doctrine and therefore, varying degrees of the self-manifestation of the Tathāgata-embryo (*Tathāgatagarbha*) within the phenomenal consciousness of sentient beings, it is only in the Lord, the *Tathāgata,* that it has become what it truly is, has attained complete self-realization as the Absolute Body (*Dharmakāya*). In a manner somewhat abrupt and in too summary a fashion, the *Śrī-Mālā* simply states:

> Lord, I suppose the embrace of the Illustrious Doctrine is thus the great striving (*mahāvīrya*). In this case, the Lord himself is the Eye, is the knowledge (*jñāna*), is the root of all the Doctrines. The Lord is omnipotent, is the resort.[21]

Though it awaits further supportive elaboration from later sections of the sūtra, the interpretation drawn at this point is that the Tathāgata can be rightly credited with salvific ultimacy as "the imperishable refuge, the permanent refuge, the steadfast refuge at the uttermost limit,"[22] not so much because He has "gained the

21. *Lion's Roar*, trans. Wayman and Wayman, p. 76.
22. *Ibid.*, p. 93.

Absolute Body" (*Dharmakāya*). It is, rather, the Tathāgata-embryo (*Tathāgatagarbha*) that has gained an absolute self-witnessing, self-confirmatory consciousness of itself as the Great Vehicle, the One Vehicle. The *Tathāgata-Arhat-Samyaksambuddha* is the Eye, the perfect knowledge through which the Tathāgata-embryo comprehends itself as what it is as "the Refuge with imperishable nature, permanent, steadfast nature."[23] The Dharma and Saṃgha properly considered, can be mere ancillary, temporal refuges. The former can only teach the path of the One Vehicle leading to the ultimate realization of the Absolute Body (*Dharmakāya*). Its role remains that of a directive, and is not itself the consummation as the rightly completed enlightenment. Likewise, the Saṃgha is a representative term for all those of the three vehicles (that are in fact only one) who, through fear, have themselves taken refuge in the Tathāgata, and who, while they seek methods, study practices and train in disciplines, are yet en route toward that perfect maturity.

Soteriology now becomes more acutely defined as epistemology, since the Tathāgata's status as absolute refuge is dependent upon his exact and pluperfect knowledge. His alone is the authentic Lion's Roar because He alone has achieved an unqualified understanding of all natures; has become omniscient and all-seeing, unrestrained from all the faults, liberated from all defilements, and possessed of infinite merit.

> Having been made Lord of the Doctrine, unhindered in all stages of the knowable, he rightly saw that there is no duty or stage beyond this to be leftover or to be understood. Having properly entered the supreme incomparable stage which is fearless and endowed with the power of the ten powers, and having clearly seen all the knowable with unhindered knowledge, he uttered the Lion's roar with the knowing, 'There is nothing to be known beyond this'.[24]

While the Arhats and Pratyekabuddhas may utter a similar proclamation attesting their goal of freedom from the bondage of *saṃsāra*, it nevertheless lacks the epistemic finality, the gnoseologic

23. *Ibid.*, p. 92.
24. *Ibid.*, pp. 90–91.

profundity of the genuine Buddha Roar. They may think to themselves that their births are finished, that there is nothing to be known beyond what they have already encompassed, and thus conclude to themselves, "Without dependence on another, I have attained the (Nirvāṇa) stage, with remainder; I am certainly in the incomparable rightly completed enlightenment."[25] The *Śrī-Mālā* insists that though they have undoubtedly experienced an authentic liberation "in the supreme Nirvāṇa stage of arrested breath," characteristic of the fourth dhyāna,[26] theirs is merely a "fractional Nirvāṇa," a skilful means (*upāya*) established by the Tathāgata.[27]

TATHĀGATAGARBHA AND EPISTEMOLOGY

The sūtra now engages itself in an epistemological critique of various stages of realization from the wayward views of the spiritually immature to the pure, yet incomplete knowledge of the Arhat and Pratyekabuddha. In achieving its most incisive obser-

25. *Ibid.*, p. 92.

26. On the significance of the fourth dhyāna see *ibid.*, n. 70, pp. 91-92.

27. For a second time, a striking resonance is sounded between the *Śrī-Mālā* and the *Lotus of the Wonderful Law* (*Saddharma-Puṇḍarīka sūtra*). This latter's doctrine of *upāya* as testimony to the Buddha's tactful mode of teaching, is celebrated and exemplified several times throughout its text with regard to *nirvāṇa* and the three vehicle system. While its tenet that all existence has, from the very beginning, been in the state of *nirvāṇa*, is not obviously apparent in the *Śrī-Mālā*, other comparisons are obvious. The parable of the magic city, created by the wise and astute guide in the midst of an alien wilderness, serves as a compelling image for the *nirvāṇa* of the Śrāvakas and Pratyekabuddhas who would otherwise have been too fearful and disheartened by the journey towards the supreme enlightenment of the Buddha's perfect knowledge. Though not as graphic, the *Śrī-Mālā's* validation of the Arhat and Pratyekabuddha realization as genuine, yet "fractional," accords very well with the *Lotus Sūtra's* basic intent. With regard to the mistaken finality that characterises the *nirvāṇa* of the Arhats and Pratyekabuddhas in the *Śrī-Mālā*, a parallel text in the *Lotus sūtra* reflects the similar error in this confession by the Śrāvakas:

> "(Because we fancied that) all things were altogether void,.., we, for long, neither coveted nor were attached to the Buddhawisdom, nor had we any will or wish (for it). But we, in regard to the Law, considered we had reached finality. We, for a long time practising the Law of the Void,.., dwelling in the final bodily state of nirvāṇa (in which form still) remains;.., (we thought) we had, without a doubt, attained the Way."

Threefold Lotus, trans. Katō, Tamura and Miyasaka, p. 122.

vations throughout this section, the *Śrī-Mālā* simultaneously realizes its most lucid and significant understanding of the Tathāgata-embryo (*Tathāgatagarbha*).

The *nirvāṇa* of the Arhats and Pratyekabuddhas is merely fractional because it remains a state lacking the totality, immeasureability, purity and inconceiveability of merit that accompanies the Nirvāṇa-realm of the *Tathāgata-Arhat-Samyaksaṃbuddha*. Stated more positively, this lack of the highest merit entails the presence of fear, and subtle defilements which, not recognized, are not eliminated, and which will necessarily occasion their rebirth. While validating their attainment of the fourth dhyāna stage and crediting their realization of the four knowledges, the *Śrī-Mālā* judges that they are yet "attended with remainder and have not final meaning." Its elucidation of what it intends here, involves the scripture in a still greater degree of technicality.

In the framework of the sūtra there are two main classes of people. Those of "discontinuous transference" encompass ordinary persons, Disciples, Self-Enlightened ones, and Bodhisattvas newly entered on the path. Their designation is such because they have not eliminated the four "static kinds of defilement," which are accompanied by innumerable "mobile defilements." The second class are persons of "inconceiveable transference" including the Arhats, Pratyekabuddhas, and the Bodhisattvas who have attained power (i.e., belonging to the 8th Bodhisattva stage), since they have eliminated the four static kinds of defilement. All three are characterized as having "bodies made of mind," this, because they have not yet eliminated the "nescience entrenchment" described as "the static kind in attraction to supramundane gestation."

Interpreted in the light of the *Mahāyāna-Sūtrālaṃkāra*, the two main divisions are initially understood from the perspective of the goal. While the first group are those considered to be "in progress," the second have already passed through those stages and are currently judged to be the "in fulfilment" set. Although not exactly delineated as such by the *Śrī-Mālā*, there would seem to be no conflict with such a classification in the light of its One Vehicle doctrine, which makes clear, as has already been demonstrated, that no matter what the level or designation, all beings are destined to the one goal.[28]

Now if the classical interpretation of the "discontinuous passing away or transference" belonging to ordinary persons, Disciples and Self-Enlightened ones, has been that of "rebirth" in a new corporeal body (*pratisaṃdhi*),[29] does "the inconceiveable transference" of the second group transcend and overcome that experience? Obviously not, since the *Śrī-Mālā* has already criticized the Arhats and Pratyekabuddhas with "rebirth remainder." The term "bodies made of mind" (*manomayakāya*) is here of critical interpretative significance, while at the same time remaining one of the most difficult phrases in the entire sūtra. Relying on the *Mahāvastu*, a work like the *Śrī-Mālā* belonging to the *Mahāsāṅghika* sect, and the *Daśabhūmika-sūtra,* Wayman and Wayman clarify the term as indicative of a saintly variety of perception and motivation, and therefore a special case of rebirth, where the "body made of mind" refers to a duplicate of the coarser, corporeal body, and is assigned to the nonfluxional realm of immaculate actions.[30] Therefore, the Arhats and Pratyekabuddhas have gained control over the "discontinuous passing away" of corporeal form, because they have gained control of the four static defilements and the accompanying mobile defilements generated by them. The four static defilements are equivalent to the *Abhidharma*'s four subdivisions of indulgence (*upādāna*), the ninth member in the chain of dependent origination (*pratītya-samutpāda*). Thus, the static kind based in a particular viewpoint corresponds to the *dṛṣṭiupādāna* or the indulgence in any of the sixty-two views of the *Brahmajālasūtra;* the static kind in attraction to desire corresponds to the *kāma-upādāna* or indulgence in the five sense objects; the static kind in attraction to form is equivalent to the *śīlavrata-upādāna* or the indulgence in useless rules and vows; finally, the static kind in attraction to mundane gestation stands for the *ātmabhāva-upādāna* or indulgence in embodiment.[31]

28. See the Introduction in *Lion's Roar*, trans. Wayman and Wayman, pp. 26–28.

29. See *ibid.*, n. 53, p. 82.

30. For the technicalities of their interpretation see the Introduction to the *Lion's Roar*, pp. 29–33.

31. *Ibid.*, n. 56, p. 84.

THE NESCIENCE ENTRENCHMENT

Though the Arhats and Pratyekabuddhas have eradicated those four static kinds of defilements (primary ones) and the numerous mobile defilements (secondary ones) generated by them, and thinking that "There is nothing to be known beyond this," they have in fact, neither eliminated all defilements nor avoided all rebirth. The primordial and abysmal center of ignorance, "the nescience entrenchment" still remains operative within them, and accounts for the formation of their rebirth in the form of a body made of mind (*manomaya-kāya*); this is the explanation for its designation as "static kind in attraction to supramundane gestation."

> Lord, the nescience entrenchment which has existed from beginningless time is unconscious. The great power among those four static kinds is the substratum of all the secondary defilements, but those four cannot bear comparison with the great power of the nescience entrenchment in terms of magnitude, portion, count, example, or cause. That being the case, the nescience entrenchment is the greatest power. . It is the foundation exceeding the Ganges sands of secondary defilements. It has cohabited a long time with the four defilements. It cannot be erased by the knowledge of the Disciples and the Self-Enlightened. It is destroyed only by the enlightenment wisdom of the Tathāgatas.[32]

Presented as the fundamental obscurative nexus, the nescience entrenchment effects a powerful blinding influence which beclouds, enwraps and ultimately deceives the Arhats, Pratyekabuddhas and even the Bodhisattvas who have attained power. Rendering them perceptually feeble, this axial entrenchment of ignorance prevents them from searching out and comprehending "this and that nature" which must be eliminated, and thus purified. Crippling their discriminative faculty, it hampers their liberation from all faults and renders them as insufficiently pure; their merits, though numerous, are therefore not complete, and their realization faulty.

32. *Ibid.*, pp. 84–85.

The ultimacy with which the *Śrī-Mālā* accords the nescience entrenchment as archetypal ground of all primary and secondary defilements, is strikingly reminiscent of the ontic status to which it has already ascribed the Great Vehicle (and therefore the Tathāgata-embryo) as the foundation and support of all mundane and supramundane virtuous natures.[33] The tendency towards a severely problematic dualism becomes obvious at this point within the sūtra, and it is significant to note the use of the same terrestrial imagery now employed for the nescience entrenchment that had earlier been descriptive of the essential nature of the Great Vehicle and the Tathāgata-embryo:

> Lord, that being the case, the nescience entrenchment is the source from which arise all the (primary) defilements and secondary defilements, which should be eliminated by contemplation. . all of them arise from the nescience entrenchment. . From time immemorial, the nescience entrenchment has been unconscious. The natures to be eliminated, more numerous than the sands of the Ganges and which are utterly eradicated by the enlightenment wisdom of the Tathāgatas, are all natures whose substratum and foundation is the nescience entrenchment. For example, whatever kind of seed it be, or grass, shrub, herb or tree, all of them are founded on soil, germinate on soil, grow on soil. Lord, in the same way, the natures to be eliminated, exceeding the sands of the Ganges River, which are all utterly eradicated by the wisdom of the Tathāgata, are founded on the nescience entrenchment, are situated on the nescience entrenchment, germinate and grow (there).[34]

Despite the repetitive assertion that the nescience entrenchment is subject to the elimination, purification and extinction by the enlightened wisdom of the Tathāgata, its status as the beginningless, originative cause and condition of all defilements remains a central problem throughout the historical development of the *Tathāgatagarbha-Ālayavijñāna* theory (though in the subsequent works, different terms may be applied to it). At the present stage

33. See quotation of n. 10 above.
34. *Lion's Roar*, trans. Wayman and Wayman, pp. 87–89.

of development, the *Śrī-Mālā's* references to the nescience entrenchment as the pretemporal abyssal center of ignorance are restricted exclusively to the fact of its presence, never to an examination of the how and why of that presence. The primary intention of the sūtra is more to state that the nescience entrenchment is the inherent epistemic impediment to the self-realization of the Tathāgata-embryo (*Tathāgatagarbha*), than to critically examine the reason and manner of its origination.

That the nescience entrenchment is the main obstruction to the complete self-knowledge of the embryo as the Absolute Body (*Dharmakāya*) of the Tathāgata, is demonstrated more by implication than by a simple, clearly defined directive. It must be recalled that the embryo is the support, holder and ground of the Buddha natures that are intrinsic and inseparable from it; they remain however, in a condition of non-recognition, concealed by the veil of the defilements. It is only when those defilements are eliminated that the Buddha natures are manifestly apparent, and known as having been forever present as "non-discrete and not dissociated." Now the *Śrī-Mālā's* critique of the Arhat and Pratyekabuddha realization as an expediential, "fractional Nirvāṇa," rests on their failure to attain by direct experience those very Buddha natures. This in turn, was explained by their incapacity to completely search out, comprehend, purify and so eliminate the subtlest of remaining defilements. And the ultimate rationale for their cognitive deficiency lay in the continued operative presence of that basal center of ignorance, the nescience entrenchment. Thus, through retrogressive implication, the sūtra establishes the latter as the primordial antithetical condition to the self-maturation of the Tathāgata-embryo (*Tathāgatagarbha*) as Absolute Body (*Dharmakāya*).

The Buddha Natures

A reconfirming clarification is provided at this point in answer to a question which immediately presents itself in regard to the subject of the Buddha natures. While they are spoken of as being essentially inconceivable and innumerable, the sūtra does in fact allude to thirty-two "chief" Buddha natures in the above quoted passage descriptive of the Tathāgata's authentic Lion Roar. It is clearly implied there, that his is the supreme incomparable Nirvāṇa-realm, because it is accompanied by what amounts to the four confidences, the ten powers and the Buddha Eye or the eighteen exclusive Buddha natures.[35] It is quite obvious that these thirty-two natures do indeed encompass and suggest inconceiveable and innumerable modalities of wisdom and knowledge. Now the question that arises is this. The *Śrī-Mālā* has stated that only when the nescience entrenchment with the primary and secondary defilements which issue from it have been completely eliminated, are the Buddha natures finally manifested in total lucidity and that thus, the Tathāgata-embryo (*Tathāgatagarbha*) attains an explicit and complete self-awareness as the Absolute Body (*Dharmakāya*) of the Tathāgata. From this perspective, the Buddha natures appear as effect, the result of the removal of the nescience entrenchment. But if the Buddha natures represent as they have been shown to, the substance of the most profound wisdom and knowledge, should they not be more properly considered as the cause rather than the effect of that removal and elimination? Put otherwise, how but by knowledge (and therefore the Buddha natures) can the beginningless core of ignorance be dissipated; if wisdom is the effect of liberation, then what is the cause?

Actually, the question itself is deceptive, and the problem if any, is one of perspective. For the Buddha natures are both the cause and the effect in the process of dissolving the nescience entrenchment and its defilements. It is here suggested that this is but an alternate way in which the *Śrī-Mālā* implicitly exposes the bivalent character of the Tathāgata-embryo (*Tathāgatagarbha*). It has been already indicated how, from the angle of finality as self-realized Absolute Body (*Dharmakāya*), the embryo is effect, result, and goal. At the same time, as the processive, self-determined movement towards that actualization, it is cause, means and progression. The relationship of the Buddha natures to the nescience entrenchment is simply a more specific, dynamic, and functional, definition of this end that is simultaneously its own becoming. In the earlier section discussing the relationship of the Illustrious Doctrine and the Great Vehicle, the scripture allowed for the possibility of different classes of beings, even though all were

35. The four confidences, ten powers, and eighteen exclusive Buddha natures are listed in appendix 1.

equally embraced by the One Buddha Vehicle. Their various stages of realization were translated as the degrees in the phenomenal manifestation of the Tathāgata-embryo (*Tathāgatagarbha*). Another way of elucidating this self-manifestation is from the complementary mechanics of the removal of the barrier. As the obstructive force of the nescience entrenchment is ever more dispersed by the diverse knowledge modes which essentially constitute the Buddha natures, these latter display themselves with greater perspicuity. This principle of self-liberation as self-explicitation explains the *Śrī-Mālā*'s understanding that as the defilements of the nescience entrenchment are eliminated or purified, there is a simultaneous attainment of the virtuous Buddha natures which are the very vehicle of their final and total self-deployment. It is this that constitutes the supreme Nirvāṇa-realm of the Tathāgata as the sūtra insists.

> It is attained by those for whom knowledge is equal; it is attained by those for whom liberation is equal; it is attained by those for whom pure knowledge and vision are equal. Therefore the Nirvāṇa-realm has a single taste (*ekarasa*). That is to say, the tastes of knowledge and liberation are identical. Lord, whichever persons do not eliminate or purify the nescience entrenchment are ones without the single taste of the Nirvāṇa-realm; that is to say, for them, knowledge and liberation taste different.[36]

Continuing its epistemological critique, the *Śrī-Mālā* now returns to focus upon the second main class of persons, those of "discontinuous transference," encompassing ordinary persons, Disciples, Self-Enlightened Ones, and Bodhisattvas newly entered on the path. While the first group just considered (the Arhats, Pratyekabuddhas and Bodhisattvas of the 8th stage on) are still subject to the continued, subtle influence of the nescience entrenchment, they had nevertheless, gained control over the four static defilements and the accompanying mobile ones. Because of their failure to attain a corresponding mastery over those same four forms of indulgence, the beings of the second class are subject to the

36. *Lion's Roar*, trans. Wayman and Wayman, p. 87.

"discontinuous passing away," the equivalent of rebirth in some new form of corporeal embodiment.

THE FOUR NOBLE TRUTHS

While the nescience entrenchment was the pivotal subject in the scriptural analysis on the imperfect realization of the Arhat and Pratyekabuddha, the four Noble Truths now assume a nuclear position for the cognitive-perceptual critique of the ordinary beings, and especially of the Disciples and Self-Enlightened Ones.[37] Here, once again the particularly Buddhistic intuition into the interdependence of knowledge and salvation, epistemology as soteriology, is clearly apparent, and the *Śrī-Mālā*'s references to the Tathāgata-embryo (*Tathāgatagarbha*) become most explicit.

According to the text, the Disciples and Self-Enlightened ones realize only a one-sided knowledge of the four Noble Truths which, while allowing a certain genuine discrimination into their nature, and removing thereby certain static defilements, is yet incapable of removing all of them. There is still a second, "supramundane, adamantine knowledge" (*vajropama-samādhi*) of the Noble Truths, perfected only by the Tathāgata, eliminating all the defilement stores, together with their originative center, the nescience entrenchment. The critical, definitive character of this ultimate, disintegrative and therefore salvific intuition, is described as the "inconceiveable voidness knowledge."

At this juncture, there appears to be a break in the logical sequence of the text. Instead of providing an immediate and straightforward elaboration of this "inconceiveable voidness knowledge" belonging to the Tathāgata alone, the *Śrī-Mālā* introduces a lengthy passage amounting to its own peculiar her-

37. While the *Śrī-Mālā* tends to confine its comments on the knowledge of the Noble Truths to the Disciples and Self-Enlightened, it does mention them in connection with the Arhats and Pratyekabuddhas. It notes that since they have not eliminated the nescience entrenchment completely, they don't adequately comprehend the four Truths. Not having attained the full manifestation of the Buddha natures, they are those "persons attended with remainder of suffering to search, attended with remainder of source of suffering to eliminate, attended with remainder of cessation of suffering to realize directly, and attended with remainder of path leading to the cessation of suffering to cultivate." Ibid., p. 86.

meneutic of the four Noble Truths. Only then does it resume its definition of the unique "voidness knowledge." Actually, the seeming hiatus is the very manner in which the sūtra renders the final purport and full extent of that particular term. For, the "inconceiveable voidness knowledge" of the Tathāgata which eliminates all defilement impressions at their very root, is the bi-polar wisdom concerning the Tathāgata-embryo (*Tathāgatagarbha*). But what the *Śrī-Mālā* intends is that the correct and exact insight into the nature of the embryo is simultaneously interdependent with one's understanding of the four Noble Truths. In its customary style the sūtra effects a direct equivalence between the two, where the explanation of the one is the very exponent of the other:

> Lord, the explanation of the meaning of the Noble Truths should be considered to be profound and subtle, difficult to understand, incapable of being judged, and not in the domain of logic... Because this profound teaching explains the Tathāgatagarbha (embryo of the Tathāgata). The Tathāgatagarbha is the domain of the Tathāgata. It is not the domain of any Disciple of Self-Enlightened one. Lord, the Tathāgatagarbha is the locus of this explanation of the meaning of the Noble Truths. Because the locus of the Tathāgatagarbha is profound, the meaning of the Noble Truths is considered to be profound and subtle, difficult to understand, incapable of being judged, and not in the domain of logic... When anyone's mind reaches the ultimate purport of the Tathāgatagarbha, the Dharmakāya of the Tathāgata and inconceiveable realm of the Buddha, he has implicit trust and the conviction in two kinds of explanation of the meaning of the Noble Truths. The two kinds of explanation of the meaning of the Noble Truths are difficult to know and difficult to understand.[38]

Actually, the dual explanations of the Noble Truths as "Create" (*kṛta*) and "Uncreate" (*akṛta*) present no great challenge, their interpretation being quite direct and simple. While the former mode of discernment into the meaning of the four Truths is imperfect due to intellectual limitation, the latter is perfect, being without such limitation. More specifically, the "Create" explanation

38. Ibid., p. 96.

of the Truths is perceptually incomplete because it essentially entails dependence on another; it fails to effect that perfect self-determined, self-witnessing probe into the very source of the phenomenal suffering that is *saṃsāra*. Without such an ultimate consciousness of the wellspring of suffering, one cannot adequately cultivate the path leading to the finality of that experience.

The designation, *Arhat-Samyaksambuddha*, is applicable to the Tathāgata since he alone is properly and perfectly enlightened as the sole one who, in sounding the profound origin and seat of suffering, perfectly realized its cessation. Thus, the Noble Truths are his discovery and subsequent gift to a world enclosed in the shell of sorrow. It is his unsurpassed, direct and unconditional intuition of phenomenal existence as suffering that validated and ensured the perfect consummation of his path to liberation. It is thus, that the *Śrī-Mālā* speaks of the Tathāgata as perfecting the "Uncreate" explanations of the Noble Truths:

> Lord, the Uncreate explanations of the meaning of the Noble Truths present the Noble Truths without intellectual limitation. Why so? Because in dependence on oneself, one seeks out all deepfelt suffering, eliminates all deepfelt sources of suffering, directly realizes the deepfelt cessation of all suffering, cultivates all the deepfelt path leading to the cessation.[39]

In an apparent attempt to rationalize its "Create" and "Uncreate" explanations of the four Noble Truths, and to integrate them with its doctrine of *nirvāṇa* and *saṃsāra*, the sūtra here injects a single declarative phrase. The synthesis it obviously intends to affect by doing so results however, in a technical schema, more abstruse than clarificatory. The designed precision involves the *Śrī-Mālā* in a somewhat forced diagrammatic structuring leaving the terms involved, more recondite than explicit. The text, without any amplification, simply states that not only is there a constructed (conditional) and unconstructed (unconditional) *saṃsāra* but, there is likewise a constructed and unconstructed *nirvāṇa*.

Evidently, in the present context of the Noble Truths, the unconstructed *saṃsāra* suggests reality as suffering which has

39. Ibid., p. 97.

already been linked to the Tathāgata-embryo (*Tathāgatagarbha*), since it alone is said to so experience it. The constructed *saṃsāra* would then amount to the defilement stores which, though constituting and occasioning the saṃsāric condition, remain nevertheless external and essentially unconnected to the embryo. On the other hand, the unconstructed *nirvāṇa* would equate with cessation of suffering, or the Absolute Body (*Dharmakāya*), while the Buddha natures would be left to round off the quadruplicate classification as the constructed *nirvāṇa*. The problem is in this last designation of the Buddha natures as constructed (conditioned) *nirvāṇa,* since it betrays an inconsistent strain within the *Śrī-Mālā*. It has already been noted that the Tathāgata-embryo (*Tathāgatagarbha*) "excludes the realm with the characteristic of the constructed." But at the same time it claimed that the embryo is the "support, holder and base of (constructed) Buddha natures that are nondiscrete, not dissociated, and knowing as liberated from the stores (of defilement)." Elsewhere, the Buddha natures assumed an ultimate value in the sūtra's description of the Absolute Body (*Dharmakāya*) which is said to be "accompanied by the Buddha natures more numerous than the sands of the Ganges, which are nondiscrete, knowing as liberated and inconceivable." There appears then to be a textual inconsistency where the *Śrī-Mālā* at one time implicates the Buddha natures to be conditioned or constructed, and at another, not so designated, but in fact, unconditioned or unconstructed. This would, of course, imply a logical incongruity as well. The schema of "constructed-unconstructed" suggests a disparity of mutual exclusion between the two. For if, as has been noted, the unconstructed *saṃsāra* (i.e., the Tathāgata-embryo as experience of suffering) excludes the constructed *saṃsāra* (i.e., the defilement stores), would not the same relation hold for the unconstructed and constructed *nirvāṇa*? In that case, the Absolute Body (*Dharmakāya*) as the cessation of suffering, would exclude the Buddha natures. But it has been the repeated insistence of the *Śrī-Mālā* that just the opposite is the case. Its reiterated critique of the Arhat and Pratyekabuddha realization consisted of the fact that their *nirvāṇa*-realm was not the supreme *nirvāṇa* of the Tathāgata, not the rightly completed enlightenment, and therefore not the perfection of the embryo as Absolute Body (*Dharmakāya*), precisely because they failed to manifest the Buddha natures that were nevertheless inherent to them as inseparable from the Tathāgata-embryo (*Tathāgatagarbha*).

Since the sūtra itself does not explain or expand upon this rather isolated and somewhat problematic statement, the noted inconsistency is not critical to the coherence of the *Śrī-Mālā*'s doctrine on the Tathāgata-embryo (*Tathāgatagarbha*). If its doctrine of an unconstructed and constructed *nirvāṇa* as well as an unconstructed and constructed *saṃsāra,* remains largely undeveloped and non-integral to the present discussion of the Noble Truths, then the hesitation it occasions as to the status of the Buddha natures must be weighed against the overall intent of the text. It is therefore suggested that the *Śrī-Mālā* simply means that the unconstructed *nirvāṇa* is "accompanied by" the constructed *nirvāṇa* and that the unconstructed *saṃsāra* is "accompanied by" the constructed *saṃsāra.* In the case of the latter pair, the Tathāgata-embryo is accompanied by the defilement stores, which nevertheless remain adventitious and non-essential to it. While in the former, the Absolute Body (*Dharmakāya*) is not only attended by, but essentially constituted of the Buddha natures. It should also be noted here, that the later śāstral commentary of the *Ratnagotravibhāga* obviates the entire question, since its quotation of the particular passage under consideration from the *Śrī-Mālā* contains no reference whatsoever to "constructed" or "conditioned" as descriptive of the Buddha natures.[40] The same work likewise provides its own uniquely creative interpretation of the *Śrī-Mālā*'s constructed and unconstructed *saṃsāra* and *nirvāṇa*, completely removing it from the restrictive schema suggested by the sūtra's own ambiguity.[41]

40. Whether this is the work of a consciously editorialized deletion or a matter of different textual source, has not been ascertained. What is important is that according to the śāstra, the Buddha natures are simply an inherent essential to the Absolute Body (*Dharmakāya*). Its quotation from the *Śrī-Mālā* includes no reference to the modifier "constructed" or "conditioned": " 'Therefore O Lord, the Matrix of the Tathāgata [Tathāgatagarbha] is the foundation, the support and the substratum of the immutable elements (properties) [Buddha natures] which are essentially connected with, indivisible from (the Absolute Entity), and unreleased from Wisdom.' " Takasaki, *A Study on the Ratnagotravibhāga*, p. 292. Significant here is the substitution of "immutable" as descriptive of the Buddha natures which, if anything, would suggest the direct opposite of "conditional" and "constructed."

41. Briefly, the *Ratnagotra* makes the constructed and unconstructed *saṃsāra*

After this lengthy but necessary excursion, it is important to return to the central intuition that there exists an exact correspondence between the proper understanding of the four Noble Truths and the correct insight into the nature of the Tathāgata-embryo (*Tathāgatagarbha*). The difficulty in totally comprehending the "Uncreate" explanation of the meaning of those Truths without intellectual limitation, is the very measure in attaining the direct and precise comprehension of the Tathāgata-embryo (*Tathāgatagarbha*).[42]

It now becomes clear that the Disciples' and Self-Enlightened Ones' incomplete, "one-sided knowledge" of the four Noble Truths translates here as the "Create explanation" of their meaning. And if it eliminates only a certain amount of the static defilements, it is because of an intellectual dependency, a percipient failure to adequately penetrate in an unqualified self-comprehensive grasp, the source of all suffering. One's intensive cultivation of the path leading to the cessation of suffering is directly contingent upon the exhaustive and unmitigated depth of that self-realization; to modulate the one is to restrict the other.

Thus, it is also apparent that the "supramundane adamantine knowledge," capable not only of eliminating all primary and secondary defilements, but of completely dissipating their causal, primordial source in the nescience entrenchment, is the "Uncreate explanation" of the Noble Truths, perfected by the Tathāgata. It is this second kind of knowledge of the Noble Truths that was accorded the "ultimate knowledge," the "Right Knowledge," and more specifically, the "inconceiveable voidness knowledge." This last designation, initially somewhat gratuitous and unexplained, now assumes critical focus as the final development in the *Śrī-Mālā*'s doctrine of the Tathāgata-embryo (*Tathāgatagarbha*).

---

and *nirvāṇa* descriptive of the Bodhisattva consciousness, which is simultaneously pure (thus partaking of *nirvāṇa*) while yet fully immersed in the phenomenal existence of *saṃsāra*. This will be more clearly amplified below.

42. "Et le savoir relatif à l'*āryasatya* devient le savoir exact...L'object de l' exposé du sens de l'*āryasatya* n' est autre que le *Tathāgatagarbha*. en tant que tel le sens de l'*āryasatya* et tres profond et difficile à approfondir, le *Tathāgatagarbha* n'étant accessible qu' au seul Tathāgata." Ruegg, *La Theorie*, p. 183.

TATHĀGATAGARBHA AS BOTH ŚŪNYA AND AŚŪNYA

If the complete cessation of all suffering is coincident with, and dependent upon the removal of the nescience entrenchment, and although the text had earlier applied the radical terminology of "extinction," "eradication," "disintegration" and "annihilation" to that act, the sūtra now insists upon the non-destructive nature of the experience. Regrounding the basic tenet on the simultaneity of liberation and knowledge, the removal of the nescience entrenchment is here stressed in terms of positive attainment. As the cessation of suffering, it is "not the destruction of Dharma" but rather, its perfection as Absolute Body (*Dharmakāya*). Soteriologically, the perfection of the Noble Truths renders the consummate liberation from the ignorance root and its defiling impressions; psychically it translates as the finality of all suffering; teleologically it defines the self-explicitated maturation of the embryo (*garbha*), in its finalized state of Buddhahood; critical to each of these interdependent modes is an epistemic precision. For, the Noble Truths are perfected by that discerning exactitude into the bipolar nature of the Tathāgata-embryo (*Tathāgatagarbha*).

It is this, that is the "inconceiveable voidness knowledge" of the Tathāgata. In the most decisive and dogmatically crucial section of the *Śrī-Mālā* a radical hermeneutic on the meaning of "emptiness' or "voidness' (*śūnyatā*) is clearly delineated, from which perspective the sūtra continues its epistemological critique, and completes its theory of the Tathāgata-embryo (*Tathāgatagarbha*):

> Lord, the knowledge of the Tathāgatagarbha is the voidness knowledge of the Tathāgatas. The Tathāgatagarbha is something not seen before or understood before by any Disciple or Self-Enlightened one. It has been seen directly and understood by the Lord. The voidness knowledge of the Tathāgatagarbha is of two kinds. The two are as follows: Lord, the Tathāgatagarbha is void [śūnya] of all the defilement stores, which are discrete and knowing as not liberated. Lord, the Tathāgatagarbha is not void of [aśūnya] the Buddha *dharmas* which are non-discrete, inconceiveable, more numerous than the sands of the Ganges, and knowing as liberated.[43]

43. *Lion's Roar*, trans. Wayman and Wayman, p. 99.

It will be recalled how the *Śrī-Mālā* initially warned that the Tathāgata-embryo (*Tathāgatagarbha*) was not the domain of anyone falling into a belief in a real personality, self, or soul, nor was it comprehensible to those "whose thoughts are distracted by voidness (*śūnyatā*)." Its intentionality is here more completely elucidated as it continues its critical examination of the percipient-cognitive failure of ordinary beings, Disciples, and Self-Enlightened ones from that precise norm of the Tathāgata-embryo (*Tathāgatagarbha*) as bipolar voidness (*śūnyatā*). Without articulating it as such, the *Śrī-Mālā* unquestionably views its doctrine as a genuine *Mādhyamika* position, advocating an authentic "middle path" within the bipolar contour of the Tathāgata-embryo (*Tathāgatagarbha*) as simultaneously void (*śūnya*)—not void (*aśūnya*). The risk of a one-sided emphasis to the exclusion of either one of the collateral terms, is the failure to realize perfectly the Noble Truth, cessation of Suffering and thus, the Absolute Body (*Dharmakāya*). In this respect, the Disciples and Self-Enlightened ones are no different from the condition of the ordinary immature beings; both fall short of the median realization, differing only in the angle of approximation to the common ideal.

Undeniably, the faculties of those judged "ordinary" and "immature" are the more grossly errant, conditioned as they are by an egotistic attachment to the five grasping personality aggregates (the *skandhas.*)[44] Corrupted by this personalistic appropriation, such beings exemplify the classical mistake with regard to the "four wayward objects"; that which is impermanent they judge to be permanent, what is suffering to be pleasure, what is nonself to be self, and what is impure as pure. Variously combined, these fundamental misperceptions (*viparyāsas*) constitute the "wayward views of the two extremes": nihilism and eternalism. Misconstruing the deterioration of body, sense organs, feelings, and volitions as final, and having no appreciation for the reality of transmigration, a nihilistic connotation characterizes the faulty judgemental designations of many led-astray beings. Opposed to them, but no less mistaken are all those who lack a sufficient, self-reflective awareness of the momentary stream of consciousness, who fail to grasp the momentary perishing of consciousness, and thus err in

44. Form or material aggregate (*rūpa*); feelings (*vedana*); ideas (*samjñā*); motivations (*saṃskāra*), and perceptions (*vijñāna*).

the belief that the objects of their superficial, everyday perceptions persist inalterably and eternally.

As it had earlier, so for a second time and just as briefly, the *Śrī-Mālā* alludes to the ever changing structure of consciousness against the background of its doctrine of the permanent, steadfast and eternal nature of the Tathāgata-embryo (*Tathāgatagarbha*). In doing so, it exposes a major problem which it will be incapable of solving and which was one of the major reasons that undoubtedly accounted for the development of the complementary notion of "the storehouse consciousness" (the *Ālayavijñāna*) as identical to the Tathāgata-embryo (*Tathāgatagarbha*) in the subsequent development of the theory in the *Laṅkāvatāra sūtra*. Merely suggestive at this point, the problem yet poses itself thus. If, as has become increasingly apparent, the Tathāgata-embryo (*Tathāgatagarbha*) is to be more properly understood as ontic subject than as ontic substance, and if in its finalized state as Absolute Body (*Dharmakāya*) it is the "domain of omniscient knowledge," of perfected self-awareness, how else but as consciousness can it be designated? Therefore, is it not implicated in the very critique by which the *Śrī-Mālā* initially established its ultimacy? Is its priority not fundamentally compromised in its definition as the very category (i.e., consciousness) that the scripture previously found wanting in permanency and stability? From such a problematic contradiction the later refinements of the *Tathāgatagarbha-Ālayavijñāna* theory would seek resolution.

The question remains only an intimation here, however, since the express purpose of the *Śrī-Mālā*'s expose of the wayward perception of ordinary beings is to prove its inadequacy to the correct knowledge of the Tathāgata-embryo (*Tathāgatagarbha*). Their views are deemed faulty "reasonings," falling "too short" as they do in the eternalistic speculations, or over-extending "too far" in the nihilistic ones. The text doesn't actually apply these two inappropriate judgements to an exact correspondence with the void (*śūnya*)—not void (*aśūnya*) of the Tathāgata-embryo (*Tathāgatagarbha*). And one might be tempted to infer that the eternalistic rationale has been led astray by an undue emphasis upon the *aśūnya* aspect, while the nihilistic suffers from too exclusive an attention to the opposite pole. But the conformity (especially in the former pair) is inexact and forced. What the *Śrī-Mālā* really intends is not so much an acute analysis of eternalism and nihilism as modes of thought, but more to condemn the egoistic attachment to the five *skandhas* which generate such delusions. As long as that false personalism persists, such beings will ever be "immature" and never attain that exact and liberating intuition of the Tathāgata-embryo (*Tathāgatagarbha*) and therefore, the coincidence of that final and absolute cessation of suffering.

If the *Sri-Mālā* validates the "voidness knowledge" of the Disciples and Self-Enlightened ones, it immediately censures that insight as the very reason why they never perceive or understand the Noble Truth of the cessation of suffering. While attaining a correct perception into the voidness (*śūnyatā*) of the four wayward objects, they fail to achieve that corresponding insight into the Absolute Body (*Dharmakāya*) as permanent, bliss, self and pure. While they are superior to the ordinary, immature beings because they have properly understood the impermanent, suffering, not-self and impure marks of conditioned phenomena, the Disciples and Self-Enlightened critically fail to realize directly the permanence which alone makes the Cessation of Suffering the highest refuge and genuine resort.[45] Their fault consists in not grasping that their cognition of the *viparyāsas* (wayward or perverted views) while authentic, remains as yet partial to the full comprehension. It is obvious that the scripture here intends an exact parallel to the Tathāgata-embryo (*Tathāgatagarbha*), against which measure the Disciples and Self-Enlightened meet only half of the gnoseologic requirement. They may very well have witnessed a realization of an unconditioned state, or *nirvāṇa* as void (*śūnya*) of the defiling wayward views. But their claim to absolute cognitive finality (and here there is a noticeable similarity to the text's earlier criticism of

45. At this juncture, the *Śrī-Mālā*, judging from the criterion of permanency, declares that the Noble Truths of suffering, source of suffering and path leading to the cessation of suffering all belong to the realm of conditioned phenomena, and therefore are considered to be illusory, untrue and non-refuges. This is consistent with its insistence on the ultimacy of the Noble Truth of cessation of suffering as the definitive state of the Absolute Body (*Dharmakāya*):

> "Anything impermanent has an illusory nature. Everything with illusory nature is untrue, impermanent and not a refuge. Therefore, the Noble Truths of Suffering, Path leading to the Cessation of Suffering are actually untrue, impermanent, and not a refuge."

Lion's Roar, trans. Wayman and Wayman, p. 100.

the Arhats and Pratyekabuddhas) is illegitimate. Though credited with a perfection of the four resorts,[46] this "pure knowledge" of the Disciples and Self-Enlightened ones fails to perceive the collateral "not void" (*aśūnya*) dimension of reality which, only when encompassed as such, can be considered absolute.

TATHĀGATAGARBHA AS SELF-EXPLICITATING KNOWLEDGE

But as soon as this has been said, an immediate corrective is demanded, bringing to a final conclusion the substance of the *Śrī-Mālā's* doctrine on the Tathāgata-embryo (*Tathāgatagarbha*). It may be correct to say that only with the exact and precise knowledge of the embryo (*garbha*) as both void (*śūnya*) and not void (*aśūnya*), a knowledge which for differing reasons both the ordinary immature beings as well as the Disciples and Self-Enlightened ones lack, one can not attain to the perfection of the Noble Truth, Cessation of Suffering, and therefore, the Absolute Body (*Dharmakāya*). But the problem with such a formulation is the erroneous implication that this "domain of omniscient knowledge" is a thing to be acquired, a conceptually obtainable object, a circumscribable precept that would thus be reified by however lofty the mode of wisdom.

Now the whole point of the sūtra's designation of the Tathāgata-embryo (*Tathāgatagarbha*) as bipolar voidness (*śūnyatā*) has been to clarify it not as the object of a knowledge external to it, a knowledge existing formally and formerly outside it, but as self-explicating knowledge itself. The embryo as realized Absolute Body (*Dharmakāya*) is simultaneously comprehended and comprehending; it is the point where the embryo knows itself as it is inherently in itself, as void (*śūnya*) of all the defilement stores, but not void (*aśūnya*) of the innumerable Buddha natures. Put otherwise, the embryo's knowledge of itself is not so much an intuition of the Absolute Body (*Dharmakāya*), as it is more precisely, the self-intuition of that Body.

It will be recalled that the scripture's earlier discussion of the

46. One should cultivate by resort to the meaning, rather than to the letter; by resort to doctrines, rather than to personalities; by resort to knowledge, rather than perception, and by resort to scriptures of final meaning (*nitārtha*), rather than ones of provisional meaning (*neyārtha*). See ibid., n. 95, p. 103.

"Illustrious Doctrine" as it moved from being initially an object to be "embraced" and relied upon with faith, to a reality that is "displayed" and actualized within phenomenal consciousness, amounted to an implicit definition of the Tathāgata-embryo (*Tathāgatagarbha*). That position is more clearly asserted now at the conclusion of the text where the Lord, with reference to the embryo as intrinsically pure consciousness that is nevertheless defiled, admits to the great difficulty in understanding it. Therefore, the embryo is originally posited as the object of a faith which becomes the primary directive, guiding the individual along the spiritual path. It is this faith in the Tathāgata-embryo (*Tathāgatagarbha*) which alone assures the perfected maturity of certitude in the reality of the embryo:

> Queen, whatever disciples of mine are possessed of faith and (then) are controlled by faith, they by depending on the light of faith have a knowledge in the precincts of the Dharma, by which they reach certainty in this.[47]

The Tathāgata-embryo (*Tathāgatagarbha*) then, is conceived initially as the content of faith and thus, as was delineated in the first stages of the present analysis, under the form of objectivity as ontic substance—the unborn, undying, permanent, steadfast, eternal and ultimate ground of *saṃsāra* and *nirvāṇa*; as such it is reality-in-itself. But as the subsequent development of the *Śrī-Mālā* demonstrated, the embryo must surmount the form of objectivity, must move from the category of ontic substance, through the generic transformation of its inherent nature, to ontic subject, fully self-explicated self-consciousness; as realized Absolute Body (*Dharmakāya*), the realm of omniscient knowledge, it is reality-in-and-for-itself. If it is originally understood as an object of faith and therefore an object of consciousness, the Tathāgata-embryo (*Tathāgatagarbha*) must ultimately be considered as the movement towards its perfect self-realization and thus, as object of self-consciousness.

The critical importance of recognizing that knowledge, far from being just an attribute of the *Tathāgatagarbha* is its very essence,

47. Ibid., p. 107.

is underlined by the *Śrī-Mālā*'s concluding warning. Emphatically cautioning that it is not to be mistaken under the notion of a self, sentient being, soul, or personality, the sūtra stresses the *Tathāgatagarbha* as embryonic absolute knowledge. Its essence is to know itself as that which it is, to be aware of itself and to bring itself about. The content of the *garbha*'s knowledge is precisely itself as void (*śūnya*) of the extrinsic defilement stores and not void (*aśūnya*) of the inherent Buddha natures. It is this content which must be made manifest; the *garbha*'s self-knowledge must be actually adequate to its content. Since the *garbha* is to possess itself as its own object, then the known can't be something parallel to knowledge any more than it can be an external object for knowledge. Knowledge is rather the self-explication of the known content and the known content is implied knowledge.

With such a clarification on the essential nature of the Tathāgata-embryo (*Tathāgatagarbha*), its relationship to the Absolute Body (*Dharmakāya*) may be more fully appreciated. The image projected by the *Śrī-Mālā* is that of a cycle that presupposes its beginning and reaches its beginning only at its end. As was previously demonstrated, the Tathāgata-embryo is initially posited as an object of faith, and it will be recalled that the sūtra presents it as such in the most didactic style. With scarcely any apologetic intent, the text definitively formulated the embryo as having an ultimate existence without beginning or end; not being born and not dying; not subject to rebirth; but permanent, steadfast and eternal; being the base and support of the intrinsic Buddha natures as well as the adventitious, discrete defilement stores. Its immediate status then amounted to that of a postulated given. However, its organic designation as embryo (*garbha*) very quickly identified this beginning as the point of departure endowed with the propensity towards its own self-transformation, a process with a most specific teleological direction. For the self-movement of the Tathāgata-embryo as that alone which experiences suffering, to the Absolute Body (*Dharmakāya*) synonymous with the cessation of suffering, is a self-teleological process of inner convergence, where the Absolute Body as *telos* is simply the point of the embryo's fully self-conscious self-revelation.

In this cycle, if the Tathāgata-embryo is the beginning or cause (*hetu*), then the Absolute Body (*Dharmakāya*) is essentially result (*phala*), the end where the Tathāgata-embryo becomes what it is in truth. The nature of the embryo is to be actual, that which becomes itself. For if it starts with itself, the *Tathāgatagarbha* reaches its consummation with itself as the Absolute Body (*Dharmakāya*). It will be recalled that the latter is characterized by the same attributes as the former and in fact, is the former when it has not yet freed itself from the adventitious defilements, i.e., when it has not yet attained full self-conscious awareness as being intrinsically and always free of such stores. Put otherwise, the Absolute Body (*Dharmakāya*) can be a result (*phala*) only because it is already present from the start in an initial embryonic ("garbic") shape or content. The cyclic transformation then, of the *Tathāgatagarbha* into the *Dharmakāya* is that of an original absolute becoming an articulate absolute, where no new elements are acquired but the latent or inherent ones (i.e., the innumerable Buddha natures) are expressed. The only transition within this sphere of self-exposition for the sake of self-understanding is that from hiddenness to manifestation.

Evaluation

Such then is the doctrine of the Tathāgata-embryo (*Tathāgatagarbha*) as presented in the *Śrī-Mālā sūtra*. Though comparatively brief in form, this early sūtra dealing with the concept successfully sketches out the major propositions of the theory. Yet, if the text provides a certain basic instruction on the fundamental premises, it likewise exposes areas for question and further refinement. Previously mentioned was the attribution "perfection of self" to the Absolute Body (*Dharmakāya*). Now, if as the *Śrī-Mālā* suggests, the latter is ultimately identical to the Tathāgata-embryo, how is one to interpret the sūtra's stricture that the embryo is not a self, soul, or personality? There exists in other words, a certain terminological ambiguity between the *Tathāgatagarbha* and *Dharmakāya* that would only be clarified by the *Ratnagotravibhāga*'s unequivocal identification of the two through *Tathatā* (Suchness).

If the *Śrī-Mālā* generally engages in an epistemological critique of the various classes of sentient beings, what is the actual value of the spiritual path? What creative role or position do the diverse disciplines and practices of orthodox Buddhism play in the process of the embryo's realization as Absolute Body (*Dharmakāya*)? Although the text clearly indicates that the embryo is fundamentally synonymous with the "Great Vehicle" (*Mahāyāna*), grounding in itself all other vehicles, what is the actual relationship between the embryo's transformation and the classical stages of the spiritual path? What are the psychological dynamics involved, noted on the level of the individual, phenomenal consciousness, that accounts for and witnesses to, the potential Tathāgatahood becoming actual? Only with the insights of the *Vijnānavāda* and its analysis of the *Ālayavijnāna* ("Storehouse Consciousness") could this critical area be elucidated.

Surely, one of the most flagrant questions posed by the *Śrī-Mālā* is its position with regard to the doctrine of *Śūnyatā* of the *Prajñāpāramitā sūtras*. Its caution against becoming "distracted by voidness (*śūnyatā*)" is by no means revolutionary or unique, since the very same warning is implicit in the *śūnyatā-śūnyatā* of the orthodox Mādhyamika of Nāgārjuna.[48] What is novel is the attribution "not void" (*aśūnya*) to the *Tathāgatagarbha* and *Dharmakāya*. To positively define them as steadfast, eternal, of ultimate existence and intrinsically replete with the infinite Buddha natures, as well as to designate the Absolute Body (*Dharmakāya*) as the perfection of permanence (*nitya*), pleasure (*sukha*), self (*ātman*), and purity (*śubha*), was a radical departure from, and confrontation with, the classical *Śūnyavāda* of the wisdom (*prajñā*) literature. Since the *Śrī-Mālā* makes no attempt to justify its position by way of an apologetic accommodation, it would be left to the *Ratnagotravibhāga* to defend and interpret the *Tathāgatagarbha* theory in the light of the earlier tradition of *Śūnyatā*.

In addition to the already noted problem of the ultimacy of the nescience entrenchment, the originative nature of ignorance per se,

48. Most specially this is illustrated in his *Mahāprajñāpāramitā Śāstra*. In his excellent commentary and generous translations from that work, K. Venkata Ramanan has written, "Nāgārjuna's criticism of the categories, the basic factors of life and understanding, is intended to lay bare these absurdities (involved in one's false imagination) thereby to reveal the conditionedness (*śūnyatā*) of the conditioned as well as the further truth that the conditionedness of the conditioned is not unconditioned (*śūnyatā-śūnyatā*)." K. Venkata Ramanan, *Nāgārjuna's Philosophy As Presented in "The Māhā-Prajñāpāramitā Śāstra*" (Rutland, Vt.: Charles E. Tuttle Co., 1966; reprinted., Delhi: Motilal Banarsidass, 1975), p. 40.

clarification is needed as to the *Śrī-Mālā's* criterion by which it delineates between reality and illusion. It will be recalled in its discussion of the Noble Truths, that the scripture judges all things (including the first three of the Noble Truths) as untrue, impermanent and illusory which "belong to the characteristic of the constructed." While the intended meaning is clear enough in its own context, this principle encounters a certain metaphysical awkwardness for the sūtra's doctrine of the *Tathāgatagarbha* as the support, base, and ground of phenomenal existence. This weakness along with the problematic schema of the constructed and unconstructed *nirvāṇa,* as well as the constructed and unconstructed *saṃsāra,* would be rectified and replaced by the introduction of the *Ratnagotra's Tathatā* ("Suchness"), and the further refinement of the tripartite metaphysics of *pariniṣpanna, paratantra,* and *parikalpita* of the *Laṅkāvatārasūtra* and the later *Ch'eng Wei-Shih Lun* of Hsüan Tsang.

Finally, the *Śrī-Mālā* itself, for a third time, yet without explicating it as such, suggests the need its doctrine of the *Tathāgātagarbha* has for the complementary notion of the *Ālayavijñāna* ("Storehouse Consciousness"). Throughout its presentation, the sūtra essentially stresses the ultimate, stable, and permanent nature of the embryo. Becoming clarified more as ontic subjectivity rather than substance, its designation (in the concluding section of the text) as innately pure consciousness is not inconsistent. Nevertheless, the *Śrī-Mālā* admits to a difficulty with such a qualification of the *Tathāgatagarbha:*

> The virtuous consciousness, being momentary, is not defiled by defilements; and also the unvirtuous consciousness, being momentary, is not defiled by defilements. Lord, since neither do defilements touch that consciousness nor does that consciousness touch defilements, in that case, how does consciousness having a noncontacting nature, get defiled? Lord, there is both the defilement and the defiled consciousness. Therefore the meaning of the defilement on the intrinsically pure consciousness is difficult to understand.[49]

49. *Lion's Roar*, trans. Wayman and Wayman, p. 106.

What is immediately apparent is that the sūtra simply reiterates its dictum that the *Tathāgatagarbha* is void (*śūnya*) of the defilements which are adventitious and extrinsic. It has not made, and does not here make, any exploration into the nature of defilement (*kleśa*) that would explain its accidental specification. That defilement exists is asserted, but its provisional status has not been sufficiently reviewed and established. Undoubtedly, this reflects the entire tenor of the *Śrī-Mālā*, the whole thrust of which has been to maintain the categorical reality of the *Tathāgatagarbha* and its identification with the Absolute Body (*Dharmakāya*). Such an emphasis tends to neglect an adequate investigation of how and why the defilements come to veil or obscure the embryo.

But the same passage indicates that a yet more serious question exists not so much concerning the nature of defilement, as with the *Tathāgatagarbha*. As already suggested in an earlier section of the present analysis, the problem is not plainly exposed by the text itself. Originally the *Tathāgatagarbha* was presented as that which "has ultimate existence without beginning or end, has an unborn and undying nature," in direct contrast to the "momentary" and "unfixed" character of the sevenfold *vijñāna* system of consciousness. The instability of the latter was the *Śrī-Mālā's* argument for establishing the "permanent, steadfast, eternal" *garbha* as the support (*niśraya*), holder (*ādhāra*), and base (*pratiṣṭhā*) of phenomenal existence or *saṃsāra*. How is it that now, in the above passage, the *garbha* (notwithstanding its designation as "intrinsically pure") is defined by the very category that the *Śrī-Mālā* had rejected as inconsistent and variable, i.e., by consciousness (*vijñānā*)?

Furthermore, the *garbha*, as consciousness, is now admitted to be momentary and of "a noncontacting nature." Does this not seriously jeopardize its claim as the ultimate ground of the phenomenal world; how can the *garbha*, thus conceived, remain the substratum (*ādhāra*) of *saṃsāra* if it is essentially unconnected and non-concommitant to it? This dual ambiguity seeks its resolution in the complementary system of the *Vijñānavāda*. However, before exploring the process of identifying the *Tathāgatagarbha* with that school's theory of the *Ālayavijñāna,* it is necessary to study the *Ratnagotravibhāga*, the complete and final systematization of the *garbha* as a separate and independent theory of its own.

CHAPTER II

THE RATNAGOTRAVIBHĀGA

THOUGH THE ŚRĪ-MĀLĀ SUTRA's importance in the development of the *Tathāgatagarbha* theory rests on the fact that it is one of the earliest Buddhist scriptures to be dedicated specifically to an exposition of the concept, it was not the first nor the last text to contribute to its elaboration. Besides the earlier *Tathāgatagarbhasūtra* with its classic illustrations of how the *garbha* is veiled by the defilements, the *Śrī-Mālā* was preceded by the still earlier *Avataṃsakasūtra*. Although that work offers no singular discussion of the concept, its major tenet of a universal penetration of sentient beings by the wisdom of the Buddha (*buddhajñāna*) was peculiarly suited to define and complement still more precisely the nature of the *garbha*. Contemporaneous with the *Śrī-Mālā* is the *Anūnatvapūrṇatvanirdeśaparivarta* with its important doctrine on the Absolute Body (*Dharmakāya*) and its identification with the "mass of living beings" (*sattvadhātu*). In addition, several other texts composed after the *Śrī-Māla*, while not treating the doctrine exclusively or even intentionally, yet contained elements complementary to a final systematic presentation of the *Tathāgatagarbha* theory. The *Dhāraniśvararājasūtra*; the *Ratnadārikāsūtra*; the *Jñānālokālaṅkārasūtra*; the *Mahāparinirvānasūtra*; the *Sāgaramatiparipṛcchā*; the *Gaganagañjābodhisattvaparipṛcchā*; the *Ratnacūḍasūtra*; the *Mahāyānābhidharmasūtra*; the *Mahāyānasūtrālaṅkāra* (*śāstra*); the *Vajracchedika*; the *Aṣṭasāhasrikā*; *Dṛdhādhyāśayaparivarta*; *Tathāgatagunajñānàcintyaviṣayāvatāranirdeśa*; *Kāśyapaparivarta,* and the *Saḍāyatanasūtra* figured principally towards the doctrinal substantiation of the *Tathāgatagarbha*.[1]

1. It should be noted that those texts beginning with the *Tathāgatagarbha sūtra* down to and including the *Mahāyānasūtralaṅkāra*, were apparently unknown to Nāgārjuna, as they appear in none of the works attributed to him. This tends to support the theory that the fully developed concept of the *Tathāgatagarbha* was a novel and fairly recent development in Mahāyāna Buddhism. Significant too, is the presence of the two texts (the *Mahāyānabhidharma sūtra* and *Mahāyānasūtralaṅkāra śāstra*) critical to the *Vijñānavāda*, as well as the representation of the *Prajñāpāramitā sūtras*, viz., the *Vajracchedikā* and the *Aṣṭasāhasrikā*.

It was not until the *Ratnagotravibhāga* however, that the various insights and developments of the above texts (all of which served as its sources) were to be comprehensively synthesised into the most authoritatively complete analysis of the *Tathāgatagarbha* theory.[2] Typical of its eclectic style, the śāstra, while employing works influential in the Vijñānavādin and *Prajñāpāramitā* traditions, exercises a highly discriminative use of those sources, drawing upon them only to accredit its already determined theme.

Consisting of an original verse section (*kārikā*) attributed to Bodhisattva Maitreya, with a later commentary in verse and prose, the final form of the *Ratnagotra* dates from the early 5th century A.D., and its authorship is credited to Saramati. Surviving in its original Sanskrit, as well as the Tibetan and Chinese versions, the text has been most recently rendered in English by Takasaki. While his translation is used as the basis of the present analysis,[3] an important digression must be noted.

Throughout, he renders *garbha* as "matrix" rather than "embryo." In English, the former has multiple meanings, depending on the context in which it is used. But in general, the interpretation of "matrix" (whether it be from a biological standpoint, and therefore connoting "womb," or from a metallurgic one, and thus translating as a "gangue" in which rock fragments are embedded) suggests a container, something which holds something else. This would seem to miss entirely the dynamic, self-transformative nature of the *Tathāgatagarbha.* Therefore, in the present study "embryo" seems more fitting to express that characteristic so peculiar to the *garbha* doctrine, and in all quotations from the text it will be substituted for Takasaki's "matrix."

Not only is this done in reliance upon Wayman and Wayman

2. In addition to those already listed, the *Ratnagotra* includes quotes from more than eight unknown sources. Although not quoting it directly, the śāstra was also undoubtedly influenced by the *Lotus of the Wonderful Law* (*Saddharmapundarika*), whose title is directly mentioned in its text.

3. An alternative translation is that of E. Obermiller from the Tibetan version alone, entitled, *The Sublime Science of the Great Vehicle to Salvation, Being a Manual of Buddhist Monism, the Work of Ārya Maitreya With a Commentary by Āryasaṅga*, Acta Orientalia, vol. 9, 1931. However, Jikido Takasaki's translation has been deemed critically superior with its translation from the original Sanskrit text in conjunction with the Tibetan and Chinese versions. See n. 3, p. 15 above for reference.

who chose "embryo" for their translation of the *Śrī-Mālā Sūtra*, but also with the approbation of Ruegg. In his excellent linguistic review of the topic,[4] he notes that the Tibetan equivalent of *Tathāgatagarbha* (*de bžin gšegs pa'i sñiṅ po*) could never be translated as "womb" (*mṅal* or *lhums*), but is more properly rendered, "embryonic essence," "kernel" or "heart." It is this last designation as "heart" (*jirüken*) that has been maintained in the Mongolian translations, where *Tathāgatagarbha* has as its equivalent, *tegüncilen iregsen-ü jirüken*. The majority of Chinese translators render *Tathāgatagarbha* as *jou lai tsang*, in which case *tsang*, as "storehouse," suggests either that which enfolds or contains something else, or that which is itself enfolded, hidden or contained by another. Obviously, the Tibetan and Mongolian interpretations indicate the latter. Ruegg then chronicles those Western translators who have chosen a similar interpretation. Whether they have used "embryo" (Tucci; La Vallée Poussin; Lamotte; Conze; Leumann), "essence" (Obermiller; Thomas; Dutt; Guenther; von Glassenapp), "germ" (Leumann; Jacobi; Murti; Frauwallner) or "nature" (Wassiljew, La Valée Poussin), all imply that *garbha* connotes a "content" rather than a "container" (which is a critical implication of "womb"). It is on the basis of such a survey, and his own interpretative analysis of the *Ratnagotravibhāga*, that Ruegg would justify the translation of *Tathāgatagarbha* as "embryo of the Tathāgata."[5]

Appearing as it does some two hundred years after the *Śrī-Mālā*, and encompassing the richness of the canonical development during that time, the *Ratnagotravighāga* reflects the wide variety of linguistic designations, suggested by its multiple sources, as applicable to the concept of the *Tathāgatagarbha*. Therefore, throughout its "analysis" (*vibhāga*) the *Ratnagotra* witnesses to

4. See *La Théorie Du Tathāgatagarbha et Du Gotra*, pp. 499-513.

5. "En d'autres termes, dans les images du *Tathāgatagarbha sūtra*, le *Tathāgatagarbha* figure comme un contenu et non pas comme un contenant (et encore moins comme une matrice); et les fragments Sanskrits des autres Sūtra traitant du *Tathāgatgarbha* qui ont été étudiés plus haut semblent également's opposer à l'interprétation selon laquelle le *garbha* serait une matrice, ou un contenant, quelconque... Dans tous les autres emplois du terme de *garbha* dans ce Śāstra [*Ratnagotravibhāga*] aussi il est naturel de voir un embryon ou une essence—autrement dit un contenu—et il serait infiniment plus difficile d'y voir une matrice." *La Theorie*, p. 506.

numerous terminological equivalences, where *garbha* ("embryo") is variously characterised by such different expressions as *gotra* ("lineage," "gene," "germ"); *dhātu* ("essence," "nature," "ground"); *hetu* ("cause," "source," "origin"); *āśraya* ("basis," "substratum"); *cittaprakṛti* ("innate mind"), and *dharmatā* ("essential nature"). Though they are by no means exact synonyms, they are often substituted for one another throughout the *śāstra*, determined substantially by the particular scriptural source which the *Ratnagotra* happens to utilize, and the particular aspect under its analysis. Of those terms, *gotra* and *dhātu* appear most frequently in the course of the text in lieu of *garbha* and it should be noted that they, together, preserve the inherent feature of the *Śrī-Mālā*'s concept of the *Tathāgatagarbha* as an ultimate, unconditional reality that is simultaneously the inherent, dynamic process towards its complete self-manifestation. While in the *Ratnagotra, dhātu* as "essence" tends to suggest the former, more ontic dimension, *gotra* as "germ" continues to maintain the organic, self-transformative implication of the latter.

As the śāstra advances its exposition, it comes to delineate in its ninth chapter an exact, triadic hermeneutic on the term *Tathāgatagarbha* in which it clarifies several of those alternating terms used in preceding chapters. But before reaching that point, the commentary introduces and examines, in depth, a conceptual refinement which, linguistically as well as doctrinally, marked a critically significant development within the *Tathāgatagarbha* theory as presented in the earlier *Śrī-Mālā-Sūtra*. The first five chapters, while elaborating somewhat, tend to merely restate that latter scripture's insistence on the *ekayāna* as *Buddhayāna*, i.e., it advocates the Buddha as the ultimate refuge and final goal of the path. Basically, those first short chapters spell out the meaning of the śāstra's title as *Ratnagotra* or, more properly, *Gotra ratnatrahasya* ("the germ as origin of the three jewels").[6] Here, the three jewels refer to the three refuges of the Buddha, Dharma, and Saṃgha. But as the second chapter illustrates, attention is directed primarily to the Buddha as "the one who has realized the Buddhahood (*buddhatva*)," which, in its eightfold quality,[7] is the goal common to all living beings by virtue of their essential

6. Takasaki, *Ratnagotravibhāga*, p. 186.
7. The eight qualities of Buddhahood are listed in appendix 1.

nature (*dharmadhātu*), here identified as the embryo (*garbha*) of the Tathāgata. Therefore, if the Buddha exercises a position of superiority, the śāstra makes it very evident that his attainment is not unique to Him alone, but only that He has realized an enlightenment which He knows to exist as a universal potentiality through an equality (*samatayā*) between His nature (*dharmatā*) and that of all beings. If the Buddha is celebrated, it is as one in whom the embryo has attained full self-explicated maturity, remaining as yet a latent possibility in all other beings. But it must be admitted that this dynamic, self-actualizing character of the embryo is only lightly suggested in comparison to the greater emphasis upon it as a basic substratum, an essential nature common to the Buddha and all sentient beings.

The Jewels of the Dharma and the Saṃgha

Following a similar pattern, the third chapter presents an eightfold quality of the jewel of the Dharma,[8] which is subdivided into the "Doctrine as the Truth of Extinction (of suffering)" and the "Doctrine as the Truth of Path." The former Truth, beyond all speculative rational categories, rises as the intuition that the irrational thought (*ayoniśomanasikāra*), or ignorant discrimination (vikalpa), the cause of action by body, word, and thought (*karman*) and the accompanying defilements (*kleśas*), is non-existent by nature. From this the śāstra concludes in an almost perfunctory brevity:

> By knowing deeply that this Irrational Thought is extinct by nature, consequently there is no origination of duality and discrimination; for this reason there is absolutely no origination of suffering. This is called the Truth of Extinction of Suffering.[9]

That this realization is of salvific efficacy, the *Ratnagotra* immediately calls upon the *Śrī-Mālā* to substantiate, which, it will be recalled, equated the Noble Truth, Cessation of Suffering with the

8. The eight qualities of the *Dharma* are listed in appendix 1.
9. Takasaki, *Ratnagotravibhāga*, pp. 166-167.

Absolute Body (*Dharmakāya*).[10] Therefore, by implication, this recognition of the irrational thought as extinct by nature is the very means by which the embryo of the Tathāgata attains its ultimate manifestation. This process is more fully elucidated under the second subdivision, the Doctrine as the Truth of Path, in which the śāstra exposes in greater detail the basic presuppositions of the Truth of Extinction, viz., the dynamics of the irrational thought, the defilements, and pursuant actions. While these latter are discussed with further clarity in the *Ratnagotra's* eighth chapter, their mention here provides certain prefatory information evidently presumed by the latter. More importantly, this preliminary treatment underscores through suggestion, the role of non-discriminative wisdom (*avikalpa-jñāna*) as the primary mode by which the Tathāgata-embryo realizes itself as the manifest Absolute Body (*Dharmakāya*).

Due to the innate tendencies of desire, hatred, and ignorance, beings fasten onto the unreal characteristic of things upon which they base their cognitive judgements, any one of which can be designated in general as the "irrational thought" (*ayoniśomanasikāra*). Once the mind has been influenced by any such thought, it is said to be actually defiled by either desire, hatred, or ignorance, i.e., what was only in the state of tendency (*anuśaya*) now emerges as fully manifest. Taking the desirable, detestable or obscure appearance of things as substantially real, one defiles the mind by depending upon such superficial characteristics as the basis for any cognitive-evaluative determination. This defiled mental condition inevitably produces actions born either of desire, hatred, or ignorance and expressed through body, speech, or consequent thoughts; from this arises the condition for rebirth. Saṃsāric existence then, arises with a critical misperception, a discriminative failure to recognize the one real essence of things (*eka-dhātu*) as it is. On the other hand, not hampered by the external characteristics,

10. The *Ratnagotra* quotes the *Śrī-Mālā* thus:

" 'O Lord, extinction of Suffering does not mean the disappearance of element. By the term, "Extinction of Suffering," O Lord, there is designated the Absolute Body of the Tathāgata...And thi very Absolute Body of the Tathāgata, O Lord, (when it is) unreleased from the covering of moral defilements, is called the Matrix of Tathāgata [*Tathāgatagarbha*].' " Ibid., pp. 167-168.

the apparent form of things, the Tathāgata is He who has perfectly realized the equality of all elements (*dharmās*), the Reality (*Bhūta*) common to all things equally.

> And thus, this realization of all natures by Wisdom, as being equal without any addition nor diminution because of these two facts, i.e., because we cannot see any characteristic nor basis of non-being [any unreal basis of characteristics], and we can see the real character of being as the absolute truth, this is to be known as the "enemy" (*pratipakṣa*) of all kinds of obstacles against the true perception.... This is indeed the Path of perception and practice based upon the non-discriminative Wisdom, which is the cause of attaining the Absolute Body (of the Tathāgata) and which is to be understood in detail according to the Sūtra named *Prajñapāramitā*.[11]

The maturation of the Tathāgata-embryo as Absolute Body is dependent, then, upon the dual operation of a non-discriminative wisdom effective on the one hand as perceiving the adventitious, contingent status of the defilements, and on the other, as simultaneously realizing the genuine essence, the essential nature of phenomena (*dharmās*). It is this conjoint function of wisdom that substantiates the principle of "neither addition nor diminution," since nothing need be added to Reality (*Bhūta*) complete in itself, nor is there necessity to remove impurities which are ultimately unreal, created and sustained by a mind deluded with hatred, desire, and obscurity.

What is important to note in this early implication of the Tathāgata-embryo is that it is not enough to gain insight into the non-existent nature of impurity; there must be a simultaneous, intuitive penetration of the fundamental ground, "the one, real essence as it is." This brief passage suggests, therefore, the axiom already introduced by the *Śrī-Mālā Sūtra*, and explicitly reformulated in the *Ratnagotra*'s tenth chapter, that the Tathāgata-embryo is at once void (*śūnya*) of the defilements and not void (*aśūnya*) of the Buddha natures. The proposition as to the ultimate non-existence of impurity closely approximates the former, while the insistence on the unconditional real essence corresponds to

11. Ibid., p. 171.

the latter dimension. And it is significant to note here the *Ratnagotra*'s reliance upon the *Prajñāpāramitā* literature as the scriptural witness and validation of its position. If the śāstra consequently assumes a critical stance towards the wisdom sūtras, its intent is to serve as a necessary corrective to a faulty interpretation of those works, rather than as a total repudiation of them.

If the third chapter stressed the spiritual path primarily as a unique mode of perception, the fourth acclaims the Bodhisattva, representative of the jewel of the community, as the one who actually exemplifies this precise discernment. He exercises a wisdom in perception, the purity of which is identical to that of the Buddha. Since this perspicuous illumination is not only for his own benefit but for the guidance of all beings, his superiority is well established over the Śrāvaka, intent on an enlightenment that remains essentially self-directed; hence, the ascription "jewel" to the Bodhisattva community.

The definitive character of the Bodhisattva's perception is discussed in terms of its manner and extent. The former aspect refers to an intuition into the quiescent nature of the phenomenal world "as it is" (*yathāvadbhāvikatā*). The Bodhisattva understands the universal non-substantiality (*nairātmya*) of what has been conventionally designated as "individualities" (*pudgalās*) and "separate elements" (*dharmās*). This of course, represents the fundamental Buddhist mandate of "not self" (*anattā*), comprehensively applied to persons and things; as such, it is by no means original to the *Ratnagotra*. What is striking however, is the śāstra's unique rationale accounting for this basic insight on the part of the Bodhisattva. According to the text, the field of this cognition, free from all attachment, is the innate purity of the essence of all beings. Because of his perception of the innate brightness (*prakṛtiprabhāsvaratā*) of the mind, and the subsequent intuition that the defilements on the mind are "destroyed from the outset," the Bodhisattva fathoms the extremity of the non-substantiality of the phenomenal world. More explicitly, under the second aspect of the Bodhisattva's perception, its extent, said to exist "as far as" (*yāvadbhāvikatā*) the limit of all knowable things, it is clear that the object of such perception is no other than the pervasive presence of the Tathāgata-embryo, the "nature of Omniscience" in, and the "Absolute Essence" of all beings:

> Because (with respect to the extent), they perceive the existence of the embryo of the *Tathāgata* in all living beings, up to those who are in the animal kingdom, by means of the supermundane intellect (*lokattara-prajñā*) which reaches as far as the limit of all knowable things..., the Absolute Essence is realized in the sense of all-pervading (*sarvatraga*).[12]

What in fact the *Ratnagotra* advocates then, is that the universality of the Tathāgata-embryo inherently pure yet veiled by the contingent and accidental defilements, and the Bodhisattva's unobstructed vision of it as such, sustains and grounds the doctrine of non-substantiality; it is the ontological presupposition for the axiomatic *anattā* dictum of elemental Buddhism. All beings are empty and devoid of self-nature because they are unilaterally grounded upon the absolute essence of the Tathāgata-embryo; to perceive the unconditional status of the latter is to understand the determinate relativity of the former. But if the reality of the Tathāgata-embryo implies the emptiness of the phenomenal world or *saṃsāra*, it is at the same time the very reason that the nature of such mundane elements is said to be "of absolute quiescence from the outset"; *saṃsāra* is itself *nirvāṇa* when correctly perceived as founded upon the indeterminate, ultimate nature which is the Tathāgata-embryo. If in the *Śrī-Mālā Sūtra saṃsāra*, said to be based upon the *Tathāgatagarbha*, tended to be antithetically opposed to it as being impermanent, unfixed, momentary, subject to birth, death, and rebirth, the *Ratnagotra* will tend more to emphasize the coincidental nature of the two. But as was typified in the three chapters preceding it, the śāstra's remarks on the Tathāgata-embryo in this fourth chapter are only allusive and suggestive of further development and refinement in subsequent chapters.

With the fifth chapter, the prefatory section of the *Ratnagotra* concludes in an explanation of the salvific valuation of the three jewels of the Buddha, Doctrine, and Community. From an empirical standpoint, the Buddha may be considered a refuge (*śaraṇa*) since He is the highest of human beings, the Doctrine because it is absolutely free of passion, and the Community since it is superior to all other communal bodies. However, the Doctrine

12. Ibid., p. 175.

and the Community are not credited as ultimate refuges; the former because it is deemed non-eternal and fundamentally "a non-existence" (*abhāva*) while the latter, because it represents those who have not yet attained the highest, perfect enlightenment, and being fearful, have themselves taken refuge in the Tathāgata.[13]

While the text plainly bases its evaluation of the Doctrine and the Community upon the authority of the *Śrī-Mālā Sūtra*, it departs notably from that source in explaining the non-ultimate status of the former. Elaborated from a twofold perspective of the Doctrine as teaching (namely, sūtras and other forms of instruction consisting of names, words and letters) and as realization (previously discussed as "Truth of Path" and "Truth of Extinction"), the scope of the *Ratnagotra* is obviously broader. The Doctrine as teaching is viewed somewhat extrinsically as the means which facilitate the acquisition of the path and therefore, point to something more ultimate, beyond themselves. If the "Truth of Path," said to be of artificial character and therefore false, deceptive, untrue, and non-eternal, reflects the *Śrī-Mālā*'s judgement that the first three Noble Truths are impermanent and illusory, the *Ratnagotra*'s interpretation of the Doctrine as "Truth of Extinction" digresses significantly from the sūtra's analysis of the "Truth of Cessation of Suffering." It will be recalled that the *Śrī-Mālā* effected a direct equation between the Noble Truth, Cessation of Suffering, and the Absolute Body (*Dharmakāya*); to realize the latter is to unqualifiably experience the former. Now in the *Ratnagotra*, the "Truth of Extinction" is interpreted with no such ultimate equivalence, being described instead as "a non-existence" (*abhāva*), a condition characterized by the mere absence of defilement and suffering. It is in fact, equated with the *nirvāṇa* of the Śrāvaka and is said to be "just like the extinction of a lamp." Therefore, whether it is considered as teaching or as realization,

13. It should be noted that, while in the fourth chapter dedicated to the jewel of the Community, the *Ratnagotra* addressed itself to the Bodhisattva as representative of the *saṃgha*, extolling the manner and extent of his perception, such is not the case in the present chapter. Here, references to the comparative weakness of the community are directly attributed to the Śrāvakas. It would appear that the śāstra has adopted a double standard in speaking of the *saṃgha*, somewhat as the *Śrī-Mālā* which likewise referred to the Arhats and Pratyekabuddhas when mentioning the non-ultimate character of the community as refuge.

the Doctrine (*Dharma*) according to the śāstra is deemed non-ultimate and, together with the Community (*Saṃgha*), can only serve as a temporary refuge.

That the *Ratnagotra* fails to adopt a significant, systematic insight afforded by its major scriptural source is curious, especially given its own highly schematic tendency to integrate and synthesize the various dimensions of the *Tathāgatagarbha* theory. Its obvious intent is to stress that the Buddha, having realized the highest, perfect enlightenment, is the sole and ultimate refuge over against the two provisional jewels of the Doctrine and Community. Yet, when it comes to describe the reason for His unconditional, salvific priority, the text states that it is His possession of the "Body of the Doctrine, the Absolute Body, *Dharmakāya*" that so qualifies the Buddha as the unique, eternal, quiescent and unchangeable refuge. There appears to be then a certain brief equivocation at this point in the *Ratnagotra* between the status of the Buddha and the Doctrine, where initially the latter is, together with the Community, considered subservient to the former, but is then indicated as being constitutive of it. Such apparent inconsistency stems from an artificial distinction between the two terms, and would have been unnecessary had the text followed more exactly the concordance developed by its prime scriptural source, the *Śrī-Mālā*. In this respect, that particular sūtra proved more effective in demonstrating the cogent assimilation of the three jewels into the one, ultimate jewel and refuge of the Buddha.

Samalā and Nirmalā Tathatā

This minor difference between the *Śrī-Mālā Sūtra* and the *Ratnagotra* is indicative of a broader perspectival variance between the śāstral examination of the *Tathāgatagarbha* theory, and its earlier scriptural treatment, an emphasis already suggested by the first five chapters of the *Ratnagotra*, and which will generally characterise the remaining sections of its analysis. While the *Śrī-Mālā* discussed the concept rather fluidly from the interdependent perspectives of ontology, soteriology, and epistemology, the *Ratnagotra* focuses its exposition from predominantly one angle. In the *sūtra*, the *Tathāgatagarbha* clearly emerges as the Absolute that is the very vehicle of its self-manifestation. While its ontic status as the unborn, undying, permanent, steadfast, eternal and ultimate ground of *saṃsāra* and *nirvāṇa* is strikingly deliberate, its designation as such is more presupposition than the object of detailed elaboration by the *Śrī-Mālā*. If it is reality-in-itself, the *Tathāgatagarbha* is much more fully explicated as the inherent movement towards its perfect self-realization as manifest Absolute Body, the realm of omniscient knowledge, and thus, as reality in-and-for-itself. Its dynamic, self-transformative character as embryonic, absolute knowledge moving towards its own complete and total self-awareness, is the principal focus of the *Srī-Mālā's* investigation; soteriology and epistemology are the primary modes through which the scripture defines the *Tathāgatagarbha*, whose ontic nature essentially remains a postulated given.

The ontic assumption of the *Śrī-Mālā Sūtra* is the very nucleus of the *Ratnagotra's* presentation. While the former emphasizes the *Tathāgatagarbha* as process, the self-evolutive potentiality of the embryo to become itself as manifest Absolute Body, the latter stresses the convergent identity of the two poles as an ontological antecedent; though linguistically distinct, the *Tathāgatagarbha* and *Dharmakāya* are one and the same reality. If the *Śrī-Mālā* evidenced a slight nebular equivocation between the pair, attributing "the perfection of self" to the *Dharmakāya* while insisting that the *Tathāgatagarbha* "is neither self nor sentient being, nor soul nor personality," all such ambiguity is removed by the *Ratnagotra* whose complete equation of the two is reflected in its consistent application of the term "essence" (*dhātu*) in reference to both the *Tathāgatagarbha* and *Dharmakāya*. What the śāstra principally examines then, is the quintessential dimension, the ultimate, ontic nature, common to both *Tathāgatagarbha* and *Dharmakāya*. This particular orientation has already been suggested by the first five chapters, where the *Ratnagotra*'s implications of, and references to the Tathāgata-embryo are that of a fundamental nature; a basic substratum; a reality common to all beings; an innate brightness: a universal Absolute to be correctly perceived and exactly understood by a non-discriminative wisdom. The śāstra's disposition then, to interpret the nature of the Tathāgata-embryo as Absolute Reality-in-itself, surfaces from the very beginning of its analysis.

Chapter 6 inaugurates the body of the text with the critically deceive definition, providing the necessary linguistic and conceptual refinement adequate to the *Ratnagotra*'s intuition of the identity of the *Tathāgatagarbha* and *Dharmakāya*. And if its multiple sources employed several distinct terms as was noted previously, a significant advance of the śāstra was to here clarify by specific designation the essential referent, common to the various determinants. Therefore, according to the text, that ultimate denominator is nothing other than Reality in its condition of absolute Suchness (*Tathatā*) which in turn, is subdivided into the two major categories of *samalā* and *nirmalā*. *Samalā Tathatā* designates that aspect of Reality "mingled with pollution" and is the *Ratnagotra*'s consistent term for the *Tathāgatagarbha*, while *Nirmalā Tathatā* is its expression for Reality "apart from pollution," and is thus synonymous with the *Dharmakāya*:

> "The Reality mingled with pollution (*samalā-tathatā*)" is a term for "the Essence (*dhātu*), unreleased from the sheath of defilements," i.e., the Embryo of Tathāgata. "The Reality apart from pollution (*nirmalā tathatā*)" is a term for the same Essence, when it is characterized as the Perfect Manifestation of Basis (*āśraya-parivṛtti*) in the Stage of Buddha, i.e., the Absolute Body of the Tathāgata.[14]

The subsequent development of the analysis focuses therefore on the nature of Absolute Suchness as one and the same reality or essence, subsistent in a two-fold modality whose very inconceivability demonstrates its non-duality. If Suchness mingled with pollution (*Samalā Tathatā* or Tathāgata-embryo) is deemed ineffable since it is both pure and defiled simultaneously, and if Suchness apart from pollution (*Nirmalā Tathatā* or Absolute Body) is likewise so stipulated because though originally not defiled, it is later purified, they are obviously non-separate in a fundamental purity. The defilement and subsequent purification inversely signify a purity common to *Tathatā* as *samalā* and thus hidden, and as *nirmalā* and therefore, manifest.

Threefold Meaning of the Tathāgatagarbha

In its seventh and briefest chapter, the *Ratnagotra* initiates its

14. Takasaki, *Ratnagotravibhāga*, p. 187.

examination of *Samalā Tathatā* with the axiomatic formulation taken from the *Tathāgatagarbhasūtra*, dogmatically asserting the universality of the Tathāgata-embryo in all animate beings:[15]

> Now with reference to "the Reality mingled with pollution" [*Samalā Tathatā*], it is said: All living beings are possessed of the Embryo of the Tathāgata [*sarva sattvās tathāgatagarbhāh*].[16]

While their detailed interpretive analysis will await the ninth chapter, the śāstra here anticipates by didactically stating in a trio of synonymous phrases, the threefold meaning of this critical theorem. The first set is somewhat obscure and becomes clear only in the light of the two other triplicate combinations. It can be said that all beings are possessed of the Buddha-embryo since they are all equally included in the Buddha's Wisdom, because their inherent "immaculateness" is non-dual by nature, and because the result of that innate purity becomes manifest "on the germ (*gotra*) of the Buddha." There follows immediately the second parallel expression specifying the same intent as the first. Accordingly, all living beings are possessed of the embryo because of the universal penetration of all things by the Buddha's Body, because Suchness (*Tathāta*) is of undifferentiated nature, and because the germ (*gotra*) of the Buddha exists in all living beings. The third set of the coincident definitions states that due to the penetration of the Absolute Body (*Dharmakāya*) into all living beings, and because the Tathāgata is the Absolute Reality or Suchness (*Tathatā*) and is therefore the "undifferentiated whole," and finally, since the germ of the Tathāgata (*Tathāgatagotra*) exists in every living being, it may be said that all animate beings are possessed of the embryo of the Tathāgata (*sarvasattvās tathāgatagarbhāḥ*).

In a threefold reiteration, the *Ratnagotra* has here established as

15. According to Ruegg, the doctrine generally admitted by the majority of schools in India and Tibet was that only the animate world (*sattvaloka*)—consisting of those beings possessed of the *Tathagatagarbha*—would attain enlightenment and become a Buddha. The inanimate world *bhājanaloka*) would thus be excluded. An exception would be the school of *T'ien-t as* (*Tendai*) which considered that the Buddha nature is the nature of all beings, animate and inanimate and included the mineral kingdom as well as the plants, See *La Théorie*, p. 152.

16. Takasaki, *Ratnagotravibhāga*, p. 196.

the ground of the unconditional presence of the Tathāgata-embryo (*Tathāgatagarbha*) among animate beings, a decisive equality through the Absolute Body (*Dharmakāya*), Suchness (*Tathatā*), and the germ of the Tathāgata (*Tathāgatagotra*). Though the text itself is rather stark, providing no further commentative elaboration at this point, certain significant ideas have been set forth by the chapter.

In its equation of the Buddha's wisdom (*buddhajñāna*) with the Absolute Body (*Dharmakāya*) the śāstra has integrated into its doctrine a cardinal precept of the *Avataṃsakasūtra*, the earliest of its multiple scriptural sources. More specifically, the universal permeating influence of the Absolute Body is a function of its character as self-born wisdom, the wisdom of omniscience, penetrating all beings equally. Subsequently, to attain the Absolute Body is to recognize the wisdom of the Tathāgata (*Tathāgatajñāna*) as the definitive, constitutive principle of one's own cognitive awareness; it is to fully comprehend the non-differentiation of the Buddha's wisdom and one's own fundamental, noetic substratum. This was clearly intended in the *Ratnagotra*'s lengthy quotation from the *Avataṃsaka* in the preceding sixth chapter which included the following reference:

> Similarly, O Son of the Buddha, the Wisdom of the Tathāgata, which is the immeasurable wisdom, the profitable wisdom for all living beings, thoroughly penetrates within the mentality [*citta-santāna*] of every living being. And every mental disposition of a living being has the same size as the Buddha's Wisdom. Only the ignorant, however, being bound by misconceptions does neither know nor cognize nor understand nor realize the Wisdom of the Tathāgata (within himself).[17]

Though it is only through implication, this passage clearly suggests the *Śrī-Mālā Sūtra*'s concept of the *Tathāgatagarbha* as embryonic absolute knowledge, whose essence is to know itself as that which it is, and thus become itself as manifest Absolute Body (*Dharmakāya*). Though the points of reference are not as sharply focused and as clearly articulated here as in the *Śrī-Mālā*, the dynamics of self-transformation through self-recognition are identical. Under

17. Ibid., p. 191.

the auspices of the *Tathāgatagarbhasūtra*, the *Ratnagotra* initially postulates an identity of the Tathāgata-embryo with the Absolute Body. Then, through the authority of the *Avataṃsaka*, it further specifies the essence of that Body (and through association, of the Tathāgata-embryo) as the absolute wisdom of omniscience. In the description of the process in which a "son of the Buddha" arrives at full equality with the Tathāgata, it is this wisdom that is the very vehicle of its final and complete manifestation; wisdom effects its own self-witnessing recognition. What, in the *Śrī-Mālā*, was the object of a lengthy and detailed definition (i.e., the relationship of the *Tathāgatagarbha* to the *Dharmakāya*) has here, in the *Ratnagotra*, been compacted within only a few brief verses. Though it might appear that the śāstra's rationale has been severely abbreviated in the process, it is more simply a testament to the linguistic differences of the two texts. As already indicated, the *Ratnagotra* focuses upon Absolute Suchness (*Tathatā*) as the essential nature, common to both the Tathāgata-embryo when veiled by the defilements (*samalā*), and Absolute Body when unobstructed by them (*nirmalā*). Its principal emphasis, therefore, is the ontic identity of the two. By contrast, the *Śrī-Mālā* had adopted a more formal soteriological and epistemological perspective, stressing the process in which the Tathāgata-embryo comes to free itself from the covering of the adventitious defilement stores, and to display the innate Buddha natures. What is significant in the present passage of the *Ratnagotra*, is its basic consistency with the more explicitly dynamic character of the *Śrī-Mālā*; this, through the instrumentality of wisdom here descriptive of the Absolute Body and therefore, by connotation, the Tathāgata-embryo.

Now, since the text designates Suchness (*Tathatā*) as the second explanation for the formula that all living beings are possessed of the embryo of the Tathāgata, it follows that its remarks concerning the Absolute Body as self-revelatory wisdom, apply equally to it. Therefore, Suchness is not only the unilateral "immaculateness" existing in all beings, the undifferentiated universal reality, but may, by affiliation, be characterised as omniscient wisdom. At this point in the analysis, such a reference is no more than suggested, and will only be further defined in the tenth chapter treating the transformation of *Samalā Tathatā* (Suchness mingled with pollution) into *Nirmalā Tathatā* (Suchness apart from pollution). But here is the nascent indication of Absolute Suchness (*Tathatā*), not statically conceived as latent and neutral entitative reality, but as dynamically operative and efficient permeation. This concept gains immediate reinforcement through the final term of the threefold equality, "the germ of the Tathāgata" (*Tathāgata-gotra*).

The Meaning of Gotra

As was stated previously, *gotra*, together with *dhātu*, serves as the most frequent and consistent synonym for *garbha* throughout the *Ratnagotra*. The ninth chapter of the text explicitly interprets it as active, causal factor (*hetu*), and thus stresses its organic, biological connotation of "germ" as most closely approximating the embryonic implication of *garbha*.[18] However, the critical importance of *gotra* within the śāstra derives from its qualification as *Tathāgatagotra* ("germ of the Tathāgata"), and its corresponding equivalence to *Dharmakāya* and *Tathatā* as explanatory of the embryo's universal presence in animate beings. By such specification, the *Ratnagotravibhāga* distinctly aligns itself with a basically Mādhyamikan rather than Vijñānavādin interpretation of *gotra* in its technical role as soteriological factor.

According to Ruegg,[19] while the highly nuanced term is found only rarely in the Pali canon, *gotra* in the Abhidharma literature clearly figures as "family," "class," "stock" and in general, represents the idea of the spiritual lineage or genotype according to which beings were classified. Those works, which became the principal corpus for the *Vijñānavāda*, substantiated that use of

18. In this case, "germ" is not to be understood in the sense of a disease-producing microorganism. Rather, it is used more accurately as "germ cell," i.e., as denoting the initial, embryonic stage, the rudimentary source for the subsequent, evolutionary development. See *Random House College Dictionary*, rev. ed. (1975), s.v. "germ".

19. While only one-third of his authoritative study, *La Theorie Du Tathāgatagarbha et Du Gotra*, is dedicated to the latter, it provides an excellent, comprehensive exposition of the numerous sources for the concept, and its wealth of scholarly research far surpasses the remaining section on the *Tathāgatagarbha*. The following review of the *gotra* substantially depends upon his text. See pp. 71-173.

gotra by applying it to the categorical distinctions of the three vehicles. Thus, the *Saṃdhinirmocanasūtra* consistently speaks of the *gotra* of the *Śrāvakayāna*, *Pratyekabuddhayāna*, and *Bodhisattvayāna*. Specifically, the *gotra* of each of the three vehicles alludes to the level of cognitive acuity, so that the faculties (*indriya*) of the Śrāvaka are designated as obtuse, of the Pratyekabuddha as medium, while those of the Bodhisattva are said to be sharply developed.

The *Mahāyānasūtrālamkāra*[20] claims that the existence (*sattva*, *astitva*) of the *gotra* is demonstrated by the differences in the spiritual qualities among beings, the differences in their levels of aspiration (*adhimukti*), which in turn accounts for their different practices (*pratipatti*) explaining why one attains the goal at a particular time, and others do not. Such differences are indicative of distinctive *gotras* which are the ultimate rationale for the various levels of result or fruit (*phala*) that constitute, according to the case, the inferior awakening of the Śrāvaka, the middling of the Pratyekabuddha and the supreme awakening of the Bodhisattva. Thus, it is that the *gotra* is compared to a seed (*bīja*). More explicitly, the śāstra notes that there are four distinguishing marks (*liṅga*) to the *gotra* of the Bodhisattva including compassion, commitment to the Mahāyāna dharma, constancy, and the accomplishment of the good, which here refers to the practice of the *pāramitās*. Likewise, the possession of the *gotra* is said to effect a fourfold advantage in that one only approaches perdition slowly, one delivers himself quickly, one suffers only mild sorrow, and one matures animate beings with a spirit touched by their sufferings. Analogously compared to a gold mine, the *gotra* is credited as the abode of knowledge, and the originative source of the roots of incommensurable goodness (*kuśalamūla*) and of the powers for obtaining the purification of the defilements.

Then, in its third chapter, the *Mahāyānasūtrālaṃkāra* refers to individuals who are not established in their *gotra* (*agotrastha*) as divided into two categories: those who temporarily lack the qualifications for attaining *parinirvāṇa* (*tatkālaparinirvāṇadharman*), and those who are *absolutely* deprived of that full and final *nirvāṇa* (*atyantāparīnirvāṇadharman*) because they are said to be (forever)

20. See ibid., pp. 77-86.

without the *gotra* of the *parinirvāṇa*, i.e., without the fundamental cause (*hetu*). However, such a possibility of a being who is completely and for all time incapable of the supreme freedom of enlightenment, is paradoxically contradicted by the śāstra's ninth chapter where it is asserted that all animate beings possess the embryo of Buddhahood in the light of the non-differentiated universality of Absolute Suchness (*Tathatā*). Now, the majority of commentators adhering to the *Vijñānavāda* tend either to ignore that particular verse (*MSA* 9.37) or adopt the position that such an axiom was not meant to be literally interpreted. By and large, the scholars of that school emphasize those passages of the text treating the *gotra* as the primary, fundamental cause of the deliverance or *bodhi*, and fully accepted the thesis that certain beings, lacking the gotra (*agotra*) will be forever denied the potentiality for attaining the supreme and perfect awakening (*anuttarasamyaksambodhi*).[21] They likewise observed and supported the śāstra's tenet of a radical distinction between the *gotra* of the Śrāvāka and that of the Bodhisattva, each leading to radically different ends. As will be seen below, the Mādhyamika tradition thoroughly repudiated such theses, and it is critically significant that one of the two major references to the *Mahāyānasūtrālaṃkāra* included within the text of the *Ratnagotravibhāga* is the former's ninth chapter argument for the universal presence of the Buddha-embryo in sentient beings.[22]

The *Bodhisattvabhūmi*,[23] the fifth section of the *Bahubhūmikavastu* of the *Yogācārabhūmi* attributed to Asaṅga, refers to the *gotra* as the seed (*bīja*), the support (*ādhāra*) and the cause (*hetu*) of the Bodhisattva's spiritual praxis, and of the realization of the supreme and perfect enlightenment. Its indispensability is underlined by the assertion that even though he be energetic and produce the *bodhicitta*, without the *gotra* the Bodhisattva will not be

21. For Sthiramati's fourfold division of those who are *agotra*, see ibid., n. 3, pp. 80-81.

22. The verse, as is quoted in the *Ratnagotra*'s chapter treating the illustrations of how the *gotra* is covered with defilements, appears as follows:

> "Though being undifferentiated among all, Reality [*Tathatā*], in case the purification is perfected, is (called) Buddhahood; therefore, all living beings are possessed of the Matrix [embryo] of Buddhahood."

Takasaki, *Ratnagotravibhāga*, p. 288.

23. See Ruegg, *La Théorie*, pp. 77-86.

able to attain the full and complete awakening. Therefore, it is the *gotra* which, furnished by nature (*prakrtyā*), and having no other function, is the essential determinant for the realization of Buddhahood, and serves as the explanation for the Bodhisattva's peculiar experience of saṃsāric conditions. When he is reborn in an evil condition of life, he is quickly delivered from it in that he does not suffer the sharp and acute sorrow as do others in the same state; this is due to the presence of his *gotra* from which he issues forth the thought of great compassion for all beings. It is his possession of the *gotra* (*gotrasampad*) and his firm abiding within it (*gotravihārin*) that enables the Bodhisattva to cultivate goodness with a natural and spontaneous excellence, rather than through violent and artificial exercises. Such a one is said to carry the seeds (*bījadhara*) of all the Buddha natures (*Buddha dharmas*) and is enabled to oppose all the defilements.

The non-accidental nature of the *gotra* is affirmed by the *Madhyāntavibhāga*,[24] and in his *Tīkā*, Sthiramati elaborates that whether a being belongs by virtue of his *gotra* to the family of the Buddha or to the family of the Hīnayāna saints, this family descent is essential; it is not accidental, coming as it does in either case from a beginningless, eternal sequence of births. What is more, the difference between such non-accidental *gotras* is as fundamental as that between the animate and inanimate world. Such again is the classical Vijñānavādin theory of the radical distinction among the *gotras* and the subsequently basic separation between the Śrāvaka and Bodhisattva.[25] Both Sthiramati and

24. See *Madhyānta-Vibhaṅga*, trans. F. Th. Stcherbatsky, Soviet Indology Series, no. 5 (reprint ed., Calcutta: Indian Studies, 1971), pp. 198-199.

25. Nevertheless, the *Samdhinirmocanasūtra* speaks of two categories of Śrāvaka. The first will never attain the *anuttarasamyaksambodhi* of the Buddha because, dreading *dukha* (sorrow), he looks only for his own rest, and having little compassion, turns away from useful action for others. The second class of Śrāvaka however, while initially motivated for their individual benefit and welfare in delivering themselves from the obstacles of the defilements, later change and turn themselves towards the highest perfect enlightenment; by this turning (*paryāya*) they are said to become Bodhisattvas. References to such an indetermined or indefinite *gotra* (*aniyatagotra*) applied to certain Śrāvakas and Pratyekabuddhas are found in *The Laṅkāvatāra Sūtra*, trans. Daisetz Teitaro Suzuki (London: Routledge & Kegan Paul, 1932), pp. 56-57; and Hsüan Tsang, *Ch'eng Wei-Shih Lun: The Doctrine of Mere-Consciousness*, trans. Wei Tat (Hong Kong: Ch'eng Wei-Shih Lun Publication Committee, 1973), p. 613.

Vasubandhu (in his *Bhāṣya* on the *Madhyāntavibhāga*) likewise attribute the differences among the faculties (*indriya*) of the profane, ordinary beings and their spiritual dispositions (*āśaya*), along with the corresponding variety of purifications necessary to them, to the diversification among their *gotras*. According to the śāstra, the *gotra*, in general, is assigned a primarily causal role in bringing forth the *bodhicitta*, eliminating the obstacles, and cultivating the counteractive virtues.

Now, in the literature of the Mādhyamika, mention of the *gotra* is rare in the more ancient śāstras of the school, and only sparse allusions to it are found in the sūtras upon which they grounded the significant tenets of their doctrine. In the *Kāśyapaparivarta* there is reference to the *aryagotra* as an uncompounded (*asaṃskṛta*), non-differentiated factor, equal in all. While it is not-self (*anātman*), this *aryagotra* is said to be in conformity with *nirvāṇa*, immaculate (*vimala*), real (*satya*), imperishable (*akṣaya*), and permanent (*nitya*). It likewise speaks of the *buddhavaṃśa* (the lineage, stock or family of the Buddha), a concept found in both the *Vimalakīrtinirdeśa* and the *Avataṃsaka's Gaṇḍavyūha.*

The *Daśabhumika* combines both terms when speaking of the eighth stage of the Bodhisattva. Such a one is said to possess the *Buddhagotra*, being brilliant with the force of the qualities of the Tathāgata and comporting himself as a Buddha. On this stage, the Bodhisattva becomes irreproachable in that he is fixed in the lineage and heritage of the Tathāgata (*Tathāgatavaṃśa*). The causal nature of the *gotra* is inferred by the text's analogy with the minerological process of polishing, heating, and cleaning a precious stone from a lump of ore. The precious stone of omniscience is said to be produced through the purifying process of the ten noble *gotras*, representing here, the ten stages or *bhūmis* of the Bodhisattva career.

It is the *Abhisamayālaṅkāra* and Haribhadra's commentary on it (*Abhisamayālaṅkārāloka*) which, together with the *Ratnagotravibhāga*, become the principal, authoritative sources for a defini-

---

While expressive of a particular mobility, the *aniyatagotra* suggests only a temporary condition of possibility. It does not challenge the main concept of radical distinction between the goal or objective, separating the determined or defined *gotra* of Śrāvakas from that of the Bodhisattvas, as espoused by the Vijñānavādin tradition.

tive Mādhyamika position with regard to the *gotra*, especially among the later Tibetan scholars of that school. In a crucial passage, the *Abhisamayālaṅkāra* identifies the *gotra* as the substratum, support, and source of the thirteen factors constituting the practice of the Bodhisattva path,[26] and concludes by identifying the *gotra* with the *Dharmadhātu*; therefore,

> A distinction between the various *gotras* (lineages) is not tenable, because the *Dharmadhātu* (or the Absolute) is undifferentiated. But it is because of the difference between the dharmas that are founded on it that their distinction is proclaimed.[27]

It is this point which ultimately separates the Mādhyamika from the Vijñānavādin interpretation of the *gotra*. Due to the universality of the *Dharmadhātu*, the Mādhyamika tradition held the impossibility of an unconditional distinction between the *gotras* of Śrāvaka, Pratyekabuddha and Bodhisattva. They claimed that the Vijñānavādin *prakṛtisthagotra* (existing by nature) could not be deemed genuinely permanent and uncompounded, since it was essentially interpreted as the seed (*bīja*), the productive cause (*kāraṇa*) of the *bodhi* still to be realized; as seed (*bīja*), it was itself subject to the perfuming (*vāsanā*) influence of other forces and factors and therefore, conditional.[28] In contrast, the *prakṛtisthagotra* of the Mādhyamika functions not only as motivating cause (*hetu* as opposed to *kāraṇa*) but also as the imperishable, permanent, unconditional, supportive ground for the practice of the

26. The *Abhisamayālaṅkāra's* thirteen factors defining the Bodhisattva path are listed in appendix 1.

27. *Abhisamayālaṅkāra*, trans. Edward Conze, Serie Orientale Roma, vol. 6 (Roma: Instituto Italiano per il Medio ed Estremo Oriente, 1954), p. 18.

28. See, e.g., Hsüan Tsang, *Ch'eng Wei-Shih Lun*, p. 123:

"It should be observed that the perfume born of hearing (*śrutavāsanā*) is not exclusively impure. In fact, when the ascetic listens to the Good Law, the innate pure Bījas are perfumed in such a way that they increase and develop progressively until they engender a mind of supramundane order. Hence these pure Bījas are also called *śrutavāsanā*. That part of the *śrutavāsanā* which is of an impure nature will be abandoned or destroyed by the *Bhāvanāmārga* (*bhāvanāheya*), the Path of Meditation and Self-Cultivation...That part of the *śrutavāsanā* which is of pure nature is not be abandoned or destroyed (*heya*). It serves as the right cause (*hetupratiyaya*) of supramundane dharmas." That the "innate pure Bījas" signify the innate Bīja-nature or *gotra*, see ibid., p. 665.

spiritual path. Its universal potential for realizing the common goal of Buddhahood opposed the fragmented capacities of the Vijñānavādin *gotras*. These latter, should they belong to the category of those who will never attain the highest *nirvāṇa* are incapable of overcoming the seeds (*bījas*) of either the *kleśāvaraṇa* (barrier of vexing passions) or the *jñeyāvaraṇa* (barrier impeding the realization of *Mahābodhi*, supreme enlightenment); depending upon the superiority or inferiority of their moral faculties, the *gotras* of the Śrāvaka and Pratyekabuddha are impeded by the *jñeyāvaraṇa* but are capable of overcoming the *kleśāvaraṇa*. Finally, the *gotra* of the Tathāgata alone, has the potency of destroying the *bījas* of both the *kleśāvaraṇa* and *jñeyāvraṇa* for those by whom it is possessed.[29]

Against such a position, the Mādhyamika adopted a nonliteral, "intentional" (*abhiprāyika*) interpretation. According to them, no one is forever incapable of rejecting impurity and of producing the proper antidotes (*pratipakṣas*). To say that there actually exist those persons who will never attain the perfect enlightenment is to disregard the salvific, penetrating efficacy of the Buddha Wisdom, and the universal extension of the *Dharmadhātu*. The theory of *agotra* (the absence of the *gotra*) is only reflective of a temporary condition, when a particular being may suffer from the delusion of a repulsion to the *Mahāyāna* (Great Vehicle); there will come a time when he is not so afflicted and will then be open for the final and complete *parinirvāṇa*. The restrictive caliber of the Vijñānavādin *gotras* is here expanded beyond their individual particularity through the *Abhisamayālaṇkāra*'s identification of the non-differentiated *Dharmadhātu* as *gotra*. This ultimate "element," coextensive with all sentient beings, became the univocal cause (*hetu*) of the comprehension of the supramundane *dharmas*, and therefore, the unconditional validation and assurance of attaining the supreme awakening.

Thus defined, the *gotra* is essentially unique. However, the text admits to the nominal distinction of three *gotras*, referring to the three vehicles of the Śrāvaka, Pratyekabuddha and Bodhisattva. In explanation, Haribhadra draws upon the example of three jars cut from the same piece of glass, fired with the same heat and cut

29. See ibid., pp. 115, 123-125. There, the *Yogaśāstra* is quoted as the authoritative text for this interpretation.

to an identical shape or pattern, and are differentiated only with respect to their particular contents, one storing meal, the other corn, and the third wheat.[30] Now, the *Dharmadhātu* as supportive *gotra* is the universal, fundamental ground for the realization of *Mahābodhi*. Nevertheless, it is said to conform to the progressive gradation of the particular comprehensions characteristic of the three vehicles. Though the goal is identical to all, there are different modes of understanding that same object, with respect to the various degrees of cognitive acuity and spiritual faculties, as well as the particular practices peculiar to each of the three paths. So then, relatively speaking, there may be three *gotras*, alluding to the comprehension and praxis of the Śrāvaka, Pratyekabuddha and Bodhisattva. But from the absolute standpoint (*paramārtha*), these nominal designations are founded upon the ultimate reality, the *Dharmadhātu*, the unique *gotra*.[31]

It is with this background that one returns to the text of the *Ratnagotravibhāga* and its third explanation for the formula, *sarvasattvās tathāgatagarbhāḥ* ("all living beings are possessed of the embryo of the Tathāgata"). Its last rationale for the universality of the Tathāgata-embryo is the universality of the *Tathāgata-gotra*; "there exists the germ of the Tathāgata in every living being."[32] In this contextual identification of the *gotra* with the Absolute Body (*Dharmakāya*) in its comprehensive permeation of all beings, and with Absolute Suchness (*Tathatā*) as the undifferentiated whole, the śāstra is in striking correspondence with the *Abhisamayālaṅkāra*'s equation of the *Dharmadhātu* as *gotra*.[33]

30. Haribhadra, *Abhisamayālaṃkārāloka Prajñāpāramitāvyākhyā*, 1.39, cited by Ruegg, *La Théorie*, pp. 131-132.

31. ...les commentaires de l' *Abhisamayālaṃkāra* qui traitent du support et de sa connexion avec le fruit enseignent que ce support a pour nature le *dharmadhātu;* et le *dharmadhātu* etant unique et indifférencié, le support qu'ést le *gotra* est en réalité lui aussi unique, d'où il s'ensuit que ce *gotra* n'est triple qu' au point de vue du supporté c'est-à-dire des trois Chemins du Śrāvaka, du Pratyekabuddha et du Bodhisattva. En somme, selon la théorie des commentaires de l' AA [*Abhisamayālaṃkāra*], le *gotra* apparaît comme triple seulement quand il est considéré sous son aspect conditionné sur le plan du Chemin..., le *gotra* ultime...étant au contraire unique." Ibid., p. 177.

32. Takasaki, *Ratnagotravibhāga*, p. 198.

33. It might be recalled that in its second chapter, the *Ratnagotra* itself defined the *Dharmadhātu* as equivalent to the *Tathāgatagarbha*. In reference to the Buddha it stated: "Essential nature (*dharmadhātu*) means the Matrix

Perhaps not as apparent, but of no less significance, is the actual equivalence of *gotra* and *garbha* effected by the *Ratna*. Undoubtedly, as indicated above in the Mādhyamika system, where the class of animate beings belonging in the last analysis to the *gotra* of the Buddha became coextensive with the class of animate beings in its totality, the primordial classificatory function of the *gotra* assumed less importance. Nevertheless, it still retained its soteriological orientation and epistemological character as the germinal faculty or gene which established the parentage of all beings with the Buddha, permitting them to become "sons of the Tathāgata," born into his "family," and furnishing them the certitude of eventually attaining the supreme and perfect awakening. So conceived, the *gotra* becomes an alternate expression for the one vehicle theory (*ekayāna*), itself, an expression of the Tathāgata-embryo from its perspective as ultimate soteriological principle, as presented by the *Śrī-Mālā Sūtra.*

Through the conjoint designation of the Absolute Body (*Dharmakāya*) and Absolute Suchness (*Tathatā*), the *Ratnagotra*'s *Tathāgatagarbha* assumes a genuinely ontological status; as such, it will be analyzed in future sections of the text as self-subsistent purity, all-pervading, unchangeable, and non-differentiated. This essentially static posture of the *garbha*, already nuanced by the character of omniscient wisdom as the very vehicle of its own self-manifestation, is more fully complemented by the alternate designation as *Tathāgatagotra*. Retaining its basic definition as active, causal factor (*hetu*), it sustains the dynamic, processive dimension of the *garbha* ultimately effecting the unique and universal goal of Buddhahood in all sentient beings. As suggested earlier, this transformational aspect of the *Tathāgatagarbha* as *Tathāgatagotra*, underlined by their mutual organic, biological tonality as "embryonic" and "germinal," when identified with *Tathatā*, contributed significantly to the animation of that concept from statically latent neutrality to effective and persistent permeation.

[embryo] of the Tathāgata which is not different from his own quality by nature." Ibid., p. 161. Therefore, its similarity with the *Abhisamayālaṃkāra* is quite evident since here, in its seventh chapter, the *Ratnagotra* equates the *garbha* with the *gotra*, both identified with the *Dharmadhātu*.

CHAPTER III

CHARACTERISTICS OF THE EMBRYO REALITY: ITS SELF-NATURE

INTERCHANGEABLY EMPLOYING *gotra* ("germ"), *dhātu* ("essence"), and *garbha* ("embryo") as representative of *Samalā Tathatā*, the *Ratnagotra*'s eighth chapter systematically analyses "Absolute Reality mingled with (hidden by) defilement," from a tenfold perspective.[1] Being pure always, absolutely and innately, the *svabhāva* ("self-nature") of the Tathāgata-embryo is undefiled by nature (*prakṛtyasaṃkliṣṭa*). This inherent purity, initially asserted simply and directly, is then translated in a rather forced and recondite style, as powerful, universally non-differentiated, and compassionate. Since the Absolute Body (*Dharmakāya*), Absolute Suchness (*Tathatā*), and the germ (*gotra*) have already been identified as the *trividhasvabhāva* of the Tathāgata-embryo (*garbha*), their respective peculiar characteristics of power, unilateral identity, and mercy are here the illuminants through which fundamental purity becomes expressive.

As such, the passage is rather inconclusive and goes non-developed. What is important to recognize is that Suchness (*Tathatā*) remains what it is, regardless of whether it is manifest or not. And what it is, its self-nature (*svabhāva*), is perfect purity. As *samalā*, *Tathatā* is simply covered over, concealed, non-manifest; yet it retains intact its *svabhāva*, technically designated "the innate purity" (*prakṛtiviśuddhi*). When *Tathatā* becomes unconcealed and manifest as *nirmalā*, its *svabhāva* will be formally referred to as "the purity as the result of purification" (*vaimalyaviśuddhi*) in the later sections of the *Ratnagotra*. The point to note here is that *Tathatā* as *samalā* is synonymous with *Tathāgatagarbha*, *Tathāgatagotra* and *Tathāgatadhātu*, and though it is "associated" with phenomenal defilements, they are accidental to it, and it thus retains its *svabhāva* of an innate and radiant purity (*prakṛtiviśuddhi*).

1. The ten perspectives of the *Ratnagotra*'s analysis are listed in appendix 1.

The Cause of the Embryo's Purification

If the third chapter had initiated a certain discussion on the nature of ignorance, that focus is more acutely defined here in the eighth chapter. And the *Ratnagotra*'s analysis of the cause (*hetu*) of the Tathāgata-embryo's purification, necessarily involves mention of the obscurations (*āvaraṇa*) which are said to defile it: enmity to the doctrine of the Great Vehicle (*Mahāyānadharmapratigha*); the conception of the self (*ātmadarśana*); the fear of suffering in the phenomenal life (*duḥkhabhīrutva*); indifference to the welfare of living beings (*sattva-artha-nirapekṣatā*). Characteristically, the text chooses to examine these conditions not through a formal epistemological investigation, but rather indirectly through a correlative study of the classes of human beings, each of which exemplifies a peculiar trace of the fourfold obscurations. Such expositional typology initially reveals three categories of beings: those who cling to worldly life, those who seek deliverance from it, and those who desire neither mundane existence nor an escape from it. Subsequently, the first group is further delineated as those who have no interest in the path of emancipation; desiring only phenomenal existence, they direct no thought toward *nirvāṇa*. As such, they constitute the class of beings who never belong to the family of the perfect *nirvāṇa* (*aparinirvāṇagotraka*). They are referred to as the *Icchantikas*, along with the second subdivision, consisting of those Buddhists who have fallen into a similarly lapsed state, and include those who are abusive to the doctrine of the Great Vehicle. While the śāstra has adopted the specific designation of *Icchantika* as belonging to the *gotra* of those who will never attain the perfect enlightenment, it repudiates the traditional valuation of the term, retaining it only as descriptive of a temporary condition. This will be made explicit in a later section, and it should not be mistaken here as the text's acceptance of a permanent exclusion from *nirvāṇa*; its qualified status is conditioned by the *Ratnagotra*'s overall theory of the Tathāgata-embryo.

Those who seek deliverance from worldly life have either fallen into a "methodless way" (*anupāyapatita*) or follow the correct path. The former include all heretical outsiders to the Buddhist faith such as the Carakas, the Parivrajakas and the Jains.[2] But in

2. According to the Chinese version of the *Ratna*, the Carakas are regarded

the same category are those Buddhists who adhere to the erroneous conception of a substantial ego (*pudgaladṛṣṭi*) and who have no faith in the "Highest Truth," i.e., non-substantiality (*Śūnyatā*). In addition, any Buddhists who, with pride, have become "intoxicated" with the conception of non-substantiality (*Śūnyatā*) and cling to it with attachment, are deemed woefully misdirected. In fact, following a passage of the *Kāśyapaparivarta,* the *Ratnagotra* finds these last to be the most offensive:

> O, Kāśyapa, really even such a conception which maintains substantial Ego as much as Mt. Sumeru is better than the conception of Non-substantiality on the part of those who are proud of it.[3]

Though the Śrāvakas and Pratyekabuddhas are said to follow a correct method, as opposed to those preceding groups, they nevertheless belong to the general category of beings who seek for deliverance from mundane existence (*vibhāvabhilāṣin*); as such, they are not as perfect as the Bodhisattvas who are free from all desire of either extreme. Merely sketching the rudiments of what will later evolve as a thorough review of his character, the text extolls the Bodhisattva as having entered the path to attain the synthetic integration of reality, fragmented into antithetical polarities by the *Icchantikas* from one extreme, and the Śrāvakas and Pratyekabuddhas from the other; the Bodhisattva's intentionality is wholly directed toward the intuitive equality of phenomenal existence and *nirvāṇa*, rather than remaining fixedly in the latter condition alone (*apratiṣṭhitanirvāṇa*). And while their activities are based in mundane reality, they remain undefiled by it, purely grounded as they are in firm compassion and superior resolve. In contraposition to the defects of the *Icchantikas,* heretics, Śrāvakas, and Pratyekabuddhas, the spiritual observances of the Bodhisattva are aligned as the antidotal remedies for those respective hindrances. If those four groups are unable to understand or realize the essence of the Tathāgata (*Tathāgatadhātu*), the Bodhisattva praxis becomes the counteractive agent of its reve-

---

as the adherents of the *Sāṃkhya*, and the Parivrajakas represent the philosophy of the *Vaiśeṣika*.

3. Takasaki, *Ratnagotravibhāga*, p. 204.

lation. It is the Bodhisattva's practice of faith in the Great Vehicle (*mahāyānadharmādhimukti-bhāvanā*) that serves as the antidote (*pratipakṣa*) for the *Icchantika*'s enmity toward it; the exercise of supremacy in the transcendental intellect (*prajñāpāramitābhāvanā*) is the vehicle that disperses the heretical conception of the self (*ātmadarśana*); to the Śrāvaka fear of suffering in *saṃsāra* (*duḥka-bhīrutva*), the Bodhisattva practice of meditations (*samādhi-bhāvanā*) is the antidote, and the Pratyekabuddha's indifference to the welfare of living beings (*sattvārtha-nirapekṣatā*) is offset by the Bodhisattva's exercise of great compassion (*mahākaruṇā-bhāvanā*). But such "therapeutic" measures are more than revelatory of the Tathāgata-embryo (here referred to as *dhātu*); they are the causal factors for its maturation as the highest truth, the Absolute Body (*Dharmakāya*), whose four supreme virtues are said to be the result (*phala*) of the purification of the essence of the Tathāgata (*Tathāgatadhātu*) in all animate beings.

The Four Supreme Virtues: Antidotal Methodology

The *Ratnagotra*'s discussion of the four *guṇa-pāramitā* of purity (*śubha*), unity (*ātma*), bliss (*sukha*), and eternity (*nitya*) is of significant propaedeutic value for its later doctrine concerning *Śūnyatā*. While the *Śrī-Mālā-Sūtra* has only alluded to the Absolute Body (*Dharmakāya*) as possessing the perfections of permanence (*nitya*), pleasure (*sukha*), self (*ātma*) and purity (*śubha*), the *Ratnagotra* attempts to vindicate such positive attributions by defining them through its familiar antidotal interpretation. Rather than being concrete attributes qualifying a hypostatic and substantial absolute, the four supreme virtues are merely the contrast or the corrective opposite to the fourfold non-delusion (*aviparyāsa*) when mistakenly applied to the Absolute Body (*Dharmakāya*).

In the very first chapter, the śāstra had established its antithetical principle, legitimizing the contrast of the unconditional (*asaṃskṛta*) and the conditional (*saṃskṛta*):

> The word [*asaṃskṛta*] should be understood as being opposite to being conditioned or caused (*Saṃskṛta*). Here, "being conditioned" (*saṃskṛta*) means the thing, of which origination [*utpāda*], lasting [*sthiti*], as well as destruction [*bhaṅga*] are con-

ceivable. Because of the absence of these characteristics, the Buddhahood should be seen as having neither beginning, middle nor end, and being represented as the immutable [*asaṃs-kṛta*] Absolute Body.[4]

Therefore, in the present section it simply applies this distinction, along with its antidotal methodology to the classical Buddhist dictum of the fourfold delusion (*viparyāsa*) and proceeds accordingly. If it is perverse to posit the notions of eternity, bliss, purity, and substantial ego to conditional phenomena which are in fact non-eternal, full of sufferings, impure, and of no substantial ego, then the antidote is the fourfold non-delusion (*aviparyāsa*); in reference to all such phenomena, the necessary corrective is to see them as they are, viz., non-eternal, full of sufferings, of no substantial ego, and impure. However, this very inversion, also called the fourfold opposite of delusion (*viparyāsaviparyaya*) itself becomes delusive and a perversion (*viparyāsa*) when taken as unconditional, and erroneously attributed to the Absolute Body of the Tathāgata (*Dharmakāya*). Remedially applying its antidotal dialectic to such a mistaken notion, the *Ratnagotra* establishes the supreme eternity (*nitya-pāramitā*), the supreme bliss (*sukha-pāramitā*), the supreme unity (*ātma-pāramitā*) and the supreme purity (*śubha-pāramitā*) of the Absolute Body (*Dharmakāya*).

Before analyzing further the status of the four *guṇa-pāramitā*, it is critical to recognize the *Ratnagotra*'s intentionality to posit them as the resultant antidotes (*pratipakṣa*) to various specific distortions, characteristic of specific classes of beings. Failure to understand the śāstra's practical, pastoral dimension in this regard would be a serious underestimation and would misconstrue the important psychological and pedagogical significance of those supreme virtues. Therefore, in characteristically concordant fashion, the text summarily coordinates purity as the result (*phala*) of the Bodhisattva's practice of faith in the doctrine of the Great Vehicle (*Mahāyāna*), and as the corrective antidote (*pratipakṣa*) to the *Icchantika*'s delight in the impure phenomenal life; unity or the perfection of self as the result of the Bodhisattva's practice of supremacy in the transcendental intellect (*prajñapāramitā*) and as

4. Ibid., pp. 156-157.

the antidote to those heretics who perceive an ego where there exist merely the five personality aggregates (*skandhas*); bliss as the result of the Bodhisattva's practice of various kinds of meditation, and the antidote to the Śrāvaka's fear of suffering and their singular delight in the cessation of those phenomenal torments; and finally, the perfection of eternity as the result of the Bodhisattva's practice of great compassion and the only antidote to the Pratyekabuddha's delight "in the isolated abode," and subsequent indifference to the welfare of all animate beings.

Even when the text translates the perfection of these four practices in reference to the Tathāgata who fulfils and masters them completely, its mention of the four *guṇa-pāramitā* is peculiarly understated and only indirectly implied. Again, the focus tends to be more strictly pedagogical, with the emphasis upon their antidotal function in the realm of spiritual praxis. Thus, the supreme virtue of self or unity (*ātma-pāramitā*) is suggestively defined as the consummate realization of the universal non-substantiality of all beings (*pudgalas*) and material phenomena (*dharmas*); the supreme virtue of eternity is implicated as the Buddha's comprehensive mercy towards all beings, exceeding all spatial and temporal limitation; the supreme virtue of bliss is allusively inferred as the perception of the omnipresent "power of the highest truth." Only the supreme virtue of purity is directly (and simply) mentioned as characterizing the loftiest state of the Absolute Essence.

The question immediately arises as to whether the *Ratnagotra* is necessarily advocating a substantialist or even "quasi-vedāntic" conception of the Absolute, thus countering the fundamental Buddhist tenet of impermanence and non-substantiality or emptiness (*Śūnyatā*). The final implication of its doctrine cannot be fully assessed until the tenth and eleventh chapters, where the text openly addresses itself and declares its stance in reference to *Śūnyatā* as the true nature of the Tathāgata-embryo (*garbha*). Nevertheless, the status of the four supreme virtues as definitive of the Absolute Body (*Dharmakāya*) does demand qualification.

Because they posit themselves by the process of inversion as the counteractive antidotes to the error of treating the Absolute Body (*Dharmakāya*) as an ordinary mundane dharma, and present themselves simply as the contrast (*viparyaya*) of that which on the mundane level is the fourfold delusion (*viparyāsa*), the four *guṇa-pāramitā* are more indicative than concrete. In other words, the comprehension of the Absolute Reality of the *Dharmakāya* is dependent upon an initial inversion whereby one eliminates the error or faulty and grasping perception (*graha*) that predicates purity, bliss, eternity and self to conditioned phenomena that are in fact, *aśubha*, *asukha, anitya* and *anātman*. However, these classical epithets can, in their turn, become the objects of dogmatic attachment, and be themselves counter-truths and erroneous misapprehensions, definitionally inadequate to the unconditional Absolute Reality of the *Dharmakāya*, which is precisely exempt from all mere description of phenomenal thought processes (*prapañca*). And in fact, the *Ratnagotra*'s first two chapters insist that *Tathatā* (Absolute Suchness) whether it be considered as *samalā* and therefore veiled by the adventitious defilements, or as *nirmalā* and manifestly free of them, is "beyond the sphere characterized as being caused and conditioned." The text stresses: that it is incapable of being explained and is to be realized by oneself and understood "as like a thunderbolt"; that it is invisible, unutterable, and immutable; that it has neither beginning, middle nor end by nature, being "a quite marvelous and unthinkable sphere"; that it is free from all dualistic views (*prapañca*) and false discriminations (*vikalpa*); that it is unimaginable, indiscriminitive, not being seen, heard, smelt, tasted or touched, and possessing no characteristic mark. Summarizing its unthinkability (*acintyatva*), non-duality (*advayata*) and non-discriminativeness (*nirvikalpatā*), the śāstra's third chapter sharply stipulates that the Absolute Dharma,

> is not a sphere of speculation even by the four categories (of existence) [*catuṣkoṭikā*], i.e., non-being, being, being and non-being together, and neither being nor non-being; it cannot be explained by any sound [*śabda*], voice [*bhāṣā*], speech [*vacana*], way of speech [*vākpatha*], explanation [*nirukti*], agreed term [*saṃketa*], designation [*vyavahāra*], conversation [*abhilāpa*], (and so forth); and it is to be revealed by the introspection of Saints.[5]

5. Ibid., p. 166.

Equally notable is the same chapter's specification that the mode of introspection, the path of perception and practice leading to the attainment of the Absolute Body is the non-discriminative wisdom "which is to be understood in detail according to the sūtra named *Prajñāpāramitā*."[6]

It is against this striking assertion of the translogical and indeterminable status of the Absolute Reality that is *Tathatā*, situated beyond the standard terms of the *catuṣkoṭi*, on a plane where analysis based on *prapañca* and *vikalpa* is no longer valuable, that the assessment of the *Ratnagotra*'s secondary antidotal inversion must be made. It should likewise be understood that the śāstra's reliance upon such "corrective" methodology is by no means unique to itself. As has already been indicated, the four perverted views (*viparyāsa*) were a cardinal tenet of Buddhist doctrine from its earliest intuition. Basically conceived as fundamental misapprehensions of truth, these "upside-down views" or "wrong notions" were opposed by the wisdom which perceived all conditioned phenomena under the threefold common features or marks (*lakṣaṇa*) of impermanence, ill, and not-self. Perceptually, cognitionally, and emotionally, these three marks, systematically applied to the data of everyday experience, became the antidotes or remedies (*prātipakṣa*) to the delusion that sought permanence in what was impermanent, bliss in what was suffering, the self in what was not selfhood, and purity in what was actually repulsive.

While the Mahāyāna considerably expanded and transformed the traditional interpretation of *viparyāsa*,[7] the notion of remedial or antidotal truth remained a functional principle of Buddhist pedagogy. And although Nāgārjuna's critique of the notion of

6. Ibid., p. 171.

7. According to Edward Conze, there were six major innovations which included: the addition of a fifth *viparyāsa*, viz., "the realistic error"; the idea that any form of discrimination was considered an intellectual perversion; the claim that the perverted views themselves have no real existence; the repudiation of "conditional" and "unconditional" dharmas, upon which the Hīnayāna theory of *viparyāsa* was based; a distinction of several stages in the rejection of perverted views; and the belief that only a Bodhisattva, exercised in perfect wisdom, could totally overcome them. For an elaboration of each point see his *Buddhist Thought in India: Three Phases of Buddhist Philosophy* (Ann Arbor: University of Michigan Press, Ann Arbor Paperbacks, 1967), pp. 204-211.

perversion (*viparyāsa*) in the *Mūlamadhyamikakārikā* is of a very different orientation and intentionality than the *Ratnagotra,* it will be shown that the latter's exposition of the supreme virtues of unity (*ātma-pāramitā*) and eternity (*nitya-pāramitā*) more closely approximate the ultimate intuition of the former than would seem apparent.

But at present, it is Nāgārjuna's clarification of remedial statements as one of the four *siddhāntas*[8] that is most germane to an understanding of the *Ratnagotra*'s method of antidote, by inversion of the mistake of attributing the fourfold opposite of delusion to the *Dharmakāya* (*viparyāsaviparyaya-pratipakṣa*). Following the critical norm that the truth of any teaching depends solely on whether one is non-clinging or clinging in regard to it, the exponent of the *Madhyamā-pratipat* (the Middle Way) repeatedly stresses that the relativity of all conditional phenomena is itself not unconditional; to cling to relativity or *śūnyatā* as itself absolute is the most serious of errors.[9] Therefore, if ignorance consists in an initial misconstruction that mistakes the relative as absolute and the fragmentary as complete, typified by the classical formulation of the delusion that seeks permanence in the impermanent, pleasure in what is actually suffering etc., the teaching that all is impermanent and suffering is remedially applied as the antidote. But if these same notions of impermanence and suffering themselves become the perverse occasions for clinging and attachment, and are distortedly seized as the ultimate nature of reality, they are to be amended by a secondary, reflexive counterpoise:

> People mostly cling to permanence and pleasure while they do not cling (so much) to impermanence and suffering. Therefore through (the relative truths of) impermanence and pain the

8. Representing four different statements of one and the same truth, but from differing perspectives, the *siddhāntas* include the mundane (*laukika*), the individual (*prātipauruṣika*), the remedial (*pratipakṣika*), and the ultimate (*pāramārthika*).

9. In his *Mūlamadhyamakakārikā*, Nāgārjuna states: "The wise men (i.e., enlightened ones) have said that *śūnyatā* or the nature of thusness is the relinquishing of all false views. Yet it is said that those who adhere to the idea or concept of *śūnyātā* are incorrigible." *Nāgārjuna: A Translation of his Mūlamadhyamakakārikā with an Introductory Essay*, trans. Kenneth K. Inada (Tokyo: Hokuseido Press, 1970), p. 93.

> perversion of permanence and pleasure is rejected....But if people would cling even to impermanence and suffering, then the Buddha would teach that even these are *śūnya,* not ultimate.[10]

That, essentially, is what the *Ratnagotra* has advocated. The obvious difference, of course, is not in the remedial procedure, or antidotal methodology common to both the *Ratnagotra* and Nāgārjuna, but in the express nature of the antidote that each employs. Given the universal relativity of all things in the light of the total emptiness of any independent, self-subsistent nature or own-being (*svabhāva-śūnyatā*), Nāgārjuna's concept of perversion (*viparyāsa*) assumes a much more comprehensive scope; to graspingly apprehend or cling to anything is the fundamental perversion. While it is obviously wrong to superimpose permanence on what is impermanent, that does not legitimize one to regard the impermanent as impermanent. For how can one attribute impermanence, suffering, etc., to emptiness (*śūnyatā*) or to *dharmas* that are fundamentally empty of self-nature? If it is a perversion (*viparyāsa*) to perceive permanence in impermanence, it is just as perverse to perceive impermanence in what is fundamentally *śūnya.*[11] If all things are equally *śūnya*, then the notions of independent perceivers, objects of perception, and acts of perception are all false misconstructions. Thus, if perception in itself does not exist, how ultimately, is perversion (*viparyāsa*) possible?[12] Therefore, while Nāgārjuna may accept impermanence, pain, not-self, and the repulsive as antidotes to the common-place perversions of

10. Nāgārjuna, *Mahāprajñāpāramitā Śāstra*, quoted in Ramanan, *Nāgārjuna*'s *Philosophy*, p. 193.

11. "If perception is a perversion such that permanence is in impermanence, then it is not possible for impermanence to be in *śūnya.* How then could that perception be a perversion? If perception is a perversion such that permanence is in impermanence, then again, how is it that the perception of impermanence with respect of *śūnya* is not a perversion?" Nāgārjuna, *Mūlamadhyamakakārikā*, p. 140.

12. Thus, several verses later, Nāgārjuna presses the point:

> "Perversions do not come about even in one who perverses. Again, they do not come about even in one who does not perverse. Perversions do not come about even in one who is presently perversing. Consider seriously by yourself...in whom will the perversions arise? How could there be non-originated perversions? When perversions have not occurred, how could there possibly be one who perverses?" Ibid., pp. 140-141.

permanence, bliss, etc., that is only from the plane of relativity. From the absolute standpoint (*pāramārthika*), *Śūnyatā* is the elemental and comprehensive antidote, the remedy that destroys the primordial perversion of attachment and clinging in its most subtle as well as obvious manifestations. The *Śūnyatā* of the composite negates the acquisitive apprehension of conditional phenomena and is thus the initial non-delusion (*aviparyāsa*), the original *pratipakṣa*. However, should that primal antidote itself turn out to be a perversion (*viparyāsa*), giving rise to a clinging tendency towards the incomposite or unconditional, then by means of the *Śūnyatā* or indeterminate nature of that uncompounded, unconditional reality, the clinging to the incomposite is also denied; the binary *śūnyatā-śūnyatā* is the secondary medicinal corrective—the antidote therapeutically applied to the antidote.[13]

Despite the shared antidotal dynamic, operative in both the *Ratnagotra* and Nāgārjuna, is there not ostensible difference then, in their respective understanding of what that remedy is? While on the one hand the śāstra accepts the cardinal fourfold non-delusion (*aviparyāsa*) in opposing the perversions of permanence, eternity, bliss, and selfhood with regard to conditioned reality, Nāgārjuna, though allowing the relative truth of such notions, ultimately rejects their validity through the logic of *Śūnyatā*. And while both are aware of the danger of the antidote itself becoming a delusion, and the need of recourse to a further prescriptive remedy, is not the *Ratnagotra*'s fourfold attribution of the *Dharmakāya* as supreme bliss, supreme eternity, supreme unity, and supreme purity totally opposed by the Mādhyamikan *śūnyatā-śūnyatā*, an

13. Candrakīrti in his *Prasannapadā* clearly emphasizes the remedial (*prātipakṣika*) nature involved in the dual emptiness of emptiness, i.e., the emptiness of all *dharmās* as empty of that emptiness:

> "Emptiness is not a property, or universal mark, of entities, because then its substratum would be non-empty, and one would have a fixed conviction (*dṛṣṭi*) about it. In fact it is a mere medicine, a means of escape from all fixed conviction. It is taught so that we may overcome attachment, and it would be a pity if we were to become attached to it. It is not a positive standpoint, but a mere turning away from all views and thought constructions. To treat it as an object, and to oppose it to non-emptiness, is to miss the point." Candrakīrti, *Prasannapadā*, XII, quoted in *The Large Sūtra on Perfect Wisdom with the divisions of the "Abhisamayālaṅkara"*, trans. Edward Conze (Berkeley: University of California Press, 1975), n. 4, p. 144.

absolute insistence on the indeterminate nature of the unconditioned reality?

Before examining more closely the meaning of two of the supreme virtues (*ātma-pāramitā* and *nitya-pāramitā*) so as to better elucidate the intentionality behind the śāstral designation of the Absolute Body (*Dharmakāya*), it should be recalled what had previously been said concerning the doctrine of non-substantiality or *Śūnyatā*. In a critically revelatory passage already noted, the text's unequivocal position with regard to *Śūnyatā* is finely delineated. Among those considered to be "of no method" (*anupāya-patita*) are those heretical Buddhists who adhere to erroneous conceptions (*durgṛhītagrāhin*); both involve the doctrine of *Śūnyatā*. On the one hand, there are those who persist in the faulty perception of a substantial ego (*pudgaladṛṣṭi*) and are said to "have no faith in the Highest Truth." That *Śūnyatā* is the intended referent is unmistakably clear since the text, quoting an unknown source, immediately stipulates that "one who has no faith in Non-substantiality [*Śūnyatā*] is not different from the Heretics";[14] those who stand at the door of emancipation adhere to *Śūnyatā*. However, should they become "intoxicated" by it, transforming *Śūnyatā* itself into a conceptual attachment, they fall into the second heretical mire, more treacherous than the first.

What is of greatest interest here, is that the *Ratna* has chosen a passage from the *Kāśyapaparivarta* to substantiate its censure of such misguided Buddhists. To fully appreciate the scope of the śāstra's acquaintance and concurrence with the classical interpretation of *Śūnyatā* as fundamental remedial antidote, it is expedient to position the particular reference within the focus of its exact context:

> Those, Kāśyapa, that (mis)apprehend Śūnyatā [non-substantiality] as a negative fact, I consider them the forlorn, the irrevocably lost....*Better it is to entertain, the substance-view (pudgaladṛṣṭi) of the magnitude of Mt. Sumeru than the Śūnyatā-view [the conception of non-substantiality] of the nihilist (abhāvābhiniviśinaḥ).* Why is it so? Of all theories Kāśyapa, Śūnyata [non-substantiality] is the antidote. Him I call the incurable

14. Takasaki, *Ratnagotravibhāga*, p. 203.

> who mistakes Śūnyatā itself as a theory (dṛṣṭi). It is as if a drug, administered to cure a patient, were to remove all his disorders, but were itself to foul the stomach by remaining therein. Would you, Kāśyapa, consider the patient cured?...Likewise, Kāśyapa, Śūnyatā [non-substantiality] is the antidote for all dogmatic views; but him I declare incurable who misapprehends Śūnyatā itself as a theory.[15]

The point to stress is that the *Ratnagotra,* at least at this point in its thesis, fully subscribes to the doctrine of *Śūnyatā* as the superior truth of a universal non-substantiality, the antidote counteracting the heretical stance of independent, self-subsistent individuals (*pudgalas*) and entities (*dharmas*). It is likewise cognizant of the mind's fallacious tendency "to substantiate" non-substantiality (*Śūnyatā*) into a distorted advocation of total nihilism. It is, in fact, this very concern over just such a perversion of *Śūnyatā* that accounts for the final development of the *Ratnagotra*'s doctrine on the subject in its tenth and eleventh chapters.

But it is necessary to more closely examine the śāstra's meaning of the four supreme virtues attributed to the Absolute Body (*Dharmakāya*). Most indicative is its explanation of *ātma-pāramitā* and *nitya-pāramitā*. At first reading, the former is undoubtedly the most problematic of the four designations and requires special attention, though the *Ratnagotra* itself does not expend any extra time in defining its position on this one "supreme virtue" as opposed to the other three; its treatment of all four is unassumingly brief.

Ātma-pāramitā: Supreme Unity

The rationale for Takasaki's rendering of *ātma-pāramitā* as "supreme unity" becomes apparent when the text explains that this particular sublime virtue is acquired through the "practice of

15. *Kāśyapaparivarta*, quoted in T.R.V. Murti, *The Central Philosophy of Buddhism: A Study of the Mādhyamika System* (London: George Allen & Unwin, 1960), p. 164. The underlined sentence alone is quoted in Takasaki, *Ratnagotravibhāga*, p. 204. The only difference is that Takasaki has chosen throughout his translation to render *Śūnyatā* as "non-substantiality" and I have supplied that to Murti's translation.

supremacy in the transcendental Intellect" (*prajñāpāramitā*), expressly opposing the heretical perception (*graha*) of multiple, independent, self-subsistent ego-natures.[16] Distorting the skandhic reality of all phenomena with the superimposition of the notional ego, the heretics lack the supreme wisdom of the Tathāgata's perception into the non-substantiality of all things (*sarvadharma-nairātmya*). In a severely compact and consequently abstruse fashion, the text argues that though this very non-substantiality conforms to the characteristic mark of non-ego (*anātmalakṣaṇa*), it may yet be interpreted as ego (*ātmabhipretaḥ*); non-substantiality is posited as ego (*nairātmyam evatmani kṛtvā*) much in the same paradoxical idiom of the *Prajñāpāramitā* literature, as for instance: "He stands by application of no standing place."[17] While such invocation of the Wisdom texts is intended here primarily as a stylistic defense of the apparent self-contradiction of non-substantiality as the perfection of self (*ātma-pāramitā*), it is not without doctrinal significance.

The *Ratnagotra*'s supreme unity of a universal non-substantiality is psychologically translated throughout the *Prajñā* literature by the repeated emphasis on non-apprehension, non-basis, non-settling down, non-reliance, and non-assertion. Cognitively, the Bodhisattva takes nothing as basic fact, apprehending nonseparate

16. Another reason for his translation is that the Chinese text of the śāstra employs the character, which, as *paramâtman*, suggests "supreme or universal self or soul." See *Ratnagotravibhāga*, n. 66, p. 207.

17. "And this very non-substantiality as has been perceived by the Tathāgata is quite consistent with the characteristic of non-ego, hence there is always the implication of Ego (*ātman*), by taking non-Egoity (*nairātmya*) in the meaning of Ego, as has been said: 'He stands by application of no standing place.' " Ibid., p. 211. Although Takasaki states the source of the last quotation is unknown, there is an obvious similar reference in the *Aṣṭasāhasrikā Prajñāpāramitā*, descriptive of the Bodhisattva who, not taking his stand on any skandhic basis, coursing in the non-objectified Dharma-element, "not stationed in the realm of the unconditioned, nor in the things which are conditioned, but freely wandered without a home: just so, without a support or a basis a Bodhisattva stands. A position devoid of a basis has that position been called by the Jina." Or again later: "But he does not come to a standing place in the Suchness of the Dharma-element. He becomes as one who, like a cloud, stands in the sky without anywhere to stand on, as a sorcerer who, like a bird, rides on the wind which offers him no support." *The Perfection of Wisdom in Eight Thousand Lines & its Verse Summary*, trans. Edward Conze, Wheel Series, no. 1 (Bolinas, Cal.: Four Seasons Foundation, 1973), pp. 13 and 59.

entities since he knows they are empty of any independent, self-subsistent own-being (*svabhāva*); this very emptiness must itself never serve as an object of clinging. He proceeds unobstructedly among worldly and supramundane realities (*dharmas*), conditioned and unconditioned ones, since he has realized there is absolutely nothing to apprehend; contemplating all dharmas, he neither settles down nor clings to them.

According to the *Ratnagotra*, the highest supremacy of universal non-substantiality is the result of a wisdom of the truth of things as they really are (*yathābhūta-jñāna*), non-dual, non-distinct. According to the Wisdom texts, such non-duality, and therefore unity, is had by the knowledge that all dharmas, all phenomenal reality, are non-produced:[18]

> At the time when a Bodhisattva, who courses in perfect wisdom investigates those dharmas, at that time he does not approach form etc., does not grasp it, does not take his stand on it, does not settle down in it, does not make it known as "form, etc., is that." For a Bodhisattva who courses in perfect wisdom, does not review form, etc. And why? Because the nonproduction of form, etc., is not form, etc. Form, etc., and nonproduction are not two nor divided....Inasmuch as one calls anything "form," etc., one makes count of what is non-dual.[19]

Taking nothing as a basis, not seizing upon any particular marks or signs, the Bodhisattva intuitively knows that nothing is either produced or stopped, defiled or purified, grows or decreases, comes or goes, because all are empty of own-being, and therefore rest in the unaltered, non-false Suchness of their dhārmic nature; it is that Suchness which displaces all concept of duality. Most fundamentally, what is preserved is the absolute identity of emptiness and the *skandhas;* form is nothing but the emptiness of the essential nature (the own-being), and the emptiness of essential nature is the very definition of form, and so for all the other dharmas. The non-duality of the *Prajñā* literature inveighs against any essential

18. See Nāgārjuna's primary tenet: "At no where and at no time can entities ever exist by originating out of themselves, from others, from both (self-other), or from the lack of causes." *Mūlamadhyamikakārikā*, p. 39.

19. *The Large Sūtra*, trans. Conze, p. 193.

particularity, and especially adjures the subtle opposition of form, etc., over against some extrinsic, substantiated and reified "emptiness".

> "Therefore, the Bodhisattva, coursing in the perfections which are the emptiness of essential nature, does not upset form, etc., (by assuming that it is) empty or not empty. And why? Because the emptiness of form, etc., does not upset form, etc., (by assuming) this is form, etc., this is the emptiness of form, etc.... Because they have no own-being which could (be) upset, (by assuming that) this is form, etc., and this is emptiness."[20]

If the attainment of enlightenment precludes any dependence upon the apprehension of self-subsistent bases, which would necessarily admit of dualism, one would be just as mistaken to seize upon non-duality as some form of correct or proper method; the supreme attainment is realized only where there is neither duality nor non-duality, since the implied dichotomy would itself suggest an intellectual bifurcation. So it is, that an alternate expression for the non-dual non-substantiality, found (however sparingly) throughout the Wisdom texts, and closely approximating the intuition of the *Ratnagotra*, is the assertion that all persons and things are non-different, the same (*sama*):

> In the sameness of Dharma there is no intellectual multiplicity, for the nature of Dharma is without intellectual multiplicity.... The sameness of Dharma is where there is no existent, no non-existent, no own-being,...outside the sameness of Dharma no dharma can be apprehended, the sameness of Dharma has transcended all dharmas... the dharmic sameness of the common people, and that of the Streamwinners, etc., [to that] of the Tathāgatas, that is just one single sameness, and in this sameness, there is not any difference. Since the sameness of the common people and that of all holy men is just one single sameness, there is no duality in it.[21]

One cannot fail but to recall the *Ratnagotra's* initial invocation

20. Ibid., pp. 604-605.
21. Ibid., p. 638.

of the *Prajñāpāramitā sūtras* in its third chapter, when it referred to the Tathāgata's wisdom of the equality of all things, equal "without any addition nor diminution," because perceptive of neither characteristic marks nor bases, but only the common Reality (*Bhūta*). According to the śāstra, it is just such "prajñic" perception, based upon non-discriminative wisdom that is the cause of attaining the Absolute Body, the perfect realization of the Tathāgata-embryo.[22]

Against such a background (brief though it be), the dogmatic significance of the *Ratnagotra's* interpretation of non-substantiality and non-duality as the supreme virtue of unity is not without vindication. However, as was initially stated, the current reference to the *Prajñā* literature, by the inclusion of the antiphrastic, "He stands by application of no standing place," would seem to be primarily a stylistic justification for the śāstra's linguistic paradox of non-substantiality as the perfection of self (*ātma-pāramitā*) or supreme self (*paramātman*). Evidently, what the *Ratnagotra* intends is that to antidotally posit the antithesis of the heretical concept of individuated, self-subsistent egohood, viz., the universal non-substantiality of skandhic phenomena, as the genuine ego or self, amounts to nothing more than a mental substitution. It is to take recourse in the methodology of ulterior motivation (*abhisaṃdhi*) and implied meaning (*abhiprāya*), whereby one should implicitly understand non-substantiality (*nairātmya*) or "non-egoity" whenever the conventional term of "ego" (*ātman*) is employed. It is in this spirit that the śāstra considers itself in absolute fidelity with the linguistic inversions of the *Prajñāpāramitā sūtras,* as illustrated by the following citations: "A non-coursing is the Bodhisattva's coursing in perfect wisdom";[23] "Moreover, Subhuti, the Tathāgata's perfection of patience is really no perfection";[24] "And yet, after beings have thus been led to Nirvāṇa, no being at all has been led to Nirvāṇa";[25] or again, "Self-identical through the absence of a self, a being, a soul, or a person, the utmost, right and

22. See *Ratnagotravibhāga*, p. 171.

23. *The Large Sutra*, trans. Conze, p. 512.

24. *Buddhist Wisdom Books*, containing "*The Diamond Sutra*" and "*The Heart Sutra*", trans. Edward Conze (New York: Harper & Row, Harper Torchbooks, 1972), p. 54.

25. Ibid., p. 57.

perfect enlightenment is fully known as the totality of all wholesome dharmas. 'Wholesome dharmas, wholesome dharmas,' Subhuti—yet as no dharmas have they been taught by the Tathāgata. Therefore they are called 'Wholesome dharmas'.[26]" Thus, the supreme virtue of unity or the perfection of self not only involves a conceptual transmutation which takes its contrary for its point of support, but it is not without its effect on the linguistic plane which expresses the true intent, the actual meaning, through the peculiar semantics of paradox.[27]

The idea of non-substantiality as the perfection of self is rendered all the more explicit by the Chinese text of the *Ratnagotra* which, omitting the quotation from the *Aṣṭasāhasrikā Prajñāparamitā*, inserts the following verse with a prose commentary on it:

> Having attained the highest Non-substantiality, as the pure and real emptiness, the Buddhas obtained the pure body. Therefore, it is said that they attained the great body.[28]

Defined as the Absolute Body, the *Dharmakāya*, "the great body," descriptive as neither "being" nor "non-being" is yet the highest pure Reality. Having attained this, the Buddhas are said to have attained the pure, controlling power. "In this sense the Buddhas could be the highest powerful Ego in the Immaculate Sphere."[29]

26. Ibid., pp. 61-62.

27. "*Non seulement l'obtention de la deliverance—l'Éveil—mais aussi la Réalité elle-meme peut se présenter comme l'inversion des caractéristiques du composé, c'est-a-dire des* saṃskṛtalakṣaṇa...; *et dans cette perspective spéciale l'*asaṃskṛta..., *peut se concevoir comme caractérise par des qualitiés inversées par rapport aux* saṃskṛtalakṣaṇa *vu qu'elles en sont comme les contrecarrants. Cette inversion tenant à la transmutation a ensuite un contrecoup sur le plan linguistique, car lorsqu'on veut donner expression à la Realitié conçue de la façon qui vient d'etre décrite le langage est susceptible de subir à son tour une sorte de transmutation* (pariṇāmā). *De ces considérations il semble ressortir qu'il n'est pas question, les textes faisant état du* nitya *et de l'*ātman, *d'un enseignement de tendence nécessairement substantialiste ou quasi védântique... mais bien plutôt d'un procédé servant à 'indiquer' la Realitié inexprimable. Or, une indication pareille étant forcément indirect, on recourt souvent à l'expression indirecte comportant éventuellement une intention* (abhiprāya) *ou une arriére-pensée* (abhisaṃdhi)." *Ruegg*, La Théorie, *pp.* 375-376.

28. Takasaki, *Ratnagotravibhāga*, n. 96, p. 211.

29. Ibid.

Since no further clarificatory remarks are included, it would appear that this peculiar Chinese addendum was intended not as doctrinal justification or more cogent explanation, but simply as a stronger, more demonstrative reassertion of the preceding paragraph. Yet, it should be noted that the so called "highest powerful Ego" could not possibly be interpreted as some sort of self or ego (*ātman*) existing as a self-subsistent entity, since it corresponds to the Absolute Body which, as the highest Non-substantiality, is realized precisely as the denial of the erroneous dichotomic split of self and non-self, being and non-being.

More informative is Takasaki's footnoted inclusion of a lengthy Sanskrit passage taken from the ninth chapter of the *Mahāyāna-sūtra laṅkāra,* paralleling the identical theme of non-substantiality considered as the perfection of self. "In the very pure Emptiness the Buddhas have acquired the highest exaltation of the self, due to the attainment of the most excellent self of non-substantiality, since they have obtained the pure self."[30] According to the accompanying commentary,[31] the implication is that the perfection of self or supreme self (*paramātman*) of the Buddhas is a term applied only in the immaculate sphere (*anāsravadhātu*) of absolute Emptiness (*Śūnyatā*), and implies nothing more than the realization of universal non-substantiality. This supreme non-substantiality is in fact Absolute Suchness (*Tathatā*), which is likewise referred to as the self of the Buddhas, in the sense of being their essential proper nature (*śvabhāva*). It is when this *Tathatā*, normally veiled by the adventitious defilements, (to borrow a phrase from the *Ratnagotra* itself) becomes purified and fully manifest, that the Buddhas are said to have attained the pre-excellent non-substantiality: the pure self. Consequently, it is with the hermeneutic of non-substantiality alone, that the Buddhas are to be understood as having attained the highest exaltation of the self (*ātmamahātmatām*), the supreme self (*paramātman*), and the pure self (*śuddhātma*).

30. "Śūnyatāyāṃ viśuddhāyāṃ nairatmyān mārgalābhataḥ/buddhāḥ śuddhatmalābhitvād gatā ātmamahātmatām//." Ibid., p. 212.

31. "Tatra cânāsrave dhātau buddhānāṃ paramatmā nirdiśyate//kiṃkāraṇam?/agranairātmyatmakatvāt/agraṃ nairātmyaṃ viśuddhā Tathatā sā ca buddhānām ātmā svabhāvarthena tasyām viśuddhāyām agraṃ nairātmyam ātmānam buddhā lābhante śuddham/ ataḥ śuddha-ātmalābhitvād buddhā ātmamahātmyaṃ prapta iti paramatmā vyavasthāpyate // Ibid., p. 212.

Elsewhere in the same *Sūtrālaṅkāra*,[32] a text which in general was authoritative for the Vijñānavādin tradition, and therefore adopting a rather different stance than the *Ratnagotra* in many ways, mention is made of a belief in the great self (*mahātmadṛṣṭi*) which is directly opposed to the heretical concept of an independent, self-subsistent ego or *ātman*. According to the fourteenth chapter of that text, this *mahātmadṛṣṭi* consists of the Bodhisattva's attainment of the steadfast mental conviction that all animate beings are equal to himself (*sattvātmasamānabhāva*); the great self (*mahātman*) is nothing more than the belief in a universal equality, and its importance derives from the fact that it is said to be the cause of the Bodhisattva's activity for the welfare of all beings, whom he knows to be his own self. The resonance with the *Ratnagotra*'s understanding of the perfection of self as the perfection of unity, the unity of all phenomena as universal non-substantiality, is striking. The *Sūtrālaṅkāra* further alludes to the determination or affirmation of the self as of capital importance (*agratvātmāvadhāraṇa*). This affirmation, always accompanied by the committed adherence to the universal equality of all dharmas, is said to result from the Bodhisattva's understanding that his self is of principal importance in virtue of the cultivation of the perfections (*pāramitās*). Consequently, in its eighth chapter it is said: "Thus, he of whom the self is fortified in the perfections, who has thus become capable of maturing others, and of whom the self is continually fortified by that which is good is always the supreme parent of the world."[33] The significance of the self of the Bodhisattva then, is its salvific function through which he accomplishes the good of others. Joined to the perfections (*pāramitās*), this self that is no-self, becomes the great self (*mahātman*), accounting for the Bodhisattva's epithet, *Mahāsattva* ("Great Being"), stemming from his magnanimity (*māhātmya*), selflessly accomplishing the welfare of all beings who are no other than himself.

Though not articulated as such, the *Ratnagotra*'s supreme virtue of self, interpreted as the supreme unity of all phenomena as non-substantial, and the supporting references from the *Prajñāpāra-*

32. See Ruegg, *La Théorie*, pp. 370-377.

33. "Iti navavidhavastupācitātmā paraparipācanayogyatām upetaḥ/ śubhamayasalalapravardhitātmā bhavati sadā jagato' grabandhubhūtaḥ//". Ibid., p. 372.

mitā literature and the *Mahāyānasūtrālaṅkāra*, demonstrates the unerring sense of self, the non-clinging notion of individuality. While the false sense of self is indicative of a differentiating, particularizing tendency, the genuine "virtue of self," functions under the light of non-discriminative wisdom as a universalizing, and thus, liberating factor. Obviously opposed to the heretical *satkāyadṛṣṭi*, the erroneous view in which the body-mind skandhic complex is imagined to be absolute and unconditional, and which splits the whole of experience into the "I" and "Not-I" (equally considered with the same false absolute exclusiveness), the śāstra's *ātma-pāramitā* as self-reference is nothing other than a reference to the real self, the real nature of one's nature as universally co-relational, neither exclusive of other selves nor as anything ultimate and absolute in its empirical mundane reality. As the truth of non-substantiality, this perfection of self clings neither to the specific, individual, body-mind complex, nor to the idea that this determinate and conditional entity is absolutely so, i.e., unconditionally conditioned, and therefore cut off from the ultimate reality, the pure and absolute Suchness (*Tathatā*). On the one hand, it respects the concept of the ordinary empirical self which (as demonstrated by the *Sūtrālaṅkāra*), may be meaningfully (because non-clingingly) employed by the common man, as well as by the Bodhisattvas and Buddhas, as that through which one works for the good and welfare of all sentient beings, because on the other hand, it knows the universal inclusiveness of just those beings in the truth of absolute non-substantiality (as asserted by the *Ratnagotra*). Finally, it must never be lost sight of, that the śāstra's assertion of the supreme self as the highest supreme unity derives from its intuition of the pure, non-dual essential nature of absolute Suchness (*Tathatā*) in all animate beings. And it is this Reality, conceived as the undifferentiated whole (*Tathatā'vyatibhedataḥ*), that is the text's more accustomed expression for the truth of non-substantiality as the universal selfhood of all beings. In fact, it should be recalled here, the fourth chapter's direct implication that the Bodhisattva's perception of the universal non-substantiality of "individualities" (*pudgalas*) and "separate elements" (*dharmas*), was due to his unattached cognition into the innate purity of the essence of all beings. It was advocated there, that the Bodhisattva's unobstructed vision of the Tathāgata-embryo

(*Tathatā* in its condition as *samalā*), the innate brightness of the mind (*prakṛtiprabhāsvaratā*), grounded and sustained the doctrine of non-substantiality; all beings are empty and devoid of self-nature because they are universally grounded upon the absolute essence of the Tathāgata-embryo (*Samalā Tathatā*). To perceive the unconditional status of the latter was to understand the determinate relativity of the former. Finally, it should be noted by anticipation that in the ninth chapter, under the inspiration of the *Jñānālokālaṃkārasūtra*, the śāstra interprets *Tathatā* in the nomenclature of selfhood whereby the Tathāgata, having understood the truth of his own most fundamental nature (*atmāpādānamūla*), knows the comprehensive selfhood of all beings in the non-dual purity of Absolute Suchness:

> Having in view (this) Innate Mind, the pure and non-dual Essential Nature, it is said by the Lord: "Here, O Mañjuśrī, the Tathāgata is one who has full knowledge about the root of his own substratum. Through the purification of his own self, he has understood the purity of living beings. That which is the purity of his own self and that which is the purity of the living beings, these two are one and the same, they cannot be divided into two."[34]

NITYA-PĀRAMITĀ: SUPREME ETERNITY

It should now be more fully appreciated that the *Ratnagotra*'s following discussion on the second virtue of supreme eternity (*nitya-pāramitā*) is totally lacking any implication of a concrete attribute, qualifying some quintessential concrete hypostasis. Its insistence upon the doctrine of non-substantiality as the antidotal remedy to the dualism that would posit on the one hand, the independent self-subsistent ego, and on the other, the erroneous

34. Takasaki, *Ratnagotravibhāga*, pp. 287-288. It is significant to note that in his *Mahāprajñāpāramitā Śāstra*, Nāgārjuna expresses very nearly the same equation, considering the ultimate status of the unerring sense of self in its non-duality with unconditional Suchness: " 'The ultimately real nature of the "I"........the ultimately real nature of the Tathāgata, all this is one reality, not two, not divided. When the bodhisattva realizes this reality (Tathatā) he is called Tathāgata.' " Ramanan, *Nāgārjuna*'s *Philosophy*, p. 269.

notion of non-substantiality as nihilism,[35] preserves it from any such accusation. Its remarks on the virtue of supreme eternity should leave no doubt that the śāstra's major intent in advancing the four *guṇa-pāramitā* is more properly pastoral and spiritually pedagogical, than it is ontological. While not without profound metaphysical implications (soon to be explicated), its primary psychological orientation focuses clearly upon the exposition of the exact praxis of those who would walk the correct and genuine path of the Great Vehicle. It is only with an appreciative understanding of this inherent methodology, that one can avoid misconstruing the practical, expediental doctrine of the *guṇa-pāramitā*, and hence better assess the originality through which the *Ratnagotra* presents its genuinely philosophical tenets on the doctrine of the Tathāgata-embryo (*garbha*).

Adhering to its corrective analysis, the text directs its argument against those who subscribe to the vehicle of the Pratyekabuddha, condemning their aversion to the profit of living beings (*sattvārtha-vimukhatā*) and their total indifference (*nirapekṣatā*) to their salvation. It is this, that is said to obstruct the virtue of supreme eternity, and the remedial antidote is the practice of great compassion (*mahākaruṇā-bhāvanā*) on the part of the Bodhisattva. Seeking neither the crass enjoyments of phenomenal existence, nor the headlong retreat from it in the soporific extinction of complete and final *nirvāṇa,* the Bodhisattva aims at the perfect integration of the two antipodal tendencies, and thus all the false contrasting distinctions arising from them, viz., the natural and supernatural, the mundane and supermundane, the finite and the infinite.

On the more superficial level, the text first implies that the supreme eternity simply means that the Bodhisattva, filled with compassion, will remain based in the phenomenal sphere (*saṃsāra-gata*) without interruption, "as long as the world exists"; that his

35. In reference to the Tathāgata as the highest unity, the śāstra explains that He is absolutely quiescent, having destroyed the dualistic view of ego and non-ego. It continues: "The Supreme Unity, too, should be understood by two reasons: (1) because of the removal of false imagination of Ego by rejecting the extremity peculiar to the Heretics, and (2) because of the removal of false imagination concerning non-substantiality by rejecting the extremity peculiar to the Śrāvakas." Takasaki, *Ratnagotravibhāga*, pp. 218-219.

mercy is so comprehensively universal, that it extends "beyond the limitation of time (lasting) as long as the utmost limit of the world." But according to such a formulation, the supreme eternity has only a remote and extrinsic connection with the *mahākaruṇā* of the Bodhisattva; the latter's eternity is functionally dependent upon the eternity of phenomenal existence. In such a case, it exercises none of the creative coalescence that defines the intuitive equality of *saṃsāra* and *nirvāṇa*. Such a compassion may be figuratively descriptive of the "eternal" resolve of the Bodhisattva's salvific intention, but it is scarcely adequate to the claim of synthesizing the mundane and the eternal; and in fact, left as it is, such a compassion "lasting as long as the world exists" could easily be implied as positing an erroneous "eternalistic view" (*śāśvatadṛṣṭi*). If the supreme eternity (*nitya-pāramitā*) results from the cultivation of the Boddhisattva's compassion, and if this *mahākaruṇā* functions to the limit of phenomenal existence, then is there not the suggestion that worldly reality has no end, since the compassion establishing the supreme eternity is said to parallel that existence?

So it is that, several verses later on, the *Ratnagotra* considerably amplifies its presentation of the virtue of supreme eternity since, far from advocating any such heretical stance, it is properly defined as that mode of perception that no more asserts a nihilistic extremity (*ucchedadṛṣṭi*) than an eternalistic one. It is now said that the supreme eternity is realized when the Bodhisattva, avoiding the former view, does not diminish his neglect of the non-eternal phenomenal life, simultaneously by-passing the latter error by not intensifying the eternal *nirvāṇa*. The awkward stylistics expressive of the Bodhisattva's dual avoidance of the extreme views translates more simply as, on the one hand, his detachment from involvement with sentient beings, having completely exterminated without remainder all tendency of desire; on the other hand, he is never totally remote from them, since his great compassion never abandons them to their sufferings. The attainment of supreme eternity is contingent then, not only upon the practice of great compassion (*mahākaruṇā-bhāvanā*), but equally upon the exercised cultivation of perfect wisdom (*prajñāpāramitā-bhāvanā*). Only through the conjunctive operation of these complementary perfections (*pāramitās*), can the Bodhisattva enter the "Unstable

Nirvāṇa" (*apratiṣṭhitanirvāṇa*), or perhaps more elegantly, if not less paradoxically, the "Unstable Stability" (*apratiṣṭhita-pada*). This is the *Ratnagotra's* expression for the classical Nāgārjunine formulation that phenomenal existence is itself *nirvāṇa*, and that no difference exists in their spheres of action.[36]

It is of critical significance, both for the correct appreciation of its current doctrine on the *guṇa-pāramitā* (supreme virtues) as well as for its later evaluation of the Mādhyamikan *Śūnyavāda*, to note again the śāstra's close affinity to, and reliance upon, the major intuitions of the *Prajñāpāramitā* literature and, at least here, its accord with certain principal tenets of Nāgārjuna. Its adherence to the dogma of universal non-substantiality has already been demonstrated in the examination of the perfection of self as supreme unity (*ātma-pāramitā*). The non-discriminative wisdom which alone was accredited with that lofty perception of *sarva-dharmanairātmya*, is again operative in knowing the equality of *saṃsāra* and *nirvāṇa*, through its non-distinction between the two (*ubhayatha'vikalpana*). It follows logically therefore, that the non-apprehension of such a distinction would be translated into the *Ratna's* description of the Bodhisattva as neither extinguishing and diminishing (*anapakarṣana*) phenomenal existence, nor as intensifying (*asamāropaṇa*) and superimposing anything upon the nirvāṇic condition; nothing need be subtracted from the one nor added to the other, for no difference exists between them in a non-substantiality that transcends all dichotomic concepts of being and non-being, finite and infinite, permanence and impermanence.[37] If the text asserts that the Bodhisattva, "being deeply

36. "*Saṃsāra* (i.e., the empirical life-death cycle) is nothing essentially different from *nirvāṇa. Nirvāṇa* is nothing essentially different from *saṃsāra*. The limits (i.e., the realm) of *nirvāṇa* are the limits of *saṃsāra*. Between the two, also, there is not the slightest difference whatsoever." Nāgārjuna, *Mūla-madhyamikakārikā*, p. 158.

37. It might be noted that Nāgārjuna's chapter on "the examination of *nirvāṇa*" (*Nirvāṇa parīkṣā*) likewise stresses the error of conceptualizing *nirvāṇa* as some particular state of being, which then gives rise to speculations about pre- and post-existent modalities of life. But once one firmly renounces the basic notions of being and non-being, realizing that there is absolutely nothing to grasp, then *nirvāṇa* is properly intuited to transcend the realm of both existence and non-existence; to attain it, nothing need be discarded, but grasping itself.

"What is never cast off, seized, interrupted, constant, extinguished and intent towards the Nirvāṇa for his own sake, *does not stay* in the phenomenal life," by no means is this to be interpreted as any manner of physical departure on his part; "he does not stay" in *saṃsāra* because for him, it has completely lost its saṃsāric character. He has protected himself through the perfection of wisdom against the saṃsāric web of the defilements by utterly uprooting all tenacious desires without remainder.[38] Likewise, the fact that "he does not abide in the Nirvāṇa" has no suggestion of privation or lack, but is simply the śāstra's barb against all those motivated solely by the search for self-quiescence (*śamaikayāna-gotra*); the Bodhisattva cannot "lack Nirvāṇa" since it has been realized within *saṃsāra* (this phenomenal life) itself, where he continues his salvific activity abiding through non-apprehension; non-appropriation; non-attachment; non-reliance; and no-settling-down, inspired and supported only by his great compassion.

If there is any temporal connotation in the *Ratnagotra*'s virtue of supreme eternity it is the evocation of a supra-transient mode of perception, a condition of profound psychic equilibrium where the things of phenomenal reality continue to come and go, to change and pass away. But because there is not the slightest tendency to seize and grasp, to cling and desire, the compassionate Bodhisattva, while perceiving the relative and the determinate, understands fully in the light of *prajñā*, that this very conditioned existence is, in its ultimate nature the unconditioned *Tathatā*, the

---

produced...this is called *nirvāṇa*...The status of the birth-death cycle is due to existential grasping (of the *skandhas*) and relational condition (of the being). That which is non-grasping and non-relational is taught as *nirvāṇa*. The teacher (Buddha) has taught the abandonment of the concepts of being and non-being. Therefore, *nirvāṇa* is properly neither (in the realm of) existence nor non-existence....The various views concerning the status of life after *nirodha*, the limits of the world, the concept of permanence, etc., are all based on (the concepts of) *nirvāṇa*, posterior and anterior states of existence. Since all factors of existence are in the nature of *śūnya*, why (assert) the finite, the infinite, both finite and infinite, and neither finite nor infinite?" *Mūlamadhyamakakārikā*, pp. 154-158.

38. However lofty an attainment, this nevertheless does not imply that the Bodhisattva has totally extirpated the succeeding origination of their subconscious impressions (*vāsanā-anusandhi*). In other words, he is still conditioned by "the body made of mind" (*manomayakāya*) which, despite its purity, hampers the final attainment of the Absolute Body (*Dharmakāya*). See *Ratnagotravibhāga*, n. 141, p. 219.

Nirvāṇa.[39] The supreme eternity is realized neither by those who cling to the determinate nor those who cling to the indeterminate, for both commit the error of exclusiveness; they cling to extremities. To seize the phenomenal as itself ultimate is to adhere to an eternalistic view (*śāśvatadṛṣṭi*), while to imagine that the indeterminate (*nirvāṇa*) is wholly exclusive of the determinate (*saṃsāra*) is to commit the error of negativism; the latter amounts to the false notion that the diminishing (*anapakarṣaṇa*) and annihilation (*uccheda*) of the phenomenal world of *saṃsāra* is the necessary condition to realize *nirvāṇa*. These exclusive views conceive the conditional and the unconditional as separate from each other. The comprehension definitive of the supreme eternity, compassionately sensitive to the determinate status of the former (i.e., *saṃsāra*) as the (possible) source of impermanence and suffering, devoid of substantiality, nevertheless wisely perceives its non-dual character with the latter (*nirvāṇa*) as its ultimate ground and nature.

Supreme Bliss and Supreme Purity

It should now be briefly noted how the text defines the remaining two *guṇa-pāramitā*, the supreme bliss (*sukha-pāramitā*) and supreme purity (*śubha-pāramitā*). Though not explicated as such by the śāstra, there is a definite resemblance between the supreme eternity and supreme bliss in their common opposition against an erroneous response to phenomenal life. While the former is realized by the Bodhisattva's practice of great compassion and wisdom against the Pratyekabuddha's indifference to the living beings of this existence, the supreme bliss is the remedial antidote to the delight of the Śrāvakas in the absolute cessation of the sufferings of phenomenal life, which is the foundation and cause of their great fear. The *sukha-pāramitā* is the joyful response of the Bodhisattva in "all matters, mundane and supramundane," and results from his practice of various kinds of lofty meditations, specified only as *Gaganagañjā*. However, one may gauge the superiority

39. Cf. Nāgārjuna's *Mahāprajñāpāramitā Śāstra*. "When one fares by seizing, by clinging, then (in one's case) the world would be a (mass of) perversion; but when one fares free from seizing, free from clinging, then the world itself is *Nirvāṇa*." Ramanan, *Nāgārjuna*'s *Philosophy*, p. 97.

of such meditations, since they are the immediate occasion for the abandonment of the "body made of mind" (*manomayakāya*). This latter (likewise referred to as the "mind made aggregate" [*manomaya-skandha*]) obtains even with those Bodhisattvas who have achieved the ten controlling powers and abide on the tenth and highest stage (*bhūmi*) of the path.[40] The supreme bliss (and by consequent inference, the three other supreme virtues) therefore, is realized only on the stage of Buddhahood. The sublime meditations of the Bodhisattva immediately effect the removal of the *manomayakāya*; more specifically, they fathom the ultimate cognition that all suffering (*duḥkha*) has been extinguished by nature, thereby removing the origination of all sufferings (which, in fact, do not exist, in the ultimate sense) as well as the total extirpation of all and any successive, subconscious impressions (*vāsanā-anusandhi*). The perfect joy of the *sukha-pāramitā* is therefore, the proximate effect of those meditations destroying all fear through the profound conviction on the original status of *duḥkha*. It witnesses then, to the total interdependence of the four *guṇa-pāramitā*, since its remedial meditations function in accord with the universal non-substantiality propounded by the *ātma-pāramitā*, and its comprehension of the ultimate nature of suffering might be a suitable expression for the transformation of *saṃsāra* as *nirvāṇa* and thus, the realization of *nitya-pāramitā*. Finally, it could easily serve as an alternate expression for the fourth *guṇa*, the supreme purity (*śubha-pāramitā*), which has an almost identical definition as the culmination of the practice of faith in the doctrine of the Great Vehicle, manifesting itself through the expurgation of the "dwelling-place of ignorance" (*avidyā-vāsanā-bhūmi*) and the accompanying "removal of all the dusts of defilements with their bad-smelling impressions" (*daurgandhya-vāsanā*).[41] Nothing more is added to the definition of supreme purity here, since the *Ratnagotra* had already insisted on this feature as the *svabhāva* (own-being or self-nature) of *Tathatā*, even in its condition of non-manifestation or concealment (*samalā*) as indicated above.

40. For a more detailed discussion of this *manomayakāya* see p. 19 above which discussed the term from the perspective of the *Śrī-Mālā Sūtra*, the source for the *Ratnagotra*'s present discussion in pp. 214-218.

41. See *Ratnagotravibhāga*, pp. 214-217 for the śāstra's understanding of the *avidyā-vāsanā-būmi* which is again based entirely on its presentation in the *Śrī-Mālā-Sūtra*, discussed in pp. 61-64 above.

It is this very point that now regrounds the lengthy, though necessary, excursions on the nature of the *guṇa-pāramitā* into the śāstra's original ten-pointed schematic analysis of the Tathāgata-embryo (*garbha*), conceived as *Samalā Tathatā*. Having stipulated its self-essence (*svabhāva*) as innate purity despite the adventitious covering of the defilements, the text exposed the perspectival obscurations, exemplified by the erroneous attitudes of the four classes of beings. Applying the particular remedial antidote (*pratipakṣa*) to each of the mistaken views, there is brought about the result (*phala*) of *Tathatā*'s purification; it is no longer "mingled with pollution" (*samalā*), but is established as the Absolute Body of the Tathāgata (*Dharmakāya*). The latter's fourfold supreme virtue, the result of such purificatory practices is itself interpreted as the antidote (*pratipakṣa*) to the "fourfold non-delusion" (*aviparyāsa*) with reference to the *Dharmakāya;* rather than being non-eternal, full of sufferings, of no substantial ego, and impure, the Absolute Body of the Tathāgata is realized as *nitya, sukha, ātma* and *śubha-pāramitā.*

It is especially significant at this juncture to reiterate the basic perspective adopted by, and operative throughout the *Ratnagotra-vibhāga.* Unlike the *Śrī-Mālā* which maintained a fluid, dynamic tension between the Tathāgata-embryo and Absolute Body as the polar phases of a transformational process more formally epistemological and soteriological, the śāstra evidences a more obvious ontological stance. Whereas the earlier scripture stressed the processive character of the *garbha* as embryonic absolute knowledge advancing towards its final and complete self-aware, self-manifestation as *Dharmakāya*, the active emergence of itself to itself from a latent to an articulate ultimacy, the *Ratna* examines the ontological non-duality between the two, under the category of Absolute Suchness (*Tathatā*). While preserving a certain elemental transformational nuance through the qualifying determinants of *samalā* and *nirmalā*, the śāstra's focus is quite deliberately on the all pervading, unchangeable, non-differentiated, self-subsistent purity of *Tathatā*. Yet, though this basically static posture of the Tathāgata-embryo as *Tathatā* (despite its hidden concealment by the adventitious defilements) remains a dominant motif, its alternate designation as *Tathāgatagotra* as active causal factor (*hetu*) still sustains the dynamic, processive dimension as that which effects the unique and universal goal of Buddhahood in all sentient beings. It is this equivalency of *garbha* and *gotra,* this "embryonic" and "germinal" character, now ascriptive of *Tathatā* as *samalā,* that must be retained when interpreting the present section on the supreme virtues of purity, unity, bliss and eternity.

The Result of the Embryo's Self-purification

Now if, as is expressly stated by the *Ratnagotra,* these four *guṇa-pāramitā* "are brought about on the Absolute Body of the Tathāgata as the result of Bodhisattva's four kinds of practices," it is to be noted that the object of the śāstra's analysis remains essentially the same, i.e., *Tathatā.* The only change that has been effected is in its condition of hiddenness and concealment. For it will be recalled that the text's alternate expression for the Absolute Body (*Dharmakāya*), is *Nirmalā Tathatā,* Absolute Suchness in its perfect manifestation as free of all adventitious defilements. Consequently, if *Nirmalā Tathatā* or *Dharmakāya* is here presented fundamentally as result (*phala*) of various spiritual exercises (faith in the doctrine of the Great Vehicle; the exercised cultivation of perfect wisdom; a definite series of meditations; and the practice of great compassion), the process is merely one of inner convergence where the end (*Nirmāla Tathatā or Dharmakāya*) lies in the self-revelation or self-manifestation of the beginning (*Samalā Tathatā or Tathāgatagarbha*). *Tathatā* as *nirmalā* can be a result (*phala*) only because it is present from the start in an initial shape and content, however much it may be veiled and obstructed as *samālā*; whether it be manifested or not, revealed or not, Absolute Suchness remains forever what it inherently is as supreme purity, unity, bliss, and eternity. If the nature of *Samalā Tathatā* (the *Tathāgatagarbha*) is to be actualized as *Nirmalā* (*Dharmakāya*), the movement is merely from an implicit to an explicit fullness; no new elements are acquired, it is only the latent or inherent ones that become fully expressed, i.e., the four *guṇa-pāramitā.* If there is a transition, it is in the sphere of a fullness that moves from an opaque to a lucid explicitation. The fourfold Bodhisattva praxis imputes nothing new or extrinsic, but as antidotal remedies, simply expose those aspects of *Tathatā* present from the beginning, though concealed by the defilements. Since the activity of such spiritual exercise or *bhāvanā* stems from the perfection which *Tathatā* is (despite its status as *samalā*), there is nothing that can be said to be created by that activity. The four practices are merely the self-exposition, the self-articulation of *Tathatā* as innate purity, unity, bliss, and eternity.

The Union with the Purifying Factors

This generic process of *Tathatā's* self-unfoldment to itself from *samalā* (and thus from the *Tathāgatagarbha*) to *nirmalā* (and so, *Dharmakāya*), its essential endowment with the propensity towards its self-transformation, is all the more decisively stated under the category of *yoga* ("union"). It is there clearly stipulated that the *Buddhagotra* (synonymous with the Tathāgata-embryo) is an inexhaustible storage, endowed with properties indivisible from it. More specifically, the essence (*dhātu*) of the Tathāgata is intrinsically united to, and provided with, the causal factors of its own purification (*hetū-semanvāgama*). These latter are in fact the fourfold practices which, under the former category of result (*phala*), were indicated as "bringing about" the supreme purity, unity, bliss, and eternity on the Absolute Body (*Dharmakāya*).

Initially, there may appear to be a discrepancy between the effects of the four practices as expressed under the category of result (*phala*), and here under the category of union (*yoga*). For instance, the practice of faith in the doctrine of the Great Vehicle formerly said to antidotally "bring about" the supreme purity on the Absolute Body, is now identified simply as "the cause of purification of the Absolute Body" (*Dharmakāyaviśuddhihetu*). Whereas the practice of supremacy in the transcendental Intellect (i.e., the cultivation of perfect wisdom) was said to result in the supreme unity, and the exercise of the Bodhisattva's meditational praxis in the realization of supreme bliss, they are now taken as a unity and designated as "the cause of the attainment of Buddha's Wisdom" (*buddhajñānasamudāgamahetu*). And while the Bodhisattva's practice of great compassion remedially brought about the supreme eternity on the Absolute Body, under the formal category of *yoga*, it is here defined as "the cause of the attainment of Buddha's Great Compassion" (*tathāgatamahākaruṇāvṛttihetu*). If however there is an observable modification, it is one more of expression than of content. For, to say that the practice of faith causes the purification of the Absolute Body, is but an alternate specification for the resultant supreme purity which the *Dharmakāya* is. So too, the Bodhisattva's cultivated initiation into the *prajñāpāramitā*, along with the dedicated exercise of the required *samādhis* as the constitutive bases for the attainment of the Buddha wisdom, is but the functional expression of the resultant supreme unity and bliss through which that wisdom manifests and realizes itself. Finally, if the supreme eternity is the prescient goal towards which the Bodhisattva's *mahākaruṇā* has already been initiated, its ultimate culmination in the stage of Buddhahood alters nothing in the nature of that compassion, except to demonstrate its perfection and signify the end of its imperfect, itinerant (and thus, causal) status.

It must also be demonstrated that though, in the interest of the śāstra's characteristically schematic structure, the text has tended to separate the Absolute Body as one thing, the Buddha's wisdom and meditative acuity as another, and his great compassion as still another, against which it has paired off the four causative factors, there is an absolute, interdependent coherence (*saṃbandha*) that cannot be forgotten; the very nature of the Absolute Body is sublime wisdom and compassion. Such likewise is the case with the four purificatory practices (*bhāvanās*) for, as the text states, the practice of faith in the doctrine of the Great Vehicle is likened to a receptacle containing as it does, the jewel of *prajñā* and *samādhi* as well as the water of *karuṇā*; these latter evidence a similar mutual concomitance, collaterally functioning indiscriminatively and further endowed with a multiplicity of "inconceiveable and powerful virtues." So then, if the dominant feature of the *Ratnagotra*'s category of *yoga* ("union") is its assertion of the absolutely inseparable accompaniment (*samanvagāma*) of *Samalā Tathatā* (or *Tathāgatagarbha*) with the features essential to its resultant self-purification as *Nirmalā* (or *Dharmakāya*), there is an implicit, secondary, though no less important, application of the term: the mutually inclusive nature of those same features among themselves (understood as cause), and the coexistent, interdependent status of the Buddha's Absolute Body, supreme wisdom and great compassion (interpreted as result).

CHAPTER IV

FURTHER CHARACTERISTICS OF THE EMBRYO

THE FUNCTION OF THE EMBRYO TOWARDS SELF-PURIFICATION

THE INHERENT SUBJECTIVITY which has emerged from the *Ratnagotra's* analysis of *Samalā Tathatā* as the embryo endowed with the factors for its complete self-realization as *nirmalā,* is strongly reinforced under the category of *karman* (the "*functions*" of the *garbha* towards its purification). Adopting the authoritative assertion of the *Śrī-Mālā Sūtra* on the Tathāgata-embryo as reactivity against the pain of phenomenal existence (*saṃsāra*) and the simultaneous intentionality toward the emancipation of *nirvāṇa,* the śāstra here discusses the essence of the Buddha (*Buddhadhātu*) (an alternate designation for the *Tathāgatagarbha*) as "the perfectly pure germ (*viśuddhigotra*), even of those people who are fixed in the wrong way." Being the unconditional perception into mundane reality as the (possible) source of suffering, the germ effects a responsive "disgust" with the causes of saṃsāric misery, and a concurrent movement of longing, desire, and earnest wish towards the joy which it knows *nirvāṇa* to be. *Tathatā*, here represented as *gotra* ("germ"), and thus as *samalā* (concealed by the adventitious defilements), is consequently identified as comprehensive awareness and consciousness of conditioned reality not only as the locus of pain and suffering, but as the very possibility for the transformational realization of total emancipation. And the usage of *gotra* ("germ") as descriptive of *Tathatā* supplements its status as ontic subjectivity by its technical inference as primary soteriological principle. Its active conative function is no more indeterminate volition or undefined aspiration, but is the universal potentiality common to all sentient beings to reach the one, unique goal of supreme enlightenment.

Here, the *Ratnagotra* advances its polemical insistence against the theory of the *Icchantikas* as those beings who are forever and absolutely deprived of the full and final awakening to *parinirvāṇa*;

no one is forever incapable of rejecting impurity and producing the proper antidotal remedies (*pratipakṣas*). That the *Icchantikas* are those who belong to the lineage of never attaining the perfect *nirvāṇa* (*aparinirvāṇagotraka*) is a mere conventional expression, reflective of a non-literal, "intentional" (*abhiprāyika*) interpretation. Wherever it has been taught, it is meant only as a pedagogical expedient (*upāya*) to remove the hatred against the doctrine of the Great Vehicle (the cause of one's designation as an *Icchantika*), and its reference is to a limited, temporal determination. While it may be used to indicate the conditional period when a being may suffer the delusion of a repulsion to the doctrine of the Mahāyāna, there will come a time when he is not so afflicted, and will thus be open to attain the ultimate self-purification, by nature of his endowment with the germinal essence of Buddhahood:

> The saying: the Icchantikas are of no Nirvāṇa, is only conventional...Indeed, as there exists the germ [*gotra*] which is pure by nature, none could be of the absolutely impure nature. Therefore with reference to the fact that all living beings, with no difference, have the possibility of being purified, the Lord has said again: "Though being beginningless indeed, [*saṃsāra*] has its end; being pure by nature, it is endowed with Eternity [*dhruvadharma*]; being covered from outside by the beginningless sheath (of defilements), (this nature) is however invisible, just as the gold concealed (in sand and dust)."[1]

It should be reiterated at this point that if the earlier five chapters of the *Ratnagotra* tended to discuss the Tathāgata-embryo as a fundamental nature (*dharmatā*); a basic substartum (*āśraya*); an original essence (*dhātu*); an unconditional Reality (*Bhūta*) common to all sentient beings; the universal Absolute that is to be correctly perceived and exactly understood by a non-discriminative wisdom; such determinations were not altered, but merely subsumed under the inclusive category of *Tathatā*. As such, it retained and preserved the unmistakably ontic status implied by each of those various designations, even in its condition of

1. Takasaki, *Ratnagotravibhāga*, pp. 223-224. The source of the secondary quotation is said to be unknown.

concealment by the adventitious defilements (*samalā*). If Absolute Suchness tended thereby to suggest a certain substantial character, this dimension was nevertheless complemented by the text's repeated reference to its processive, intentional modality as embryonic absolute knowledge, inherently endowed with the properties necessary to its self-transformed realization as *nirmalā*. The *Ratnagotra*'s insistence upon the germinal aspect of *Samalā Tathatā* as *gotra* ensures its correct, definitive posture not as ontic substance, but rather, ontic subjectivity. It will be recalled that under the triplicate set of coincident definitions, attesting the universal presence of the Tathāgata-embryo among all animate beings (*sarvasattvās tathāgatagarbhāḥ*), the śāstra established a decisive equivalency of *Dharmakāya, Tathatā* and *gotra* (Absolute Body, Absolute Suchness, and germinal essence). It was there further specified under the mandate of the *Avataṃsakasūtra*, that the universal permeating efficacy of the Absolute Body (and through associative implication, the undifferentiated Absolute Suchness, and the germinal essence), was the function of its nature as self-born wisdom, the wisdom of omniscience. Now once again under its analysis of *karman* (the functions of the germinal essence towards its purification), the *Ratnagotra* applies the *Avataṃsaka*'s imagery of the cosmic penetration of all beings, even those who are confined to erroneous paths (or no path at all), by the efficacious radiation of the Tathāgata's "solar" wisdom.[2] A reasonable inference is that, since the present section of the śāstra discusses the activity of *Samalā Tathatā* as *gotra,* the dynamic, germinal essence of Buddhahood, perfectly pure by nature and universally present in all beings, the *Ratnagotra* intends to define the specific nature of that embryonic essence as wisdom. The alignment of the *Avataṃsaka*'s description with the perspicuous function of the *gotra* in its all-inclusive awareness of both *saṃsāra* and *nirvāṇa*, is indicative not only of the comprehensive extent of its presence, but also the nature of that universal potentiality as self-emergent wisdom.

2. Said to be taken from the thirty-second chapter of the *Avataṃsakasūtra*, the *Ratnagotra*'s quotation reads as follows:

"After this the rays of the disk of the sun-like Tathāgata fall upon the bodies of even those people who are fixed in the wrong way and make benefits for them. And furthermore producing the cause of future (bliss) (in them), they cause them to thrive with virtuous qualities." Ibid.

This primal subjectivity that now characterizes *Samalā Tathatā* is obvious not only from the cognitive-perceptual definition of the *gotra's* profound acuity into the very nature of reality, and its conative responsiveness away from suffering and active intentionality towards joyful liberation. In addition, it is said that the *gotra* is endowed with the five supernatural faculties (*abhijñā*),[3] and the wisdom by which the evil influence of the mental predispositions and moral defilements is destroyed (*āsravakṣayajñāna*). The diaphonous tonality attributed to the *gotra,* here said to resemble the light and heat of a flame, is the *Ratna's* figurative expression for a wisdom which, in the process of extinguishing the darkness and "consuming the fuel" of ignorance, becomes self-manifest.

So it is to be understood that Absolute Suchness (*Tathatā*), generally presented rather statically as the latent, all pervasive, unchangeable and non-differentiated self-subsistent purity, even in its condition of concealment (*samalā*) is, in that same state, the active animation of omniscient wisdom, embryonic and germinal in its movement towards full, self-expressive disclosure as actually free of the contingent defilements (*nirmalā*).

The Embryo's Manifestation

This critical interpretation of Suchness (*Tathatā*) as ontic subjectivity is clearly recognized under the terms of the next three categories of the śāstra's analysis. Under the aspect of "manifestation" (*vṛtti*), it is strikingly evident that the status of the three major classes of beings—ordinary persons, saints, and Buddhas—is idealistically defined as the threefold self-perception of Absolute Suchness (*Tathatā*). The latter is not reified as the objective possession of the former; rather, through them, it arrives at varying degrees of self-witnessing self-possession. In the ordinary people, those "of erroneous conception" (*viparyasta*), the Buddha-embryo (*jinagarbha*) or essence of the Tathāgata (*Tathāgatadhātu*) fails to attain any significant perception of itself as what it really is, "the perfect purity, the Suchness of all the elements." While in "those of the right conception" (*aviparyasta*), the saints, a greater measure

3. See Ibid., n. 210, p. 227.

of self-cognition is attained, until finally in the Buddhas "of perfectly right conception" (*samyag-aviparyasta*) all obstructions of moral defilements and knowable objects having been dispelled, *Tathatā* becomes perfectly self-aware in the supra-dualistic knowledge of itself as the Absolute Suchness of all reality.

The *Ratnagotra's* insistence upon the trans-personal definition of *Tathatā* is further specified under the category of *avasthāprabheda* where it further translates the mainfestation of Suchness from the vehicle of the threefold classes of individuals into the more impersonal reference to its "different states" of revealed purity. So it is that in the impure state (*aśuddha*), the essence of the Buddha is conventionally designated by the term "ordinary beings," in the partly pure and partly impure state (*aśuddhaśuddha*) it is known commonly as "the saints" or, more properly, "the Bodhisattvas". Finally, it is known as "the Tathāgata" in the perfectly pure state (*suviśuddha*) of its manifestation. What is being emphasized in this further refinement of the previous category is the absolute subjectivity of *Tathatā*. While under *vṛtti* this was presented in terms of its self-reflective awareness in and through the conceptual modalities of the three classes of persons, here it is expressed under the varying conditions of its self-disclosed innate purity. Under the inspiration of the *Anūnatvāpūrṇatvanirdeśaparivarta,* the śāstra unequivocably equates not only the Tathāgata, but the Bodhisattvas and the ordinary living beings as well, with the Absolute Body (*Dharmakāya*); the respective status of each of the three groups is defined in terms of their strict identity with the latter.

The designation, "ordinary living beings," is nothing other than the Absolute Body in the impure state of its concealment by the sheath of the adventitious defilements, subject to the phenomenal processes of birth and death in the wheel of *saṃsāra*. What is conventionally referred to as "the Bodhisattva" is merely descriptive of the same Absolute Body in the median condition of both purity and impurity, when it has become averse to the suffering of existence and attained a certain degree of freedom from all objects of desire through various spiritual praxes. Finally, "the Tathāgata, the Arhat, the Perfectly Enlightened One" is the supreme epithet for that Body having released itself from the defilements and their successive impressions, surpassing all sufferings and realizing itself as the unexcelled, innately pure, absolute essence of all things (*Paramaviśuddhadharmatā*).

The universal dimension of that essence is formally stipulated under the following category, *sarvatraga* ("all-pervading") where it is compared to the cosmic extensions of space. Just as the latter's expanse penetrates the totality of things in an all-encompassing presence, the *Tathāgatadhātu* indiscriminately permeates all beings irrespective of their apparent defects or virtues. Since it has already insisted upon the comprehensive scope of the Tathāgata-embryo under the precise formula *sarvasattvāś tathāgatagarbhāḥ*, what is of particular significance here is the *Ratnagotra*'s radical implication as to the subject and object of this pervasive influence. Continuing the emphasis noted in the previous sections, the śāstra strongly suggests that if the essence of the Tathāgata, Absolute Suchness, is the efficacious permeating principle throughout all levels of sentient reality, it is simultaneously the object of that very self-activity. Undoubtedly, the inclusion of the following passage from the authoritative *Anūnatvāpūrṇatvanirdeśaparivarta* is intended to substantiate such a conception:

> Therefore, O Sariputra, the (ordinary) living beings and the Absolute Body are not different from each other. The living beings are nothing but the Absolute Body, and the Absolute Body is nothing but the living beings. These two are non-dual by meaning, and different merely by letters.[4]

While the *Ratnagotra* fails to make any deliberate and methodical analysis on the exact nature of such non-duality, it does add a further, more exact specification; the essence of the Tathāgata is not only equated with the Absolute Body (*Dharmakāya*), but is defined moreover as "the immaculate nature of the mind" (*cittaprakṛti-vaimalyadhātu*).

Thus far, the text has employed the threefold equivalence of *Dharmakāya* (Absolute Body), *Tathatā* (Suchness), and *Tathāgatagotra* (germinal essence of Tathāgatahood) in its systematic articulation of *Tathāgatagarbha*, often referred to as *Tathāgatadhātu* (essence of the Tathāgata). Through the combined interchangeability of the former, the *Ratnagotra* has substantiated

4. Ibid., p. 234.

the unconditional status of the latter. More precisely, it has been argued that the ontic character afforded the Tathāgata-embryo as both the unmanifest Absolute Body and the immanence of Suchness concealed by the adventitious defilements, had been significantly nuanced by its designation as *gotra*. As "germinal" absolute knowledge and active intentionality away from saṃsāric suffering towards the liberation of ultimate *nirvāṇa*, the embryo assumed the role of an ontic subjectivity. This interpretation is now expressly certified by the *Ratnagotra's* explicit determination of *Tathāgatadhātu as* "the indiscriminative Innate Mind" (*Cittaprakṛti*), clearly synthesizing the absolute transcendence of *Dharmakāya* with the immanence of *Tathatā* under a decisively noetic category. And if the śāstra does not attempt any detailed clarification on the non-duality of *Dharmakāya* (Absolute Body) and *sattvadhātu* (the mass of human beings)[5] as noted by the *Anūnatvāpūrṇatva*, it is suggested that the introduction of *cittaprakṛtivaimalyadhātu* ("the immaculate nature of the mind") contributes towards that explanation.

The threefold strata of humanity are understood as the varying states in which the innate purity of the Absolute Body is manifest. As the conditions of impurity, purity and impurity, and perfect purity, the human sphere is initially and extrinscially interpreted as the field upon which the *Dharmakāya* is revealed. However, as the different cognitive levels—those of erroneous conception, of right conceptions, and of perfectly right conception—human consciousness is more precisely focused as the vehicle through which the Absolute Body gains self-conscious recognition of its inherent nature. The all-pervading Innate Mind is the immanent mode by which the *Dharmakāya* becomes fully self-aware in and through phenomenal human consciousness. By defining the human intellect simply in terms of *Cittaprakṛti* (the noetic substratum common to ordinary people and to Buddhas alike), the *Ratnagotra* implies the diverse planes of conceptual awareness to be, in fact, the self-reflective moments in which the Absolute Body affirms

5. *Dhātu* is used here in the sense of "group" or "collection", and principally denotes the totality of human beings; it is used as a collective noun for *sattvas*. However, it also retains the implication, used so often throughout the text, of being "the essence of the living being". In this case, the two interpretations need not be conflicting.

itself as the perfectly pure essence, the Suchness of all reality. "Innate Mind" is then the epistemic-noetic determination of *Tathāgatagarbha* (known also as *Tathāgatadhātu*) in the latter's appositional reference to all persons; at the same time it is the specification of immanent primal subjectivity, attributed to the *Dharmakāya* in its all-pervasive (*sarvatraga*) presence within those beings.

Cittaprakṛti : the Innate Mind

Under the ninth category, *avikāra*, the text reinforces the unconditional status of *Cittaprakṛti*, taken in its latter designation by means of a lengthy analysis of its "unchangeability". Largely inspired by the *Gaganagañjā-paripṛcchā*, the *Ratnagotra* grounds the absolute nature of the Innate Mind through the standard parallel to the infinity of space:

> The Innate Mind is like space, being of no cause or condition, or complex (of producing factors); it has neither origination nor destruction, nor even stability (between two points). The innate nature of the mind is brilliant and, like space, has no transformation at all; it bears however, the impurity by stains of desires, etc., which are of accident and produced by wrong conception.[6]

The śāstra then proceeds to establish correspondence between the macro-and micro-phase of popular Buddhist cosmogony, where the earth is supported by water, water by air, and air by space which is itself, as the ultimate dimension, unsupported by anything. While the first three primary elements are themselves subject to appearance and disappearance, evolution and devolution, the omnipresent *ākāśa* transcends all causation and conditioning. In similar manner, all the constituent factors of phenomenal existence, classified into five elementary groups (*skandhas*), eighteen component elements (*dhātus*), or twelve bases of cognition (*āyatanas*), are akin to earth. They, in turn, have their foundation upon the active force and defilements which resemble the expanse of water. As this latter was said to rest upon air, so *karman* and *kleśa* exist on the basis of the "irrational thought" (*ayonimanas-*

6. Takasaki, *Ratnagotravibhāga*, p. 237.

kāra). This last, signifying the originative force of ignorance, is nevertheless grounded upon the space-like, firm, immoveable, unoriginated, indestructible essence—the naturally radiant, Innate Pure Mind.

In this critically significant passage, the *Ratnagotra* comes closest to explaining the inexplicable mystery, first asserted by the *Śrī-Mālā Sūtra* and repeated several times throughout the śāstra itself. The permanent, steadfast and eternal *Tathāgatagarbha*, beyond all that is caused, conditioned or compounded, is the supportive ground or base of the innumerable Buddha natures, which are inseparable and indivisible from it. At the same time, it is said to be the foundation of the "defilement stores" which are however, separate from and extrinsic to it. This metaphysical formulation is translated more specifically into the problem of the simultaneity of an innately pure consciousness and a defilement on that consciousness. If the radiant purity of the mind cannot be touched by those defilements, how is it possible that it can be affected by darkness, since it is nevertheless said that "there is defilement and there is a defiled mind"?

The intent in the *Ratnagotra*'s abbreviation of the classical twelvefold link of conditioned co-production (*pratītyasamutpāda*) is its insistence upon the conditioned nature of ignorance (*avidyā*). In its third chapter analysis, the śāstra explained the presence of defilement by initially focusing upon the innate tendencies of desire, hatred, and ignorance which severely pervert the apprehensive faculty of the individual. Fastening upon the desirable, detestable, or obscure appearance of things as substantially real, and taking them as the basis for cognitive-evaluative determinations, there occurs the "irrational thought" (*ayonimanaskāra*); the crucial misperception, conditioned by the impulsive predispositions, when actualized as particular judgemental moments—"irrational thoughts"—become the concrete defilements of either desire, hatred, or ignorance. In their turn, these defiled thoughts are translated into actions of body, speech, or consequent thoughts themselves, the proximate conditions of future rebirth. And so, this explanatory cycle would go on in an endless series of repetitions. Therefore, when the text comes to simplify the explanation by reducing conditions of phenomenal existence through the active force (*karman*) to the defilements (*kleśas*) and thence to the "irrational thought," it apparently intends to avoid the erroneous extremity of concluding either a total devoidness of all beginning and end, or an absolute beginning and an absolute end. Rather, the "irrational thought" is expressive of the principle of ignorance itself, *avidyā*, understood here as the root and source of those subtle, dormant tendencies that condition the individual to proceed in an endless series of rebirths. One is not to seek for the further condition of ignorance which would only lead to the extremes, or at least to an infinite regression within the cycle of ignorance itself. Instead, one must recognize and understand the true nature of *avidyā* as "abiding in" (*ālīna*) and founded upon the Innate Pure Mind, "stable with its own essence, of no cause nor condition, being of no root and no support." Ignorance is not any substantial entity, any ultimate element but, as "the irrational action of mind" (*ayonimanaskāra*) is itself dependent upon *Cittaprakṛti*; the latter is the condition for the possibility of the former which, while it may be manifested as an unwise discrimination or a "wrong conception" (*abhūtakalpa*), cannot take place without that fundamental substratum. So then, if the "irrational thought" is grounded upon the Innate Mind, *avidyā*, in its ultimate nature, is not different from *Cittaprakṛti*.[7] If defilements exist, they do so as deluded modes of consciousness, taking their particular appearance as forms (no matter how distorted) of one elemental reality—the Innate Pure Mind.

However, the *Ratnagotra* fails to develop this notion further and simply adheres to its cosmogenic model where the cyclic origination and destruction of the primary elements of earth, water, and air is accepted at face value against the immutability of space. Just as the ultimate rationable for that periodic process lies in the

7. This conclusion is strikingly reminiscent of a passage from Nāgārjuna's *Mahāprajñāpāramitā Śāstra*:

"In order to put an end to ignorance, the bodhisattva seeks to know its true nature. And in the course of his investigation, he enters the comprehension of complete *śūnyata*...When the Bodhisattva thus seeks to understand the true nature of *avidyā*, at that very time (in that very act) he sees it to be in truth the *prajñā*, the universal reality, itself. Then he sees that all things are in truth comparable to magical creations; he sees that it is out of perversion that people give rise to *kleśas*, do evil deeds and revolve in the five states of existence and suffer the pain of birth and death." Ramanan, *Nāgārjuna's Philosophy*, p. 242.

essential conditionality of those organic components, so too for the microphase.

There, the interrelated combination of irrational thought, active force, defilements, and the constituents of individual, phenomenal existence have their rise and fall on the space-like foundation of *Cittaprakṛti*. While the former are essentially qualified, originated by a complex of causes and conditions, the latter is unproduced, uncaused, of absolutely unchangeable character, having neither origination nor destruction. Quoting the *Gaganagañjā-paripṛcchā*, the *Ratna* concludes:

> Therefore, it is said: all phenomena are completely devoid of any root and based upon an unreal and unstable foundation, (because they are of unreal nature, but at the same time) they are founded on a pure (essence) which is, in its turn, of no root.[8]

Now, it should be recalled that the third chapter had already stipulated this twofold intuition as the essence of salvific wisdom. To understand thoroughly the universal non-substantiality (*nairātmya*) of individualities (*pudgalas*) and separate elements (*dharmas*) is contingent upon the perception of the Tathāgata-embryo (*Tathāgatagarbha*) as the absolutely pure and all-pervasive essence (*dhātu*). All beings are empty and devoid of self-nature because they are unilaterally grounded upon that universal reality; to realize the unconditional status of the latter is to understand the determinate reality of the former.

But recognition must proceed further, comprehension become more incisive. The most profound insight into the nature of ignorance (here referred to as the "irrational thought") automatically eliminates it by showing that it does not exist as an ultimate fact in its own right. Ignorance is itself conditioned by its own misperceptions, and when one correctly understands the compounded nature of things in their universal non-substantiality, one puts a halt to the cycle of false imagination upon which ignorance regenerates itself. Undoubtedly, this functional contingency is understood when the śāstra designates the irrational thought to be

8. Takasaki, *Ratnagotravibhāga*, p. 241.

itself, "caused and conditioned". However, a more radical interpretation of the nature of ignorance had been suggested earlier, once again in the third chapter of the text. Formulated as the "Truth of the Extinction of Suffering," it was said that by fully comprehending the irrational thought to be extinct by nature, one would definitely effect the end of the origination of duality and discrimination and consequently, the origination of all suffering.

What the *Ratnagotra* advocates then for the complete cancellation of ignorance and its consequent defilements is not the conscious resistance to it, but the simple non-apprehension of it. If, as has been constantly reiterated in the present section, the irrational thought (ignorance) is like all other factors of experience (*dharmas*), devoid of any independent self-subsistent nature (*niḥ-svabhāva*), then any cognitive activity directed towards it is without factual basis. To regard the irrational thought as a thing to be opposed and removed is the very attitude that occasions its further retrenchment; it is a serious misperception which, as a form of ignorance, becomes a remedy that strengthens the disease. Since the irrational thought is synonymous with faulty discrimination (*vikalpa*), to identify it as the deliberate objective to be overcome by the cultivation of a specific path, is itself a discriminatory judgement. It is only with the firm conviction of the unreality of the irrational thought that ignorance is extracted at its root; through non-apprehension there is no self-contradictory reversion to the principle of ignorance as the vehicle for its own removal. Instead, the irrational thought is intuitively dispelled through the psychological disarmament of approaching it as it truly is—absolutely empty, "extinct by nature".[9]

9. The *Ratnagotra* has already indicated its adherence to the teachings of the *Prajñāpāramitā* texts. Although not so noted by the śāstra itself, there is a striking similarity here in its methodology of overcoming ignorance by relying on the fact of its "natural extinction", and "the non-apprehension of a basis" as found in the wisdom literature. See, for example, chapter thirty-eight on the "Full Understanding of All Modes" in *The Large Sūtra,* trans. Conze, pp. 312-317. Referring to the perfection of wisdom as the perfection of non-apprehension it states:

> "This is a perfection which cannot be crushed...Because all dharmas cannot be apprehended...This is a nameless perfection...Because feelings, perceptions, impulses and consciousness cannot be apprehended...This is a perfection without an agent...Because no agent can be apprehended...This

To return then to the question posed initially by the *Śrī-Mālā-Sūtra* and adopted by the *Ratnagotra*, how is it possible to have an innately pure consciousness and a simultaneous defilement upon it, how can the mind be pure and defiled at the same time? The earlier scripture had presented the primordial abysmal center of ignorance, "the nescience entrenchment" (*avidyāvāsabhūmi*), as the archetypal ground of all primary and secondary defilements. Despite that sūtra's repetitive assertion that it is subject to the elimination, purification, and extinction by the enlightenment wisdom of the Tathāgata, the status of the nescience entrenchment as the beginningless, originative cause and condition of all defilements remained somewhat problematic. It had been accorded such a degree of ultimacy, that the *Śrī-Mālā's* designation of the defilement stores (which were founded upon and arose out of the nescience entrenchment) as adventitious and accidental, lacked conviction. Granted that the "inconceivable voidness knowledge", the knowledge of the *Tathāgatagarbha* as both *śūnya-aṣūnya*, as the wisdom which is capable of uprooting the nescience entrenchment, is an assertion of the latter's conditionality; ignorance is not any absolute state. But still the question persists, since the knowledge that the *Tathāgatagarbha* is void (*śūnya*) of the defilements that are adventitious doesn't explain why they are so. While the *Śrī-Mālā* discussed the nescience entrenchment and its accompanying defilements as the inherent epistemic impediment to the self-realization of the *Tathāgatagarbha*, it failed to critically examine the reason and manner of its origination; its remarks then, on the adventitious status of the defilements remained rather gratuitous.

While the *Ratnagotra* accepts the "inconceivability" of a consciousness that is at once innately pure and yet defiled, it is now apparent that it does so merely as a conventional expression. With a clarity not found in the *Śrī-Mālā*, the śāstra disperses the enigma of the "defiled pure mind" through the logic of the *Prajñāpāramitā*. It is of course possible to conclude the nonessen-

---

perfection is free from defilement...Because the own-being of the defilements cannot be apprehended...This perfection knows no purification... Because no defiled being can be apprehended...This is the perfection of Emptiness...Because no false views are apprehended...no meanness...immorality...ill will...indolence...distraction...stupidity is apprehended."

tial character of the defilements as a *post factum* realization; once one has attained the goal of the path and freed oneself from all obstacles, one can experientially attest to their transience. However, the *Ratnagotra* insists upon the perception of defilement "as being destroyed from the outset" (*ādikṣaya*).[10] The text had already established the unconditional nature of the Innate Mind as the designation for the immanent subjectivity of the Absolute Body in its all-pervasive presence within animate beings. It next proceeded to depict through metaphorical analogy how ignorance, as the irrational action of mind, is grounded upon and thus conditioned by *Cittaprakṛti*. Now if ignorance is the illusory belief in the reality of separate entities, to regard the irrational thought (signifying the principle of ignorance) and the consequent defilements as independent particularities, is a perversion as consequential as it is subtle; it is to initiate the path to full cognition on a falsely conceived premise which, through self-contradiction, ultimately perpetuates the ignorance that such a path is said to dispel. While the *Ratnagotra* may have adopted the modification, "adventitious" (*āgantuka*), in reference to the defilements, it is actually superfluous. Since the irrational thought is unreal, empty of any substantial referent, the ensuing defilements are by definition, nonessential. Therefore, when the śāstra accepts that the mind is defiled it does so only as conventional truth (*vyavahāra*), reflecting the empirical presence of greed, hatred, and ignorance. However, these latter are not ultimate facts, but originated by a series of causes and conditions; as such, they cannot alter the pristine nature of the Innate Mind upon which they ultimately depend.

It is precisely because the Bodhisattva has correctly understood the unborn, unoriginate, indestructibility of that innately radiant Mind that he clearly perceives the defilements as the production of incorrect discrimination which is itself, like all separate elements (*dharmas*), "of no real essence, of no creator, of no substance, nonexistence, lifeless, of no personality and of no owner." Knowing then, that the irrational thought and its subsequent defilements are

10. In fact, the Chinese text particularly stipulates that "Real perception means the perception of the non-existence and quiescence of individuality and separate element from the outset, and not such a perception as existing after the realization by dispelling the defilements." Takasaki, *Ratnagotravibhāga*, n. 11, p. 174.

empty (*śūnya*), having no power whatsoever to penetrate and distort the *Cittaprakṛti* of living beings, the Bodhisattva raises his intention to liberate those beings by teaching them the doctrine on the innate purity of the Mind; he himself witnesses to the contingency of ignorance for, if it were absolute, his self-reflective awareness of defilements as defilements would be impossible. Therefore, following the *Sāgaramati-paripṛccha*, the *Ratnagotra* directly relates the salvific activity of the Bodhisattva career to the specific cognition of the *Tathāgatagarbha* as the unconditional purity of the Innate Mind in its ultimate freedom from the obscurative defilements. Not only the inspiration of his redemptive vow and the substance of his teaching, but also his basic psychic equilibrium is grounded upon his intuition of *Cittaprakṛti* and *āgantukakleśa*. Far from being demoralized by the enormity of his task, the Bodhisattva's knowledge of the universal non-substantiality of all beings and separate elements preserves him from all fear of and disgust for, phenomenal existence; knowing the essential nature of all things, he is aware that there exists absolutely nothing that is capable of either benefit or harm.

Now if birth in the phenomenal world is due to the combination of irrational thought, active force, and the defilements (the *Ratna's* abbreviated summation of the twelvefold link of conditioned coproduction), the Bodhisattva's intuition of their fundamental unreality liberates him from the dynamism of corporeal embodiment. Thus, the śāstra posits the attainment of the body made of mind (*manomayakāya*), the vehicle through which the Bodhisattva appears to undergo birth, old age, illness, and death, as the result of truly perceiving the essence of the Tathāgata as *Cittaprakṛti*, unborn and subject to neither origination nor destruction. But how is that peculiar body of the Bodhisattva able to abide in the phenomenal world (*saṃsāra*) if that very existence is conditionally determined by the defilements which the Bodhisattva has now dispelled as illusory? According to the text, the exact mechanism that accounts for the paradoxical residence of the undefiled Bodhisattva in a world originated by defilement, is his production of virtuous roots (*kuśalamūla*). The Bodhisattva's great motivating compassion is realistically translated through his skill of means (*upāya-kauśalya*) into these eight modalities,[11] expressive of the

11. The eight virtuous roots (*kuśalamūla*) are listed in appendix 1.

activities which engage him in the phenomenal world and, as such, are the virtuous powers which define his attachment to it.

It is here that the *Ratnagotra* clarifies through simplification the passage in the *Śrī-Mālā* on the conditioned ("constructed") and unconditioned ("unconstructed") *saṃsāra*, the conditioned and unconditioned *nirvāṇa*. What, in that earlier scripture, had amounted to an obscure schema on the inter-relation of *Tathāgatagarbha* and defilements, *Dharmakāya* and Buddha natures,[12] has been condensed by the śāstra as a definition of the Bodhisattva nature. Specifically, *saṃsāra* for the Bodhisattva refers to his body made of mind, through which he appears in the phenomenal world. But because that body is not manifested under the influence of the passionate *karman* ("active force") and *kleśas* ("defilements"), but instead through those eight "immaculate roots of virtue", the Bodhisattva is said to already partake of *nirvāṇa*. Thus, while approached from differing perspectives, the unconditioned *saṃsāra* and the conditioned *nirvāṇa* define a common convergence in the existential mode of the Bodhisattva. If the conditioned *saṃsāra* indicates phenomenal existence as originated from and maintained by *karman* and *kleśa*, and signifies the sphere of ignorance and defilement, it is directly antithetical to unconditioned *nirvāṇa*, the state of absolute freedom from all defilement. As already discussed in the section on the supreme virtue of eternity (*nitya-pāramitā*) attributed to the *Dharmakāya*,[13] it is within the consciousness of the Bodhisattva that this antipodal distinction is resolved.

Due to his exact comprehension of the *Tathāgatagarbha* as the innate essence, the absolutely pure mind of sentient beings, the Bodhisattva severed the normal chain of causality originated and sustained by ignorance; his appearance in the world of transmigration (*saṃsāra*) is thereby no longer conditioned by extraneous impulsions, but is the free decision and effect of his compassionate will. This unconditioned *saṃsāric* experience is alternately expressed as the conditioned *nirvāṇa* of the Bodhisattva, reflecting his non-realization of absolute release (*mokṣa*). According to the *Ratnagotra*, the Bodhisattva, having perfectly purified his mind

12. See pp. 22-25 above.
13. See pp. 90-95 above.

through the four contemplations and the exercise of the five supernatural faculties,[14] produces the unobstructed intellect in the sixth stage of the path (*Abhimukhī*, i.e., "ready for the Enlightenment"). It is at this juncture, having obtained the power for realizing the complete and final extinction of all evil influences, and through abiding in the desireless world of form, that the Bodhisattva voluntarily assumes again existence in the world of desire. The *nirvāṇic* purity to which the consciousness of the Bodhisattva directly witnesses is, in this sense, "conditioned" by his choice to return to the world of transmigration and labour for the awakening of all beings; it is the temporary postponement of the final release from the contingency which the Bodhisattva's vow now assumes in the body made of mind (*manomayakāya*).

Throughout this section, the text has discussed the "unchangeability" (*avikāra*) of the *Tathāgatagarbha* in terms of the absolute purity of the Innate Mind (*Cittaprakṛti*). If it now concludes with a simple reiteration of the *Śrī-Mālā's* definition of the Absolute Body (*Dharmakāya*) as eternal (*nitya*), everlasting (*dhruva*), quiescent (*śiva*), and constant (*śāśvata*), a certain inference regarding the Bodhisattva's position is not unfounded. It is in him that the Tathāgata-embryo attains some definite awareness of itself as the unoriginate, unborn (and thus eternal) essence of the existent world. From that self-recognition in the consciousness of the Bodhisattva, it derivatively effects its freedom from the illusion of ignorance and its causal sequents (*karman* and *kleśa*) that lead to phenomenal rebirth. In the body made of mind it actualizes, though still imperfectly, its constancy, quiescence, and everlasting character, since it is no longer impelled by the compulsive defiling forces, the suffering that they entail, and the death which they occasion. If the Tathāgata-embryo (*Tathāgatagarbha*), in the intuition of the Bodhisattva, comes to self-understanding as the temporal modality of the Absolute Body (*Dharmakāya*), it executes that self-perceptive liberation through its epistemic-noetic designation as the absolutely pure Innate Mind (*Cittaprakṛti*).

14. The four contemplations (*dhyānas*) and five supernatural faculties (*indriyas*) are listed in appendix 1.

Buddhahood and Nirvāṇa

The tenth and final category in the *Ratnagotra's* analysis of the *Tathāgatagarbha*, studies its undifferentiated nature (*asaṃbheda*) at its ultimate point of perfected purification. Initially, the text merely assembles a tissue of scriptural quotations demonstrating the synonymous correlation of four terms, applied to the *garbha* in its final stage of self-transformation. As the "immaculate essence" it is simultaneously known as the Absolute Body, the Tathāgata, the Holy Truth and the Highest Nirvāṇa. Of the four, the śāstra's explanation of the second term is illuminating. Here translated, "Tathāgata" signifies the germinal essence (*gotra*) having been perfected as it is (*tadgotrasya tathāgamah*). The text had earlier established the equivalence of *gotra* and *Tathatā*, along with *Dharmakāya*, as the *trividhasvabhāva* of *Tathāgatagarbha*. Stemming from that, illusions have been made suggesting that, as the germinal essence (*gotra*) within sentient beings, Absolute Suchness (*Tathatā*) may be characterized as the dynamic movement within phenomenal existence toward its own self-manifestation. Here, under the auspices of the *Ṣaḍāyatanasūtra*, the śāstra underlines this processive dimension, stating directly how *Tathatā* has come down since beginningless time from one existence to another, assuming the form of various living beings. Thus, it finally arrives at the point of its complete manifestation and so is said "to have been perfected", albeit in an "inconceivable manner." The text offers no further clarification, and presumably one is to recognize *tathāgamah* ("perfected as it is") as a variant form of *tathāgata*.[15] Thus rendered, there is no explicit reference to the person of the Buddha, nor is there an explanation to account for how Absolute Suchness as the undifferentiated universal reality, the unilateral "immaculateness" in all beings, can undergo a process which is said to perfect it; how can that which is unalterable as Reality without any specific character or nature, be subject to a transformation implying its imperfection? Some elucidation may be possible against the more comprehensive background of the *Ratnagotra's* thesis.

The ontological status of *Tathatā* as the essence (*dhātu*) of

15. See Takasaki, *Ratnagotravibhāga*, n. 449, p. 259.

phenomenal existence had been asserted early in the text. Its own nature (*svabhāva*) as "the innate purity" (*prakṛtiviśuddhi*) remains thus, regardless of whether it is manifest or not. In its non-manifested condition, *Tathatā* is covered over and concealed; it is *samalā* ("mingled with pollution"). When unconcealed and manifest as *nirmalā*, *Tathatā's* innate purity is technically designated, "the purity as the result of purification" (*vaimalya-viśuddhi*). As demonstrated above, the process is one of conscious self-explicitation. *Tathatā*, initially mistaken as ontic substance, is soon recognized as the inherent movement of self-realization and thus, as ontic subjectivity. This takes place through and in the phenomenal consciousness of sentient beings whose various stages along the spiritual path are interpreted as the germinal ("gotral") advance of *Tathatā* toward final and complete self-revelation. And it is in the person of the Buddha that Suchness, overcoming all duality, "has come" (*tathāgata*) to possess itself in total self-awareness; if it "has been perfected" (*tathāgama*), it is through the self-maturation in consciousness of what it always is. As embryonic ("*garbic*"), Suchness is essentially replete with the factors of its own purification (*hetu-samanvāgama*), its own self-unfoldment; in its movement from implicit to explicit fullness nothing need be super-added upon *Tathatā* which, as reality-in-itself, necessarily moves towards its own self-possession, i.e., as reality-in-and-for itself.[16]

If the category of *yoga* had detailed the inherent union of the *Tathāgatagarbha* with those factors essential to its self-perfected removal of the adventitious defilements, *asaṃbheda* attests to a similar union, the "non-differentiation" of Buddhahood and *nirvāṇa*. Founded on the principle of the identity of knowledge and liberation, the śāstra's conclusive remarks here are the reflection and compendium of the detailed analysis worked out by the *Śrī-Mālā-Sūtra*. According to that scripture, it will be recalled that because they have not effected the dispersion of the nescience entrenchment (*avidyāvāsabhūmi*) as the originative seat of ignorance, the Arhats and Pratyekabuddhas still evidence a degree of fear and various subtle defilements which, not recognized, are not

16. See pp. 101-104 above for the more exact and detailed analysis of this process under the categories of *yoga* ("union") and *karman* ("the function towards self-purification").

removed, and necessarily occasion their rebirth. Unable to completely search out, comprehend, purify and thus eliminate those remaining defilements, they never directly experience and realize the totality (*sarva*), immeasurability (*aprameya*), inconceivability (*acintya*), and purity (*viśuddhi*) of the Buddha natures that are intrinsic and inseparable from the *Tathāgatagarbha*, and of which it is thus said to be *aśūnya* ("not empty"). Because of their non-realization of those innumerable *Buddhaguṇāh*, the *Śrī-Mālā* determined the *nirvāṇa* of the Arhats and Pratyekabuddhas as merely expediential (an *upāya* of the Tathāgata) and "fractional."

The *Ratnagotra's* "non-differentiation" of Buddhahood and *nirvāṇa* represents, therefore, its insistence upon the indissolvable union of the Absolute Body (*Dharmakāya*) and those sublime "natures." *Nirvāṇa* is not the ultimate liberation of the Tathāgata if it is not simultaneously accompanied by the conscious realization and manifestation of the *Buddhadharmāḥ*.[17] And according to the text, these latter are brought forth through a most specific practice:

> Now in the Immaculate Sphere, the Buddhas are possessed of all kinds of properties since they have accomplished the non-substantiality endowed with all sorts of excellency.[18]

The meaning of this highly unusual designation, *sarvākāravaropetaśūnyatā*, is obscurely suggested through the inclusion of a parable concerning a group of painters commissioned to execute the portrait of a king. Now, if one of them were to journey abroad, the picture would remain incomplete, since the skill of each is unique to himself and unknown to the others. The painters are then said to represent the six perfections (*ṣaṭ-pāramitaḥ*) and,

17. According to Takasaki, the terms *buddhaguṇāh* and *buddhadharmāḥ* are synonymous and refer to "the qualities of the Buddha". See *Ratnagotravibhāga*, n. 23, pp. 144-145. However, throughout his translation, he has rendered them as "the properties of the Buddha". On the other hand, Wayman and Wayman consistently translated *buddhadharmāḥ* as it appears in the *Śrī-Mālā-Sūtra* as "the Buddha natures", i.e., "being of the nature of the Buddha". It is this rendition that I have adopted and used throughout the study of the *Ratnagotra*.

18. Takasaki, *Ratnagotravibhāga*, p. 263.

"being endowed with all kinds of these excellencies, the non-substantiality is called the picture". Aside from a verse inserted into the Chinese translation explaining that the non-completion of the king's portrait represented the "non-endurance of the knowledge of non-substantiality", there is no further information. It is therefore conjectured that "the non-substantiality endowed with all sorts of excellency" does not imply (as might be suggested by a literal interpretation of the parable) that *Śūnyatā* is constituted by the six *pāramitāḥ* in a cause-effect relationship. Rather, the wisdom of the non-substantiality of all things never realizes an enduring perfection unless it is embodied and actualized in and through the practice of all six perfections; it is dependent upon them not as the source and ground of its intuition, but as the concrete expression of its universal applicability. *Śūnyatā* exercises logical priority over the virtues of charity, moral conduct, patience, effort, meditation, and wisdom as the knowledge which alone ensures their non-clinging practice in total detachment, and thus accounts for their designation as "perfections" (*pāramitāḥ*).[19] These latter in turn are the necessary forms through which the principle of non-substantiality becomes functionally operative in the phenomenal realm.

According to the text, the practice of meditation on this "non-substantiality endowed with all sorts of excellency" leads to the realization of the non-origination of all the elements (*anutpattika-dharma*). Rejecting the ultimacy of all particular natures, the Bodhisattva, through *Śūnyatā*, comprehends all things as absolutely unproduced and not different from the unconditional reality itself. Because of this intuition into the ultimate truth of all the elements, "the *dharma* devoid of birth" (*anutpāda-dharma*), he ascends to the eighth stage of the path, *Acalā* ("Immovable", "Irreversible"). There his knowledge is unimpeded, being itself indiscriminative and faultless, and it is on the basis of such know-

19. This is clearly demonstrated in the wisdom literature as "the supramundane perfection of wisdom". Understanding the principle of *Sūnyatā*, one practices the perfections, having no basis upon which to stand, i.e., through the non-apprehension of self; beings; gift; morality; endurance; physical and mental vigor; trances, concentrations, attainments; all dharmas; and enlightenment, one "perfects" the virtues of *dāna*; *śīla*; *kṣānti*; *vīrya*; *dhyāna*; and *prajñā* respectively. See *The Large Sūtra*, trans. Conze, pp. 199-200.

ledge that the totality (*sarva*) of the Buddha natures "in the Immaculate Sphere" is complete.[20] Then, on the ninth stage of *Sadhumati* ("Perfect Knowledge"), by means of countless forms of meditation and magic formulas, the Bodhisattva obtains the knowledge to assume the immeasurability (*aprameya*) of the Buddha natures. This inconceivability (*acintya*) is witnessed on the tenth and final stage of *Dharmameghā* ("Dharma-cloud") through the knowledge that reveals the secret state of all the Buddhas. As an immediate consequent of this, having attained the knowledge which removes the residual impressions of the defunct defilements, the highest purity (*viśuddhi*) of the Buddha natures is manifest.

Under the category of *asaṃbheda*, the *Ratnagotra* concludes to a dual non-differentiation:

> Thus, within the essence (of the Buddha) which is endowed with the virtuous qualities as its own nature constantly associated since beginningless time, there exists the essential nature of the indivisible properties of Tathāgatas.[21]

Accordingly, the *Tathāgatagarbha* is replete with the knowledge that is *Śūnyatā* in its self-explicating modes of charity, morality,

20. Now since "the Immaculate Sphere" is a synonym for *Dharmakāya* the *Ratnagotra* indicates that on the eighth stage, the Bodhisattva realizes the totality of the *Buddhaguṇās* because he has attained that Absolute Body of which they are an intrinsic element. It should be noted that the *Mahāprajñā-pāramitā Śāstra* corroborates and clarifies that, having attained the *anut-pattika-dharma-ksānti*, the Bodhisattva abandons his last physical body and on the eighth stage, obtains the *Dharmakāya* and, unimpeded by factors of limitation, no longer needs to be taught the factors of the Path. But while his defilements (*kleśas*) have become extinct, their residual impressions (*vāsanā*) remain. It is due to their persistence that he is said to retain his individuality, even when he receives the *Dharmakāya*. Having gained the ability to penetrate into the minds of other people and know their mental constitution, he is said to exercise all the *abijñās*, the elements of extraordinary power and understanding. Capable of spontaneously assuming corporeal embodiments, he returns to phenomenal existence on account of his great compassion and in order to complete his attainment of the rest of the factors of Buddhahood. For, as long as the residual impressions continue, he is not a Buddha in whom they are totally extinct; yet, he is still considered as embodied in the *Dharmakāya*. See Ramanan, *Nāgārjuna's Philosophy*, pp. 307-310.

21. Takasaki, *Ratnagotravibhāga*, p. 266.

patience, vigor, meditation, and wisdom. Though the designation as "the non-substantiality endowed with all sorts of excellency" may be novel, the concept is not. In fact, this is but the reiteration of what had already been stated more elaborately under the earlier category of *yoga*, the intrinsic union of the embryo with the factors of its self-purification. In addition to faith in the Great Vehicle and the observance of various meditational practices, the Bodhisattva's cultivation of "supremacy in the transcendental intellect" (*prajñāpāramitā-bhāvanā*) and the exercise of great compassion (*mahākaruṇā-bhāvanā*) were said to be the features essential to the *garbha's* self-realization as *Dharmakāya.* The inseparable coherence of *prajñā* and *karuṇā* is but an alternate expression for the present determination of *sarvākāravaropetaśūnyatā.* For *prajñā* is the very wisdom that perceives the universal non-substantiality, while *karuṇā* is the integral expression, the active translation in charity, morality, endurance, etc., of that sublime intuition. As *karuṇā* is the emotive correlate of *prajñā,* so too are the excellent modalities, the indissoluble complement to the profound knowledge of non-substantiality. And according to the text, these perfections that are implicit to *Śūnyatā*, function with it as revelatory of still another level of non-differentiation, that of the *Dharmakāya* with the totality of the Buddha natures that are immeasurable, inconceivable and pure. This latter union is to be explored in greater detail in remaining sections of this text.

CHAPTER V

NINE ILLUSTRATIONS OF THE *GARBHA*

IN ITS NINTH CHAPTER, the *Ratnagotra* turns to the *Tathāgatagarbhasūtra* with its graphic illustrations, depicting the concomitance of the adventitious defilements and the essential nature (*dharmatā*) of the Innate Mind (*Cittaprakṛti*) which remains essentially unconnected (*asaṃbaddha*) to them. Understood as the figurative analogues to the *Ratna's* own more formally philosophic exposition, the nine similes are here given in as succinct a form as possible.

The Buddha perceives his own nature as identical with that of even the lowest of all beings, yet covered with the sheathlike stains of desire, hatred, etc. Through compassion he destroys such obscurations (*āvaraṇa*) and releases beings to realize their own inherent Buddhahood. This idea is captured by the image of the ugly withered lotus flowers symbolizing the defilements, while the essence of the Tathāgata (*Tathāgatadhātu* which is equivalent to *Tathāgatagarbha*) is compared to the presence of the apparitional Buddha resplendently abiding within the petals.

The second illustration uses the image of honey bees as the defilements, that completely swarm over and cover the essence of the Tathāgata, depicted as the precious honey. With the eye of omniscience, the Buddha perceives the immaculate wisdom (again typified by the honey) of all creatures and "accomplishes the non-connection (*aśleṣa*) of the essence with the bees-like obscurations, completely".

Or, like an outer husk covering an inner kernel, so do the defilements shroud the *Tathāgatadhātu*. The interpretation here given is that unless the Buddhahood, abiding within sentient beings is freed from the polluting stain of defilements, it will never be actualized to perform the immaculate acts of a Buddha, and to grant the good taste of the doctrine to all who are afflicted with the hunger of those same defilements.

The fourth illustration employs the image of a filthy mire of dirt (the defilements) into which a valuable piece of gold (*Tathāgatadhātu*) is accidentally dropped by a traveller and remains hidden without losing its quality for hundreds of years. It is the Buddha who perceives the precious quality of all creatures drowned in the muck of defilements. Moved by compassion, he pours the cleansing rain of the doctrine that they may be restored, and themselves realize their intrinsic purity.

A fifth image conceives the essence of the Tathāgata as a priceless treasure of jewels hidden under the ground (the defilements) of a poor man's hut. The entire purpose of the Buddha's appearance in the world is to allow people to discover "within the house of the mind" the inconceivable properties of the Buddha nature.

Like the bark-covering of a seed, the defilements envelope the germ within a seed, here akin to the *dhātu* of the Tathāgata. The expanded interpretation depicts the pure absolute essence, gradually growing with the aid of the various virtues from within the bark of the fruit of ignorance, and attaining the highest state of manifest Buddhahood, "the tree of Highest Truth".

The essence of the Tathāgata is akin also to a precious jewel-studded image, wrapped within a tattered garment (the defilements) and discarded on the open road. It is only the Lord's "eyes of no-obstacle" that detect the nature (*ātmabhāva*) of the Buddha concealed by the stains and tatters of the defilements, even among those of the animal world. It is for the sake of its final revelation and deliverance that he provides the purifying means of the doctrine.

The eighth illustration from the *Tathāgatagarbhasūtra* uses the image of a pregnant, abandoned woman to symbolize the defilements, while the essence of the Tathāgata is portrayed as a future emperor, now in the form of the embryonal elements. Thinking that she is alone and wretched, the woman, reduced to living in an orphanage, unknowingly bears the glory of royalty within her:

> The generation of worldly existence is like an orphanage, like a pregnant woman are the impure living beings, and the immaculate essence in them is like that embryo, owing to the existence of which, they become possessed of protection..., [those] whose mind is not quiet by the power of defilements, imagine themselves without a protector though the good protectors are residing in their own bodies.[1]

1. Takasaki, *Ratnagotravibhāga*, p. 275.

The final illustration compares the defilement-covering to an earthen mould, encasing the priceless golden statue of the *Tathāgatadhātu*. The mind (*Cittaprakṛti*), in the quiescence of its indiscriminative non-dualistic nature, is understood by the Buddha to be like pure gold. With the single stroke of the doctrine, the clay-like-mould of the obscurations crumbles to reveal that innate purity of all sentient beings.

What was alluded to in an earlier section of the present thesis can be clearly identified here. In all nine analogies, the various images signifying the essence of the Tathāgata specifically suggest the idea of a content, not a container. Interpreted spatially, each represents an interior condition, a position within something else. And in the eighth example there is an explicit distinction between the embryo (representing the immaculate *Tathāgatadhātu*) and the womb which carries it. This latter, signifying the woman, is a direct referent to impurity. These two factors (the concept of content in general, and the image of the embryo specifically) help to convalidate the overall interpretation of *Tathāgatagarbha* as "embryo" rather than "womb" of the Tathāgata.

At the same time, it will be admitted that only two of the similes (that of the seed that grows into a tree, and that of the embryo maturing into the person of an emperor) capture the processive, self-sufficient dynamic of the *garbha's* self-revelatory transformation as *Dharmakāya*. But if the images of the apparitional seated Buddha, the honey, the kernel of grain, the gold, the treasure, the precious image, and the golden statue evoke a more static and neutrally passive connotation, it is simply the figurative recognition of the everlasting (*nitya*), quiescent (*dhruva*), constant (*śiva*), and eternal (*śāśvata*) nature of *Tathatā* as ontic reality. That must be understood if there is to be no mistake concerning its role as universal self-emergent subjectivity. Therefore, when six of the illustrations speak of the Buddha as the agent who frees the immaculate essence from the defilements, the *dhātu* (or *garbha*) is not to be misconstrued as mere object. If the Buddha exercises a position of superiority, it is as the one who has fully awakened to the innate radiance of the Mind (*Cittaprakṛti*) which he knows to be the essential nature (*dharmadhātu*) of all beings. While he is recognized as the teacher of the doctrine, it is as the exemplar and concrete actualization of its truth; it is in him that the essence of omniscience has attained the self-witnessing eye, the unimpeded perception of its absolute freedom from defilements as the pure suchness of all existence. The Buddha is the historical articulation of the Mind's doctrine concerning its association with, but independence from the covering of the defilements, and the validation of its self-purifying capacity:

> for all living beings, the defiling elements (which cover) over their mind from the beginningless time are (merely) of an accidental nature, whereas the purifying elements existing in the mind since beginningless time were born together (with the mind), and hence they are of an indivisible nature. Therefore, it is said: "Owing to the impurities on the Mind, the living beings are defiled; owing to the Mind itself, pure (by nature), they are purified."[2]

The *Ratnagotra* next coordinates each of the nine illustrations with the particular defilement represented, explaining where each one functions among the classes of beings, what are the causes of the defilements, and what mode of knowledge is necessary for its removal.

The lotus flower, appearing at first delightful but soon withering and turning foul, represents the dormant state of desire (*rāgānuśayalakṣaṇa-kleśa*) found in all worldly persons who are however freed from actual desire. This defilement causes the forces which account for the motionless state, and give rise to the material and immaterial sphere (*rūpārūpyadhātu*). It can only be removed by the supermundane wisdom (*lokottarajñāna*).

The honey bees that sting symbolize the dormant state of hatred (*devṣānuśaya-lakṣaṇa-kleśa*) while the dormant state of ignorance (*mohānuśayalakṣaṇa-kleśa*) is depicted as the husk concealing the pure kernel within it. Both defilements follow the first, and are found in the worldly beings freed from desire (*laukikavitarāga*), give rise to the *rūpārūpyadhātu*, and are extinguished by the *lokottarajñāna*.

The intense outburst of desire, hatred, and ignorance (*tīvrarāgadveṣamohaparyavasthāna-lakṣaṇa-kleśa*) is likened to the filthy mire of impurities, and is found in those living beings who indulge

2. Ibid., p. 277.

in desire, hatred, and ignorance. This *kleśa* occasions the forces that accumulate merit and demerit, giving rise to the sphere of desire (*kāmadhātu*), and is only removed by the wisdom obtained through the contemplation of impurity (*aśubhādibhāvanā-jñāna*).

The ground under which the treasure is hidden, represents the defilement contained in the dwelling place of ignorance (*avidyā-vāsabhumisaṃgṛhīta-kleśa*) as found in the condition of the Arhats. It causes the immaculate actions, resulting in the birth of the pure body made of mind (*manomayakāya*) and is removed only by the Tathāgata's wisdom of enlightenment (*tathāgatabodhi-jñāna*).

The defilement to be extirpated by means of perception (*darśana-prahātavya-kleśa*) burdens those ordinary beings who are training on the Path (*pṛthagjanaśaikṣa*) and is designated as the impure stage (*aśuddhabhūmi*). It is illustrated by the sprout of seed breaking forth and growing out of the husk. The wisdom obtained through the first perception of transcendental truth (*prathama-lokattaradharmadarśana-jñāna*) is credited with its removal.

The tattered garment is the image of the defilement to be extirpated by means of practice (*bhāvanāprahātavya-kleśa*) from which the saints training on the Path (*āryapudgala*) suffer. This too, is the impure stage (*aśuddhabhūmi*), and is removed by the wisdom obtained through the transcendental practice of the truth according to their transcendental perception (*yathādṛṣṭalokottaradharma-bhāvanā-jñāna*).

The defilement remaining in the impure stage of the Bodhisattva (*aśuddhabhūmigata-kleśa*), tainting those Bodhisattvas who haven't reached ultimate perfection (*aniṣṭhāgatabodhisattva*) is symbolized by the royal embryo within the abandoned woman. This defilement is the enemy to the wisdom attained on the first seven stages of the Bodhisattva, and can be removed only by the wisdom obtained through the practice of the eighth, ninth and tenth stages (*aṣṭamyā-dibhūmitrayabhāvanā-jñāna*).

The last defilement is that which remains in the pure stage of the Bodhisattva (*śuddhabhūmigata-kleśa*) and characterises those who have reached the ultimate perfection (*niṣṭhāgatabodhisattva*). The image used here is that of the earthen mould, and this final *kleśa* is the enemy to the wisdom attained through the practice of the last three Bodhisattva stages. It can be removed only by the wisdom of the Buddha obtained through the meditation called, "the diamond-like" (*vajrōpamasamādhijñāna*).

Threefold Nature of the Tathāgatagarbha

Having specified with some detail the nature of the defilements covering the Innate Mind, the text turns to re-examine the threefold nature of the *Tathāgatagarbha* (*trividha svabhāva*), here stipulated as the elements of *Cittaprakṛti* which account for its actual purification from the defilements. Elaborating upon its seventh chapter, the *Ratnagotra* here effects a more exact linguistic hermeneutic on its cardinal tenet that all living beings are possessed of the embryo of the Tathāgata (*sarvasattvās tathāgatagarbhāḥ*). It does so through an interpretation of each member in the triadic definition of the essence (*dhātu*) of the Tathāgata, viz., *Dharmakāya, Tathatā, Gotra.*

As the nature (*svabhāva*) of the *dhātu* or *garbha* of the Tathāgata, the Absolute Body is to be understood in two aspects; it is the perfectly pure Absolute Entity in itself (*Dharmadhātu*), and it is likewise to be known as the natural outflow of that Entity (*Dharmadhātu-nisyanda*) in the form of the doctrine that is taught for the realization of that Entity (*deśanā-dharma*). As the Truth realized by the Tathāgata through introspection (*pratyātmādhigamadharma*), the Absolute Entity in itself is identified simply as "the acting sphere of Non-discriminative Wisdom", while *deśanādharma* is subdivided into the subtle and the extensive modalities in which the doctrine is taught. The Code of the Bodhisattva (*Bodhisattvapiṭika*) represents the most profound means of exposing the doctrine in the light of the highest truth (*paramārthasatya*). Then there are those teachings in the form of scriptures, aphorisms, prophecies, solemn utterances, and various statements which all employ empirical truth (*saṃvṛti-satya*) as the medium for leading the Śrāvakas, Pratyekabuddhas and all others to the final realization of *Dharmadhātu*.

Content with this cursorily formal determination of *Dharmakāya*, the śāstra reverts to the imagery originally inspired by the *Avataṃsakasūtra*, adapted by the *Tathāgatagarbhasūtra*, and included in its earlier seventh chapter describing the cosmic permeation of all things by the Absolute Body in its nature as the wisdom of omniscience.[3] Here, the text defines the universality of the Tathāgata-embryo through the unilateral penetration of all living beings by the Absolute Body; understood collectively, all animate existence is "the interior" (*garbha*) of the Tathāgata, i.e., the *garbha* into which the Tathāgata penetrates (*tathāgatasya ime garbhāḥ sarvasattvāḥ*).[4] By means of amplification, the familiar imagery of all-pervasive space (*ākāśa*) is prototypically applied to the infinite expansion of the Absolute Body; as the one is said to encompass all physical forms, so the other comprehensively pervades all sentient beings as elemental wisdom.

A certain clarification is in order here, since all along it has been understood by the *Śrī-Mālā Sūtra* and the *Ratnagotra* that *Tathāgatagarbha* is the designation for *Dharmakāya* under conditions of defilement; a direct equivalence had been established between the two terms through their identification as Absolute Suchness (*Tathatā*) in its modality as *samalā* and *nirmalā* respectively. Initially, the current interpretation of *garbha* as collectively representing animate existence and, as such, the object of *Dharmakāya's* penetration, may seem to compromise that identity; *Dharmakāya* as one thing pervades *garbhá* as another thing. But such is not the case, and it must be clearly understood that *garbha* does not signify sentient beings per se, but rather *garbha* is the determination for sentient reality-as-essentially-permeated-by *Dharmakāya*: *garbha* is *Dharmakāya* as it wakens to itself, becomes perfectly self-aware, in and through phenomenal human consciousness. If the individual living being as *garbha* is thus conceived as embryonic absolute knowledge in the process of self-maturation, it is only because collectively as *garbha,* the totality of such beings is so

3. "The multitudes of living beings are included in the Buddha's Wisdom, ...The Buddha's Body penetrates everywhere,...the Absolute Body (*dharmakāya*), of the Tathāgata penetrates all living beings." (*Buddhajñānāntargamāt sattvarāśeh...Saṃbuddhakāya spharanat...Sarvasattveṣu tathāgata dharmakāya parispharanārtha.*) Ibid., pp. 197-198.

4. Takasaki has rendered *tathāgatasya garbhāḥ* as a Bahuvrīhi compound whose interrelation is *sarvasattvāh*, regarded as a dependent determinative (Tatpuruṣa). Since *garbhāḥ*, translated as a collective implies "interior", the compound suggests "one who is within the Tathāgata". Stemming from the penetration of the Buddha Wisdom into all things from within (*antargama* of *buddhajñāna*), it signifies the universal pervasion of the Absolute. See Ibid., n. 140, p. 286.

penetrated by *Dharmakāya* as *Dharmadhātu* (the sphere of non-discriminative wisdom) as to be non-dual with it.[5]

Perhaps the failure of the text to elucidate the nature of *Dharmadhātu* as the unconditioned reality and the intrinsic, fundamental and ultimate essence of conditioned phenomena, is due to its confluence with the second term of the threefold nature (*trividhaḥ svabhāvaḥ*) of *Tathāgatagarbha*, viz., *Tathatā*, the unchangeable, non-dual essential nature (*advayadharma*) of all things. All that the *Ratnagotra* does here is to reiterate its understanding of *Tathatā* as the immaculate Absolute Reality, the undifferentiated whole, and the common substratum (*ātmaupādāna*) of all living beings, understood as the radiant nature of their Innate Mind (*Cittaprakṛti*).[6] Then, using the same etymological method as it had employed in the previous chapter, the text states that this very Mind (as the immanent, epistemic modality of *Tathatā*), when it perfects its purification from the accidental defilements is alternatively known as "the Tathāgata".[7] Following upon this, the second interpretation of the term *Tathāgatagarbha* is made by appositionally relating the two component terms, *tathāgata* and *garbha,* to each other; understood syntacticaily, *garbha* is identical to *tathāgata*. And since *Tathāgata* is an alternate designation for *Tathatā* which is the unconditioned essence of phenomenal existence, *Tathatā* is the embryo (*garbha*) of all sentient beings, understood as their inner essence. The distinction between *Tathāgata*

5. This non-duality is suggested by an unusual phrase found later in the *Ratnagotra's* tenth chapter which, for the first and only time within the text, describes the *Tathāgatagarbha* as "being united with" (*avipralambha*) the Absolute Body (*Dharmakāya*). Takasaki admits that the reading is unclear and that the Tibetan and Chinese versions also suffer from poor and inexact translation of the original. If the wording *avipralambha* is not a corruption, it can only be rendered properly as "not disunited". But this designation is highly irregular and such non-duality of *Tathāgatagarbha* and *Dharmakāya* is never explicitly investigated by the text in any formal sense. See Ibid., n.1, p. 294.

6. "Their immaculateness [i.e., the multitudes of living beings] is non-dual by nature,...Reality is of undifferentiated nature." (Tam-nairmalyasyādvayat-vat,...*Tathatā'vyatibhedatah.*) Ibid., p. 197.

7. It was said that the germinal essence (of *Tathatā*), having been perfected in an inconceivable manner "as it is" (*Tadgotrasya tathāgamaḥ*), was an explanation for the appellation, *Tathāgata*. Since the principle is identical, see my remarks on this etymology in pp. 118-119 above.

and *Tathāgatagarbha* is therefore only apparent. The first represents *Tathatā* when it has perfected its purification (*śuddhim āgatā tathatā*), while the second is still *Tathatā* only as yet hidden by the defilement-covering; *Tathāgata* and *Tathāgatagarbha* both signify Absolute Suchness in its respective conditions as *nirmalā* (undefiled) and *samalā* (defiled).

It will be recalled from the lengthy analysis already made in an earlier section that *gotra*, as the final term of the threefold nature (*trividha-svabhāva*) of *Tathāgatagarbha*, possesses a dual aspect. As *prakṛtistha gotra*, it is the innate germ existing since beginningless time, and as identified with *Dharmadhātu* (in the *Abhisamayālaṅkāra*) it was understood as the imperishable, permanent, unconditional and supportive ground for the realization of Buddhahood by all classes of persons; the *prakṛtistha gotra* represented as such, the unqualified assurance and validation of a universally attainable supreme enlightenment. At the same time, the germ of the Buddha is designated *samudānīta* or *paripuṣṭa gotra* as "that which has acquired the highest development". It was variously indicated that this twofold *gotra* represented the immanent, processive movement of the Absolute toward the perfect realization of itself as the unconditional Suchness of reality. Put otherwise, sentient beings could develop into and mature as perfect Buddhas (signifiying the functional dynamic of *gotra* as *paripuṣṭa*) only because they already and always possessed the innate germ of Buddhahood (the *gotra* as *prakṛtistha*). The *Ratna* now formalizes these joint aspects of *gotra* as the germinal essence (*dhātu*) that is the cause (*hetu*) of its own self-attainment. As applied to it, this conception of *gotra* accounts for the third interpretation of *Tathāgatagarbha*. As embryo, the *garbha* is the causal essence of the Tathāgata (i.e. Buddhahood) within all sentient beings (*Tathāgatadhātur eṣām garbhaḥ sarvasattvānām*); in every living being there exists the essence of the Tathāgata, arisen and actively present in the form of embryo (*garbhagata*).

Now since Buddhahood is manifested in the threefold body of the Buddha (*trikāya*), the *Ratna*, preserving the dual character of *gotra* subsumed under *garbha*, explains the Body of the Absolute Essence (*Svābhāvika-kāya*) by virtue of *prakṛtistha gotra*. One can realize this essential nature of *Dharmakāya* because it has always existed as "the innate germ" within sentient existence since beginningless time. And it may be noted that *Svābhāvikakāya* is a representation of *Dharmadhātu* (the perfectly pure Absolute Entity in itself) which has already been identified as *prakṛtistha gotra*. The śāstra's rationale for "obtaining" the twofold *Rupakāya* (the Body of Enjoyment, *Sāmbhogakāya*, and the Apparitional Body, *Nirmānakāya*) as a function of *paripuṣṭa gotra* is not specified. Presumably, the correlation of *prakṛtistha gotra* with *Svābhāvikakāya* indicates the immutable, unconditional, innate purity of the Absolute Essence (*prakṛtiviśuddhi*) despite the presence of the adventitious defilements which conceal it; it remains "as such" (*tathā*) regardless of whether it is manifest or not. On the other hand, the conditional qualification of *paripuṣṭa gotra* reflects the temporal, developmental process through which the innately pure Absolute Essence existentially realizes its total freedom from the defilement-coverings. While this perfection of the germinal essence (*gotra*) as *paripuṣṭa* (fully developed) contributes nothing (by some additional super-imposition from without) to its innate purity, the actual liberation of the Absolute Body which it signifies is the necessary condition for the manifestation of *Sambhogakāya* and *Nirmānakāya;* in that way, they are said to be "obtained" from *paripuṣṭa gotra*. Further elaboration on the nature of the threefold Body of the Buddha will be made in the śāstra's analysis of *Nirmalā Tathatā*.

Chapter VI

THE *TATHĀGATAGARBHA* AND *ŚŪNYATĀ*

In its tenth and eleventh chapters, the *Ratnagotra* advances its critical axiom that the embryo of the Tathāgata (*Tathāgatagarbha; Tathāgatadhātu; Tathāgatagotra; Samalā Tathatā*) represents the true conception of non-substantiality (*Śūnyatā*), and formally evaluates the doctrine of the *Prajñāpāramitā* literature as an earlier, and thus incomplete codex of Buddhist teaching.

Understood as the "Highest Logical Truth" (*Paramārtha*), the existence of the Tathāgata-embryo within all animate beings is accessible neither to the imagination (*kalpana*) nor to discrimination (*vikalpa*); as was stated by the *Śrī-Mālā Sūtra,* it can be understood only by faith. Following the lead of that earlier scripture, the *Ratnagotra* reviews the four classes of individuals whose common blindness (*acakṣumat*) regarding the nature of the Tathāgata-embryo is symptomatic of a notional misapprehension concerning non-substantiality; though from differing perspectives, they share a myopic focus on *Śūnyatā* which hinders their exact perception of the *Tathāgatagarbha*. The *Ratnagotra's* criticism of the erroneous positions is the crucial, though implicit, medium through which it defends the basic orthodoxy in its own irregular exegesis of non-substantiality (*Śūnyatā*).

If not the most serious, then the crassest deviation from the proper conception of *Śūnyatā* characterizes all those "ordinary beings" maintaining the existence of independent, self-subsistent individualities (*satkāyadṛṣṭi*). Analytically feeble, they never grasp the skandhik constitution of persons and things, and seizing upon them as real entities, persistently define themselves in terms of substantial egohood (*ahaṃkāra*); their relation to other persons and things is largely a function of their craving and possessive self-reference, i.e., their sense of "mine" (*mamakāra*). So steeped are they in this falsely realistic framework, that they cannot even conceive the immaculate essence of the Tathāgata-embryo as an object of faith because (and here the *Ratnagotra* punctuates its own view) the very nature of that *anāsravadhātu* "represents the annihilation of the conception of the existence of real individuality" (*satkāya-nirodha*).

If the former group reflected no sensitivity to *Śūnyatā* as the relative, determined, and conditional status of phenomena, the Śrāvakas and Pratyekabuddhas combined (representing the second and third classes of individuals) dissipate its comprehensive applicability as "the highest true nature of the elements". For if it signifies the non-substantiality of all things in their existential mundane reality (*vyavahara*), *Śūnyātā* at the same time is the ultimate, essential, and true nature of all that is qualified and contingent; as such it is a cognate expression for *Tathatā*, the Absolute Suchness of reality. While they witness to the dynamic function of *Śūnyatā* as the analytic reflection on and critical awareness of phenomena as dependent and provisional, the Śrāvakas and Pratyekabuddhas lack sufficient appreciation for it as the unconditional, indeterminate and undivided real nature of existence. Differing from the superficiality of the ordinary beings, they have attained a genuine perception into the truth of things; their failure consists in mistaking the ultimates of their investigation as ultimate in reality. Specifically, the Śrāvakas and Pratyekabuddhas fasten upon the evanescence (*anitya*), suffering (*duhkha*), non-egoity (*anātma*) and impurity (*aśubha*) of phenomena, and attaching themselves dogmatically to such factors, neglect to realize *Tathatā* as the real essence of things (*dharma-tattva*). Repeatedly indulging in this particular focus of meditational praxis, clinging to it as the only orthodox methodology, the Śrāvakas and Pratyekabuddhas actually constrict the complete manifestation of Absolute Suchness. As "those who are attached to delusion", they become bound by the very terms of their own analysis. Dogmatizing the relativity of all things (*śūnyatā*) they misapprehend the conditional as itself unconditional, and thus subvert the genuine principle of universal non-substantiality. The *Ratnagotra* characteristically does not counter this subtle substantiation of the factors of non-substantiality (i.e., the assumption of the unqualified reality of evanescence, suffering, non-ego, and impurity) by the Mādhyamikan application of the binary *śūnyatā-śūnyatā*. Instead, it proposes an alternate meditational subject. Rather than the continual contemplation of phenomena as *anitya, duhkha, anātma* and *aśubha*, one should concentrate upon and comprehend the Tathāgata-embryo as the supreme eternity (*nitya-pāramitā*), the supreme bliss (*sukha-pāramitā*), the supreme unity (*ātma-pāramitā*) and the supreme purity (*śubha-pāramitā*).

Now it has already been argued in a lengthy preceding analysis[1] that these four supreme virtues (*guna-pāramitā*), understood as the antidotal inversions of the error that would attribute "the fourfold non-delusion" (evanescence, suffering, non-egoity, impurity) to the Absolute Body, are not to be understood as specific attributes, qualifying some quintessential, concrete hypostasis. Rather, they refer to the absolute Suchness of reality (*Tathatā*) whose translogical and indeterminable status was clearly recognized by the *Ratnagotra* as incapable of being explained; invisible, unutterable, and immutable; unimaginable, indiscriminative, and unthinkable; beyond the standard terms of the *catuṣkoṭi* (being, non-being, being and non-being together, and neither being nor non-being) on a plane where analysis based on *prapañca* (dualistic views) and *vikalpa* (false discriminations) is of no value. The positive designation of the four *guṇa-pāramitā* nevertheless does not compromise this understanding of *Tathatā* as the unqualified Absolute.

For, upon examination, they translate as nothing other than non-substantiality (*Śūnyatā*) understood not only as the supreme remedial antidote (*pratipakṣa*) for the various erroneous views, but as "the Highest Truth", the ultimate essence of things. So then, the perfection of self or supreme unity (*ātma-pāramitā*) indicated the absolute reality of phenomenal existence (i.e., *Tathatā*) as the universal non-substantiality of independent, self-subsistent persons and things (i.e., *Śūnyatā*). Likewise, the supreme eternity (*nitya-pāramitā*) represented the identity of *saṃsāra* and *nirvāṇa* in a non-substantiality (*Śūnyatā*) that transcends all dichotomic concepts of being and non-being, finite and infinite, permanence and impermanence. The profound cognition into the emptiness of all suffering as being extinguished by nature (i.e., there is no *duhkha* in the ultimate sense) occasioned the perfect joy of the *sukha-pāramitā*, while the supreme purity (*śubha-pāramitā*) similarly reflected the non-substantiality of the dwelling-place of ignorance and its accompanying defilements and impressions.

1. See pp. 72-81 above.

The dominant thrust in the *Ratnagotra's* critique of both the ordinary beings on the one hand and the Śrāvakas and Pratyekabuddhas on the other is their mutual, though non-identical, disregard of the underlying reality, the transcendent ground of phenomena. Though differing in perspective, their convergence is the same, since the attention of both groups revolves around the ultimate factuality of existent things. The ordinary beings assume the uncritical view of an infinite multiplicity of independent, self-sufficient, mutually exclusive entities. Theirs is the most obvious denial of an undifferentiated, unconditionally real essence, universally common to all phenomena.

Such absolutistic particularity is denied by the Śrāvakas and Pratyekabuddhas whose detailed examination of individuality and materiality revealed the dependent, correlative structure of existence. As fundamentally qualified by a whole series of causes and conditions, persons (*pudgalas*) and things (*dharmas*) in and of themselves, were perceived as totally lacking (*śūnya*) the permanence and substantiality accorded them by the majority of superficial, ignorant beings; consequently, they are regarded as impure sources of pain and suffering. Yet, despite their initial success in overcoming the illusion of the gross substantiality of existent elements, the *Ratnagotra* implies that they become entrapped by the very categories of their analysis. Having reduced phenomena to the major "dharmic" classifications of the five heaps (*skandhas*), the twelve sense-fields (*āyatanas*), and the eighteen elements (*dhātus*), and unilaterally defining them as evanescent, suffering, non-ego and impure, they still do not escape from an implicit realism of those same factors. Besides turning these ascriptions of conditionality into dogmas of unconditional fact (i.e., a belief in the ultimate reality of *anitya, duhkha, anātma* and *aśubha*), the Śrāvakas and Pratyekabuddhas with a concentration centred so intensely upon the discrete components of phenomena, never attain the realization of the undivided, absolute essence, the real nature (*Tathatā*) of things.

Opposing the substantive view on phenomena held by the ordinary beings, and the absolute relativity of phenomena held by the Śrāvakas and Pratyekabuddhas, the *Ratnagotra* directs attention to Absolute Suchness as the essential complement lacking to both perspectives and therefore, as the genuine middle path (*madhyamā-*

pratipat) between the two. And as the supreme eternity, bliss, purity, and unity, its conception of *Tathatā* has been shown not to deviate from, but to be a valid expression of *Śūnyatā* as "the highest truth" of things.

If the ordinary beings, the Śrāvakas, and Pratyekabuddhas betrayed erroneous notions on the nature of phenomena due to the total ignorance of *Śūnyatā* (non-substantiality) on the one hand, and only a partial and thus false understanding of it (as an absolute relativity) on the other, there remain those who regard *Śūnyatā* as the ultimate reality, but who are no less deluded. In censuring this group, referred to as Bodhisattvas who have recently entered the Great Vehicle (*Mahāyāna*), the *Ratnagotra* further illuminates and clarifies its own interpretation of the term. Here, the śāstra openly reveals its intentionality by alternately describing the Bodhisattvas as those who fail to recognize the *Tathāgatagarbha* as representing the true meaning of *Śūnyatā* (*tathāgatagarbha-śūnyatārthanaya*). The common feature of this group is their aberrant tendency to substantiate non-substantiality. Among them are the ones who cling to *Śūnyatā* as "the medium of liberation"; approaching it as the perfect *nirvāṇa*, they misapprehend it as the unconditional reality, absolutely transcendent and separate from the realm of conditioned phenomena. This dualistic split is completely antithetical to the genuine *Śūnyatā*, the principle and ground of comprehensive non-exclusion and universal harmony.[2] Such a notion of *Śūnyatā* amounts to a nihilistic view (*ucchedadṛṣṭi*) since one is thought "to attain it" by an absolute disavowal of mundane reality, the implied extinction of phenomenal existence. Such a false concept of *Śūnyatā* had been specifically countered by the *Ratnagotra's* antidotal supreme eternity (*nitya-pāramitā*) which exposed the authentic nature of non-substantiality as the very identity of *saṃsāra* and *nirvāṇa*.

Validation of its own orthodoxy with respect to *Śūnyatā* is further suggested by the śāstra's repudiation of another misrepresentation of non-substantiality which perceives it as a thing existing outside of and apart from the five skandhas. Over against and opposed to form, feelings, perceptions, impulses, consciousness and

2. "Whatever is in correspondence with *Śūnyatā*, all is in correspondence (i.e., possible). Again, whatever is not in correspondence with *Śūnyatā*, all is not in correspondence." Nāgārjuna, *Mūlamadhyamakakārikā*, p. 147.

the entire conditioned world that is coextensive with them, this *Śūnyatā* is very similar to the preceding notion. While the former resulted in a nihilistic denial of conditional elements, the present formula postulates an eternalism as applied to *Śūnyatā*; it exists absolutely and independently of everything else. By opposing such a dichotomising *Śūnyatā*, the *Ratna* significantly, though implicitly, identifies itself with the loftiest intuitions of the *Prajñāpāramitā* texts. If non-substantiality is not some reified object, an extrinsic other subsisting in a dimension exclusive of form, etc., then it must be coexistent with phenomenal reality. Classically expressed in the *Heart Sutra* (*Prajñāpāramitā-hṛdaya sūtra*) there exists a complete and reciprocal identity in extent and content between emptiness and form; taken as abstract concepts as well as the concrete events to which they apply, *Śūnyatā* and *rūpa* are thoroughly coincidental:

> Here, O Śāriputra, form is emptiness and the very emptiness is form; emptiness does not differ from form, form does not differ from emptiness; whatever is form, that is emptiness, whatever is emptiness, that is form, the same is true of feelings, perceptions, impulses and consciousness.[3]

Though not included among the vast collection of its quotations, this passage is one to which the śāstra would undoubtedly subscribe. It is an adequate commentary on its own briefly indicated position.

Thus far the *Ratnagotra* has witnessed, through the implication of its criticisms, a basic fidelity to the *Śūnyatā* of the *Mādhyamika*. It has successfully represented it as the authentic middle path, challenging all errors of misplaced absoluteness. On the one hand, it refuted the tendency of ordinary beings to seize the relative and determinate as ultimate and unconditioned. Then, against the Śrāvakas and Pratyekabuddhas it equally countered the reverse

3. *Buddhist Wisdom Books*, trans. Conze, p. 81. Cf. likewise:
"It is wonderful O Lord, that the Bodhisattvas should course in dharmas which are all empty of essential nature, and yet do not upset this emptiness of essential nature (by assuming that) form is one thing and the emptiness of essential nature another. And so up to enlightenment. Form is just the emptiness of essential nature, just the emptiness of essential nature is form. And so up to enlightenment." *The Large Sūtra*, trans. Conze, p. 604.

movement to assert the absolute relativity of all specific, particular entities. And if those two positions signified a one-sided phenomenal perspective, the *Ratnagotra* censured the two groups of novice Bodhisattvas for their polarized rejection of the same. Clinging to *Śūnyatā* as unconditional, they misapprehend the distinction between the determinate and indeterminate as an absolute exclusion, the one from the other. Basing their position on an erroneous conception of and attachment to non-substantiality, they foster a dual extremism from which they are no more liberated than the ordinary beings, Śrāvakas and Pratyekabuddhas are from theirs. The comprehensive non-duality of *Śūnyatā* is preserved and manifested in the *Ratnagotra's* opposition to an eternalism projected upon phenomena by the ordinary beings, as well as that applied to *Śūnyatā* as an absolute thing-in-itself by certain Bodhisattvas; likewise, in the śāstra's rejection of any nihilistic devaluation of mundane reality, be it proposed by the specific stipulation of some Bodhisattvas in the name of an exclusively independent *Śūnyatā*, or through the unqualified relativity of the Śrāvakas and Pratyekabuddhas.

Tathāgatagarbha as Śūnya and Aśūnya

This unspoken adherence to the authentic *Śūnyatā* as the rejection of the manifold forms of extremity commonly arising from the error of misplaced absoluteness, remains at the heart of the *Ratnagotra's* more formal articulation, that the *Tathāgatagarbha* represents the real meaning of non-substantiality (*Śūnyatā*). Critical to its thesis is the following explanation:

> Here there is nothing to be removed and absolutely nothing to be added; the Truth should be perceived as it is, and he who sees the Truth becomes liberated. The Essence (of the Buddha) is (by nature) devoid [*śūnya*] of the accidental (pollutions) which differ from it; but it is by no means devoid [*aśūnya*] of the highest properties which are, essentially, indivisible from it.[4]

4. Takasaki, *Ratnagotravibhāga*, pp. 300-301.

Absolute Suchness (*Tathatā*), represented throughout the text as the essence (*dhātu*) or embryo (*garbha*) of the Tathāgata, being perfectly pure by nature cannot possibly be the object of any negation. Because of their intrinsic adventitious status, no defilement need be removed from it. Conversely, no purifying element need be imputed from without since, by nature, *Tathatā* is indivisible from the pure properties (of the Buddha). Its very definition as the "Suchness" of existence is indicative of its absolute freedom from the extremities of imputation (*samāropa*) and negation (*apavāda*); as the true state of things, *Tathatā* represents a condition empty (*śūnya*) of any specific nature, either positive or negative.[5] Brief as it is, this conveys the extent of the *Ratnagotra's* explanation on the axiom that the *Tathāgatagarbha* signifies the real meaning of *Śūnyatā*.

A striking parallel to the first sentence of the above quote is found in the fifth chapter of the *Abhisamayālaṅkāra* which, along with corresponding passages from the *Pañcaviṁśatisāhasrikā Prajñāpāramitā Sūtra*, offers further elucidation on the *Ratnagotra's* rather abbreviated remarks. Speaking of enlightenment, the *Abhisamaya* agrees that it is constituted by the absolute extinction of the obscurations of the defilements (*kleśāvaraṇa*) and the conceptual obscurations (*jñeyāvaraṇa*) so that they are never again manifested in the future. But it immediately qualifies that this is to be effected through the cognition that knows "the absence of extinction and the non-existence of production (in all *dharmas*)." What the text challenges is the independent reality of the two obscurations, implicit in the very judgement that they are "things" to be repudiated and extinguished. And in fact, to believe in the real existence of the defiling *dharmas*, and at the

5. "Thusness is the ultimate foundation of Buddhist thought concerning the real state of all that exists...To see the true nature or the true state of all things is not to find one in many or one before many, nor is it to distinguish unity from diversity or the static from the dynamic. *The true state is the state without any special condition.* It is in fact, 'the true reality without a reality', i.e., without any specific character or nature...When any Buddhist speaks of the true state of reality he means the state without a specific nature...When the view is negatively expressed it indicates the true negation or Void, because any special state of things is denied altogether." Junjirō Takakusu, *The Essentials of Buddhist Philosophy*, 3d ed., edited by Wing-Tsit Chan and Charles A. Moore (Honolulu: Office Appliance Co., 1956), pp. 45-47.

same time to accept the possibility of eventually terminating *jñeyāvaraṇa*, is to posit a contradiction in terms. As long as one regards any *dharma* (including the defiling passions) as an absolute fact, existing in and of itself, one intensifies the obscurative force of ignorance which is engendered precisely by the erroneous belief in the reality of things. In the very attempt to overcome *kleśāvaraṇa*, falsely conceived under the notion of realism, one aggravates through unconscious reinforcement the deeply rooted *jñeyāvaraṇa* which will continue all the more to obstruct the perfect realization of *sarvākārajñāta*, the knowedge of all forms. Only when one perceives the essential original nature of all things as *svabhāvaśūnya*, as empty of any ultimately separate, particular own-being, can one traverse the path of practice and meditation free from error. Originally unborn and unproduced, no *dharma* can be extinguished; one cannot halt that which, from the beginning, remains essentially non-existent (i.e., as any particular thing). "Since the essential original nature of *dharmas* is not in reality ever stopped, how could the force of the path of vision extinguish that which has been born by way of false discrimination, or how could it reach a state of non-genesis?"[6] So it is that *nirvāṇa* represents an emancipation in which nothing is really ever taken away or removed, and in which nothing is superimposed; it is rather, a liberation through the perception of things as they genuinely are, i.e., *śūnya*.

Similarly, both the *Pañcaviṁśatisāhasrikā* and the *Aṣṭasāhasrikā Prajñāpāramitā Sūtras* stipulate that the Bodhisattva should aspire after and consummate the perfection of wisdom through non-extinction.[7] Specifically, following the principle that of which there is no production, no extinction can be conceived, the texts declare that not only is the perfection of wisdom limitless, boundless, and inexhaustible, but so too are all *dharmas*. Reviewing the five *skandhas*, the twelve links in the chain of conditioned coproduction, as well as all facts of experience as nonextinct, the Bodhisattva avoids

6. *Abhisamayālaṅkarā*, trans. Conze, pp. 85-86. For the logical analysis on the impossibility of origination and cessation see the seventh chapter, "Examination of the Created Realm of Existence", in Nāgārjuna, *Mūlamadhyamakakārikā*, pp. 64-70.

7. See *The Large Sūtra*, trans. Conze, pp. 448-491. An almost exact reference can be found in the *Aṣṭasāhasrikā Prajñāpāramitā Sūtra*. See *Perfection of Wisdom*, trans. Conze, pp. 270-272.

the extremes of eternity and annihilation, since he surveys them all as without beginning, end, or middle. Knowing the correlational interdependence of all things in the comprehensive emptiness of their essential original nature, he reviews no *dharma* as an independent particularity. Thus, he is free from the erroneous judgements concerning their permanency or impermanency, ease or ill, selfhood or non-self, appeasement or non-appeasement. Comprehending their original non-substantiality (*Śūnyatā*) and consequent non-production and non-extinction, the Bodhisattva consummates the perfection of wisdom by neither attributing nor denying anything to the real nature of things, their absolute Suchness.[8]

So, therefore, when the *Pañcaviṁśatisāhasrikā Prajñāpāramitā Sūtra*, enumerating the twenty modalities of emptiness, refers to the emptiness of non-repudiation (*anavakāraśūnyatā*) it may be understood in the same context.[9] Ostensibly, this indicates the untenability of holding to an Absolute, conceived as the remnant which alone abides after all existing superficialities have been repudiated; but since "the non-repudiated" is itself relative to "the repudiated", it is nothing in itself but a sign and concept. The point to be noted here is the sūtra's depiction of *nirvāṇa* as that of which absolutely nothing needs removing. As the non-repudiation, it opposes all activities which suggest that there are things to be rejected, cut off, or spurned. Ultimately, such activities are non-activities, they are not real entities, for their objects, perceived as various defilements and impurities, are in fact empty (*śūnya*). When no false reality is superimposed upon the universal nonsubstantiality of all *dharmas,*

8. Cf. *The Large Sūtra*, trans. Conze, pp. 349-350:
"Moreover, the Tathāgata, thanks to this perfection of wisdom, perceives form, etc., as identical with Suchness and nonfalseness, as immutable, indiscriminate, signless, impassive, unimpeded and inapprehensible...It is thus that the Suchness of the Tathāgata and the Suchness of all beings are just one single Suchness, an indistinct Suchness. As indistinct this Suchness is indistinguishable and because it is indistinguishable it is not divided. This is the Suchness of all dharmas which, thanks to the perfection of wisdom, the Tathāgata has fully known...For Suchness, Subhuti, is inexhaustible. And why is it inexhaustible? Because of the inexhaustibility of all dharmas."

9. "What is the emptiness of non-repudiation? Of that dharma there is no repudiation. 'Repudiation' means casting off, spurning, letting go. The non-repudiation is empty of the non-repudiation, on account of its being neither unmoved nor destroyed. For such is its essential nature." Ibid., pp. 145-146.

nirvāṇa as the intuition of that comprehensive *Śūnyatā*, realizes itself free from all negation.[10]

The entire perspective of the *Ratnagotra* is dominated throughout by its study of *Tathatā*, analysed in its condition of concealment by the adventitious defilements (*samalā*) and its existential liberation from the same (*nirmalā*). On the other hand, the literature of the *Prajñāpāramitā* has as its primary focus the exposition of *Śūnyatā* and the elaboration of its pervasive application. While the *Ratnagotra* speaks of non-substantiality (*Śūnyatā*) in terms of its doctrine on Suchness ("The *Tathāgatagarbha* represents the true meaning of non-substantiality"), the wisdom texts tend to illuminate *Tathatā* through their more explicit amplifications on the nature of *Śūnyatā*. But as was suggested by their common adherence to the basic intent of the classical formulation, "Here there is nothing to be removed and absolutely nothing to be added; the Truth should be perceived as it is, and he who sees the Truth becomes liberated", the *Ratnagotravibhāga* and the *Prajñāpāramitā sūtras* understand *Tathatā* and *Sūnyatā* as cognate conceptions; as the indeterminate, unconditional reality, they are mutually inclusive, coincidentally interreflective.[11]

10. The emptiness of essential nature (*prakṛtiśūnyatā*) as the twelfth mode of *śūnyatā* correspondingly emphasizes that no dialectical reflection on the part of Śrāvakas, Pratyekabuddhas or Tathāgatas either contributes or removes anything. Dharmas exist in their own right (*prakṛtyā*), and as such they lack any independent reality in and of themselves. This essential *śūnyatā* is neither made nor removed by any activity directed toward them. "The dialectic does not deprive them of their reality; things themselves are void, lack essential reality of their own." Murti, *Central Philosophy of Buddhism*, p. 354. Likewise see *The Large Sūtra*, p. 146.

11. At the conclusion of his excellent study on the *Mahāprajñāpāramitā Śāstra*, K. Venkata Ramanan writes:

"Negation is not an end in itself; its end is the revelation of *tathatā*. With the rejection of the falsely imagined nature, the true nature of things comes to light. As the true nature of things, *śūnyatā* is *tathatā* which is comprehended at different levels, mundane and ultimate. The way that the Mādhyamika employs to reveal the true nature of things is negative; but the truth that is thus revealed is the nature of things as they are. At the level of the mundane truth the error lies in imagining the substantiality of the non-substantial, the self-containedness of the relative and the truth that is revealed by rejecting this false imagination is that all things are essentially relative; the basic elements of existence are not substance, but kinds of conditioned becoming. The error in regard to the ultimate truth consists in imagining conditionedness, relativity, as itself the ultimate nature of things and the truth that is revealed

It is against this majority of evidence corroborating the *Ratnagotra's* overall fidelity to the orthodox conception of *Śūnyatā*, that one must evaluate a single, problematic phrase which might easily suggest otherwise if taken as an isolated statement. Having exemplified the principle of neither imputation nor negation through its application to the *Tathāgatagarbha* as void (*śūnya*) of the adventitious defilements, but not void (*aśūnya*) of the intrinsic *Buddhadharmas*, the śāstra concludes: "Thus, wherever something is lacking, this is observed as 'void' (*śūnya*) in that place (*tena*), whatever remains there, one knows that this being must exist here: this is really the true (conception of non-substantiality)."[12] However, such a notion is explicitly downgraded by the *Laṅkāvatāra sūtra* as the lowliest and most mundane interpretation of *Śūnyatā*; it is to be eschewed by the Bodhisattva.

Designated the "emptiness of mutuality" (*itaretaraśūnyatā*) and listed as the last of the seven kinds of emptiness, it is illustrated through a passage in the Pali canon in which the monastery of Mṛigārama is said to be empty of elephants, bulls, and sheep, but not empty of the Bhikshus abiding there; while they may be found elsewhere, they are not there (in the monastery). Therefore, this is an emptiness only of extrinsic and non-characteristic things, a relative emptiness; it is applied only of certain things with respect to certain other things, not to things in and of themselves:

> It is not that the lecture hall is devoid of its own characteristics, nor that the Bhikshu is devoid of this Bhikshuhood,..., here one sees all things in their respect of individuality and generality, but from the point of view of mutuality (*itaretara*) some things do not exist somewhere. Thus one speaks of the emptiness of mutual (non-existence).[13]

---

by the rejection of this error is that the conditionedness of the conditioned is not ultimate, that in their ultimate nature, the conditioned and the contingent are themselves the unconditioned reality, the Nirvāṇa." *Nāgārjuna's Philosophy*, p. 317.

12. "yad yatra nāsti tat tena śūnyam iti samanupaśyati/yat punar atravasiṣṭaṃ bhavati tat sad ihāstiti yathābhūtam prajānāti." Takasaki, *Ratnagotravibhāga*, pp. 301-302.

13. *Laṅkāvatāra Sūtra*, trans. Suzuki, p. 67. The reference here is to a passage in the *Cūlasuññatāsutta* of the *Majjhimanikāya* (123, tome III). For a discussion of this and a more extensive listing of Pali texts revealing parallel conceptions of *suññatā* see Ruegg, *La Théorie*, pp. 320-321.

What the *Laṅka* condemns is the tendency to adopt this purely empirical, relational connotation as the singular definition of *Śūnyatā*. While it is credited with a certain validity as descriptive of a particular existential fact, *itaretaraśūnyatā* when transferred from this conventional context (*vyavahāra*), and applied as a statement of absolute truth (*paramārtha*), is a serious perversion. This "emptiness, the one of the other" when accorded such ultimate status would insinuate the notion of some hypostatic absolute entity, existing in reality as empty of all extrinsic and relative factors, without however itself being empty of an essential own-being (*svabhāva*).

This is specifically refuted by the twentieth mode of *Śūnyatā* as given in the *Pañcaviṁśatisāhasrikā*.[14] The emptiness of the other-being (*parabhāvaśūnyatā*) directly challenges any ultimate distinction between *dharmas*, be they conditioned or unconditioned. It does so by pointing to the unaltered, non-discriminative, universal nature of all *dharmas*, established whether Tathāgatas appear or not. "Suchness", "Not-falseness", "unaltered Suchness", "the Reality limit", are expressions indicative of the essential non-differentiation not only among all phenomena, but also between the conditioned and unconditioned realms. Any attempt to posit some absolute entity as separate from and empty of *dharmas*, considered as fundamentally extrinsic to it (as suggested by *itaretaraśūnyatā*), is a failure to adequately comprehend *Tathatā* as universal non-substantiality (*Śūnyatā*). Since the central theme of the *Ratnagotra* has focused upon just such an interpretation of Absolute Suchness as the nondual, immaculate essence, it is of one accord with the *Pañcaviṁśatisāhasrikā* in opposing the relative emptiness as abjured by the *Laṅkāvatāra*. The argument that the *Ratna's* reference to *itaretaraśūnyatā* represents its definitive acceptance of such a heterodoxical conception is to accuse the śāstra of a major self-contradiction which simply cannot be sustained by the bulk of evidence to the contrary.

Again, the text is in total harmony with *Paramārthaśūnyatā* as the sixth form of emptiness listed by the *Pañcaviṁśatisāhasrikā*.[15] The emptiness of ultimate reality similarly proscribes any attempt

14. See *The Large Sūtra*, trans. Conze, p. 148.
15. See Ibid., p. 145.

to consider *nirvāṇa* as a separate reality. As but a further specification or more concrete application of the principle advocated by *itaretaraśūnyatā*, the view of *nirvāṇa* as a real entity engendered by the cessation of the defiling forces or manifested by their repudiation is flatly criticized by the *Ratnagotra*. This was clearly indicated by its disapproval of those Bodhisattvas who would bifurcate reality into the polarization of an invidious *saṃsāra* and *nirvāṇa* through an erroneous conception of non-substantiality (*Śūnyatā*). It rejected both the eternalism that regarded *Śūnyatā* as an absolute existent, independent of the entire conditioned world and its corollary, a nihilistic devaluation of phenomenal elements.

Another form through which *itaretaraśūnyatā* is manifest, and which is equally spurned by the *Ratnagotra* applies to the Śrāvakas and Pratyekabuddhas. Though evidencing a degree of meditative acuity in grasping the truth of conditioned coproduction, knowing that the facts of normal experience are empty of permanence, bliss, and self, they fail to perceive the emptiness of own-marks (*lakṣaṇa-śūnyatā*).[16] While things may be empty of a soul or permanent ego, they nevertheless continued as discrete, unique entities (*dharmas*). The five skandhas, the twelve sense-fields and the eighteen elements considered devoid of (*śūnya*) *anātman*, still persisted as real elements, possessing any number of precisely defined, real attributes. So for example, the body-mind complex may be lacking any actual referent to some real egosubstance, but it is constituted of form, feelings, perceptions, impulses, and consciousness each of which, as independent realities, possesses in its turn unique and equally real traits or characteristics (*lakṣaṇas*). Therefore, in terms of *itaretaraśūnyatā*, the *ātman* as lacking to the psycho-physical organism is void (*śūnya*) in it, but *rūpa*, *vedanā, saṃjñā*, *saṃskāra* and *vijñāna* "remain there", and consequently are believed to truly "exist here". As was demonstrated above, the *Ratnagotra* faulted the Śrāvakas and Pratyekabuddhas since the analytical factors exposing the relative conditionality of phenomena, became for them in turn, determinations existing as unconditionally real.

As further indication that the śāstra repudiated any departures from the comprehensive nature and scope of *Śūnyatā*, which would amount only to notions of a relative emptiness (*itaretaraśūnyatā*),

16. See Ibid., pp. 146-147.

is its alternate designations for *Tathāgatagarbha*. The embryo of the Tathāgata may be referred to as the embryo of the Absolute Essence (*Dharmadhātugarbha*) since it is the sphere not accessible to those who in any way, no matter how subtle, maintain the conception of separate individuality (i.e., *satkāyadṛṣṭi*). Characteristically, the *Ratna* defined *Dharmadhātu* as the antidote (*pratipakṣa*) against all such erroneous conceptions. As synonymous with *Tathatā* and *Śūnyatā*, it represents the indeterminate, incomposite, real nature of all things, and as universal essence, it invalidates all assertions of ultimate distinctions among separate, individual entities.[17] And any inclination to cling to impermanence, suffering, not self, and impurity as ultimate conditions is countered by the *Tathāgatagarbha* as the embryo of the Absolute Body (*Dharmakāyagarbha*) and of the Transcendental Element (*Lokottaradharmagarbha*). Remedially countering any such absolute relativity through the antidotal indications of supreme eternity, bliss, unity, and purity these two represent the highest truth of universal nonsubstantiality as discussed above.

Therefore, from several different perspectives the *Ratnagotra* has resisted all views that either neglect entirely or else significantly misapprehend the true intent of *Śūnyatā*. Whether it be the gross materialism of the ordinary ignorant beings, the unqualified contingency of the Śrāvakas and Pratyekabuddhas, or the eternalistic and nihilistic extremities of the novice Bodhisattvas, the śāstra testifies to a non-substantiality which, as revelatory of the universal, dependent correlativity among phenomena, is simultaneously the non-dual, unconditional, essential nature of the same.

17. In his *Mahāprajñāpāramitā Śāstra*, Nāgārjuna writes:
"Within the heart of everything there is the ultimate reality, (the everpresent) self-being...But when one's capacity to comprehend is little, one cannot make all things enter *śūnyatā*, (and therefore one cannot realize the ultimately real nature of all things)...Nirvāṇa is the unborn, unextinct *dharma*; it is the ultimate reality, the supreme end...It is not itself anything born. In truth all things are in their ultimate nature, the Nirvāṇa itself,...It is (the real nature itself of) all things that is called the *dharmadhātu*...(All beings are ultimately identical with the unborn *dharma*). For the thing that is unborn and undestroyed (in its ultimate nature) is the same as the *dharmadhātu*. The *dharmadhātu* is itself the *prajñāpāramitā*, (which is the same as the bodhisattva and the Buddha)." Ramanan, *Nāgārjuna's Philosophy*, pp. 262-263.

The Ratnagotra and the Prajñāpāramitā Tradition

But if the śāstra is essentially free from any heretical misrepresentation of *Śūnyatā*, it nevertheless presents itself within the Buddhist tradition as the standard critique upon, and legitimate corrective for the abuses of the *Śūnyavāda*. Authoritatively styled as the "Treatise on the Ultimate Doctrine of the Great Vehicle" (*Mahāyāna-uttaratantra-śāstra*), the *Ratnagotravibhāga* is conscious of the need to justify its claim of supersession with regard to "the previous doctrine" (*pūrva tantra*) of the *Mādhyamika*. In doing so it once again exposes the strong practical and pastoral orientation, the important psychological and pedagogical significance that animates and inspires its formal ontology. To ignore the explicit, prescriptive intention of its criticism, is to confuse its censure of the detrimental effects of the *Śūnyavāda* for an outright castigation of *Śūnyatā*. But that would clearly be untenable in light of what has been demonstrated above. And in fact, the text recognizes the scriptural validity of the doctrine teaching that all things are "unreal, like clouds, visions in a dream, and illusions"; opposed to that, it freely admits the problematic of teaching "that the essence of the Buddha 'exists' in every living being". Accordingly, it is to offset the potential harm of the former that the truth of the latter is stressed.

The text alleges five defects against the Śūnyavādin insistence that existent phenomena, being caused and conditioned, without independent, self-subsistent own-being (*svabhāva*) are likened to dreams, magical illusions, and clouds.[18] This focus on the unreality of the world can easily engender severe depression within the mind of the seeker and cause a general sense of self-depreciation (*ātmāvajñāna*), depriving the will of any desire to strive for enlightenment. But even if one should not be daunted by this first defect, he might easily fall prey to the second. Having resolved to attain enlightenment, there is the danger of a subtle pride that manifests itself through a judgement of personal superiority over all other

18. See, e.g., the *Vajracchedika Prajñāpāramitā*: "As stars, a fault of vision, as a lamp, a mock show, dew drops or a bubble, a dream, a lightning flash, or cloud, so should one view what is conditioned." *Buddhist Wisdom Books*, trans. Conze, p. 68. Likewise see *The Large Sūtra*, trans. Conze, p. 209.

beings who are not as advanced. No matter how slight, this contempt against those who are deemed inferior is aggravated and sustained by a tendency to cling to what is actually unreal.

This third defect suggests a cognitive failure on the part of the Śūnyavādin. If he had truly perceived that the very inferiority of those other beings was itself non-substantial, he would never have fallen into any form of self-pride. But, according to the *Ratnagotra* it is the fourth that is the most serious defect of this doctrine. It applies to the one who successfully escapes the first three. The fault here is his insistence not only upon the unreality of all defects and defilements, but also of all virtues which are on the contrary, real and pure by nature.

According to the text, this depreciation of the truth of things (*Bhūtadharma*) amounts to a nihilistic denial of the real, i.e., Absolute Suchness (*Tathatā*). Finally, because of his inability to appreciate the reality of their virtues, one never realizes genuine benevolence (*maitri*) and compassion (*mahākaruṇā*) by which he regards all other living beings as equal to himself, and thus again, such a one is not without false pride and an inordinate affection for his own self.

In evaluating the validity of such observations it must first be clearly recognized and admitted that the noted dangers are by no means original to the *Ratnagotra*. For in fact, they are to be found in the very sources of the Śūnyavādin tradition, the *Prajñāpāramitā sūtras*, themselves a source for the *Ratna*. So then, when similes are listed describing the unreality of phenomena, by no means are they meant to postulate the absolute non-existence of things. Their purpose is merely to deny their ultimate, unconditional reality; they are comparative statements indicating a certain degree of entitative value, and not unqualified assertions of a total nullity. Rather than deny, they instead define the reality of phenomena which do not exist in fact, as the way they appear through ignorance.

Like stars, things in-and-of themselves are distant, unreachable, unattainable, insignificant, and seen only in the darkness of ignorance; like a lamp, they persist as independent and self-subsistent only through the fuel of craving and selfish desire; like a magic show, their semblance of individual, ultimate significance is a deception and the fraudulent pretense of ignorance; like dew-drops, their existence is temporary and evanescent; like bubbles, the factors of experience while actual, are insubstantial, and lasting but a moment, they are like a flash of lightning and as impermanent as clouds.[19] The perfection of wisdom (*prajñāpāramitā*) does not destroy the existence of anything, but is the very mode by which one investigates and truly perceives the essential nature of phenomenal reality as it is, a universal correlativity and mutual interdependence.

As to the charge that the doctrine of *Śūnyatā* can cause depression in the mind of the individual, the wisdom texts readily assent. Exposed to the absolute claims of its application, the novice Bodhisattva can easily become cowed, stolid, regretful, frightened, and even terrified. It is only by his endowment with the skill in means (*upāya*) and the assistance of good spiritual friends that enable him to go forth to all knowledge and reach the knowledge of all modes.

Confronted with the formidable truth that the *skandhas* and all *dharmas* are like a dream, an echo, an apparition or a reflection of the moon in water, the Bodhisattva might easily relent and fall into the path of the Śrāvakas and Pratyekabuddhas. But instead, he is fortified with the skill in means of an unremitting and unflagging detachment that protects him from apprehending anything as a real fact, from relying upon anything as a basis, from making anything into a sign. It is only with such psychic conditioning that he will remain unafraid as he courses in the wisdom that all things are the very emptiness themselves. Likewise, the task of disengaging himself from all things and exerting himself in such an absolute degree of purity would be impossible without the sustaining presence of spiritual friends who share the similar pursuit of realizing enlightenment not only for themselves, but working for the universal awakening of all beings. Without this social reinforcement and the necessary skill in means, the demoralising potentiality of the *Śūnyavāda* is readily admitted throughout the *Prajñāpāramitā* literature.[20]

And it is precisely through the *upāya* of comprehensive detachment that apprehends nothing and therefore leaves no opportunity to discriminate between things, that the Bodhisattva resists the

19. See *Buddhist Wisdom Books*, trans. Conze, pp. 68-70; and Conze, *Buddhist Thought*, pp. 222-225.

20. See, e.g., *The Large Sūtra*, pp. 113-114, 379-382.

insidious self-pride alluded to by the *Ratnagotra*. Throughout the wisdom texts, with specific reference to the practice of the six perfections, there are repeated warnings against the most subtle as well as crass forms of arrogance. The most obvious stricture is aimed against all and any ego reference in the pursuit of the perfections.

Should the Bodhisattva fall into "I-making and mine-making" he may very well execute the varieties of giving, morality, patience, vigour, and concentration, but without the guidance and perfection of wisdom. While applying himself to particular actions he remains ever self-conscious, ever aware of his own subjectivity. "When he gives a gift, etc., it occurs to him, I give a gift, to him I give that gift, I am a giver."[21] With such an attitude it is not easy to escape a certain smugness, especially when the Bodhisattva studiously notes his relative success in fulfilling the demands of the perfections.

But it is precisely because it abstains from the slightest discrimination, takes nothing as a basis, settles down in no *dharma* and apprehends absolutely nothing, the perfection of wisdom wards against the incipient tendencies of pride. By means of it, giving is perfected, since no notion of the act, the donor, or the recipient ever occurs in the mind of the Bodhisattva. And particularly, in the practice of morality, where the snare of self-righteous judgement upon the actions of others is difficult to resist, the *prajñāparāmitā* makes no distinction between good conduct and immorality. In the perfection of patience there is neither the one who is patient nor an awareness of what is endured. The perfection of vigour knows nothing of what has to be done, while the perfection of concentration adheres neither to the thoughts nor to the trances by which it is effected, and wisdom itself functions with no regard to the one who is wise or, by contrast, to the one who is ignorant.[22]

In its contrast between the worldly and supramundane perfection of wisdom, the *Pañcaviṁśatisāhasrikā* exposes the extent through which *Śūnyatā*, properly understood, utterly expunges every inclination "to fancy oneself" over others in the observance of the *pāramitās*. Though he may scrupulously and without reserva-

21. Ibid., p. 365.
22. See Ibid., pp. 256 and 263.

tion observe the injunctions of giving, morality, patience, vigour, concentration, and wisdom, the Bodhisattva is often unconsciously tied by the notions of self, others, donations, conduct, endurance, physical and mental energy, concentrations and attainments, and enlightenment itself. Though ostensibly he may not exalt himself or depreciate others, and may dedicate the wholesome root engendered by such self-renunciation to the supreme enlightenment of all beings, he may enjoy an undefined relish and fancy himself for all his exertions. This is due to his "leaning on a basis" with subliminal intentionality towards himself, his merit, his cognitions, and his goal, enlightenment. It is only by adhering to the profound contemplation of universal *Śūnyatā* that will liberate the Bodhisattva from all such referential attachment. Knowing deeply the non-substantiality of all things, he will perceive neither himself nor others and therefore, absolutely no foothold will obtain for pride; the invidious polarity through which it functions discriminatively will have been collapsed through a wisdom made perfect in nonapprehension.[23]

Let it suffice that the same dynamic of non-apprehension fends off the other criticism of the *Ratnagotra* that the *Śūnyavāda* tends to focus on things that are unreal, i.e., the defects of beings rather than their virtues which are real and pure by nature. But the axiom inherent to the *Prajñāpāramitā* belies this, in that "all dharmas are equally uncomprehended."[24] Due to the perception of absolute emptiness all things are unproduced, isolated, trackless, unseizeable, and non-cognizable. This applies to what are conventionally designated as defilements since they have no own-being (*svabhāva*). Because no defiled person or thing is to be discriminated, any particular regard towards "the defects" of a being betrays a wisdom not

23. "Here a Bodhisattva gives a gift, and he does not apprehend a self, a recipient, or a gift; also no reward of his giving. He surrenders that gift to all beings, but does not apprehend those beings, or himself either. And although he dedicates that gift to the supreme enlightenment, he does not apprehend any enlightenment...In the same way should the difference between the worldly and the supramundane perfections of morality, patience, vigour, and concentration be understood...He dedicates all wholesome roots to the supreme enlightenment, by means of a dedication which is undifferentiated, supreme, equal to the unequalled, unthinkable, incomparable, and measureless. This is called the supramundane perfection of wisdom." Ibid., pp. 199-200.

24. Ibid., p. 312.

yet perfect. Passion, falsehood, greed, hatred, delusion, meanness, immorality, ill-will, indolence, distraction, stupidity, lack of skill, lack of vows, and weakness are all not apprehended by *prajñā-pāramitā* which comprehends such *dharmas* as *niḥsvabhāva* (having no own-being), *vivikta* ("isolated" in their inability to act upon anything), and ultimately, nonproduced and unborn (*anutpanna*).[25]

Because the perfection of wisdom absolutely relinquishes all thought of good and evil, it alone penetrates to the truth of all things as they are. The element of Dharma (*Dharmadhātu*) is that pure essential nature, "the Dharmahood of dharmas", in which all things are firmly established. As *Tathatā*, it is the indeterminate, unconditional absolute nature of phenomenal reality. In contrast to the charge of the *Ratnagotra,* the *Prajñāpāramitā* literature indicates how *Śūnyatā* leads not to the depreciation of reality or "to speaking ill of the Truth", but rather to its exact perception and revelation. As the rejection of ultimacy regarding the specific and determinate, *Śūnyatā* recognizes the unique and special nature and function of each thing in its particularity and from there, to its essential conditionality and relativity. However, it does not stop at that point, but moves from their relativity and non-substantiality to the realization of their ultimate truth as the undivided being. Thus, the *Mahāprajñāpāramitā Śāstra* refers to a threefold *Tathatā,* the lower (ɪ), the middle (≠) and the superior (ʟ), referring first to the specific, determinate, unique nature of every particularity, secondly to the relativity and essentially qualified status of the same, and finally to the ultimate truth, the absolute reality, their unconditional nature.[26]

And it is critical to recognize that *Śūnyatā*, moving from the mundane conventional truth of things to their absolute and highest, effects no change in them whatsoever; if *Śūnyatā* exposes a difference in the levels of phenomenal truth, it is an epistemic and not an ontological one. Rather than effecting any transformation in the nature of phenomena, *Śūnyatā*, as the critical reflection on rational conceptions of and attitudes toward existent things, is the medium through which their truth is actually seen as it is (*yathābhūtam*). If *Śūnyatā* discloses the emptiness of an

25. See Ibid., pp. 313-316. For an elaboration of such designations see Conze, *Buddhist Thought*, pp. 220-222.
26. See Ramanan, *Nāgārjuna's Philosophy*, pp. 256-261.

independent self-subsistence in all *dharmas*, that does not imply the absolute nullity or non-existence of things. Rather, it brings to light the untenability of predicating any and all specific characteristics or determinations to them; no attribute or condition can logically apply to an entity which, conceived as a separate, particular thing-in-itself, is in fact devoid of reality. This recognition that "all *dharmas* are without marks, immaterial, undefinable, non-resisting, with one mark only, i.e., no mark,"[27] is a perception of their absolute freedom from all qualifications, their ultimate unconditionality, their very Suchness. "That Suchness of which no production, abiding or alteration is conceived, that is the Suchness of form, etc., in which the Bodhisattva should train."[28]

With a precision not found in the *Ratnagotra*, the *Prajñāpāramitā sūtras* elucidate *Śūnyatā* as the crucial medium which, far from degrading phenomena, preserves the essential integrity of their Absolute Suchness from the perversions of erroneous conceptions and false imagination. In its twentysixth chapter, the *Aṣṭasāhasrikā-prajñāpāramitā* includes one of the most significant passages on *Tathatā* in the whole of the wisdom literature. Its doctrine is in total accord with that of the *Ratna*, and indeed, its pre-eminence with respect to it lies in the acuity with which it relates *Śūnyatā* to Absolute Suchness. If *Tathatā* is universally undifferentiated, the non-dual immaculacy of *Tathatā* and all sentient beings, it is through a comprehensive emptiness in which all things neither come nor go, are unborn and unproduced and lack the differentiating separateness of distinct, independent particularities. Being without individual self-natures, the qualifications of names and definitions by which things are discriminated one from the other, are ultimately without value. Spatial and temporal demarcations do not apply to things which have no permanent "abiding place" where they can be localized as entities unto themselves, or substantially transmuted by processes of past, future or present occurrences. Because it liberates them from the limitation of their specific determinations, *Śūnyatā* is the perception of things as they exist in the utter freedom of Absolute Suchness where they are equally immutable, unchangeable, and unobs-

27. *The Large Sūtra*, trans. Conze, p. 544.
28. Ibid., p. 505.

tructed. *Tathatā* is itself empty of self-reference and as a "no Suchness" transcends all restrictive notions applied to it.[29]

Finally, the *Pañcaviṁśatisāhasrikā* contains a most exact definition of Suchness which functions collaterally with *Śūnyatā* to indicate *nirvāṇa* as the essential nature of all *dharmas*. In reference to *rūpa* as representative of the remaining *skandhas* as well as the whole conditioned world coextensive with them, the text notes that the Suchness of form is that "in which there is no form, and which is yet no other than form,...[thus] by a subtle device the irreversible Bodhisattva has impeded form, etc., and indicated Nirvāna at the same time."[30] Through *Śūnyatā* the incipient tendency to seize upon and cling to the relative and determinate aspect of things is checked or impeded without in any way altering their genuine nature, their true reality. If in the Suchness of form there is no form, what is denied is the false notion of a separate, individuated, self-existence. But this rejection of ultimacy merely clarifies the contingent aspect of *dharmas*, pointing first to the truth of their conditioned relativity, and then, lest that be seized upon as itself the final state of things, to their absolute truth beyond all definitions and descriptions, all speculations and disputes. It is this profound nature of all things, ever remaining unaffected by the imaginative constructions of ignorance and the perverting cravings of passion, that is *nirvāṇa*. And thus, the Suchness of form is no other than form in the unperverted purity of its original nature. This brief formulation in the *Prajñāpāramitā* resonates clearly with, and is an alternate expression for the principle of the *Ratnagotra* that in *Śūnyatā* there is nothing to be removed and absolutely nothing to be added; things are to be perceived as they are, in the truth of their Absolute Suchness.

29. "The Suchness of the Tathāgata and the Suchness of all dharmas are the same thing,...But that Suchness is also no Suchness,...And just as the Suchness of the Tathāgata, which is immutable and undifferentiated, is nowhere obstructed, so also the Suchness of all dharmas, which is also immutable and undifferentiated. For the Suchness of the Tathāgata and the Suchness of all dharmas, they are both one single Suchness, not two, not divided. A non-dual Suchness, however, is nowhere, is from nowhere, belongs to nowhere. It is because it is a Suchness which belongs nowhere that it is non-dual." *The Perfection of Wisdom*, trans. Conze, pp. 193-194. For a similar, if not identical passage see *The Large Sūtra*, trans. Conze, pp. 377-379.

30. *The Large Sūtra*, trans. Conze, p. 405.

Undoubtedly, the weakest and most fallible aspect of the *Ratnagotra* lies therefore in the quality of its critique upon the *Śūnyavāda*. Its reading of the central intuition animating that major tradition within Buddhist thought is all too superficial and facile. Its charges are not borne out against the scrutiny of the *Prajñāpāramitā* texts which are the authoritative sources and the sustaining inspiration of the Mādhyamika philosophy. The validity of its observations lies in its recognition of certain definite tendencies that, at times, earned for Buddhists the appellation of "*nāstika*". However, the wisdom literature (as well as Nāgārjuna's systematic reflections upon it) was itself sensitive to such dangers, and with an acuity unsurpassed by the *Ratnagotra*, isolated, exposed, and corrected the errors incipient within its fundamental tenets.

How then is one to interpret the śāstra's claim of embodying "the ultimate doctrine" (*uttara tantra*) in the light that its criticisms against the *Śūnyavāda* were recognized and answered within the very sources of that tradition itself? It is obvious that the *Ratnagotra's* development of the *Tathāgatagarbha* theory depends in large part upon the teaching of non-substantiality (*Śūnyatā*) and throughout, it has invoked the authority of the *Prajñāpāramitā*. So there can be no question of an outright repudiation of the profound insight of the *Śūnyavāda*; to do so would jeopardize the validity of its own doctrine, to renounce the repository and wellspring by which it advances its own thesis. In this sense the very manner in which the *Ratnagotra* posits itself as the final teaching over against what had been advanced earlier, is misleading. It has artificially separated the doctrine "that all things are to be known everywhere as being unreal like clouds, visions in a dream, and illusions", from its own axiom that the essence of the Buddha "exists" in every living being, i.e., the reality of the *Tathāgatagarbha*. The dichotomy is clearly unwarranted and spurious since the absolute reality of *Tathatā* as the undifferentiated, immaculate essence of phenomenal existence (the heart of the *Tathāgatagarbha* theory) necessarily implies the determinate and contingent qualification, the unreality of all things as independent, self-subsistent entities.

It is then, a matter of emphasis rather than content in the *Ratnagotra's* claim of superseding the *Śūnyavāda* within the Buddhist tradition. More significantly, it indicates a movement towards a more positive formulation of the Absolute Reality. *Śūnyatā* is not only the animating principle of an exacting critique upon rational processes, more than just the reflective awareness of the inherent falsities and inner contradictions of the dialectical fluctuations of reason between "is" and "not is". As critical methodology, *Śūnyatā* is the very vehicle of its own manifestation as the non-conceptual, indeterminate, unconditioned Absolute Reality, the highest truth and ultimate nature of things; as such it is a cognate expression, an alternate designation of *Tathatā*. The complaint of the *Ratnagotra* evidently lies in its estimation that *Śūnyatā* as logical critique (exercised pre-eminently in the Mādhyamika tradition) lacked sufficient cohesion with *Śūnyatā* as unconditioned, transcendent ground. Undoubtedly, it was as a corrective to what it considered an excessively negative epistemological review that the *Ratnagotra* advanced its ontology of the *Tathāgatagarbha*. But that it did so as a development upon and integration of the *Śūnyavāda* is clearly obvious from its definition of the essence of the Buddha or Tathāgata-embryo as representing the genuine meaning of *Śūnyatā*.

Chapter VII

THE PROPERTIES OF THE BUDDHA

The Tathāgatagarbha is void (*Śūnya*) of the adventitious defilements but not void (*aśūnya*) of the highest properties of the Buddha (*Buddha-guṇa*) which are inseparable from it by nature. It is this latter determination of *aśūnya* that has left the *Ratnagotra* open to the criticism of implying some substantial Absolute to which these properties inhere and by which it is qualified. Presented simply as "nondiscrete, inconceivable, more numerous than the sands of the Ganges, and knowing as liberated" by the *Śrī-Mālā-Sūtra*, the *Buddha-guṇa* assume greater specificity in the *Ratna*. Unfortunately, due to the schematic structuring of the śāstra, their treatment is somewhat artificially separated into a distinct category which tends to obscure their implicit role in the transformation of *samalā* to *nirmalā Tathatā*.[1] The critical point to recognize here is that the essence of those inconceivable and immeasurable properties of the Buddha is nothing other than absolute wisdom and knowledge; they are the self-expressive modes of its complete manifestation as the Body of Highest Truth (*Paramarthakāya*), the *Dharmakāya*. They are by no means a mere series of distinctive attributes connected, but non-essential to the *Dharmakāya*. These infinite and highest Buddha natures[2] are the intrinsic forms of wisdom's appearance and spontaneous

1. The four divisions of the *Ratnagotravibhāga* are: *Samalā Tathatā*; *Nirmalā Tathatā; Buddha-guṇa* (the properties of the Buddha); and *Jinakriyā* (the acts of the Buddha). Looked upon as a separate section, the *Buddha-guṇa* are presented primarily as resultant factors (*phala*). While it is true that they are only fully manifest on the plane of perfect enlightenment, as modes of perfect wisdom they are not without a functional, even causal aspect.

2. As already noted in chapter 5, n. 17 above, the alternate designation of *Buddhaguṇāḥ* is *Buddhadharmāḥ*. It may now be understood more clearly why the latter, as "Buddha natures" is to be preferred over "properties" (*guṇāḥ*). The former term more reliably indicates the nondiscrete, inherent character, their essential aspect as the manner in which absolute wisdom is functional. Though they "exceed the sands of the Ganges", the *Ratnagotra* nevertheless specifies thirty-two *Buddha-guṇāḥ* as indivisible from the Absolute Body (*Dharmakāya*). As such, they are listed in appendix 1.

activity; they "represent the Body of the Absolute, since they are indivisible from it, as with a gem, the lustre, color and shape." It will be recalled how the text in discussing the universality of the *Tathāgatagarbha* did so by virtue of its threefold nature (*trividhasvabhāva*) as *Dharmakāya*, *Tathatā* and *Tathāgatagotra*. Under the auspices of the *Avataṃsaka sūtra*, the unilateral permeating influence of the Absolute Body was indicated as the function of its character as self-born wisdom, the wisdom of omniscience, penetrating all beings equally. Therefore, to specify that the *Tathāgatagarbha* (which is the unmanifest *Dharmakāya*) is not void (*aśūnya*) of the highest Buddha natures is to posit nothing extrinsic, but is to simply recognize the nature of that Absolute Reality as replete with an infinite variety of knowledge modalities through which it is expressive as the Body (*Kāya*) of omniscience (*sarvākarajñatā*).[3]

Now if wisdom is the goal, it is at the same time the very vehicle of its own manifestation. The perfect disclosure of the innumerable Buddha natures on the level of *Dharmakāya* is possible only because they are already germinally present and indivisible from the *Tathāgatagarbha* which, as embryonic absolute knowledge, is the active emergence of an implicit to an explicit fullness. This reassertion that wisdom is the essential medium through which the

3. The relationship of the multiplicity of its forms to the essential unity of perfect wisdom, is noted by Nāgārjuna in his *Mahāprajñāpāramitā Śāstra*. While there are numerous levels and phases of understanding, *prajñā* is one, and as the complete knowledge of all forms existing in the mind of the Buddhas, it is designated *sarvākarajñatā*, containing all other kinds of knowledge. As the all-comprehensive eye of the Buddha, it is devoid of all divisions and distinctions, yet containing them all in itself. This would shed a certain light on the *Ratnagotra's* designation of the totality of the Buddha natures as "inconceivable". Nāgārjuna writes:

"By this true *prajñā* one can understand the distinctive features of knowing of these other kinds [of knowing], their respective objects, their mutual differences, and the special mode of each of these. In the knowledge of the true nature of all things, there cannot be obtained any character of its own, any object of its own, any distinctive, determinate nature of its own, in it all the determinate modes of knowing become extinct; in it there is not even any knowing (as a determinate mode)...When the ten kinds of knowledge enter the true, ultimate, knowledge, they lose their original names. (They merge into it and become of one essence with it.) There remains only the one kind, viz., the true knowledge." Ramanan, *Nāgārjuna's Philosophy*, pp. 289-290.

Tathāgatagarbha intuits itself as innate purity, thus signifying its manifestation as *Dharmakāya*, marks the transition within the *Ratnagotra* from *Samalā* to *Nirmalā Tathatā*:

> Here, to perceive that the Transcendental Absolute Body is perfectly pure by nature, by means of the cognition of the unique introduction to the Wisdom which is essentially connected with the Absolute Essence, implies here the True Intuition.[4]

Undoubtedly, the most creative and illuminating section of the *Ratnagotra* is that found in the first eleven chapters analysing Absolute Suchness (*Tathatā*) in its condition of concealment by the adventitious defilements (*samalā*); a fully developed exposition of the embryo of the Tathāgata (*Tathāgatagarbha*) is there presented. Within its scope, the śāstra has established the ontology of *Tathatā's* processive advance to realize itself as that which it is, the Absolute Suchness of all existence; given that this movement of the universal to possess itself in perfect self-awareness takes place in and through phenomenal human consciousness, the section contains significant epistemological and soteriological insight. And since it synthesized the binary modalities of *Tathatā*, i.e., the *Tathāgatagarbha* (*Tathatā* as *samalā*) and *Dharmakāya* (*Tathatā* as *nirmalā*) under the dynamism of self-emergent wisdom, in its treatment of *Nirmalā Tathatā* it only remains for the text to formalize the transformative moment between the two phases. It does so with little elaboration.

Nirmalā Tathatā

Despite its adoption of the basic structure through which it had analyzed *Samalā Tathatā*,[5] the doctrinal core of this section can be summarized briefly. The essential purity of *Tathatā*, its *svabhāva*,

4. Takasaki, *Ratnagotravibhāga*, p. 303.

5. While the *Ratna* utilised ten categories for its exposition of *Samalā Tathatā*, in this section on *Nirmalā* it employs only eight: own nature (*svabhāva*); cause (*hetu*); result (*phala*); function (*karman*); union (*yoga*); manifestation (*vṛtti*); and the eternal and inconceivable character (*nitya* and *acintya*) of its manifestation.

when freed from the concealment of the defilements is designated "the perfect manifestation of the basis" (*āśrayaparivṛtti*); Buddhahood, until now existing germinally (*gotra*) and in embryonic form (*garbha*), matures at full term. Once said, an immediate qualification is introduced to preserve the integrity of Absolute Suchness from a serious misconception arising from the ambivalent semantics of an original, radiant purity that is nevertheless purified.

Innately pure (*prakṛtiviśuddhi*), *Tathatā* is essentially free from all stains, even though existentially it is "mingled with" and concealed by the veil of the defilements. If there is a liberation from those accidental pollutions, "a purity as the result of purification" (*vaimalyaviśuddhi*), it is the temporal disclosure of that primordial and pristine essence; the sequential difference from purity to purity (*prakṛti* to *vaimalya*) merely reflects the inner convergence of *Tathatā* upon itself, where the end is the ratification in consciousness of the beginning. In that process, no extraneous, purifying agent is applied to *Tathatā* whose unconditional freedom remains as it is against the contingent and qualified status of the defilements. As the latter are exposed as the compound configurations of ignorance, proportionately does the utter simplicity and impermeability of Absolute Suchness become manifest; this, through its inherent movement as self-actualising wisdom. In its non-discriminative modality, this wisdom (*avikalpajñāna*) removes desire and dissipates the obstructions of the defilements (*kleśāvaraṇa*) and of ignorance *jñeyāvaraṇa*). Having effected such a liberation, that wisdom is technically designated, *tatpṛṣṭhalabdhajñāna* (a wisdom obtained after and on the basis of the former). This signifies the immediate and actual manifestation of Buddhahood in the radiance of its indivisible and immeasurable, virtuous properties in their salvific pervasion of samsāric existence. Iconographically, if *avikalpajñāna* resembles the immaculate full moon yet hidden by an eclipse, or the luminous brilliance of the sun even though concealed by clouds, *tatpṛṣṭha-labdhajñāna* represents the efficacy of the lunar rays "released from the *Rāhu* of hatred" suffusing the world with love and compassion; similarly, having penetrated the clouds of ignorance, it is the sustained energy of a "solar" wisdom as it continues to penetrate and disperse all forms of mental darkness.

Without so differentiating it, the text discusses the function of the twofold wisdom as both teleology and soteriology. Under the former, wisdom is understood as the self-purification of the Absolute Body (*Dharmakāya visaṃyoga*) as well as the fulfilment of the Body of Innate liberation (*muktikāya*). The meaning here is clarified by recalling that the *Tathāgatagarbha* is the immanent modality of *Dharmakāya* as concealed by the defilement-coverings. While it is innately liberated, it must existentially purify itself from those adventitious defilements; it does so as embryonic absolute knowledge, progressively dissipating all forms of ignorance. This accomplished, its innate liberation (*vimukti*) expresses itself in the omniscient wisdom of enlightenment.[6]

As soteriology, wisdom functions, according to the text, for the fulfilment of one's own aim and the aim of others. On the one hand, it effects the perfect emancipation of the individual from all ignorance and defilements along with their subconscious impressions and potential forces, thus resulting in "the attainment" of the undefiled Absolute Body. On the other hand, it manifests itself for the welfare and happiness of all beings in the forms of the twofold *Rupakāya*, the Body of Enjoyment (*Sāmbhōgika-kāya*) and the Apparitional Body (*Nairmāṇika-kāya*). And it is in the relationship between the *Dharmakāya*, the Body of Absolute Essence (*Svābhāvika-kāya*), and the *Rupakāya* that the *Ratnagotra* finalizes its presentation of the *Tathāgatagarbha* as it functions in the context of religious symbolism.

The text poses the question of how the immutable, unoriginated, immeasurable and inconceivable Buddhahood could be said to manifest itself in the form of the Doctrine and Path (attributed to the *Sāmbhōgikakāya*) or in the various apparitional forms of corporeal manifestation, including the fourteen *mahāvastu*[7] (i.e., the *Nairmāṇika-kāya*); how could the Buddha's Absolute Body (the *Dharmakāya*), being immaterial and invisible, without support and foundation, formless and incapable of representation, yet assume the palpable features of the *Rupakāya*? In a series of nine illustrations derived from the *Jñānālokālaṅkāra Sūtra*,[8] the *Ratnagotra*

6. Here, the Body of innate liberation (*muktikāya*) corresponds to *prakṛtistha gotra*, while the purification of the Absolute Body (*Dharmakāya visaṃyoga*) corresponds to *samudānīta gotra*. See pp. 133-134. above.

7. As presented by the *Ratnagotra*, the fourteen *mahāvastu* are listed in appendix 1.

8. "Like Indra, like the divine drum, like clouds, like Brahmā, and like the sun, like the wish-fulfilling gem, like an echo, like space and like the earth,

furnishes the answer through the dynamics of the radiant and pure Innate Mind (*Cittaprakṛti*).

The most explicit of the similes, illuminating the hermeneutic operative throughout this final section of the śāstra is the first, which refers to the peculiar quality of an immaculate stone whose clarity would reveal to the beholder a vision of Indra, surrounded by a retinue of various gods dwelling in divine glories. Being unaware of its illusory character, anyone peering at such a stone would be so entranced that they would earnestly pray and adopt the necessary virtuous conduct that would enable them to attain that same divine condition after death; the ardent seeker would undoubtedly "be borne to heaven", thus attaining the desired state. Emphasis is not upon the conjuring power of the stone, but upon the inherent potentiality of the beholder to effect the object of his own perception. Significantly, the *Ratnagotra* draws the following critical analogy:

> In the same way, the living beings, if they were pure in their faith and so forth, and were endowed with virtues, faith and the like, would perceive in their own minds the vision of the Buddha, who is endowed with the visible features and marks, who acts in manifold actual behaviour...Having seen him, the people who are filled with desire, undertake the attainment of the Buddhahood, and, having brought the factors to development they do attain the desired state...Ordinary people do not notice that this is merely a reflection of their own mind; still this manifestation of the Buddha's features is useful for fulfilling their aim. Indeed, those who, having seen this vision, have gradually established themselves in this method, perceive, with the eyes of transcendental wisdom, the Body of the Highest Truth within themselves.[9]

The *Rupakāya* is then the creation and reflection in particularized form of the Innate Mind, the noetic determination of the *Tathāgatagarbha*, Absolute Suchness under conditions of adventitious

---

—such is the Buddha (in his acts)." Takasaki, *Ratnagotravibhāga*, p. 355. Since a detailed examination of each simile is not cogent for the purposes of the present study, one may refer to pp. 355-379 of the *Ratnagotra* for the full discussion and meaning of each illustration.

9. Ibid., pp. 357-358.

defilement (*Samalā Tathatā*). In the main body of its text, the *Ratnagotra* had discussed in a more formal metaphysics the process in which the Tathāgata-embryo realizes itself as Absolute Body, the movement of *Tathatā* to possess itself in total self-awareness as the perfect Suchness of all reality. It is this same analysis that is now discussed in the final section of the śāstra through the idiom of religious symbolism. For at issue in the problematic of the relationship between the inconceivable *Dharmakāya* and the representational modes characterising the *Rupakāya,* as posed by the *Ratnagotra,* is the inadequacy of *Tathatā's* ultimate self-particularization in sensibly perceptible form.

In the *Rupakāya, Tathatā* represents itself to itself in definite shape and specific appearance; it is an essential and necessary stage towards its perfect self-comprehensive awareness. But as yet external form, *Tathatā* is not immediately present to itself; it still projects itself in the cast of an other than itself. As long as the experience of the Buddha-personality, in the multiple expressions of the *Rupakāya,* fails to be understood as the self-created reflections of the Innate Mind, *Tathatā* remains concealed by its own symbolizations, fails to know itself, to recognize itself perfectly as what it is in itself.

At this juncture it should be reiterated that the significance of the historical Buddha is as one who has fully awakened to the innate radiance of the Mind, which he knows to be the essential nature (*dharmadhātu*) of all sentient beings. While he is recognized as the teacher of the Doctrine, it is as the exemplar and concrete actualization of its truth; it is in him that the essence of omniscience has attained the self-witnessing eye, the unimpeded perception of its absolute freedom from defilements as the pure Suchness of all existence. The Buddha is the historical articulation of the Mind's doctrine concerning its association with, but independence from the covering of the defilements, and the validation of its self-purifying capacity. So it is in the present context, that the person of the Buddha is subsidiary to the attainment which he represents, viz., the enlightenment of perfect Buddhahood. If in him, Absolute Suchness successfully awakened to itself in an omniscient wisdom as the highest truth of phenomenal reality, its process of self-emergence within the consciousness of his followers is no different than the path it traversed and perfected in him.

As both the path and the goal of its self-activating movement from the concealments of the adventitious defilements to its final self-revelatory emancipation from them (i.e., from *samalā* to *nirmalā Tathatā*), Suchness defines itself ever more acutely through the infinite wisdom modalities (the innumerable Buddha-properties and virtuous perfections) that are inherently united to it. The stages of its self-explication are as many and varied as the sentient beings in whom it is universally present and through whom it advances towards itself. The *Rupakāya* is one such clearly determined, fundamental and necessary stage in *Tathatā's* self-encounter; in the perception of the visible features and marks, actions and teachings, qualities and virtues of the Buddha, the Innate Mind (i.e., *Tathatā*) projects self-reflective images for its own self-recognizance. Should the individual fail to realize this true identity of the *Rupakāya*, fail to identify those external forms as symbolizations of the one Innate Mind common to himself and all animate beings, and thus as the interior dimensions of his own authenticity, *Tathatā* becomes fixated in a form that is not the adequate medium for, does not completely correspond to, its essence. To apprehend the *Rupakāya-Buddha* as some sort of uniquely independent, self-subsistent personality over against, different from, and beyond oneself, is the failure "to perceive with the eyes of transcendental wisdom, the Body of the Highest Truth within themselves"; put otherwise in the familiar polarity of the śāstra, it is the failure of the Tathāgata-embryo (*Tathāgatagarbha*) to realize itself perfectly as the Absolute Body (*Dharmakāya*).

The final adjuration of the *Ratnagotra* is on the supreme import and efficacy of faith in the doctrine of the *Tathāgatagarbha*. While inconceivable even to the loftiest and purest minds, the *Tathāgatagarbha*, accepted in faith, initiates the self-unfoldment of all the properties and virtues necessary for the removal of ignorance and its obscurative defilements. It does so as embryonic absolute knowledge (*prajñā*) explicated through the practices and observances of the Path and the exercise of the perfections of charity, morality, patience, meditation and exertion. Only thus does it come to the perfect self-revelation in the Absolute Body as actually freed from, because essentially devoid of (*śūnya*), the defilements, and replete with, because intrinsically not devoid of (*aśūnya*), the modalities of omniscient wisdom. The *Tathāgatagarbha* begins then, as the content of faith and thus, under the form of objectivity, as ontic substance; it is *Tathatā* as the pure essence, the fundamental nature, the básic substratum, the unborn, undying, permanent, steadfast, eternal, and ultimate ground of *saṃsāra* and *nirvāṇa*. But the *garbha* must surmount the form of objectivity, must move from the category of ontic substance, through the generic transformation of its inherent nature, to ontic subject, fully self-explicated self-consciousness; as realized *Dharmakāya*, the realm of omniscient wisdom, it is *Tathatā* recognizing itself as pure Suchness in and through all forms of phenomenal reality.

The necessary movement of *Tathatā's* inner convergence upon itself, the stages towards its final and perfect self-comprehension, is the subject of the nine illustrations referred to above; they indicate the process through which *Tathatā* produces the forms of and for its own self-knowledge. The corporeal features and marks, as well as the virtues and properties exemplified in the *Rupakāya-Buddha* are the self-reflections of the Innate Mind; so too with the teachings and instructions, the prescriptions and praxes embodying the Doctrine (*Dharma*). *Tathatā* is the truth which animates and finds self-expression in all the formulations and specifications of the Buddhist Path. As the one vehicle (*ekayāna*), grounding and authenticating the multiple variations of observance and interpretation, *Tathatā*, under its determination as *Tathāgatagarbha*, is the soteriological principle of absolute efficacy. It is the warrant, intrinsic to all sentient beings, for the attainment of the supreme and perfect enlightenment of Buddhahood; thus, its designation as the Great Vehicle (*Mahāyāna*).[10]

If the Doctrine (*Dharma*) is inaugurated as an extraneous code whose faithful adherence promises the emancipation from all sorrow and suffering, it must come to be understood as *Tathatā's* self-objectifying knowledge of itself as the truth of all things. Under the primary axiom of "impermanence, ill, and not-self", *Tathatā* manifests an important insight into the conditioned relativity of phenomenal existence; it is a wisdom revealing the non-substantiality (*Śūnyatā*) of things, and thus dispelling a form of ignorance that seizes upon the determinate as indeterminate, the relative as

10. See the analysis on the *Śrī-Mālā Sūtra's* presentation of the Illustious Doctrine and its relationship to the *Tathāgatagarbha* in chapter 2, pp. 8-15. above.

absolute. But this dictum itself becomes a perversion, if its truth is constricted into a unilateral literacy, if the world is unqualified as the source of all pain and suffering.

Such is an instance where the self-explicating movement of *Tathatā* as embryonic absolute knowledge can be stagnated by its own formulations. Though necessary to it, these codified moments of its self-reflection must be surmounted and transcended by *Tathatā* if it is to attain that supreme modality in which alone it is able to recognize itself as the Suchness of reality; only as omniscient wisdom does it adequately perceive itself as the ultimate ground and unconditional nature of existent phenomena. The initial truth of "impermanence, ill, and not-self", while revealing the universal relativity of all things, must yet annul and transcend itself as incomplete. The Suchness of things may indeed be manifest in this testimony of their interdependent co-origination, their non-substantiality (*Śūnyatā*) as unique, self-subsistent entities, but its revelation is only partial. *Anitya*, *duhkha* and *anātman* are propaedeutic and not final; they must yield to the more profound and comprehensive recognition of the absolute quiescence (*śānti*) of all things, their original nirvānic status as essentially free from the adventitious defilements.

Up to that point, *Tathatā's* advance towards total and perfect self-awareness progresses through the innumerable varieties and forms, degrees and levels of self-reflective wisdom, constituting the path of the *Dharma*. At each stage, by its efficacy as innate absolute knowledge, it attains a proportionate self-liberation from the obscurative force of ignorance through the instrumentality of its self-formulations. But these latter, while the vehicles of its self-representation, are never (independently) the adequate media for the perfect self-manifestation of *Tathatā*. Instead, they are the necessary moments of self-transcending absolute wisdom as it approaches the goal, where the form in which *Tathatā* appears for its own perfect self-consciousness corresponds completely to its essence. Only as omniscient wisdom, unrestricted by the contours and moulds of material existence, does *Tathatā* universally perceive itself as the fundamental and original purity of all things, intrinsically free from the concealing defilements.

EVALUATION

The critical significance of the *Ratnagotravibhāga* lies in its presentation of the *Tathāgatagarbha* as absolutely central, the crucial axis for any satisfactory reflection upon the Absolute and relative polarity within the development of the Buddhist tradition. The *Śrī-Mālā Sūtra* had adequately represented the Tathāgata-embryo as primary epistemological-soteriological factor, germinal absolute knowledge realizing its inherent freedom from adventitious defilements, and thereby effecting its self-transforming revelation as Absolute Body (*Dharmakāya*). While acknowledging their implicit equivalence, the scripture maintained a consistent distinction throughout, between *Tathāgatagarbha* and *Dharmakāya,* strongly emphasizing the processive character of the former.

The singular advance and metaphysical refinement of the *Ratnagotra* was its explicit identification of the two terms as qualitative modalities of one and the same Reality, Absolute Suchness (*Tathatā*). As that which effects its own self-purifying manifestation, *Tathatā* is both subject and object in the processive realization of enlightenment. The very structure of the śāstra, in its two major sections of *Samalā* and *Nirmāla Tathatā,* leaves no doubt that Absolute Reality is the dominant hermeneutic through which the various classes of individuals, the spiritual path, the character of the Bodhisattva, the person of the Buddha, and the relationship of *nirvāna* and *saṃsāra* are defined and interpreted. And the principle that all sentient beings are possessed of the Tathāgata-embryo, that all animate reality has an inherent endowment for the supreme and perfect awakening of Buddhahood, is validated through an extensive metaphysical analysis of Absolute Suchness (*Tathatā*). While this remains the significant contribution of the *Ratnagotra-vibhāga,* it likewise accounts for a particular deficiency.

To argue the thesis of the universal potentiality of Buddhahood entirely from within the dynamics of Absolute Suchness, as the śāstra does, is to leave undeveloped the role of the individual human consciousness. The emphasis upon the primary subjectivity of *Tathatā,* as embryonic absolute knowledge or the germinal essence of Buddhahood (i.e., as *garbha* and *gotra*), tended inevitably to minimize the uniqueness of the phenomenal subject. Yet, in clarifying the first term, the text has implicitly defined the status of the correspondent term in the Absolute-relative polarity. And in doing so, it clearly suggests the direction in which the study of the *Tathāgatagarbha* must proceed in its complementarity with the *Ālayavijñāna.*

That *Tathatā* advances through various stages of unconcealment to its ultimate self-awareness as the Absolute Suchness of reality, specifies that both the goal (enlightenment) and the path towards it (the knowledge modalities characterizing Arhats, Pratyekabuddhas and Bodhisattvas) are noetic determinations. Consciousness then, is directly implicated in the concept of the *Tathāgatagarbha* as the very locus and form of its processive self-transformation. This became explicit in the *Ratnagotra's* reference to *Cittaprakṛti* (the Innate Mind) as a noetic determination of *Tathāgatagarbha.* In that context, it will be recalled that the human sphere was interpreted rather extrinsically as the field upon which the innate purity of the Absolute Body is manifested, i.e., as being impure (the condition of ordinary beings), as pure and impure (the Bodhisattvas) or as perfectly pure (the Tathāgata). Correspondingly, as the different cognitive levels—those of erroneous conception, of right conception, and of perfectly right conception—human consciousness was seen as the vehicle through which the Absolute Body gains self-conscious recognition of its inherent nature. The all-pervading Innate Mind is the immanent mode by which the *Dharmakāya* becomes fully self-aware in and through phenomenal human consciousness. The *Ratnagotra* thus implies that the diverse planes of conceptual human awareness are, in fact, the self-reflective moments in which the Absolute Body affirms itself as the perfectly pure essence, the Suchness of all reality.

Characteristic of its entire perspective, the text therefore only by indirection posits human consciousness as the necessary complement, the factor essential to the perfect self-awareness of *Tathatā's* inner self-convergence, of an original absolute becoming an articulate one. The only transition within this cycle of self-exposition for the sake of self-understandng is that from hiddenness to manifestation. But because it takes place within the sphere of human consciousness, the procedure might equally be discussed through the problematic of how finite, particular consciousness functions with, and is transformed into, the infinite, universal, and absolute consciousness. What must the structure of consciousness be that would allow for the coherent dynamics of such a relationship?

While the *Ratnagotra* clearly indicates that the Innate Mind (*Cittaprakṛti*) is the fundamental noetic substratum common to ordinary beings and Buddhas alike, it sustains no detailed analysis of its active interplay with and upon the phenomenal mind. The latter is depicted as the vehicle of ignorance, with little appreciation for its positive contribution to the attainment of enlightenment. Once the nature of defilement had been analysed as conditioned by, and a mode of, the Innate Pure Mind (granted, a distorted one), once defilement had been demonstrated as "non-existent by nature", then the distinction between the phenomenal mind and the Innate Pure Mind loses its definition. If the latter's identity with and/or difference from, the phenomenal mind is never directly addressed by the *Ratnagotra,* its insistence upon and description of, the ontic character of *Cittaprakṛti* dissipates the uniqueness of the finite and particular consciousness. The śāstra's psychological analysis is simply not adequate to the comprehensive scope of its metaphysics. Only the more refined nuances of the Vijñānavādin reflection upon the *Ālayavijñāna* would satisfactorily answer its ambiguities.

Another aspect of *Cittaprakṛti* suggesting its complementarity with the *Ālayavijñāna,* lay in its capacity to actively project the images and forms of the *Rupakāya-Buddha* and the multiple formulations of the *Dharma.* Ordinarily mistaken as independent, external objectivities, they are in fact, the creation and reflection in particularized form of the Innate Mind. While it is not a point of explicit reflection by the *Ratnagotra,* this reference to an ideational causation process raises the question as to its extent and inner dynamics. If the Mind is capable of projecting such apparently concrete forms, is its creativity only limited to that particular sphere; could not the range of its projection extend to the whole of phenomenal existence? What are the determining factors that govern this feature of *Cittaprakṛti* and restrict it to such a limited influence? If its ideational projection is an inherent character of the absolute Innate Mind, shouldn't the field of its activity be of a correspondingly universal extension? In the system of the *Vijñānavāda*, the *Ālayavijñāna* exercises just such a comprehensive influence; as the fundamental and absolute consciousness, it bears within itself the seeds of all phenomenal forms, and is the proximate basis for their manifestation. This suggestive correspondence of *Cittaprakṛti* with *Ālayavijñāna* is a further inducement for a more detailed investigation.

The relationship of the Innate Mind to phenomenal existence is more acutely focused in the *Śrī-Mālā Sūtra's* assertion that the *Tathāgatagarbha* is the ontic ground of *saṃsāra* and the condition for the possibility of attaining *nirvāṇa*. This was more thoroughly elaborated by the *Ratnagotravibhāga's* definition of *Tathatā* as the immaculate essence (*dhātu*) of all things. Now if *saṃsāra* represents phenomenal reality under the sway of primordial ignorance and its subsequent defilements, and if *Tathatā* is the ontological ground of that reality, how is one to avoid the implication that *Tathatā* is the metaphysical source of ignorance and defilement? To seek a solution by positing ignorance as a separate principle or force is to undercut the ultimacy of *Tathatā*, and to introduce a dualism more problematic than the original question.

It will be recalled that the *Ratnagotra* introduced the category of *Cittaprakṛti* specifically to deal with the paradox of an innately pure consciousness and a simultaneous defilement upon it; how could the *Tathāgatagarbha* be pure and defiled at the same time, how could the immaculate nature of *Tathatā* be afflicted by darkness? By choosing so deliberate a noetic context in which to discuss the question, the śāstra clearly recognized that "defilement" and its correlative "purity" are not in fact entitative realities; they are instead, determinations of consciousness. Defilements, as so many forms and manifestations of ignorance, are ultimately but the distortions in unwise discriminations or wrong conceptions (*abutakalpa*) of consciousness. As a formally psychic event, defilement of phenomenal existence (*saṃsāra*) cannot be attributed to Absolute Suchness as the formally ontic ground of that existence.

However, through its equivalence to the Body of omniscient wisdom (*Dharmakāya*) and the germinal essence of Buddhahood (*gotra*), the conception of *Tathatā* had moved from that of a neutrally static ontic substance to that of an ontic subjectivity, the unilateral and dynamic presence of absolute wisdom within animate being. The inclusion of *Cittaprakṛti* merely explicates this noetic dimension of *Tathatā*. Now if the nature of the latter is to know itself as the indeterminate, unconditional nature of all things, their unqualified Suchness, it is object as well as subject. As the pure essence of reality, *Tathatā* is the sum total of objectivity, the absolute object; it must recognize itself as such in and through human consciousness. *Tathatā* perfects itself as absolute subjectivity when it possesses itself in total self-recognition as absolute objectivity. It is this process of self-recognition that entails the process of defilement.

Until human consciousness spontaneously and continuously perceives the unconditional nature that makes of all forms and appearances a harmonious realm of interdependent coexistence, the unity of multiplicity, the identity-in-difference (i.e., the *Dharmadhātu*), *Tathatā* is never fully present to itself, never knows itself as what it really is; *Tathatā* as subjectivity is not adequate to itself as objectivity. More specifically, the tendency of the human intellect is to mistake the finite for the infinite, the particular for the universal, the conditional for the unconditional. This error of misplaced absoluteness manifests itself in the realm of subjectivity as the belief in an autonomous, self-subsistent ego which in turn, falsely discriminates a world of independent, isolated objectivities. Not comprehending its identity with the Innate Pure Mind and thus failing to understand its own universality, the idividual consciousness correspondingly constricts reality to the limited sphere of its own attachments. Defilement then, is the ongoing estrangement of the individual consciousness from its identity with *Cittaprakṛti,* and the fragmented perspective which it subsequently adopts and through which it continues to reinforce that erroneous self-definition.

But while the *Ratnagotravibhāga* clearly recognizes that defilement formally develops in the noetic aspects of *Tathatā*, namely the Innate Mind, it fails to extend its implications into a generic theory of consciousness. *Cittaprakṛti* remains essentially a metaphysical construct, representing the primordial stratum of pure awareness in all animate beings. Now, defilement presupposes a mode of consciousness, a phenomenal mind, individuated out of, but not separate from that fundamental Innate Mind. How precisely the latter becomes compromised and defiled as the individual consciousness strays from its identity with it, demands a knowledge of the structural dynamics animating the processes of sensory awareness, intelligible apperception, ideal conceptualization and objective creativity. Together, these represent the essential phases in a coherent morphology of phenomenal consciousness; they are critical mental determinations and as such, must be considered in any discussion of *Tathatā's* self-realization in and through human consciousness. While the *Ratnagotra* succeeds in establishing the metaphysical context in which to interpret the transformational event of enlightenment, it lacks this adequate psychological detail necessary for the translation of that theory into the practical discipline of the spiritual path. The introspective analysis of the Vijñānavādin reflection upon the *Ālayavijñāna* complemented this neglect, and is therefore essential to any study of the Buddha nature, articulated as the embryo of the Tathāgata.

PART TWO

THE *ĀLAYAVIJÑĀNA* IN THE *LAṄKĀVATĀRA SŪTRA* AND THE *CH'ENG WEI-SHIH LUN*

CHAPTER VIII

THE *LAṄKĀVATĀRA SŪTRA*

THE UNION OF THE TATHĀGATAGARBHA AND THE ĀLAYAVIJÑĀNA

IF THE ŚRĪ-MĀLĀ SŪTRA and the *Ratnagotravibhāga* suggest an implicit complementarity of the *Tathāgatagarbha* by the *Ālayavijñāna*, the *Laṅkāvatāra Sūtra* explicitly notes their equivalence. Like the *Ratnagotra* and roughly contemporaneous with it, the *Laṅkāvatāra's* primary scriptural allusion is to the *Śrī-Mālā* whose references to the *Tathāgatagarbha* as the innately pure, yet existentially defiled consciousness, are adopted into the psychological schema of the *Vijñānavāda* espoused by the *Laṅkāvatāra*. However, this incorporation of the *Tathāgatagarbha* into the system of the *Ālayavijñāna* is by no means a mere subsumption of the former as an empty and subsidiary form of the latter. Rather, the *Tathāgatagrabha* witnesses a creative determinacy within the structure of the *Ālayavijñāna* that is not found in the earlier classical treatises of Asaṅga and Vasubandhu. In both the *Mahāyānasaṃgraha* of the first master and the *Vijñāptimātratā-siddhitriṃśikā* of his brother, the *Ālayavijñāna* is merely the first in a series of eight levels of individual phenomenal consciousness. As a strictly individual and relative principle, it is the seat of pure subjectivity, out of which objectivity develops. Since it is the keeper of the karmic seeds, it is the locus of ignorance, and its ultimate identity with the unconditional pure mind realized in *nirvāṇa* is to that extent, strained and ambiguous.[1]

1. With reference to the *Ālayavijñāna* as presented in the thought of Asaṅga and Vasubandhu, Verdu concludes:

"Ultimately, it does not seem that the *ālayavijñāna* can be identified in any way with the universal pure mind realized in *nirvāṇa*, which together with 'space' (*ākāśa*) and 'the *dharma* of extinction', belongs to a different realm of utter absoluteness (*tathatā*, or suchness). Therefore, in Vasubandhu's thought, and this more conspicuously than in his brother's doctrine, an ontological gap seems to separate the individual *ālaya* from the absolute level of 'suchness'...The problems of his idealism still remain: ...the obscure ontological relationship between the *ālaya* as ultimate basis of subjective and

In the *Laṅkāvatāra Sūtra* however, a generic transformation has been effected within the concept of the *Ālayavijñāna* in its union with the *Tathāgatagarbha* which critically establishes its ontic status as essentially pure mind. In its second chapter, the text accepts the reality of the Tathāgata-embryo as inherently bright and pure, fundamentally undefiled and endowed with excellent qualities which, however, "hidden in the body of every being like a gem of great value", becomes soiled through greed, anger, folly, and false imagination. The concern of the sūtra is not with the embryo's designation as eternal and permanent, but that it not be mistaken as such for the ego of the heterodox philosophical systems. Instead, the Tathāgata-embryo, unborn and unqualified, is the very meaning of emptiness (*Śūnyatā*) the reality-limit (*bhūtakoṭi*), and *nirvāṇa*.[2] Implicitly, the embryo is likewise identified with Absolute Suchness (*Tathatā*), defined synonymously by the same combination of terms.[3] However cryptically, the *Laṅkāvatāra* therefore invests the Tathāgata-embryo with the ultimate significance accorded it by the *Śrī-Mālā* and elaborated upon by the *Ratnagotravibhāga*.[4] In addition, the *Tathāgatagarbha* retains its noetic-cognitive determination as embryonic absolute knowledge, defined as it is by the *Laṅkāvatāra* as that whose essence is perfect knowledge and whose realm is noble wisdom.[5]

---

individual mind and the absolute state of *nirvāṇa* as transcendental pure mind, which involves the further question of how the final destruction of the *ālaya*, as a limited and still conditioned *dharma*, may result in the accomplishment of the non-conditioned *dharma* of the *nirvāṇa* of 'no abode'." Verdu, *Dialectical Aspects in Buddhist Thought*, p. 12.

2. *Laṅkāvatāra Sūtra*, trans. Suzuki, pp. 68-69.

3. "Suchness, emptiness, the limit, Nirvāṇa, and the Dharmadhātu,...—these I point out as synonymous...Suchness, emptiness, (reality-) limit, Nirvāṇa, the Dharmadhātu, no-birth of all things...—these characterise the highest truth." Ibid., pp. 241 and 269.

4. This is not meant to imply that the *Laṅkāvatāra Sūtra* was influenced by the *Ratnagotra*. Being contemporaneous, it is probable that they were ignorant of each other, or, as suggested by Wayman and Wayman, that the *Laṅkāvatāra* briefly precedes the *Ratnagotra* which chose not to incorporate it as one of its sources in disagreement with the *garbha's* union with the *ālayavijñāna*, as found therein. The present statement merely intends that the full significance of the *Laṅkāvatāra's* designation of the *garbha* as emptiness, etc., has already been analyzed at length in the study of the *Ratnagotravibhāga* above.

5. See *Laṅkāvatāra Sūtra*, trans. Suzuki, pp. 21 and 64.

But a novel factor has now been introduced into the nature of the Tathāgata-embryo, explicitly confirming what had only been an intimation in the *Ratnagotravibhāga*.[6] In its sixth chapter, the *Laṅkāvatāra* assigns an active causal determination to the embryo as that from which arises the multiplicity of phenomenal forms:

> Mahāmati, the *Tathāgatagarbha* holds within it the cause for both good and evil, and by it all the forms of existence are produced. Like an actor it takes on a variety of forms and (in itself) is devoid of an ego-soul and what belongs to it.[7]

Yet this originative designation is sustained only by virtue of the embryo's union with the *Ālayavijñāna*, said to evolve from within itself seven alternate modalities of consciousness, and to objectify itself as a world of "body (*deha*), property (*bhoga*) and abode (*pratishṭhāna*)."[8] What has been effected, therefore, is the inter-illumination of the *Tathāgatagarbha* and *Ālayavijñāna*, and the mutual inherence of their previously distinct characteristics grounds the novel definition which each now assumes. It is through the refractive light of the *Tathāgatagarbha* as unconditional absolute, that the *Ālayavijñāna* is referred to as the realm of the *Dharmakāya*, the fundamentally pure consciousness, subsisting uninterruptedly like the depths of the ocean, permanent and unmoved despite the agitation of its waves.[9] Similarly, the *Tathāgatagarbha's* already mentioned causal function, its union with the seven *vijñānas*, and its momentary permeability by those consciousnesses,[10] reflect the nuances of its identification with the *Ālaya*.

6. See pp. 173-174 above.
7. *Laṅkāvatāra Sūtra*, trans. Suzuki, p. 190.
8. Ibid., pp. 38 and 49-50. "Body, property and abode" here signify the human organism, its material possessions and its supportive environment, respectively.
9. See Ibid., pp. 40-43.
10. There is thus a dialectic dimension in the *Laṅkāvatāra's Tathāgatagarbha* whereby it is both ontically stable and yet evolutionary, both quiescent and momentary:

"(But) when a revulsion (or turning-back) has not taken place in the Ālayavijñāna known under the name of Tathāgatagarbha, there is no cessation of the seven evolving Vijñānas...As [the Śrāvakas and Pratyekabuddhas] (only) know the egolessness of the self-soul, as they (only) accept the indi-

But, considered separately as independent concepts representing two variant traditions, it is the psychology of the *Ālayavijñāna* rather than the metaphysics of the *Tathāgatagarbha*, with which the *Laṅkāvatāra* is predominantly concerned. By comparison, the sūtra's references to the *garbha* (taken alone or as identified with the *Ālaya*) are few, though hardly incidental. Their selective incorporation into the text crucially specifies the *Ālaya* as the ultimate grounding consciousness, of which all objective phenomena are mere correlates. But just as the *Tathāgatagarbha* is susceptible of misinterpretation as an ego-soul, so is the *Ālaya* mistaken among the skandhic constituents; in fact, both represent the nirvānic absolute mind of the Buddha:

> The Ālaya where the Garbha is stationed is declared by the philosophers to be (the seat of) thought in union with the ego; but this is not the doctrine approved (by the Buddhas). By distinctly understanding it (i.e., the doctrine) there is emancipation and insight into the truth, and purification from the passions which are abandoned by means of contemplation and insight. The Mind primarily pure is the Tathāgata's Garbha which is good but is attached to (as an ego-soul) by sentient beings; it is free from limitation and non-limitation. As the beautiful color of gold and gold among pebbles become visible by purification, so is the Ālaya among the Skandhas of a being. The Buddha is neither a soul nor the Skandhas, he is knowledge free from evil outflows.[11]

Now if the nature of the *Ālaya* may be said to represent the formally noetic aspect of Absolute Suchness (*Tathatā*) through its identification with the *Tathāgatagarbha*, its function is to recognize itself as such in the multiplicity of phenomenal forms. It is

---

viduality and generality of the Skandhas, Dhatus and Ayatanas, there is the evolving of the Tathāgatagarbha. When an insight into the five Dharmas, the three Svabhāvas and the egolessness of all things is obtained, the Tathāgatagarbha becomes quiescent." Ibid. p. 191. "Mahāmati, momentary is the Ālayavijñāna known as the Tathāgatagarbha, which is together with the Manas and with the habit-energy of the evolving Vijñānas—this is momentary. But (the Ālayavijñāna which is together) with the habit-energy of the non-outflows (anāsrava) is not momentary." Ibid., p. 203.

11. Ibid., p. 282.

this recognition that defines the transformative realization of the Tathāgatas which is the intent of the *Laṅkāvatāra* to disclose. And while it adopts the epistemology and psychology of the *Vijñāna-vāda* to identify the dynamics of that recognitive process, the sūtra grounds itself in the ontology of the *Tathāgatagarbha*, i.e., Absolute Suchness (*Tathatā*). This is most clearly illustrated in the third chapter of the text through the metaphor of the hidden city which a traveller happens upon, secluded in the depths of a forest. Using the road which he finds leading into the city, he enters to enjoy its comfort and rest, its pleasures and beauty. Though previously undiscovered, the city with its delights has always been there, available to all who find its roadway. So it is with the unborn, unconditioned truth of all things (*Dharmadhātu*), and their genuine nature as unqualified and indeterminate (*Tathatā*). It is this ultimate reality, eternally abiding like a precious stone in the earth, or the city concealed within the heart of the forest, that has been perceived and recognized by the Buddhas:

> The ancient road of reality, Mahāmati, has been here all the time,...the Dharmadhātu abides forever, whether the Tathāgata appears in the world or not;...reality forever abides, reality keeps its order, like the roads in an ancient city...: Just so, Mahāmati, what has been realised by myself and other Tathāgatas is this reality, the eternally-abiding reality (*sthititā*), the self-regulating reality (*niyāmatā*), the suchness of things (*tathatā*), the realness of things (*bhūtatā*), the truth itself (*satyatā*).[12]

While the *Ratnagotravibhāga* extended the precise delineations of *Tathatā* as the universal immaculate essence of phenomenal existence, the *Laṅkāvatāra* explores the manner in which *Tathatā* (noetically conceived as absolute consciousness, i.e., the *Alaya-vijñāna*) comes to perfect self-awareness as that comprehensive totality. In doing so, it nuances the ontological context defined by the *śāstra*, and with which it implicitly agrees, by its focus upon the epistemology proper to that context. This analysis in turn, demands a coherent structure of the phenomenal mind, an adequate psychology, which was lacking to the *Ratnagotravibhāga*.

The *Ālayavijñāna* as the conscious modality of *Tathatā*, grounds

12. Ibid., p. 124.

and animates the individual human psyche whose forms are the immanent transformations of (the *Ālaya*) itself. The first five sensorial consciousness of seeing (*cakṣurvijñāna*); hearing (*śrotravijñāna*); smelling (*ghrāṇavijñāna*); tasting (*jihavaijñāna*); and touching (*kāyavijñāna*) represent the simple awareness of the respective data appearing before consciousness. It is the sixth, *manovijñāna* or mind consciousness, which is the unifying principle of that raw sense information as apprehended by the first five. It accounts for the constitution of objects within consciousness and their intelligibility or rationality. As the consciousness that "perceives ideas", it is the faculty of formal conceptualisation. Intellection proper is attributed to the seventh consciousness, the *manas*. It systematically categorises information and acts upon it, pondering, calculating, and directing means to specific ends. Thus, it is the organ of conative intentionality and the source of ego-identity with its attendent craving, thirst, and desire.

Often in the *Laṅkāvatāra*, ignorance and its defilements are credited at one time to the *manovijñāna,* at another to the *manas.* Actually, each functions coordinately with the other. The sixth consciousness is charged as the factor of objective discernment, determining distinct and isolated forms as objective realities, while *manas* attaches itself to those particularities, substantiating them with a further degree of realism by the investment of its emotional reactions for or against them in greed or hate. A cycle of mutual reinforcement thus defines the conjoint function of *manovijñāna-manas,* embodying a crucial misperception of reality.

For, according to the *Laṅkāvatāra,* the totality of phenomenal existence is nothing other than self-manifesting Mind, formulated repeatedly throughout the text under the axiom of "Mind-only" (*Cittamātra*):

> Multiplicity of objects evolves from the conjunction of habit-energy and discrimination; it is born of Mind, but is regarded by people as existing outwardly: this I call Mind-only. The external world is not, and multiplicity of objects is what is seen of Mind; body, property, and abode—these I call Mind-only.[13]

13. Ibid., p. 133.

Reality is largely determined by linguistic context, since the human mind is generically habituated to respond to appearances by naming and defining them. This denominative proclivity strengthens the false notion of independent, self-subsistent entities. Born into a world of nominally specified forms, shapes, and features, the child's experience of reality is mediated by the definitions he learns, and with parrot-like repetition, reinforces.[14] And this differentiation of appearances into objective realities, isolated one from the other, symptomatically points to a more profound distinction between perceiver and perceived, the subject over and against an external world. With insistent reiteration the *Laṅkāvatāra* asserts the reality of Mind-only; it alone constitutes the genuine subject whose object is itself in the totality of its universal extension.

The Confusion of Epistemology and Ontology in the Laṅkāvatāra

But difficult ambiguities begin to suggest themselves in the area of the sūtra's admonitions to realize the truth of Mind-only. Concerned as it is with correct perception, the text (as pointed out above) expresses itself more often through the idiom of epistemology than ontology. This is most apparent in the scripture's references to the three self-natures (*svabhāva*); *parikalpita* or purely imaginary nature, *paratantra* or dependent nature, and *parinișpanna*, ultimately real nature, all assume a distinct cognitive expression. Rather than formally indicate the respective level of entitative value or degree of self-being of the particular thing to which each refers, the three categories represent three ways of understanding. They are not so much states of self-nature, as they are modalities of knowing that nature. The idea is that existence can be understood in three different, characteristic ways, each of which is taken to be the final and true nature of reality by whom-

14. "When (the baby) is just born, it is like a worm growing in the dung; like a man waking from sleep, the eye begins to distinguish forms, and discrimination goes on increasing. With knowledge gained by discrimination, human speech is produced from the combination of the palate, lips and cavity; and discrimination goes on like a parrot." Ibid., p. 239.

ever entertains that respective viewpoint. The problem arises with the minimal distinction between *paratantra,* whose characteristic mark is the construction of appearances, and *parikalpita* whose mark is the naming and defining of those appearances. While the one recognizes and discriminates forms, shapes, etc., the other imputes indepdendent self-subsistence to them as real, objective particularities; both are discredited by the *Laṅkāvatāra* as faulty. Now in *parikalpita,* the act of imagination produces its own object, in that the seeing of the object is no different from the object seen. Substantial personality and "thinghood" (i.e., *ātman* and *dharma*) have no identity apart from the belief which posits them. With *parikalpita,* reality is a function of epistemology.

Nevertheless, the imagined thought-object, in itself having no entitative value, must be occasioned by something other than itself.[15] This other is the *paratantra.* But according to the sūtra, the *paratantra* is itself a mode of perception, a particular viewpoint. As *paratantra,* it is itself "dependent" upon other factors, from which it constructs and thus discriminates, appearances. Now the primary concern of the *Laṅkāvatāra* focuses upon this active construction, this discriminatory function, the epistemic process. It tends therefore not to distinguish accurately enough between the activity of discrimination and the content of discrimination. Throughout the text, the references to *paratantra* always imply the discrimination that makes of many factors, the appearances of particular things which *parikalpita* then imagines to be absolute in themselves. Because *pariniṣpanna* is the perfect knowledge which comprehends all things as Mind-only, transcending as it does all names, appearances, discriminations, and judgements, and functioning in "the realm of imagelessness" the impression is given that the whole constitution of the object in consciousness is caused by false discrimination, and consequently, is equal to void imagination. As presented in the *Laṅkāvatāra,* the paratantric percetion is so strongly tinged by the erroneous imagination of *parikalpita* as to be invalidated together with it as a non-veridical source of knowledge; the perfect knowledge of *pariniṣpanna* is actualized only through the complete cessation of *paratantra* and *parikalpita.*

But such an exclusive emphasis upon the epistemic interpreta-

15. So for instance, the imagined snake is occasioned by the actual rope, glimpsed in a dark room.

tion of *paratantra* as a discriminatory function, jeopardizes the ontic status of the paratantric object. It is one thing to identify the act of imagination and the content of that act, as in *parikalpita*, but the distinction between the formation of appearances and the "stuff" of which they are formed and upon which the *paratantra* is said to depend, must be maintained. It is not the constitution of formed appearances per se (the paratantric activity proper), but their projection as independent, self-subsistent entities of a world, external and separate from consciousness or Mind that is erroneous and imaginary (*parikalpita* proper). *Paratantra* as an ontic reality, a level of dependent self-being (*svabhāva*) is overshadowed by *paratantra* as a mode of cognition infected by *parikalpita*. Here, ontology is obscured by an over-extended and therefore imprecise epistemology.

This obscuration manifests itself throughout the *Laṅkāvatāra* in the ambiguous status of the phenomenal reality perceived by the eightfold system of consciousness. In addition to numerous references to the *skandhas, dhātus* and *āyatanas* as developing out of ignorance or arising from desire, the sūtra repeatedly relies upon "a metaphysics of metaphor", likening them to mere dreams, echos, mirages, reflections in water, flashes of lightening, passing clouds, the offspring of a barren woman, or the magical city of the *Gandharvas*. Through the imagery of illusion, the sūtra seeks to psychologically disarm the tenacious belief in the ultimate reality of phenemena as independent, self-subsistent entities. Thus, it discredits the imputation of the *parikalpita* (false imagination) by turning its own dynamism against it, systematically disparaging its belief in substantiality by the application of those fictive illusions. However, only the erroneous idea of their unconditional reality is censured, and not a nihilistic denial of the human organism and its material environment (i.e., the *skandhas, dhātus*, and *āyatanas*). But because the text fails to adequately attest their dependent co-originate nature (their proper *paratantra svabhāva*) they tend to be incorporated into its criticisms of *parikalpita* as the forms intrinsic to its misrepresentations. To do so however, is to confuse the psychological technique of discrediting the belief in the substantiality of things, for a statement of ontic fact.

The sūtra does give some indication that phenomena are not totally inexistent, but only that they cannot be accepted unquestionably as discrete particularities. They are really the self-representations (*vijñapti*) of the Mind but, through the impulse of generic, instinctive habit, are dualistically regarded as existing external to and separate from consciousness:

> When it is not thoroughly understood that there is nothing but what is seen of the Mind itself, dualistic discriminations take place; when it is thoroughly understood that there is nothing but what is seen of the Mind itself, discrimination ceases. Mind is no other than multiplicity, ... forms are visible but not in the way as seen discriminated by the ignorant. The triple world is no other than discrimination, there are no external objects; discrimination sees multiplicity, this is not understood by the ignorant.[16]

Given that phenomenal reality is the self-reflecting image of the *Ālayavijñāna* which, through its identity with the Tathāgata-embryo, is the noetic determination of Absolute Suchness, "phenomena" are indeed, the manifest "appearances" of *Tathatā.* But only once in the entire text is this stated explicitly,[17] suggesting again the sūtra's uneasy integration and amplification of the metaphysics of the *Tathāgatagarbha* into its basic Vijñānavādin psychology. While the doctrine of the Buddha-embryo significantly nuanced the ontic status of the *Ālayavijñāna,* it failed to creatively inform and coherently ground the extensions of that absolute Mind in the multiple forms of existence.

There is then a failure of the *Laṅkāvatāra* to clearly identify phenomena as paratantric objects and to formally accredit them as such with the degree of entitative value that is theirs as existing in proximate interdependence with one another and in ultimate dependence upon Absolute Suchness, of which they are the manifest forms. Nor is this neglect confined to the realm of objectivity. There is a correspondent ambiguity that jeopardizes the status of the phenomenal subject, understood as the sevenfold elaboration of consciousness into the five sensorial consciousnesses, the *mano-*

16. *Laṅkāvatāra Sūtra*, trans. Suzuki, p. 161.

17. "Not being born, suchness, reality limit, and emptiness,—these are other names for form (*rūpa*); one should not imagine it to mean a nothing." Ibid., p. 276.

vijñāna and the *manas*. As the immanent transformations of the *Ālaya*, they exist in differentiated identity with it; finite, relative consciousness animated and grounded upon the universal, absolute Mind. These seven constitute the structure of the phenomenal psyche, the network of human subjectivity, determined by the primordial consciousness, which they in turn modify. For, they are capable of defiling the essentially pure *Ālaya* by an ignorant misinterpretation of the forms which they perceive. Grasping at sense objects, they invariably fixate upon and cling to them as independent, self-subsisting entities, rather than perceiving their genuine nature as Mind-only. Taken as a unit, the relative consciousnesses are the seat of the *parikalpita*. But again, the sūtra fails to adequately delineate the ontic structure of the phenomenal psyche from the epistemological processes that define its function. There is a difference between the form of the human consciousness and the ignorant activities that characterize it; this distinction is absent in the *Laṅkāvatāra*. In fact, so close is the identification between the relative consciousness and ignorance, that *nirvāṇa* is defined by the absence not only of the *manovijñāna* but of the other consciousnesses that depend upon it for support:

> According to my teaching, Mahāmati, the getting rid of the discriminating Manovijñāna—this is said to be Nirvāṇa ... : With the Manovijñāna as cause and supporter, Mahāmati, there rise the seven Vijñānas. Again Mahāmati, the Manovijñāna is kept functioning, as it discerns a world of objects and becomes attached to it, and by means of manifold habit-energy (or memory) it nourishes the Ālayavijñāna... Thus Mahāmati, when the Manovijñāna is got rid of, the seven Vijñānas are also got rid of... I enter into Nirvāṇa when the Vijñāna which is caused by discrimination ceases... Like a great flood where no waves are stirred because of its being dried up, the Vijñāna (-system) in its various forms ceases to work when there is the annihilation (of the Manovijñāna).[18]

Considered by itself, such a statement might be interpreted as referring only to the cessation of the relative consciousness in its failure to accurately perceive the multiplicity of phenomenal forms

18. Ibid., pp. 109-110.

as the self-manifestations of Mind. But it would appear that the sūtra's intention is more radical. Repeatedly, the text states quite deliberately that the sevenfold development of consciousness is due to ignorance which in turn it perpetuates. Generically inherent to them, an habitual tendency to cling to the named forms of phenomenal reality as self-substantiating particularities, brands the *vijñāna* system as essentially deluded and delusive:

> Because of the influence of habit-energy that has been accumulating variously by false reasoning since beginningless time, what here goes under the name of Ālayavijñāna is accompanied by the seven Vijñānas which give birth to a state known as the abode of ignorance ...; they [the seven vijñānas] are born with false discrimination as cause, and with forms and appearances and objectivity as conditions which are intimately linked together; adhering to names and forms, they do not realise that objective individual forms are no more than what is seen of the Mind itself; they do not give exact information regarding pleasure and pain; they are not the cause of emanicipation; by setting up names and forms which originate from greed, greed is begotten in turn, thus mutually conditioned and conditioning.[19]

The principle of primordial ignorance which evokes the initial responsiveness of the relative consciousness and sustains its consequent misperceptions, is the illusion of an objective world independent of, and external to, consciousness. What is crucially significant is that ignorance is now revealed as the actual cause of phenomenal individuation.

Thus, it is more than a simple confusion between the structure of human consciousness and the deceptive activities that characterize it. What the sūtra ultimately challenges is the very integrity of phenomenal subjectivity. If it is the product of ignorance and the condition for its continued influence, then the attainment of *nirvāṇa* would indeed imply its abandonment. In the frequent image of the *Laṅkāvatāra,* the sevenfold modality of the finite consciousness would dissolve as so many waves on the surface of an otherwise tranquil ocean. Under such a conception, the asbo-

19. Ibid., pp. 190-191.

lute consciousness (the *Ālayavijñāna*) would alone remain. But such a conclusion is severely problematic.

First, is it not contradictory to say on the one hand that the essentially pure consciousness of the Ālaya-ocean is the grounding principle of the wave-like *vijñānas,* and on the other, to suggest that their form is a temporary agitation, a disturbance caused by the ignorant "winds of objectivity"? How can the noetic transformations of Absolute Suchness be said to originate from the energy of a habitual desire, clinging, speculation, and ignorance?[20] Then again, if relative consciousness is the consequence of ignorance, where in turn does that radical nescience originate? To attribute it to the *Ālaya*, would implicate the latter as the seat of delusion and involve it in direct self-contradiction as the inherently immaculate Mind. But if the primordial projection of objectivity (i.e., ignorance) is a principle alien to the *Ālaya,* the latter forfeits its status as ultimate, and dualism threatens the absolute idealism of the *Tathāgatagarbha-Ālayavijñāna.*

From still another perspective, if the relative consciousness, as a product of and vehicle for ignorance, is essentially delusive, and if it is capable of modifying the *Ālaya*, obscuring its natural luminosity like a veil, then how is it ever possible for the *Ālaya* to free itself? *Nirvāṇa* may be defined as the cessation of the deceptive sevenfold consciousness, and the self-recognition by the Mind as

20. The identity of the seven *vijñānas* with the *Ālaya* is most distinctive in the following passage:

"They are neither different nor not-different: the relation is like that between the ocean and its waves. So are the seven vijñānas joined with the Citta (mind). As the waves in their variety are stirred on the ocean so in the Ālaya is produced the variety of what is known as the Vijñānas. The Citta, Manas and Vijñānas are discriminated as regards their form; (but in substance) the eight are not to be separated one from another, for there is neither qualified nor qualifying. As there is no distinction between the ocean and its waves, so in the Citta there is no evolution of the Vijñānas." Ibid., p. 42. But the following statement is just as clear that they originate from the fourfold habit-energy (i.e., clinging to existence; form; theorising; and desire) and are different from the *Tathāgatagarbha*:

"Mahāmati, the seven Vijñānas, that is, Manas, Manovijñāna, eye-vijñāna, etc., are characterised with momentariness because they originate from habit-energy, they are destitute of the good non-flowing (anāsrava) factors, and are not transmigratory. What transmigrates Mahāmati, is the *Tathāgatagarbha* which is the cause of Nirvāṇa as well as that of pleasure and pain". Ibid., pp. 208-209.

the whole of phenomenal existence, but how does the *Ālaya* gain even the rudimentary insight that the *vijñānas* must be transcended, if their defiling presence is naturally coexistent with it? More specifically if *Tathatā* is to realize itself as the ultimate nature of existence, how is its process of self-reflective awareness possible without the relative *vijñānas*? How are the specific forms of its self-manifestation recognizable without the mediation of the five sensorial consciousnesses, the *manovijñāna* and *manas*? If it is to know itself in the otherness of those forms, be perfectly conscious of itself as the unconditional nature that makes of them a harmonious realm of interdependent coexistence, the unity of multiplicity, the identity-in-difference (i.e., the *Dharmadhātu*), *Tathatā* must first of all perceive them. Without the simple apprehension of the raw sense data proper to the five sensorial consciousnesses, their unified intelligibility proper to *manovijñāna,* and their determinate categorization proper to *manas,* there would be no "other" in whose distinctness *Tathatā* (as *Ālaya*) would recognize itself.[21] Finite, relative consciousness is an immanent development of absolute consciousness, and essential to its self-awakening. This however, is far from clear in the *Laṅkāvatāra Sūtra* which jeopardizes the value of human subjectivity by an inadequate ontology.

As was the case with the status of the objective world, the significance of its subjective counterpart is seriously compromised by

21. "The content of *Ālaya* is indeterminate objectivity. As soon as this content is known as another, its indeterminateness gives place to empirical determinations. And known it must be...The transition from the act of willing of this fundamental content to those of the determinate contents is the work of *manas*. It breaks up the monotony of the indeterminate objectivity by projecting the latter through categories; its essence is categorisation...It actualizes the empirical contents which are implicitly contained in the pure objective...The 'other' can be realised only as a determinate other and the splitting up of the pure form into determinate forms resulting in the precipitation of matter or content is intellection...Only after consciousness is determinately categorised does the awareness of the distinction between form and matter, or consciousness and its content, characteristic of empirical knowledge, arise. *Manas* is not the result of this process which are the several object-knowledges, but it is the process itself.' It is the fructification of the seeds lying dormant in the *Ālaya* into the content of consciousness. It is the ripening of the fruit, not the ripe fruit itself." Ashok Kumar Chatterjee, *The Yogācāra Idealism*, 2d ed., rev. (Varanasi, India: Motilal Banarsidass, 1975), pp. 102-103.

the confusion of content and form, epistemology and ontology. The sevenfold form of relative consciousness is not categorically identical to the quality of its knowledge. The five sensorial consciousnesses, the *manovijñāna*, and the *manas*, as the "structure" of human subjectivity, are the conditions for the very possibility of wisdom and ignorance. Whether *Tathatā* recognizes itself in the multiplicity of phenomena, or is obscured by beliefs of substantial egohood and thinghood, its faculty of perception and recognition is crucial, and cannot be forfeited. But this is what the text often suggests through its inadequate distinction between the *parikalpita function* and the *paratantric nature* of the relative consciousness.

Mutually interdependent and supportive, the seven *vijñānas* ultimately depend upon the *Ālayavijñāna* whose self-transformations they are; human subjectivity as the differentiated identity of the absolute mind has a formal ontic status, a dependent self-nature (*paratantra svabhāva*). A transcendental illusion, the projection of an objective and external world of discrete and independent entities (the principle of "beginningless ignorance") may indeed distort the interpretation with which the relative consciousness invests that which it apprehends and orders into unified forms of intelligibility. But this interpretative function of false imagination (*parikalpita*) is more formally an epistemological process than an ontic reality; it is an activity peculiar to relative consciousness but not exhaustively definitive of it. The cessation of this deceptive mode of knowing does not necessitate the end of the seven *vijñānas*. However, the distinction between ontology and epistemology, between consciousness as a stratum of being and consciousness as an interpretative process, is not acutely focused in the *Laṅkāvatāra*.

For this reason, the doctrine of the *Ālayavijñāna* had to advance beyond its elaboration in the *Laṅkāvatāra Sūtra* to arrive at the mature coherence of its fundamental implications. The historical and logical significance of the text for the present study lies in the explicit union it effects between the *Tathāgatagarbha* and the *Ālayavijñāna*. If the *Ratnagotravibhāga* had specified the *garbha* as the immanence of Absolute Suchness within the phenomenal order, the *Laṅkāvatāra* gave it a more exact noetic determination as the grounding principle of human consciousness through the *Ālayavijñāna*. It established the necessary psychological context, lacking to the *Ratnagotra*, in which the relationship of *Tathatā* as ontic subjectivity and individual, human subjectivity might be meaningfully discussed. It simultaneously accorded the *Ālaya* a degree of entitative value not found in the earlier texts of the Vijñānavādin tradition, establishing it as the unconditional absolute.

But this validation of the *Ālaya* as the conscious modality of *Tathatā*, paradoxically contributed to the ambiguity of the sevenfold relative consciousness. By its categorical insistence upon the essential purity and non-delusive character of the *Tathāgatagarbha-Ālayavijñāna*, the *Laṅkāvatāra* removed the suggestion of earlier texts that the *Ālaya* represented only an individual and relative principle of finite, deluded consciousness. But inevitably, this revaluation shifted the seat of ignorance and its beguiling influence onto the *manas*, *manovijñāna*, and the five sensorial consciousnesses. Then, given the clumsy approximation of ontological fact through epistemological statement, the sūtra lacks a necessary clarity on the precise nature of the phenomenal world and the ultimate value of the phenomenal consciousness; this obscurity, as noted above, jeopardizes the integrity of the sūtra's framework through the contradictions it suggests. An answer to those problems will be found in the mature reflections on the *Ālayavijñāna* in Hsüan Tsang's *Ch'eng Wei-Shih Lun*, where the present study must now advance.

Chapter IX

THE *CH'ENG WEI-SHIH LUN*

The Metaphysics of Mere-Consciousness

Representing a two hundred year development within the Vijñānavādin tradition subsequent to the *Laṅkāvatāra*, the *Ch'eng Wei-Shih Lun* (the *Doctrine of Mere-Consciousness*) is an exhaustive study of the *Ālayavijñāna* and the sevenfold development of the *manas*, *manovijñāna*, and the five sensorial consciousnesses. As a creative and elaborate exposition of Vasubandhu's *Vijñaptimātratāsiddhitriṃśikā* (*Treatise in Thirty Stanzas on Consciousness Only*), it synthesized the ten most significant commentaries written on it,[1] and became the enchiridion of the new *Fa-hsiang* (*Dharmalakṣaṇa* or *Hossō*) school of Buddhist idealism.

In both style and content, the *Ch'eng Wei-Shih Lun* represents a superior advance over the earlier *Laṅkāvatāra Sūtra*. Instead of the latter's cryptically aphoristic form, Hsüan Tsang's treatise is a detailed and coherent analysis, a scholastic apologetic on the doctrine of consciousness only (*vijñaptimātratā*). Its most significant contribution to the psychology of the former scripture lies in its critical amplification of the union effected between the *Ālayavijñāna* and the *Tathāgatagarbha*. The *Laṅkāvatāra's* failure to sustain the ontological implications of that bivalent reality undermined the ultimate value of human subjectivity and risked the self-contradictions noted above. Without any reference to the *Tathāgatagarbha* itself, the *Ch'eng Wei-Shih Lun* firmly grounds its pan-consciousness on Absolute Suchness (*Tathatā*), the immanent modality of which had been signified by the *garbha* throughout the *Ratnagotravibhāga*. Although the latter was not a consciously appropriated source, the *Ch'eng Wei-Shih Lun* shares the fundamental intuitions of that extensive ontology. This is strikingly evident in the final two books of the work, treating of

1. The ten great *śāstra*-masters whose thought is reflected in the *Ch'eng Wei-Shih Lun* are listed in appendix 2.

the three self-natures (*svabhāvas*) and the five stages in the holy path of attainment.

If the *Laṅkāvatāra* suffered from the clumsy equivalence of the epistemological significance and the ontological reality of *parikalpita, paratantra,* and *pariniṣpanna,* the *Ch'eng Wei-Shih Lun* is free of all such ambiguity. In its eighth book, the three terms clearly signify the varying degrees of entitative value, the ontic status, of that to which they refer. *Parikalpita* represents that level of self-being that is totally null and void, indicating a purely imaginary figment. Those entities whose existence is defined by a mutual interdependence and encompass the universal extension of phenomenal forms are designated, *paratantra.* They reciprocally contribute to and mutually inhere a common identity, and this interdependent, correlational totality is ultimately sustained by and dependent upon *pariniṣpanna*, as the ultimately real, self-subsistent absolute. As equivalent to genuine Suchness (*Bhūtatathatā*), *pariniṣpanna* is the essential nature (*dharmatā*) of phenomenal existence (i.e., the *paratantra*). Defined as the "eternal freedom from the *parikalpita* nature of the *paratantra*", *pariniṣpanna* is neither identical with nor different from *paratantra.* It is the self-identical universality, the grounding truth of finite particularity which, through false imagination, had been distortedly conceived as a multiplicity of discrete, self-subsistent individualities.

By way of exemplification, the text applies the three *svabhāvas* to ten categories, extending from the unconditioned non-active *dharmas* (*asaṁskṛtas*) to the two modes of existence (designated or real).[2] What emerges from this section is a more precise focus on *paratantra* in the peculiar light of the treatise's fundamental doctrine of consciousness-only. The forms of phenomenal existence mutually participate in the being of each other, everyone inclusively implicating all the others, every one essential to the integrity of the others. But this universal interdependence of phenomena is itself only "the image aspect" or perceived division of consciousness (*nimittabhāga*), correlatively dependent upon "the perceiving aspect" (*darśanabhāga*). As will be seen in greater detail shortly, the sole reality of consciousness manifests itself as

2. The ten categories through which the text analyses the three *svabhāvas* are listed in appendix 2.

the unity of subjectivity (that part of consciousness that perceives, *darśanabhāga*) and objectivity (that part of consciousness that is perceived, *nimittabhāga*). Since the *dharmas* that constitute the phenomenal world (the *skandhas*, *āyatanas* and *dhātus*) are the forms (*nimitta*) in which consciousness (as *darśana*) appears to itself, they are *paratantra* primarily because they appear only as the result of numerous conditioning factors within consciousness itself. False imagination assumes that the images and forms constituting the perceived aspect of consciousness (*nimittabhāga*) are self-subsistent particularities, autonomous not only from one another, but more fundamentally, from consciousness itself. However, through the sustained wisdom of the two voids (*pudgalaśūnyatā* and *dharmaśūnyatā*), it is revealed that the ultimate reality (*pariniṣpanna*) of genuine Suchness (*Bhūtatathatā*) is the true nature of both the perceived and perceiving aspects of consciousness (the *paratantra*).

This clear identification of absolute Suchness as the genuine nature of mere-consciousness (*Vijñaptimātratathatā*) is all the more pronounced in the final book of the treatise on the holy path of attainment. With each of the tenfold stages (*bhūmis*) of the Bodhisattva's spiritual ascent, *Tathatā* progressively delineates the nuances of its own plenitude, in and through the respective realizations attained by him. Advancing from the simple awareness of its universality as the essential nature of all *dharmas* in the first *bhūmi*, it reveals itself as provided with infinite sublime qualities in the second; as the source of excellent teachings in the third; as independent and self-subsistent in the fourth; as the identity of *nirvāṇa* and *saṃsāra* in the fifth; on the sixth stage, as essentially and always pure despite its adventitious concealment; as self-identical in all its varied definitions as *Paramārtha*, *Pariniṣpanna*, *Dharmadhātu*, etc., in the realization of the seventh *bhūmi*; as invariably transcending all notions of increase and decrease, remaining essentially unaffected by purity and defilement—this in the eighth; while in the ninth and tenth stages, *Tathatā* reveals itself as the basis of transcendental wisdom and the unhindered powers for the interpretation of the Dharma.[3] The ontic primacy of Suchness which these stages of realization collectively reflect, is nowhere more emphatically stated than in the *Ch'eng Wei-Shih*

3. See Hsüan Tsang, *Ch'eng Wei-Shih Lun*, pp. 747-49.

Lun's presentation of the psychic transformation of enlightenment, the *āśrayaparāvṛtti.*

Bhūtatathatā is alternately referred to as the *āśraya* or basis which is to be transformed, and again, as the *āśraya* which is the result of the transformation. Its self-coherence from the one to the other identifies it as the absolute that is the vehicle of its own self-manifestation. In the one passage it is the condition for the very possibility of both ignorance and knowledge:

> On the other hand, [there is] the *āśraya* of confusion (delusion) and intelligence (awakening), i.e., the Bhūtatathatā. It serves as the root of confusion and intelligence; it is by depending thereon that defiled and pure dharmas are born. The Holy Path transforms it in such a manner that it rejects the defiled and acquires the pure.[4]

In the other, it is equivalent to *Mahāparinirvāṇa*, the essential purity freed from the adventitious defilements that had concealed it (the *Anādikālika-prakrtiśuddha-nirvāna*):

> This is the Bhūtatathatā, the ultimate principle or essential nature of all dharmas. Despite adventitious contamination it is pure in itself; possessed of innumerable and measureless excellent qualities; free from birth and destruction, being absolutely tranquil and placid, like space; equal and common for all sentient beings; neither identical with all dharmas nor different from them (for it is the Dharmatā); free from all *nimitta* (because it is not apprehensible: the *grāhyanimitta* is lacking in it); free from all *vikalpa* (mental discrimination) (because it does not apprehend: the *grāhakavikalpa* is lacking in it); beyond the path of the intellect (that is to say, it is "realized" internally: it transcends ideation and ratiocination); beyond the path of names and words; and realized internally by true Āryas (saints and sages).[5]

The joint significance of these two passages is the emergence of Suchness as the primal consciousness (the presupposition of both

4. Ibid., p. 755.
5. Ibid., p. 759.

knowledge and ignorance) whose essence is to know itself in the universality of its extension as the essential nature of all things. For the Holy Path is inherent to it as the germinal presence of omniscient wisdom, deploying its luminosity the more it disperses the tenacious force of ignorance. Since the point of the Path's culmination in the supreme wisdom of *Mahābodhi* is co-instantaneous with the perfect revelation of *Mahāparinirvāṇa*, it is the moment of *Tathatā's* absolute self-awareness, its immediate self-coincidence as subject and object. This is specified in the treatise's description of the fourfold modality of *Mahābodhi*: the Great Mirror Wisdom (*Mahādarśajñāna*); the Universal Equality Wisdom (*Samatājñāna*); the Profound Contemplation Wisdom (*Pratyavekṣaṇājñāna*); and the Perfect Achievement Wisdom (*Kṛtyānuṣṭhānajñāna*). With the exception of the last, each of these wisdoms is the dual expression of *nirvikalpakajñāna* and *pṛṣthalabdhajñāna*. The former is a non-discriminative, immediate intuition, while the latter is based upon and subsequent to it. In the Great Mirror, Universal Equality, and Profound Contemplation Wisdoms, the object of *nirvikalpakajñāna* is *Bhūtatathatā*; it is the sheer, unmediated presence of Absolute Suchness to itself.[6] In those same wisdoms (and exclusively in the Perfect Achievement Wisdom), *pṛṣthalabdhajñāna* functions with regard to the multiple variety of phenomenal forms; its objects are the *paratantric dharmas*. The Great Mirror Wisdom is said to carry all objects without failure of memory or perceptive errors, since it is eternally present to them. Basing itself upon the *Mahāyānasūtrālaṁkāra śāstra* and the *Buddhabhūmi Sūtra*, the text explains:

> (Just as images appear in a mirror, so) in the Mirror Wisdom of the Tathāgata there appear all images of the six āyatanas (eye, ear, etc.,) the six viṣayas (color, sound, etc.), and the six consci-

6. In its section on the stage of unimpeded penetrating understanding (*Prativedhavastha*), the text had determined that *nirvikalpakajñāna* was the imageless apprehension of *Tathatā*:

"It is said in the Yogaśāstra, 73: 'It has no images to apprehend. It does not apprehend images.'...Although it has no perceived division (*nimittabhāga*), it can be said that it is born by adhering to *Tathatā*, because it is not separate from *Tathatā*...If it develops into an image of the *Tathatā* which it perceives, then it will not be the immediate realization of *Tathatā*. It will know *Tathatā* as the Subsequent Jñāna (*pṛṣthalabdha*) knows it and, like the

ousnesses (visual consciousness, auditory consciousness, etc.). (This is why the Bhagavat is omniscient.)[7]

Similarly, it notes that the Perfect Achievement Wisdom focuses upon "the 84,000 states of mind of sentient beings" and the totality of *dharmas* past, future, and present. Like the Profound Contemplation Wisdom which bears on the individual and common characteristics of all *dharmas*, the Universal Equality Wisdom has as its object both *Tathatā* and *saṃvṛti*. Perceiving the profusion of phenomena, it penetrates to the essential nature (*Tathatā*) which makes of their forms and appearances a harmonious realm of interdependent coexistence, the unity of their multiplicity. It does so through the knowledge of the non-substantiality of persons and things (*pudgalasūnyatā* and *dharmaśūnyatā*).

Thus, in the simultaneity of *Mahāparinirvāṇa* and *Mahābodhi*, *Tathatā* is at once comprehended and comprehending. Appearing initially as ontic substance, the permanent, absolute, self-identical ground of phenomenal existence, it quickly assumes a formal noetic status and moves as primal consciousness (and thus, as ontic subject) to unqualified self-awareness as the indeterminate nature of that existence, its utter Suchness. The *Ratnagotravibhāga* had suggested the same thesis. But despite its reference to the Innate Pure Mind (*Cittaprakṛti*) as the psychic determination of *Tathatā*, it failed to articulate as radical and absolute an idealism as that of the *Ch'eng Wei-Shih Lun*. In the *Ratnagotra* there remains a certain equivocation between phenomenal existence and absolute Suchness. While the latter is the immaculate essence and the fundamental nature of the former, and while it actualizes itself as dynamic wisdom, perceiving itself in the manifold of phenomenal forms, the material density and exteriority of those forms remain unexplained. That they present no ultimate hindrance to the self-manifesting wisdom of *Tathatā* is never questioned. But it can at least be raised, how concrete sensibility is permeable by absolute non-substantiality.

What was only an implication in the *Ratnagotra* is plainly stated by Hsüan Tsang, for the *Ch'eng Wei-Shih Lun* answers out of the

---

Subsequent Jñāna, it will be *savikalpaka* (discriminating). It should therefore be admitted that it has *darśanabhāga*, but no *nimittabhāga*." Ibid., p. 689.

7. Ibid., p. 775.

central axiom of Yogācāra Buddhism, categorically denying all such dichotomy as matter and spirit, exteriority and interiority, object and subject. There is but one reality: mere-consciousness (*vijñaptimātratā*). The self-transparency of *Tathatā* in the totality of phenomena is accordingly, the self-recognition of consciousness in the multiplicity of its forms. For to say that consciousness is the sole reality, is not to consign material existence to the realm of illusion, but to interpret its sensible shapes and contours as the immanent developments and structured modalities of consciousness itself. Illusion is to imagine the independent self-subsistence of those sensible forms apart from consciousness, when they are instead the integral patterns of that one reality. If *Tathatā* is the essential nature of consciousness, and if consciousness is in turn the essential nature of phenomena, the following passage presents the psychic morphology of *Tathatā*: the structures of phenomenal existence as the ideal forms of Absolute Suchness.

> Verily, the expression *Vijñaptimātratā* has a profound meaning. The word 'consciousness' generally expresses the idea that each sentient being possesses eight consciousnesses, which are consciousness in their essential nature; six categories of mental activities which are associated with consciousness; the two Bhāgas of *Nimitta* and *Darśana*, which are evolved from consciousness and its caittas; the Viprayuktas which consist of three categories of dharmas (the caittas, rupa, and dharmas not associated with the mind); and Tathatā (True Thusness or True Reality) which is revealed through the realization of Śūnyatā (Voidness of ātman and dharmas) and which is the true nature of the four preceding categories. Hence all dharmas, whichever they may be, are not separable from consciousness. For this reason, the general term 'consciousness' has been created. The word 'mere' (*mātra*) is employed to deny the existence of real matter, etc., as distinct from the various consciousnesses, which existence is admitted by ignorant people, including the adherents of the two Vehicles.[8]

Tathatā (*Parinispanna*) can know itself as the indeterminate, unconditional nature of all things (*paratantra*) because they are the

8. Ibid., pp. 523-25.

radically ideal manifestations or transformations (*pariṇāma*) from within itself, noetically conceived as absolute consciousness (*Ālaya-vijñāna*). In its presentation of *nimittabhāga* and *darśana-bhāga*, the text illustrates just how extensive that self-manifestation is.

The Ālayavijñāna and the Bījas

The *Ālaya* determines itself through a twofold activity: "internally" it takes the form of a physical body possessed of the five sense organs and also, as the storehouse of its own creative potentialities, the seeds (*bījas*) of its future self-modifications[9]; "externally" it assumes the form of the physical universe which supports all living things. These thoroughly ideal transformations of the *Ālaya* are collectively known as its image aspect (*nimittabhāga*), and it is in relation to this objective dimension of itself (*ālambana*) that the *Ālaya* defines its subjectivity. For, it continually perceives those self-manifested images (*nimitta*). This subjective pole of the *Ālaya* is known as its perception or vision aspect (*darśanabhāga*). Together, the image aspect and perception aspect cohere in the self-corroboratory aspect of consciousness (the *svasaṃvittibhāga*). As the awareness that perception has taken place, the latter is the formal moment of self-consciousness; in every act of perception, consciousness reflects back upon itself and thus, in knowing anything, it knows itself.[10] Distinct only with regard to their particular form, the three *bhāgas* attest the ultimate cohesion of consciousness-only (*vijñaptimātratā*):

9. The more exact and detailed discussion of the *bijas* and their function will be treated below. Here, let it suffice that they are the dynamic potentialities of consciousness itself.

10. So for instance, a patch of blue may be considered the *nimittabhāga*, the object which is then perceived by the *darśanabhāga*, the action of knowledge "which sees the blue". The *svasaṃvittibhāga* is the awareness of having seen the blue. (To know that I see the blue.) Technically, there is another fourth *bhāga*, the reflection of consciousness upon itself as active knowing. (To know that I know that I see the blue.) This is the *svasaṃvitti-saṃvittibhāga*. But the text notes that this fourth may be included in the third *bhāga*, the *svasaṃvittibhāga*. See Hsüan Tsang, *Ch'eng Wei-Shih Lun*, pp. 141-43. See also *Vijñaptimātratāsiddhi: La Siddhi de Hiuan-Tsang*, trans. Louis de La Vallée Poussin, 2 vols. (Paris: Librairie Orientaliste Paul Geuthner, 1928), 1:132.

> As taught in a stanza of the *Pramanasamuccaya*: "The *nimitta* or internal image which resembles an external thing, is the object of the act of perception. What perceives this image and the consciousness behind the perception (*svasaṃvitti*) are respectively the act of perception and the fruit of that act. The substance of these three is not differentiated.[11]

It is by virtue of its common or universal *bījas* that the *Ālaya* develops into the manifold appearances of the physical universe, while it is its non-common or non-universal *bījas* that account for the unique formations of the individual physical bodies and accompanying sense faculties. The consciousness of each sentient being manifests itself in a peculiar and distinctive manner, but inherent to the *Ālaya* of every being there are archetypal determinations of consciousness (i.e., of and by the *Ālaya* itself) which ensure a common manifestation of the phenomenal world. The uniformity of the physical shapes and localities of this specific world system (mountains, rivers, etc.,) attest the universal self-particularizations of consciousness. The apparent solidity and uniform stability of those forms by no means invalidates their origin in, and persistence as, consciousness-only. As K'uei Chi points out,[12] "the abiding homogeneity" of physical forms refers not to them in and of themselves, but to the uninterrupted continuity of the *Ālaya's* self-manifestation. Before the beginning of time, the matter of the seemingly external world arises and continues to be evolved in an endless sequence.

Nor do the spatial and temporal determinations of things along with their functional capabilities necessarily imply their self-subsistence apart from consciousness.[13] The classical refutation is

11. Hsüan Tsang, *Ch'eng Wei-Shih Lun*, p. 141.

12. K'uei Chi was the most eminent of Hsüan Tsang's disciples, whose authoritative commentaries on the *Ch'eng Wei-Shih Lun* (*Ch'eng Wei-Shih Lun Shu-chi*) and Vasubandhu's *Wei-Shih Erh Shih Lun* have been incorporated at various places into Wei Tat's translation of Hsüan Tsang. For K'uei Chi's interpretation of the solidity of phenomenal forms see Ibid., pp. 519-21.

13. At this point in the *Ch'eng Wei-Shih Lun*, the text simply states that all doubts concerning such matters "may be dispelled by comparison with the world of dreams." p. 511. What is presupposed here is the discussion in Vasubandhu's *Vijñaptimātratāsiddhi viṃśatikā* (*Wei-Shih Erh Shih Lun*) (*The Treatise in Twenty Stanzas on Consciousness Only*). For the precise arguments

based on the dream experience. There, the projected phenomena, admittedly possessing no reality apart from the mind, are similarly bound by the laws of spatial and temporal designation. The seeming reality of the dream episode is intensified by a certain logical coherence of the things perceived; their appearance is not haphazard, but follows the demands of place and time for their basic recognizability. The apparent reality dreams possess derives not from any concrete, objective world, but merely from the idea of objectivity; the plausibility of the dream world lies in its projected objectivity. Not only does consciousness create in dreams the contents of perception, but more importantly, infuses them with a reality through the primordial category of objectivity. In addition to such ideal creativity, the dream has an efficacy within the physical realm as well. Vasubandhu's graphic example of nocturnal emission can easily be amplified by the evidence of numerous organic reactions (from increased heart rate to sleep-walking) induced through the experience of a nightmare.

The implication in all of this is that since even dreamed objects reflect a certain concretion in time and space and can exercise an observable influence on the dreamer, the presence of those characteristics in the objects of the waking world doesn't necessarily authenticate the claim of their independent self-subsistence. Whether or not the dream as the norm of the real is adequately convincing, the present argument is highly illuminative. For it clearly dispels the popular notion that the things of consciousness-only are but flimsy transparencies, devoid of all fixed cohesion. Physical consistency and concrete tangibility are not inimical to consciousness-only. Because it is ideal it does not mean that the empirical world is subject to no laws; idealism is not to be construed as the negation of precise and rigorous spatio-temporal determinations. Instead, they are the very forms in which absolute consciousness manifests itself. It is not the material solidity of empirical phenomena, but only the notion or idea of their externality (apart from consciousness) that is disputed by the doctrine

---

see stanzas one, two, and three in Vasubandhu, *Wei Shih Er Shih Lun or The Treatise in Twenty Stanzas on Representation-Only*, trans. Clarence H. Hamilton, American Oriental Series, vol. 13 (New Haven, Conn.: American Oriental Society, 1938), pp. 19-29.

of consciousness-only.[14] The universal *bījas* as the innate self-determinations of the *Ālaya* are actively and persistently projected by it as the multiple forms of the phenomenal universe. Since the *Ālaya* is the seat of the primordial a priori category of objectivity, specified in the general categories of space and time, and since it (the *Ālaya*) is the grounding principle of phenomenal consciousness, to perceive those forms (whether in a dream or the waking state) is to perceive them as objective.

The error is to misunderstand this fundamental function of consciousness (the projection and objectification of phenomena) and to interpret the perceived objectivity of things as evidence of their independent self-subsistence. In the familiar terms of Vijñānavādin ontology, to impute substantiality to empirical phenomena (the *paratantra*) is the failure to perceive them as ultimately dependent on absolute consciousness (the *parinispanna*), and thus to accord them a reality that is purely fanciful (the *parikalpita*). Phenomena are forms of consciousness and as such are real. Their objectivity is only the mode of its appearance. They seem to be "out there" possessing independent self-subsistence; in fact, that is only the way in which the *Ālaya* projects its contents, its own self-determinations or universal *bījas*.

That the sense faculties and their supporting physical body evolve from the non-universal and unique *bījas* of the *Ālaya*, needs clarification. It had been a disputed question among the earlier masters of the *Vijñānavāda* whether all *bījas* were eternally innate. Candrapāla believed that they existed since beginningless time as the inherent, though non-manifest, self-determinations of the *Ālaya*. Nanda and Śrīsena contested just the opposite. According to them, all *bījas* come into existence and are created within the

14. "We cannot choose the objects of our experience. One can avert one's eyes, but if one sees at all, one cannot help seeing the empirical objects as they are...No system of philosophy can afford to tamper with the least factor of the empirical experience...The Yogācāra is an idealist only transcendentally; in empirical matters he has no quarrel with the realist. All philosophical issues lie between conflicting interpretations of facts and not between the facts themselves. It is not the case therefore that idealism violates the empirical activities...That our experience is manifold and variegated cannot be gainsaid; the point is whether the content experienced is wholly within it, or enjoys an existence even when not experienced. Even if it does not, experience as such remains what it would be were the content real." Chatterjee, *Yogācāra Idealism*, pp. 74-75.

Ālaya through the influence of the phenomenal consciousness. Hsüan Tsang accepted the mediating view of Dharmapāla according to whom there exist *bījas* of both categories. To deny the creativity of the phenomenal consciousness to modify itself either through a more exact wisdom or a regressive ignorance, is to dispense with the spiritual path as useless; if all *bījas* are predeterminately fixed, excluding the novel influence of phenomenal consciousness, how does one explain the progress from delusion to enlightenment? Therefore, there must be *bījas* that are created by the activity of phenomenal consciousness which exist within the *Ālaya* as residual impressions and potential sources that could modify consciousness in a more perfect knowledge or a greater obscurity, depending upon the activities that occasion them.

On the other hand, where does the sevenfold structure of the phenomenal consciousness itself come from? The *manas*, *manovijñāna*, and the five sensorial consciousnesses evolve from *bījas* that have innately existed within the *Ālaya* "since before the beginning of time". In other words, the form of human individuality is part of the inherent self-patterning of the *Ālayavijñāna*. The *bījas* that project the constituents of the psycho-physical organism (the *skandha-āyatanadhātus*), which when developed into the sevenfold phenomenal consciousness are capable of creating within the *Ālaya* new and dynamic impressions (new *bījas*) of wisdom or ignorance, are themselves not created. Therefore, both the universal *bījas* (consciousness projected as the objective forms of the empirical universe) and the non-universal *bījas* (consciousness projected as the sevenfold phenomenal consciousness and its supporting sense faculties and physical body) are the natural self-determinations of the *Ālayavijñāna*.

What is important to clarify is that although the *Ālaya* as the universal grounding consciousness of human individuality innately contains the *bījas* developing into the form of human consciousness, each individual consciousness possesses the freedom to create itself. Within the predetermined forms of *manas*, *manovijñāna*, and the sensorial consciousnesses, grounded upon the *Ālaya* and supported by the physical body and the larger universe, human subjectivity can transform itself through every activity of body, voice, and mind. These latter are actually volitions (*cetanās*) which, as modes of consciousness, leave their impressions (*bījas*) within the fundamental consciousness of the *Ālaya* to become potential sources of future activities of the same moral category as the activities that originally impressed them. It is these impressions or unique and personal non-universal *bījas* that determine the sense faculties and the physical body of the next rebirth, as will be explained below.

Although the phenomenal consciousness which is capable of creating new impressions within the *Ālaya* is itself born of innate *bijas* of that fundamental and absolute consciousness, the priority of those innate *bījas* is merely logical and not temporal. In actuality, there is a simultaneous, reciprocal causality eternally existing between the *bījas* that engender the basic structure of the phenomenal consciousness and the consciousness itself which immediately creates and stimulates new impressions (*bījas*) which in turn sustain the functioning of consciousness. Revolving cyclically from all time, those ideal, archetypal self-determinations (*bījas*) of the *Ālaya* and the forms of the phenomenal consciousness evolving from them are mutually cause and effect, "just as a candle-wick engenders the flame and the flame engenders the incandescence of the wick."[15]

Thus far explanation has been given only for the origin of the form or basic structure of the phenomenal consciousness. Once evolved, it defines itself through the spontaneous and continuous dynamics of self-transformation. The *Ch'eng Wei-Shih Lun* explains this process in the context of "the perfumable" and "the perfumer". The latter is the collective designation for the *manas*, *manovijñāna*, and the five sensorial consciousnesses in their function of either strengthening and renewing, or mitigating old impressions and creating new ones within the *Ālaya*, referred to as "the perfumable". As the universal ground of the phenomenal consciousness, the *Ālaya* is the non-defined and neutral medium capable of receiving and retaining the seeds or creative, residual impressions from every thought, feeling, or deed originated as the volitions of the empirical consciousness. The *Ālaya* as the noetic determination of Absolute Suchness is the primal consciousness, and thus it is the sheer presupposition for the development of both wisdom and ignorance. Every activity of the phenomenal

15. Hsüan Tsang, *Ch'eng Wei-Shih Lun*, p. 133.

consciousness, good or bad, pure or impure, leaves its impression within the *Ālaya* where it remains as a habitual, dynamic presence, a persistent tendency to manifest itself in the form of the empirical consciousness that produced it. And that is what happens, because these impressions (*bījas*) "which possess a superior power of activity" spontaneously engender and animate those particular modes of actual consciousness which had created or nurtured them. The *Ālaya* or that which is perfumed, the *bījas* or perfuming impressions, and the empirical consciousness or that which perfumes or impresses, are simultaneously present to each other, being neither identical to nor different from one another; differing in form and function, they are essentially mere-consciousness (*vijñaptimātratā*), consciousness in a state of constant self-manifestation and self-transformation (*pariṇāma*).

This tri-partite self-modification of consciousness is formally termed *hetupariṇāma* and refers to the two forms of psychic energy (*vāsanā*) stored in the *Ālaya*. The "similar efflux energy" (*niṣyanda-vāsanā*) represents the creative influence of every act of body, voice, and mind originating from the phenomenal consciousness. Abiding within the *Ālaya* as seed-like impressions, these *bījas* are instantaneous and momentary (*kṣaṇika*), perishing as soon as they are born. Yet, each one possesses a dynamic efficacy whereby it produces another *bīja* similar to itself, and thus the residual impressions persist within the *Ālaya* in a continuous, homogeneous, uninterrupted series. Depending upon their various strengths and weaknesses and certain other conditioning factors (*pratyayas*),[16] these unmanifest tendencies can then engender and animate the same acts of empirical consciousness (good, evil, or indifferent, pure or impure volitions which prompt physical deeds, produce speech or elicit mental deliberations and judgements) that had created or nurtured them. With this similar efflux energy as the fundamental "condition quā cause" (*hetūpratyaya*),[17]

16. "To realize their capacity to produce an actual dharma, the Bījas require a concourse of conditions. This definition rules out the cause called 'spontaneity' admitted by certain Tīrthikas, i.e., the cause which engenders its fruit spontaneously without depending on any conditions...This definition shows that, since the conditions are not always present, the Bīja does not produce its fruit at all times and all at once." Ibid., pp. 127-29.

17. According to the text, causality is of consciousness-only and is defined by the combination of four principal conditioning factors (*pratyayas*). The

the phenomenal consciousness as grounded upon the *Ālaya*, becomes manifest and qualitatively determined; as such they (the sevenfold constituents of phenomenal consciousness) are called *niṣyandaphala*, they are the fruit or effect of their own *bījas* (thus the designation, "similar efflux"). Therefore, at any one particular moment, the moral quality of an individual's mind and the activities (physical or mental) that are produced by it is primarily a function of the residual impressions (*bījas*) created by the immediately preceding state of empirical consciousness, or by those impressions registered by any past state of consciousness. No matter how remote, they all remain within the *Ālaya* as a habitual dynamic presence, spontaneously self-regenerative in a perpetual series of instantaneous moments, actively predisposed to manifest themselves once again as moments of empirical consciousness.

The constant self-modification of consciousness then, includes the unceasing self-propagation of the subliminal contents of the *Ālaya* (every particular residual impression or *bīja* regenerates itself); the increase and thus amplification of the force of certain subliminal impressions through repeated similar experiences of the empirical consciousness; the creation of new impressions through novel experiences of the empirical consciousness; the manifestation and the persistence of any particular mode of empi-

---

fundamental condition quā cause (*hetūpratyaya*) are both the *bījas* or creative residual impressions within the *Ālaya*, and the sevenfold forms of the phenomenal consciousness (the *manas*, *manovijñāna* and the five sensorial consciousnesses) which engender them, and are in turn engendered. The condition quā antecedent (*samānāntara pratyaya*) represents the preceeding moment of each of the eight consciousnesses as the condition for the emergence of the succeeding moment, given that the *Ālaya* and the sevenfold empirical consciousness are momentary. The condition quā perceived object (*ālambana pratyaya*) is the particular *dharma*, upon which the mind (the eight consciousnesses) is based, and which is perceived and known by the mind. The condition quā contributory factor (*adhipatipratyaya*) represents any *dharma* that is capable of promoting or counteracting the evolution of another *dharma*; essentially, it refers to any of the twenty-two organs or powers (*indriyas*) that contribute to the activities of consciousness (e.g., the five sense organs, the two sexual organs, the five moral powers, etc., all of which are ultimately the forms of consciousness-only). The existence of any particular *dharma* is dependent, therefore, upon the particular combination of these four conditioning factors, the estential nature of which is mere-consciousness (*vijñaptimātratā*). See Ibid., pp. 535-51.

rical consciousness, through the accumulated force of the subliminal tendencies identical to it, accompanied by the proper combination of other conditioning factors.

If the similar efflux energy and fruit (*niṣyandavāsanā* and *niṣyandaphala*) describe the self-transformation of consciousness over the course of one lifetime, the retributive energy (*vipākavāsanā*) stored in the *Ālaya* accounts for the continuity of consciousness (the phenomenal consciousness grounded on the *Ālaya*) through the successive rebirths. When death intervenes, the activity of *vipākavāsanā* forces the *Ālaya* into a new stream, beginning from the next birth of the individual. It represents the accumulated force of all impure impressions engendered by the impure deeds of the *manovijñāna* and the five sensorial consciousnesses from all past incarnations. Specifically, it is the collective impressions from what are called the *ākṣepaka deeds* that determine whether the *Ālaya* of the new rebirth will belong to that of a human being, a god, a ghost, etc., while the impressions from the *paripūraka deeds* account for the general development of the *manovijñāna* and the sensorial consciousnesses that complement it. What is important to note is that those impressions that "project" the *Ālaya* (*ākṣepaka*) into a new stream and those that "complete" it (*paripūraka*) with the other six consciousnesses, are those non-universal and uniquely personal *bījas* created throughout the totality of one's past rebirths by every activity of body, voice, and mind, originating from the individual empirical consciousness. It can now be understood that when the text stated that it is from the non-universal *bījas* of the *Ālaya* that the sense faculties and the physical body evolve, they do so in correspondence with, and as the supporting basis for, the phenomenal consciousness "projected" at the end of one lifetime into a new one.

It has been necessary to detail the complex dynamics of the non-universal and universal *bījas* in order to validate the ontic status of the phenomenal universe and of the empirical human consciousness as paratantric realities. They are the radically ideal manifestations or transformations (*pariṇāma*) from within the *Ālayavijñāna*, the noetic determination of Absolute Suchness (*Tathatā*). It is only when they are falsely considered to be self-subsistent particularities, independent of consciousness, that they are designated as mere imaginations (*parikalpita*). Collectively, the forms of the phenomenal universe and of human individuality are the images (*nimitta*) in and through which *Tathatā* appears to, and recognizes itself. Since the structure of the phenomenal consciousness (the *manas*, *manovijñāna*, and the five sensorial consciousnesses) evolves from immanent, archetypal self-patternings of the absolute consciousness (i.e., from beginningless time, the form of human subjectivity pre-exists as the *innate bījas* of the *Ālayavijñāna*), and since that phenomenal consciousness exists as the differentiated identity of the absolute consciousness,[18] the perceptions of the phenomenal consciousness are the perceptions of the *Ālaya*. It is this perceptive activity of *manas*, *manovijñāna* and the five *pravṛtti-vijñānas* that must now be analyzed.

18. It has been said of the *bījas* that they are neither identical nor different from the *Ālaya* nor from the empirical consciousness which they engender. See Ibid., p. 109. Likewise, "the perfumed consciousness" (the *Ālaya*) and "the perfuming consciousness" (the sevenfold empirical consciousness) were said to be simultaneous with, and mutually present to, each other and thus, neither identical nor different from one another. See Ibid., pp. 131-33. Finally it is stated:

"The eight consciousnesses cannot, in their essential natures, be said to be definitely one (i.e., forming a single whole). This is because their modes of activity, the conditioning causes on which they depend, and their associated qualities are different....At the same time they are not definitely different (i.e., being separate units), for, as is noted in the sūtra (*Laṅkāvatāra*), the eight consciousnesses are like the waves which cannot be differentiated from the water. This is because, if they were definitely different, they could not be as cause and effect to one another." Ibid., p. 499.

CHAPTER X

THE *ĀLAYAVIJÑĀNA* AND IGNORANCE

ĀTMAGRĀHA AND DHARMAGRĀHA

THROUGHOUT THE *Ch'eng Wei-Shih Lun*, the manifestation of ignorance is said to assume two primordial forms: the tenacious belief in the reality of an independent, autonomous ego (*ātmagrāha*), and the even more radical adherence to the notion of discrete, self-subsistent particularities or things-in-themselves (*dharmagrāha*). The former gives rise to "the barrier of vexing passions" (*kleśāvaraṇa*), consisting of six fundamental passions (*mūlakleśas*), and twenty secondary ones (*upakleśas*), the nuanced forms of the primary six.[1]

Dharmagrāha on the other hand, is the basis for "the barrier impeding supreme enlightenment and hindering absolute knowledge" (*jñeyāvaraṇa*). The consideration of any reality (*dharma*) as a self-sufficient entity, essentially distinct from all other realities and independent of consciousness, would constitute a barrier of ignorance, a hindrance to perfect knowledge. Translated into the metaphysics of mere-consciousness (*vijñaptimātratā*), *jñeyāvaraṇa* is any moment of empirical consciousness that fails to perceive the mutual interdependence of all phenomena in their ultimate dependence as the forms of absolute consciousness (*Ālayavijñāna*). In every instance in which the mind misapprehends the dependent reality of *Paratantra* for an unconditional thing-in-itself, it is a barrier to absolute knowledge; *jñeyāvaraṇa* is thus equivalent to the false imagination of *parikalpita*.[2]

Of critical significance is the twofold origin of both *ātmagrāha* and *dharmagrāha*. On the one hand, there is the extrinsic influence

1. The ten fundamental vexing passions (*mūlakleśas*) and the twenty secondary vexing passions (*upakleśas*) are listed in appendix 2.

2. While this is the specific definition of *jñeyāvaraṇa* (see Hsüan Tsang, *Ch'eng Wei-Shih Lun*, p. 671), it is also used in the more general sense to indicate various states of ignorance, blocking the Bodhisattva's progress through the ten stages (*bhūmis*) of the path. The barriers of ignorance (*jñeyāvaraṇas*) peculiar to each of the ten *bhūmis* are listed in appendix 2.

of erroneous teachings, purporting the reality of the self (*ātman*) and independent particularity (*dharma*). Since it is the faculty of ideal conceptualization, the *manovijñāna,* adverting to such teachings, constructs mental images or ideas of the supposed *ātman* and/ or *dharmas* to which, through discrimination and speculation, it adheres as real. So for instance, hearing of the elements and categories of *Sāṅkhya* philosophy or of *Hinayāna* doctrine, the *manovijñāna* transforms these into imaged concepts, and through sustained reflection upon and consideration of them comes to accept them as real, and as such attaches itself to them. This form of belief in selfhood and individuality is said to be caused by mental discrimination; the *manovijñāna* responds to teachings about the *ātman* and *dharmas* by forming ideas and concepts of them and adhering to them as veridical facts. This adherence in turn creates a residual impression (*bīja*) within the *Ālaya*, where it remains as a dynamic tendency, subliminally reinforcing the erroneous attachment of the *manovijñāna*, and thus predisposing it towards repeated similar responses.

The Manas and Manovijñāna

In addition to the accessory condition of teachings arising from various external sources, there is an innate, "natural" belief in the reality of an autonomous ego and independent things-in-themselves. From beginningless time, the *manas* as well as the *manovijñāna* instrinsically assumes the existence of the *ātman* and *dharma,* individual selfhood and thinghood. While the *Ch'eng Wei-Shih Lun* maintains an initial distinction between innate *ātmagrāha* and innate *dharmagrāha,* it is obviously more scholastic than essential. The attention of the text quickly focuses upon innate *ātmagrāha* which is in fact, but a more specific form of *dharmagrāha.*[3] And while *ātmagrāha* is attributed to both the *manas* and

3. Innate *dharmagrāha* is defined as the spontaneous activity of the *manas*, forming "a mental image" or idea about the *Ālayavijñāna* "to which it adheres as a real *dharma*." Hsüan Tsang, *Ch'eng Wei-Shih Lun*, p. 89. While this is a constant and continuous activity, there is an occasional *dharmagrāha* involving the *manovijñāna*. Whenever it directs its attention to the *skandha-āyatana-dhātus* and "produces from them a mental image to which it adheres as a real

manovijñāna, the latter's error is but a derivative of the primordial, innate attachment which defines the *manas*. This essential constituent of phenomenal human consciousness, without which the knowledge from the five sensorial consciousnesses and the *manovijñāna* would remain inchoate and non-functional,[4] is intrinsically accompanied by (*sahita*) a fourfold ignorance.

Evolving out of and grounded upon it, the *manas* has a constant and spontaneous awareness of the *Ālayavijñāna*. But instead of recognizing it as the unconditional reality, the universal absolute consciousness, the generic animating principle of all sentient beings, the *manas* appropriates it as the determinate center of its own, discrete self-identity (the *ātman*). It does so through the influence of an ignorance unique to it (*āveṇikī avidyā*) and perpetually continuous (*nityācarini*) with it since beginningless time. Specifically, this cardinal ignorance is self-delusion or *ātman*-ignorance (*ātmamoha*) which, obscuring the genuine nature of the *Ālaya* and hindering the wisdom of egolessness (*nairātmya*), induces the *manas* to adhere to the *Ālaya* as a substantial nucleus of personal identity. With this explicit self-belief (*ātmadṛṣṭi*), there is a correspondent self-conceit (*ātmamāna*) and self-love (*ātmasneha*), in which the *manas* considers itself superior and lofty to all others in its possession of a unique selfhood, to which it develops a profound attachment.

---

dharma", there is erroneous attachment. Ibid. An identical procedure defines innate *ātmagrāha*. The only difference is that the *manas* adheres to its mental image or idea of the *Ālaya* "as though there were a real *ātman*" and the *manovijñāna* similarly clings to its image of the five tenacious aggregates (*upādānaskandhas*) "as though there were a real *ātman*". Ibid., p. 21. The innate attachments of both the *manas* and *manovijñāna* to the idea of self-subsistent individuality (*dharmagrāha*) is merely specified in a more determinate form when they misinterpret the *Ālaya* or the *skandhas* to be a center of independent, unique personality. The basic non-distinction between *ātmagrāha* and *dharmagrāha* is explicitly noted by the text in a later section where it points out that whenever there is the belief in the imaginary *ātman* there is necessarily an implicit belief in the reality of individual things-in-themselves (*dharmas*); the former takes the latter as its supporting basis. See Ibid., p. 673.

4. The raw sense data of the sensorial consciousnesses is unified into intelligible form by the *manovijñāna*, the faculty of ideal conceptualisation. But it is the *manas* that systematically categorizes this information and acts upon it, pondering, calculating and directing means to specific ends. As the center of personal identity "it supplies the requisite element of stability which makes discursive knowledge possible." See Catterjee, *Yogācāra Idealism*, p. 104.

These four rudimentary vexing passions (*kleśas*) are complemented by an additional eight subsidiary passions (*upakleśas*).[5] The text leaves no doubt as to the critical significance of this ignorance which inherently distorts the *manas'* perception of the *Ālayavijñāna,* and thus the perfect self-awareness of Absolute Suchness (*Tathatā*):

> The Pṛthagjanas [ordinary, unenlightened beings] ... whether their mind is good, bad or non-defined, always produce an avidyā called *āveṇikī*, which causes errors in the understanding of right principles, obscures Bhūtatathatā, and obstructs the eye of Transcendental Wisdom or Prajñā. Thus one gatha from the *Mahāyāna-saṃparigrahaśāstra* says: "When the Mind of Reality is about to be born, it is always obscured and obstructed by something which actively operates at all times; it is the *āveṇikī avidyā.*"..., since before the beginning of time, this avidyā has always been stupefying and bewildering the mind, resulting in its failure to realize Ultimate Reality. This failure is entirely due to the powerful nature of self-delusion... The avidyā associated with manas has been in action at all times since before the beginning of time, impeding the manifestation of the supreme intelligence of Bhūtatathatā. Such an important function is lacking in the avidyā of the other consciousnesses. This avidyā that belongs exclusively to the seventh consciousness (*manas*) is called *āvenikī.*[6]

Because the *manas* is the supporting basis (*āśraya*) of the *manovijñāna* and the five sensorial consciousnesses, its persistent misapprehension of the *Ālaya* decisively nuances their own perceptive functions; *ātmagrāha,* having its inception in the *manas,* pervasively dominates the whole structure of phenomenal consciousness. Basing itself upon the *Yogacaryābhūmiśāstra,* the text describes

5. Of the six fundamental *mūlakleśas,* these four that are peculiar to *manas* incorporate delusion (*moha*), conceit (*māna*), and erroneous views (*kudṛṣṭi*). Of the twenty secondary vexing passions, the eight associated with the *manas* are: torpidmindedness (*styāna*); agitation (*auddhatya*); unbelief (*āśraddhya*); indolence (*kausīdya*); thoughtlessness; forgetfulness (*muṣitasmṛtitā*); distraction (*vikṣepa*), and nondiscernment (*asaṃprajanya*). See Hsüan Tsang, *Ch'eng Wei-Shih Lun,* pp. 291-303.

6. Ibid., pp. 323-25.

this condition of human consciousness as "the binding or entrammelling of the perception-aspect (*darśanabhāga*) of the mind by the image-aspect (*nimittabhāga*) with the result that deliverance or emancipation cannot be attained... It consists in our inability to understand the true nature and character of external objects as having the same mode of existence as illusions and mirages."[7] This briefly noted, non-elaborated passage translates the error of the *manas*' attachment to egohood and thinghood (*ātmagrāha* and *dharmagrāha*) and the subsequent attachment of the *manovijñāna* and the sensorial consciousnesses, into the broader question of perception and objectivity.

It will be recalled that the sole reality of consciousness (*vijñapti-mātratā*) manifests itself as the bipolar unity of that which perceives (*darśanabhāga*) and that which is perceived (*nimittabhāga*). More specifically, the *Ālayavijñāna* determines itself into the forms of the phenomenal universe and of human subjectivity. These thoroughly ideal transformations of the *Ālaya* are collectively known as its image aspect (*nimittabhāga*), and it is in relation to this objective dimension of itself (*ālambana*) that the *Ālaya* defines its subjectivity. For, it continually perceives those self-manifested images (*nimitta*); this subjective pole of the *Ālaya* is known as its perception or vision aspect (*darśanabhāga*). Now, if the *Ālaya* is to know itself perfectly *in* the universal extension of its self-manifested forms, it also comes to that self-recognition *through* certain of those forms, viz., the sevenfold phenomenal consciousness.

As previously demonstrated, the *manas, manovijñāna,* and the five sense *vijñānas,* having evolved from immanent, archetypal self-patternings of the absolute consciousness (the innate *bījas* of the *Ālaya*), become the faculties through which it perceives itself in the multiplicity of its forms. For, the seven modalities of human consciousness share a common function of perception; the *manas* perceives the *Ālaya*, the *manovijñāna* perceives the *manas* and the sensorial consciousnesses, which in turn perceive the elements of the material universe. Depending upon the interpretation accorded those perceptions,[8] the perfect self-awareness of the *Ālaya* is realiz-

7. Ibid., p. 333.

8. This interpretative function belongs only to the *manas* and *manovijñāna* as the consciousnesses of deliberation, speculation and imagination. The

ed or hindered. In the broadest sense then, "the binding or entrammelling of the perception-aspect (*darśanabhāga*) of the mind by the image-aspect (*nimittabhāga*)" can refer to the fact that the self-perception of the *Ālaya* is dependent upon and at times constricted by, human consciousness whose seven-fold structures are ultimately the self-transformed appearances (*nimitta*) of the (*Ālaya*) itself. But in the context of the *manas'* innate *ātmagrāha*, a more exact interpretation may be rendered.

As a mode of consciousness, the *manas* itself has an image aspect (*nimittabhāga*) and a perception aspect (*darśanabhāga*). Due to the intrinsic delusion unique to it (*āveṇikī avidyā*), the *manas*' continual perception of the *Ālayavijñāna* is fettered by its attachment to it as an *ātman*; its conception of the *Ālaya* as an independent ego (i.e., its image-aspect or perceived-aspect, *nimittabhāga*) distorts and thus "entrammels" its perception-aspect (*darśanabhāga*). This dominant belief in the reality of autonomous selfhood is spontaneously adopted by the *manovijñāna*, grounded upon and conscious of the *manas*. Its collateral perception of the five sensorial consciousnesses and their corresponding sense organs is subsequently hampered by its implicit assumption of their independent self-subsistence; under the sway of the *manas*, defiled by ignorance, the *manovijñāna* instinctively imputes an ego identity to the constituents of the phenomenal personality. In addition, its function of organizing the raw sense data apprehended by the sense consciousnesses into forms of intelligibility, is over-shadowed by its adherence to the idea of self-hood. The objects of the physical universe constituted by it through the mediation of the sense consciousnesses, are invested by the *manovijñāna* with a similar degree of self-reality. If the psycho-physical organism is a discrete, self-determining center of unique identity (an *ātman*), it is so, over and against a plurality of similarly unrelated egos and a world of unconnected, self-standing objects and things (*dharmas*). When the text referred above to "our inability to understand the true nature and character of external objects as having the same mode of

---

sensorial *vijñānas* are without cogitation and have the simple task of perception; the *manovijñāna* interprets and provides the intelligibility of the raw sense data apprehended by them. The *manas* instinctively speculates upon and applies an interpretation for the *Ālaya* which it continously perceives. See Ibid., p. 627.

existence as illusions and mirages", it is this peculiar misconception of the *manovijñāna* that is meant. Rather than perceiving the sense consciousnesses, sense organs and sense objects as the self-manifested forms of the *Ālayavijñāna,* the sixth consciousness, pervaded by the *manas*' appropriation of the *Ālaya* as an independent self-entity, becomes ensnared by the self-reality it in turn attributes to them; its *nimittabhāga* "binds or entrammels" its *darśanabhāga.*

In summary, the *Ch'eng Wei-Shih Lun* identifies an erroneous sense of exteriority as the specific dynamic through which the *manovijñāna* invests the objects perceived by the sensorial consciousnesses with the illusion of independent reality. They are not external to, but the manifest forms of, consciousness; they are the proximate perceived aspect (*nimittabhāga*) of the sensorial consciousnesses, and through their mediation, of the *manovijñāna*:

> When the external spheres are apprehended through immediate perception, they are not regarded as external. It is only later that Manovijñāna, through its discrimination, erroneously creates the notion of externality. Thus, the objective spheres immediately apprehended are 'the perceived division' (*nimitta-bhāga*) of the consciousnesses themselves. Since they are manifestations of consciousness, we say they exist.
> But inasmuch as they are regarded by Manovijñāna as constituting external and real matter, etc., and are thus erroneously imagined to be existent, we say they are nonexistent. Furthermore, objective spheres of color and so forth are not colors though they seem to be so, and are not external, though they seem to be so. They are like objects in a dream, which cannot be regarded as real and external.[9]

All this can be expressed quite succinctly in the metaphysics of mere-consciousness (*vijñaptimātratā*). Genuine Suchness (*Bhūta-tathatā*) is equivalent to the ultimately real, self-subsistent absolute (*Pariniṣpanna*) which can know itself as the indeterminate, unconditional nature of all things because they are the radically ideal manifestations or transformations (*pariṇāma*) from within itself, noetically conceived as absolute consciousness (*Ālayavijñāna*). The

9. Ibid., p. 521.

structures of the material universe and of the phenomenal human consciousness meaningfully cohere through the mutual interdependence of various conditioning factors (*pratyayas*), whose ultimate reality are the innate self-determinations (the *bījas*) of the *Ālaya*. Commenting upon a stanza of Vasubandhu's *Vijñaptimātratāsiddhitriṃśikā*, the text stresses the *bījas* as the primary causal factor:

> If only consciousness exists, without any external causation, from what are generated the many kinds of distinction (e.g., the eight consciousnesses, the associated mental activities, the two Bhāgas, the unassociated mental activities)? The stanza says: "From the consciousness which contains all bījas, such-and-such evolution or transformation takes place. Through the force of the mutual cooperation of the actual dharmas, such-and-such kinds of distinction are engendered." By "consciousness which contains all bījas" are meant the various powers and potentials (bījas) in the root consciousness (Mūlavijñāna or Ālayavijñāna) which are capable of engendering spontaneously their own fruits (i.e., all conditioned dharmas, saṃskṛta)... The stanza, employing the term *sarvabīja*, considers the bījas in their immediate casuality, which is to produce all kinds of distinction, all saṃskṛtas, all paratantras.[10]

The *manas* and *manovijñāna* fail to perceive that their own status is dependently originated and sustained by the universal grounding consciousness of the *Ālayavijñāna*. Their principle of subjectivity, while authentic, is conditional and secondary; they are formally *paratantra*. But under the influence of the *manas'* innate *ātmagrāha*, they misrepresent the consciousness upon which they are contingent (the *Ālaya*) as the validation of their own ultimacy and independence; they appropriate it as a function of their own ignorant attachment. Their faulty self-regard spontaneously affects their interpretation of all other persons and things as constituting a world of unrelated egos (*ātmans*) and discrete particularities (*dharmas*). This falsely imagined isolation and self-sufficiency

10. Ibid., p. 529. In addition to the phenomenal consciousness, the three other conditioning factors ultimately derive from the *bījas* of the *Ālaya*. See chapter nine, n. 17, pp. 208-09 above.

(*parikalpita*), arises from the *manas'* failure to perceive the universal extension of the *Ālayavijñāna* as the grounding principle of *all* phenomena, the thoroughly ideal manifestations and transformations of which, they are. As long as this fundamental misapprehension remains the dominant mental horizon informing all acts of consciousness which prompt physical deeds, produce speech, or elicit deliberation and judgement, those acts are rendered impure and defiled. Despite its inherent excellence, the practice of the moral perfections (*pāramitās*), including the various meditations and contemplations, is all too often tainted by the *manas*' persistent belief in an independent and unique selfhood; the aspirant frequently devotes himself to such virtuous activities, animated by the subtle desire for self-advancement on the spiritual path.[11]

In its involved discussion of the twelve links (*dvādaśāṅgas*) of conditioned co-production, the *Ch'eng Wei-Shih Lun* clearly identifies *ātmagrāha* and *dharmagrāha* as the primary causal delusions in the saṃsāric chain of birth-death-birth. This bifocal ignorance manifests itself on the one hand through the *manas*' erroneous misapprehension of the *Ālayavijñāna* as the center of independent, personal self-identity (the *ātman*). As stated above, all deeds initiated as conscious volitions (*cetanākarman*) expressed through the body, the voice, or the mind under the pervasive influence of such delusion (*ātmagrāha* as *avidyāṅga*) become the accumulated force of active predispositions (*saṃskārāṅga*). These remain as subliminal tendencies (*bījas*) within the *Ālayavijñāna,* and at the moment of physical death they "project" (*ākṣepaka*) it (i.e., the *Ālaya* as the *vijñānāṅga*) along with its innate *bījas* of names and forms

11. "Pṛthagjanas [ordinary, unenlightened beings] have thoughts of three natures (good, bad, and non-defined). While externally producing, by the power of the first six consciousnesses, various acts of a corresponding nature, they produce, internally and in a continuous manner, through the influence of Manas, Ātmagrāha, adhering to their Ātman. Because of this Ātmagrāha, all their actions through the six consciousnesses, such as their practice of the Six Pāramitās,...are not free from...attachment to the image-aspect of the mind....As with Pṛthagjanas, so will it be with Śaikṣas (ascetics who have not yet attained Arhatship); their thoughts, even those that are good, are impure because their Manas or seventh consciousness is defiled or tainted by Ātmagrāha. The impure dharmas of Aśaiksas (Arhats), although not accompanied by impurities, proceed from past, impure Bījas and are, for this reason, impure....Good dharmas etc., are rendered impure by a Manas which, without cessation, produces Ātmagrāha." Ibid., pp. 333-37.

(*nāmarūpāṅga*, i.e., the four non-material *skandhas* and the *rūpa-skandhas*); the six sense organs (*sadāyatanānga*); touch or contact (*sparśāṅga*); and sensation or feeling (*vedanāṅga*) into a new birth (*jātyaṅga*).[12]

On the other hand, in its collateral "outward" focus upon the objects of the phenomenal universe, through the natural orientation of the *manovijñāna*, ignorance falsely represents them as discrete particularities, independent from one another and from consciousness. This coordinate form of ignorance which fails to perceive the true nature of things (*dharmagrāhạ* as *avidyāṅga*) spontaneously leads to a craving-thirst and desire (*tṛṣṇāṅga*) and subsequently to the four graspings or clingings (*upādānāṅga*).[13] These two "links" in the chain of causation embody all the vexing passions (*kleśas*) whose cumulative residual impressions (*bījas*) habitually "moisten" (i.e., powerfully reinforce and exacerbate) the projecting influence of the subliminal predispositions (the *bījas* of the *saṃskāras*) arising from *ātmagrāha*.[14] Thus it is that a new existence (*bhavāṅga*) becomes actualised and progressively determined through the stages of birth (*jātyaṅga*) and old age-death (*jaramaranāṅga*).

12. The difference between the *saṃskārāṅga* and the *aṅgas* of *vijñāna*, *nāmarūpa*, *ṣaḍāyatana*, *sparśa* and *vedanā* is a working example of the difference between *bījas*. While the *bījas* of *saṃskārāṅga* are created and impressed upon the *Ālaya* by every act of empirical consciousness, the *bījas* of the other five *aṅgas* exist as the natural self-determinations of the *Ālaya* which, when manifest, become the constituents of the psycho-physical organism. See Ibid., p. 595 and also pp. 205-208 above.

13. Clinging to desire (*kāmopādāna*); clinging to ideas arising from the conception of *ātman* (*ātmavadopādāna*); clinging to erroneous views (*dṛṣṭyupādāna*); and clinging to false moral precepts (*śilavratopādāna*). See Hsüan Tsang, *Ch'eng Wei-Shih Lun*, p. 591.

14. Since it had already been established that *ātmagrāha* is the source of the vexing passions (*kleśas*) (see p. 213 above), the distinction here between *ātmagrāha* as that which produces impure deeds (*karma*), and *dharmagrāha* as that which augments and moistens them through *kleśas*, is an artificial, schematic one. K'uei Chi points out that in fact, both forms of ignorance lead to defiled activity, and that each is the auxiliary of the other in "moistening" or amplifying their impure effects, occasioning rebirth. "In reality, the delusion respecting the internal mundane suffering [a technical reference to the failure of perceiving the genuine nature of the *Ālayavijñāna*] also moistens birth. The delusion respecting the external objects also produces deeds." Ibid., p. 591 Likewise see p. 595.

The Ultimate Origin of Ignorance

While the text's implication of the *manas* and subsequently the *manovijñāna* in saṃsāric causality is abundantly clear, a subtle qualification must be noted. Ignorance, in the form of *ātmagrāha* and *dharmagrāha*, is inherently associated with (*saṃprayukta*), but not exhaustively definitive of these two constituents of human consciousness; *avidyā* is only an associated mental activity (*caitta*), not the essential nature (*svabhāva*) nor the essential mode of activity (*ākāra*) of either the *manas* or the *manovijñāna*. Cogitation or intellection is both the essential nature and mode of activity of the *manas*. It is a permanent condition which specifies the *manas* after, as well as before, the psychic transformation of *āśrayaparāvṛtti*; what changes is its object (*ālambana*), not its *svabhāva* or *ākāra:*

> Manas, when it has not been "revolutionized" (*aparāvṛtti*), has as its object the Ālayavijñāna only. When revolution or inner transformation has been achieved, it has its object, besides the eighth consciousness, also the Bhūtatathatā and the other dharmas... When it has not yet been revolutionized it constantly meditates and cogitates upon the supposed ātman; after the revolution (*parāvṛtta*) it meditates and cogitates also upon nairātmya, i.e., egolessness.[15]

Unlike the *Laṅkāvatāra Sūtra,* the *Ch'eng Wei-Shih Lun* clearly distinguishes ignorance as a qualified condition (viz., a *caitta*) rather than the absolute state of the phenomenal consciousness.[16] While in the former scripture, the cognitive processes of the *manas*-

15. Ibid., pp. 283-287.

16. The determinate nature of the associated mental activity (*caitta*) is clarified by Chatterjee; they do not exhaust the essence of consciousness, but are only temporal phases and subsidiary aspects of it:

"In early Buddhism, these [*caittas*] were really distinct realities, besides the one contentless citta. They were ultimate existents, independent and absolute. Here, [in the Yogācāra] on the other hand, they are merely the phases in which the complexity of consciousness is exhibited. They are so many hues as it were, radiated by the prismatic consciousness...In early Buddhism one moment of consciousness is constituted by the moments of citta *and* the appropriate caittas: in the Yogācāra, it is merely one unitary moment in which different aspects however can be distinguished." *The Yogācāra Idealism,* p. 113.

manovijñāna are radicaly compromised as originated by *avidyā*, the latter text preserves their integrity as the innate self-determinations (*bījas*) of the *Ālayavjiñāna* through which it perceives itself in the universality of its self-manifested forms; *manas* is the essential basis and the necessary faculty for the Universal Equality Wisdom (*Samatājñāna*) which perceives the identity of all *dharmas* and the non-distinction of all sentient beings, while the *manovijñāna* is the consciousness through which the Profound Contemplation Wisdom (*Pratyavekṣaṇājñāna*) discerns their unique as well as their common characteristics.

In the *Ch'eng Wei-Shih Lun*, the status of ignorance has been clearly altered. Rather than the cause of phenomenal individuation, as stipulated by the *Laṅkāvatāra*, *avidyā* is sequential to, and a subsidiary mode of human consciousness. Likewise, though the *manas* is originally deluded by innate *ātmamoha* (self-delusion), it is not by that fact, itself essentially delusive; it may well be the vehicle through which ignorance is manifested and perpetuated, but it is not its elemental source and productive cause. Just as the structure of the phenomenal human consciousness originates and assumes its sevenfold form from the innate self-determinations (*bījas*) of the absolute consciousness, so too does the ignorance which accompanies it germinally develop from within the very ground of the *Ālayavijñāna*; it does so along with the innate seeds (*bījas*) of wisdom and virtue:

> The Ālayavijñāna contains both pure and impure seeds. The pure seeds spontaneously produce pure dharmas or things, and the impure seeds impure dharmas. Thus, from the Ālaya are produced all dharmas, pure and impure alike, and these in turn react upon the Ālaya by "perfuming" it.... The Ālayavijñāna and the impure dharmas interact on one another as cause and effect, ... It is only through these two (the Ālaya and the impure dharmas) that causality is established. There need be no other causality. Precisely the same process of reciprocal causation also operates between the Ālaya and the pure dharmas. Thus the Ālaya is in itself both cause and effect, and in itself is capable of producing all things, both pure and impure. What is the need, then, to look for external causation? The fact that all sentient beings are bound to the perpetual flux of life and death "springs

from internal causation, independent of external causes. Therefore, there is nothing but consciousness."[17]

Such a doctrine is critically significant to the entire theory of the *Tathāgatagarbha-Ālayavijñāna*. Thus far, it has been established that Absolute Suchness (*Tathatā*) can know itself as the indeterminate, unconditional nature of all things because they are the radically ideal manifestations or transformations (*pariṇāma*) from within itself, noetically conceived as absolute consciousness (*Ālayavijñāna*). It attains this plenary self-awareness in and through phenomenal human consciousness of which it is the fundamental ground and animating principle. However, instead of perceiving it as the unconditional nature (*Parinispanna*) that makes of itself and all things a totality of interdependent co-existence (*paratantra*), the human mind constricts the *Ālaya* to a mere unit of discrete personal autonomy. Rather than comprehending it as the dynamic center of a universal correlativity, the *manas* adheres to the eighth consciousness as a faculty of exclusive self-definition; as an ego it provides and sustains an impression of distinct identity only through an on-going process of differentiation. Initiated through an act of separation that posits it as a self-subsistent entity, independent of the universal absolute consciousness, human selfhood perpetuates that act by discriminating a plurality of similarly unrelated egos and a world of unconnected, self-standing objects. Instead of actualizing itself in conscious union with the *Ālayavijñāna*, the human mind projects its radical self-alienation onto all other persons and things over against which it proceeds to define itself, thereby only to reinforce that original self-estrangement.

But if the primordial self-delusion is inherent to human consciousness, it is not its sole determination. For there exists concomitant to and simultaneous with it, germinal innate wisdom which actively informs the mind through five stages of progressive illumination.[18] What is critical to recognize is that human consciousness is a product neither of ignorance nor of wisdom; its natural condition is the very interplay of their mutual presence. Human con-

17. Hsüan Tsang, *Ch'eng Wei-Shih Lun*, pp. 531-33.
18. The five stages of the holy path of attainment are listed in appendix 2.

sciousness is by nature the processive advance to an ever more perfect *self*-consciousness in which it finally awakens to the plenitude of its identity with the *Ālayavijñāna*. That the latter grounds and posits the phenomenal mind with seeds (*bījas*) of both ignorance and wisdom, specifies the mind's active self-emergence as the necessary opposition between the two. Only in the expansive illumination of wisdom, gradually dilating the restrictive vision of ignorance, does human consciousness attain the awareness of its own universality. Only against the fragmented universe of multiple, discrete, isolated persons and things, projected by *ātmagrāha* and *dharmagrāha*, can the mind begin to comprehend, and at last to utterly witness the truth of consciousness-only (*vijñāptimātratā*). The natural co-existence of ignorance and wisdom is decidedly creative, defining the context and providing the stimulus for the mind's definitive transformation in the fourfold wisdom of *Mahābodhi*.

According to the *Ch'eng Wei-Shih Lun* then, consciousness is its own becoming, and ignorance is a necessary contributive factor to that self-evolution. So far from being the problematic dualism which the obscure ontology of the *Laṅkāvatāra Sūtra* was incapable of avoiding, ignorance is here integrated into the essential dynamic through which the mind realizes itself in the omniscience of Buddhahood. Originally posited with it, ignorance is incorporated as a preliminary mode and auxiliary dimension of wisdom's movement towards perfect self-manifestation in and through the phenomenal consciousness.

Chapter XI

THE HOLY PATH OF ATTAINMENT

The Stage of Moral Provisioning

The general stages of that noetic itinerary (i.e. wisdom's movement towards perfect self-manifestation in and through the phenomenal consciousness) are discussed in the final book of the text, on the holy path of attainment. At the initial level of moral provisioning (*saṃbhārāvasthā*), the innate belief in, and attachment to the autonomous ego and its universe of isolated, disparate particularities is radical, and so instinctive that the doctrine of consciousness-only (*vijñaptimātratā*) appears totally incomprehensible. Exposure to its profundity through reading or instruction, accompanied by reflective meditation stimulates innate seeds (*bījas*) of wisdom which manifest a nascent understanding combined with deep faith. Subsequently, the novice Bodhisattva begins the cultivation of the moral virtues, and through great effort is able to inhibit the crudest of the vexing passions. However, his practice of meditation is hampered by many distracting thoughts and his concentration is weak. Since he is totally incapable of comprehending the emptiness (*śūnyatā*) of the concepts *ātman* and *dharma*, and of the absolute division between subject and object, his success in halting the passions and vices is strictly superficial; they are merely the symptoms of that more profound ignorance.

Nevertheless, the text credits this earliest stage with an incipient transformation (*āśrayaparāvṛtti*) by the very fact that there is a reduction in the active manifestation of *kleśāvaraṇa* (the barrier of vexing passions) and *jñeyāvaraṇa* (the barrier to absolute knowledge). That the *Ch'eng Wei-Shih Lun* expands the technical designation *āśrayaparāvṛtti*, generally applying it to the earliest stages of the spiritual path, rather than reserving it strictly for the moment of *Mahābodhi*, further suggests the generic interpretation of human consciousness as dynamic transformation: processive self-realization through a self-revolution in which wisdom actively opposes the disruptive, alienating attachments of ignorance.

The great dichotomy perpetuated by that ignorance and which

in turn sustains the ego's manipulative appropriations of all other persons and things, is that between subjectivity and objectivity. Failing to recognize itself and all phenomena as the immanent, ideal transformations of the absolute consciousness (the *Ālaya-vijñāna*), the human intellect misses the vital link between itself and them. It thus projects its own profound (though illusory) self-alienation upon them and proceeds to define itself over against them as isolated, autonomous persons and discrete, self-standing entities; there is an absolute gulf separating it as an independent, self-determining subject (*grāhaka*) and them as so many objects (*grāhya*) which it encounters and perceives. The human intellect, erroneously conceiving itself as an *ātman*, has therefore no essential cohesion with any other person or thing (*dharma*); their relationship as *grāhaka* and *grāhya* is strictly functional—something which "grasps" and something which "is grasped"

The Stage of Intensified Effort

In the second stage of intensified effort (*prayogavasthā*), germinal absolute wisdom having exercised itself in the stage of moral provisioning, awakens the mind to that fallacy and confirms it in the truth of consciousness-only (*vijñaptimātratā*). Through the successive influence of four meditative realizations (the *nirvedha-bhāgīyas*),[1] human consciousness understands the mutual implication and interdependence of the perceiving subject and the perceived object. There is a systematic reflection upon the names (*nāman*) and essences (*vastu*) of things, together with their self-natures (*svabhāva*) and differences (*viśeṣa*), all of which conventionally denote the unique, singular reality of the particular entities. Under scrutiny, however, the mind realizes through the first three *samādhis* that these four *dharmas* which are "grasped" as objects (*grāhyas*) are nothing but the manifestation of itself, that they exist merely as figurative designations or mental constructions, and that they are not real existences. Then, in the third *samādhi* there emerges the spontaneous recognition that if all *grāhyas* have no other reality apart from the consciousness that

1. The *nirvedhabhāgīyas* are listed and explained in appendix 2.

perceives them, it in turn has no meaning without them; consciousness without a content is meaningless:

> Since no real objects exist apart from the consciousness which takes them, how can real consciousness itself exist apart from the objects which are taken by it? For what is taken and what takes are in mutual dependence, one on the other.[2]

This conviction of the mutual implication and emptiness of subjectivity and objectivity is capable of suppressing and eliminating the influence of *ātmagrāha* and *dharmagrāha* arising from the extrinsic sources of those erroneous teachings purporting the reality of an autonomous self and equally independent, self-standing entities. It is a powerful insight into the conditional structure of reality which strongly persuades the intellect as to the illusion of any such doctrines. But as efficacious as these *samādhis* are, they are incapable of removing the residual impressions (*bījas*) which an initial adherence to those teachings created within the root consciousness (*Mūlavijñāna*, i.e. *Ālayavijñāna*) where they persist as an habitual dynamic presence, actively predisposing the empirical consciousness to a renewed explicit adherence to such doctrines.

Even less capable are those meditations to remove the primordial, inherent attachment of the *manas* and *manovijñāna* to the existence of individual selfhood and thinghood (innate *ātmagrāha* and *dharmagrāha*) and the subliminal impressions created by it and by the multiple passions (*kleśas*) arising from it. It is not sufficient then, to merely understand that the concepts of the *ātman* and *dharmas*, understood as a self-subsistent subject (*grāhaka*) which grasps at a multiplicity of similarly autonomous objects (*grāhya*), are not autonomous at all, but mutually dependent correlatives. It is not enough to indicate that the logic of the concepts, subject and object, perceiver and perceived, what grasps and what is grasped, necessarily imply and demand each other. The mind must fully comprehend not only the logical, mutual implication and relativity of the concepts, their emptiness, but must realize the ultimate, unconditional nature of that which they signify.

2. Hsüan Tsang, *Ch'eng Wei-Shih Lun*, p. 681.

Persons and things, understood through the empty concepts of *ātman* and *dharma*, *grāhaka* and *grāhya*, and thus spoken of as non-existent, actually contribute to a mutual inherence, a universal interdependence where each one implicates all the others, every one essential to the integrity of the others. Finally, the persons and things of this shared reality are ultimately dependent upon and sustained by the unconditional reality of absolute Suchness (*Tathatā*). The human mind attains its maturity in the perfect awareness of it as the fundamental, indeterminate nature of phenomenal existence. It can do so because *Tathatā*, in its noetic determination as absolute consciousness (*Ālayavijñāna*) projects those forms as the radically ideal manifestations or transformations (*pariṇāma*) from within itself. And human consciousness then, grounded upon and animated by the *Ālayavijñāna*, is able to recognize the sensible shapes and contours of phenomenal existence as the immanent developments and structured modalities, the ideal forms of Absolute Suchness. It is this recognition which begins to emerge in the fourth *samādhi*, in "the superior knowledge of Absolute Reality by which the emptiness of the two graspings is confirmed and the first worldly truth is established.... From this stage the yogin immediately and necessarily enters the *Darśanamārga* (the path of insight into Truth)."[3] Here, it is convincingly known through a radical intuition of *Tathatā* as their ultimate, essential nature, that persons and things are indeed devoid of the independent self-subsistence attributed to them as *ātman* and *dharma*; it is the experiential ratification of previous theoretical analysis.

The Stage of Unimpeded Penetrating Understanding

The *Darśanamārga* or *Prativedhāvasthā* (stage of unimpeded penetrating understanding) successfully removes all the residual impressions (*bījas*) produced by an adherence to the false speculations and erroneous teachings on the reality of the *ātman* and *dharma*. Through the psychic and ethical disciplines of the first two stages, wisdom, in exposing the fragmentation of reality

3. Ibid., p. 683.

occasioned by ignorant attachment and desire, progressively deploys its own plenitude. At this third stage of the spiritual path, it assumes the definitive mode of its future self-manifestation up to and including its perfection as *Mahābodhi*: it functions as both the non-discriminating transcendental wisdom (*nirvikalpakajñāna*) and as the wisdom subsequent to it (*pṛṣṭhalabdhajñāna*). By virtue of the first, the mind "is now said really to abide in the genuine and transcendent nature of Vijñaptimātratā, that is to say, it experiences the Bhūtatathatā (Absolute Reality). Its wisdom and the Bhūtatathatā are on the same plane, both being equally divorced from the aspects of subject and object (*grāhaka* and *grāhya*)."[4] Although further cultivation is still necessary, the realization of consciousness-only has been attained, since *nirvikalpakajñāna* signifies an immediate self-coincidence of *Tathatā* as both subject and object.

Human consciousness, thoroughly informed by and exercised in the truth of *pudgalaśūnyatā* and *dharmaśūnyatā*, is liberated from its instinctual self-attachment and no longer discriminates among the different objects of its perception. In what the text again notes as a mode of inner transformation (*āśrayaparāvṛtti*), the Universal Equality Wisdom (*Samatajñāna*), a form of *nirvikalpakajñāna*, manifests itself through the *manas* which comprehends the identity of all things and the complete equality between itself and all other sentient beings. What it perceives is the universal, essential nature common to all of them, their Absolute Suchness. Now since the *manas*, *manovijñāna*, and the five sensorial consciousnesses evolve as the self-determinations of the *Ālaya-vijñāna* (the noetic aspect of *Tathatā*), and are thus endowed with the germinal wisdom of perfect enlightenment inherent to it, their transformed perception of a multiplicity of independent, isolated persons and things to an immediate grasp of their fundamental unconditionality (their Suchness), is the self-intuition of that Absolute. Thus, it is said that the non-discriminating transcendental wisdom (*nirvikalpakajñāna*) has the perception or vision aspect (*darśanabhāga*) but no longer the perceived or image aspect (*nimittabhāga*).[5] The mind constructs no image or concept (*nimitta*) of *Tathatā*, but intuits it in a sheer immediacy.

4. Ibid., p. 687.
5. See Ibid., p. 689.

This self-intuition of *Tathatā* in and through human consciousness, transformed in the non-discriminating transcendental wisdom (*nirvikalpakajñāna*), in no way devalues the significance of phenomenal reality whose shapes and forms are the ideal transformations of *Tathatā* itself. On the path of unimpeded penetrating understanding (*Darśanamārga*), *Tathatā* not only attains a radical self-presence in which it knows itself directly as the ultimately real, self-subsistent absolute. Through a subsequent wisdom (*pṛṣṭhalabdhajñāna*), it continuously reflects upon the common and the unique characteristics (*lakṣaṇas*) of the interdependent phenomena (paratantric *dharmas*) projected by, and grounded upon it. In them it contemplates the richness of its own diversity, since this *jñāna* scrutinizes all forms, thoroughly expelling all concepts of *ātman* and *dharma* with an exact, structural analysis of reality as mere-consciousness (*vijñāptimātratā*). Up to this point, the objects of the physical universe and the components of the phenomenal personality, constituted by the *manovijñāna* through the mediation of the sense consciousnesses, had been invested by it with an erroneous autonomy. But upon entrance into the *Darśanamārga*, the *manovijñāna* is progressively transformed (*parāvṛtti*) in the Profound Contemplation Wisdom (*Pratyavekṣaṇājñāna*). This mode of *pṛṣṭhalabdhajñāna* which comprises the observation of innumerable *dhāraṇīs* and *samādhis*, acutely penetrates the apparent density and exteriority of all sensible phenomena, revealing their contingent status as the ideal self-determinations of *Tathatā*. With regard to sentient beings, it is capable of discerning their precise mental condition, and of providing them with those teachings most beneficial to their progress.

The Stage of Exercising Cultivation

In the fourth stage of the spiritual path (*Bhāvanāmārga/vasthā*) there is a continuous cultivation of *nirvikalpakajñāna* and *pṛṣṭhalabdhajñāna*, a continuous transformation of the human consciousness into the perfect wisdom of *Mahābodhi*. For, although the self-intuition of *Tathatā* had been realized on the path of unimpeded penetrating understanding (*Darśanamārga*), it remained only temporary, and interrupted by the emergence within the empirical consciousness of various forms of the primordial *ātmagrāha* and *dharmagrāha*. Those instinctive, innate attachments to the reality of autonomous selfhood and thinghood are the persistent sources of all passion (*kleśāvaraṇa*) and the most subtle as well as the crassest forms of ignorance impeding supreme enlightenment (*jñeyāvaraṇa*). While the active manifestation of these dual forces had been largely suppressed from the first stage of the spiritual path on up through the fourth, the residual impressions (*bījas*) created by them remain as dynamic subliminal tendencies within the fundamental consciousness of the *Ālayavijñāna*. Until they are thoroughly dispersed, they are capable of reappearing in explicit acts of the empirical consciousness. But even if they were to remain only as unmanifest contents of the *Ālaya*, their habitual, spontaneously self-regenerative presence would still obscure its perfect self-luminosity.[6]

Since their nature consists of an attachment to the exclusive reality of multiple persons and things, they are removed by the constant cultivation of the non-discriminating transcendental wisdom (*nirvikalpakajñāna*) which grasps at nothing and knows no multiplicity, but comprehends the identity of all things in an immediate intuition of the unconditional nature common to all of them, their Absolute Suchness. The *Ch'eng Wei-Shih Lun* presents the continuous practice of *nirvikalpakajñāna* and its dispersal of the *bījas* of innate ignorance as the principle of a progressive transformation, characteristic of the *Bhāvanāmārga*. It does so in the metaphysical context of *vijñaptimātratā*, interpreting the *bījas* as the effects of a false imagination which, failing to perceive the universal co-relativity of phenomena as the interdependent forms of mere-consciousness, imputes an empty autonomy to them:

> By the repeated cultivation of the non-discriminating wisdom, the two "heavy" barriers within the primary consciousness

6. "(The term *dauṣṭhulya* signifies something crude and heavy, i.e. inaptitude, incapacity, infirmity.) This name of *dauṣṭhulya* is given to the Bījas of the two Āvaraṇas (barriers), because these Bījas, compared with those of the unconditioned non-discriminative Jñāna, are crude and heavy and therefore 'incapable' of serving as one of the causes for the attainment of Reality." Ibid., p. 705.

(*Ālayavijñāna*) are cleared away. Thus, through the process of "turning over" (i.e. inner transformation,) it is possible to discard the product of the false imagination (*parikalpita*) which lies upon the surface of the principle of "dependence on others" (*paratantra*) and to acquire "the nature of Ultimate Reality" (*Parinispanna*) which abides underneath this principle. By rolling away the vexing passions (*kleśas*), the *Mahāparinirvāṇa* (true and ultimate emancipation) is gained; by rolling away the barrier that impedes absolute knowledge [*jñeyāvaraṇa*], Mahābodhi or Supreme Enlightenment is experienced.[7]

But if the direct, intuitive experience of *Tathatā* attenuates the residual impressions of *kleśāvaraṇa* and *jñeyāvaraṇa*, it is only with the simultaneous complementarity of the ten moral perfections (*pāramitās*) that they are thoroughly and forever removed. While these reciprocally inclusive virtues are practiced from the very first stage of moral provisioning (*saṃbhārāvasthā*), it is in the stage of *Bhāvanā* that their characteristics are most clearly manifested, and in which they are said to constitute the essential nature and basis, "the land or bhūmi", for all the moral qualities that must be cultivated.[8]

The *Ch'eng Wei-Shih Lun* isolates ten singularly obstinate forms of innate ignorance[9] and defines the classical ten *bhūmis* through

7. Ibid., p. 705.

8. "Thus the ten Bhūmis comprise and have as their self-nature all the 'meritorious virtues', both conditioned (*saṃskṛta*) and unconditioned (*asaṃskṛta*)...they are the supreme supporting basis for all moral qualities that have to be cultivated. They cause them to come into being and grow up. Therefore, they are called Bhūmis or Lands." Ibid., p. 711. Also: "The ten Pāramitās are practised in all the ten Bhūmis; nevertheless, one may attribute to each of the Bhūmis the Pāramitā which is dominant in it. Innumerable are the moral practices of the ten Bhūmis; however, they are all comprised in the ten Pāramitās." Ibid., p. 727.

9. The text only mentions those obstacles embodying the ignorance impeding supreme enlightenment and hindering absolute knowledge, i.e. the *jñeyāvaraṇa*, and not the obstacles of the vexing passions (*kleśāvaraṇa*). This reflects the fact that while the Bodhisattva suppresses the actual manifestation of all the *kleśas*, thereby preventing any future *bījas* from being impressed upon the *Ālayavijñāna*, he willingly retains all prior residual impressions of them. By failing to remove these subliminal traces of the vexing passions he willingly

their active repudiation of them and removal of every trace of their subliminal impressions (*bījas*). In each *bhūmi* the tenacious influence of ignorance is increasingly weakened by the expansive exercise of wisdom in the tenfold form of the *pāramitās* which are said to reveal in each "land" the particular modality of Absolute Suchness peculiar to it. For as the text notes:

> Although Tathatā, in itself, is free from varieties and differences, nevertheless these ten species are distinguished by reason of their excellent qualities. Although from the first Bhūmi the Bodhisattva understands the ten Tathatās, nevertheless he has not yet experienced and practised them in a perfect manner. The Tathatās are therefore established in order that, progressively, in the course of the ten stages of the path, they may be perfectly understood and practised.[10]

Though obscured by the text's failure to provide a more cohesive interpretation for the ten *bhūmis*, ten *āvaraṇas*, ten *pāramitās*, and ten *Tathatās*, a generic pattern of psychic transformation is intended. Through *nirvikalpakajñāna*, human consciousness is transformed in the self-intuition of *Tathatā*, in which all cognizance of a distinction between self and other, subject and object, interior and exterior, is transcended in the sheer, metarational awareness of absolute reality. But despite the intensity of such an experience, the subliminal persistence of ignorance (the *bījas* of *kleśāvaraṇa* and *jñeyāvaraṇa*) prevents its perfect sustenance. Through the systematic cultivation of the *pāramitās*, innate wisdom so pervasively and concretely informs the mind, that the habitual impressions of the *āvaraṇas* "are contradicted by their antithesis, just as darkness is countered by light; they are therefore cut off and destroyed."[11] In even its most subtle and latent forms, ignorance is annulled as its psychic basis within the *Ālayavijñāna* is

---

accepts the rebirth which they occasion and thus fulfils his vow to lead all sentient beings to liberation before he himself enters perfect *nirvāṇa*. Though not manifested within the empirical consciousness, the persistence of such *kleśas* induces a continuous rebirth which the Bodhisattva freely enjoins to thus accomplish his salvific work. See Ibid., p. 731.

10. Ibid., p. 749.

11. Ibid., p. 757.

progressively and consistently illumined by the perfections of wisdom. The individual phenomenal consciousness experiences this liberation by the *pāramitās* which it cultivates, as a more thorough and precise understanding of absolute reality. While the non-discriminating transcendental wisdom (*nirvikalpakajñāna*) afforded it an immediate, non-conceptual intuition of *Tathatā*, the praxis of the *pāramitās* in each of the *bhūmis* yields a secondary wisdom (*pṛṣṭhalabdhajñāna*), a more formal, rational analysis and comprehension of "the excellent qualities" of Absolute Suchness; it is the knowledge and realization of such characteristics that constitute the revelation of the ten *Tathatās*.

But on a more fundamental level, they are to be understood as various refinements in the self-explicitness of that absolute. Suchness, in its noetic activity as *Ālayavijñāna*, having become fully self-conscious in and through the human mind's experience of *nirvikalpakajñāna*, delineates that immediate self-intuition in the more deliberate conceptions of that mind. Since the *Ālaya* contains the seeds (*bījas*) of perfect wisdom that assume the particular form of the *pāramitās*[12] within the phenomenal consciousness which it grounds, the realizations of the ten *Tathatās* which "they attain" are in fact the moments of its perfect self-comprehensive elucidation. *Tathatā* does not remain a mere abstract universal, an object of a knowledge external to, and distinct from itself. As *Ālayavijñāna*, it projects the sensible forms of phenomenal existence as the ideal manifestations or transformations (*pariṇāma*) from within itself.

Grounding as it thus does individual human consciousness, the *Ālaya* animates it with the germinal creativity of *Mahābodhi* which informs the perceptions of the *manas* and *manovijñāna*, enabling them to comprehend the indeterminate Suchness, the essential nature of all things as mere-consciousness (*Vijñaptimātratathatā*). In the reversal (*parāvṛtti*) of their instinctive tendencies to frag-

12. This is not to imply that perfect wisdom is exhausted by its particular manifestation in the *pāramitās* or that they are its sole expression. They are inherent, constituent practices of the holy path of wisdom, and may well imply and include the innumerable variety of other moral and meditative exercises. It is simply to be noted here that they are not the only forms of wisdom's self-explicitness. For a similar discussion within the *Ratnagotravibhāga* see pp. 118-20 above.

ment reality by positing a multiplicity of independent, self-subsistent persons and things, the *manas* and *manovijñāna* are respectively transformed in and by the Universal Equality and the Profound Contemplation Wisdoms. Conjointly, they illumine the mind that it may discern precisely the unique features and peculiar characteristics of all *dharmas*, while at the same time comprehending their complete equality as the thoroughly ideal forms of absolute Suchness. Both wisdoms are exercised throughout the ten *bhūmis* of the *Bhāvanāmārga* and both are perfected by the complementary exercise of the ten *pāramitās*. While the moments of the *manas*' direct intuition of *Tathatā* through *nirvikalpakajñāna* (of which the Universal Equality Wisdom is an expression) are intensified and prolonged, the more deliberate reflection upon, and consequent understanding of the ten characteristics of *Tathatā* by the *manovijñāna* through *pṛṣṭhalabdhajñāna* (of which the Profound Contemplation Wisdom is an expression) is more clearly defined. It is in this manner that Suchness, as the absolute ground of human consciousness (the *Ālaya*), informing it with the seeds of perfect wisdom, realizes a concrete self-consciousness.

Thus, in the first "land of great joy" (*Pramuditā bhūmi*) through the germinal wisdom of omniscience innate to it as *Ālayavijñāna* and manifested as the knowledge of the non-substantiality of persons and things (*pudgala* and *dharmaśūnyatā*), *Tathatā* witnesses its universality as the indeterminate Suchness of phenomenal existence. In the second "land of perfect purity" (*Vimalā bhūmi*), through the wisdom of the pure moralities (*śīla*), it counters the subtle delusion that gives rise to slight offences of body, speech, and thought and all of its residual impressions (*bījas*). In completely cutting off this *mithyāpratipattyāvaraṇa* through the transformation of human consciousness in the practice of ethical truth, *Tathatā* recognizes itself as the most sublime of all *dharmas* since it is replete with the infinite virtues and properties of Buddhahood.[13]

13. This interpretation of *Tathatā* as the basis of the *Buddhadharmas* has been exhaustively discussed in pp. 72-99, 141-49, 161-63 above on the *Ratnagotravibhāga's* axiom that the *Tathāgatagarbha* is void (*śūnya*) of the adventitious defilements that conceal it, but not void (*aśūnya*) of the highest properties that are indivisible from it.

In the third "land of luminosity" (*Prabhākarī bhūmi*) it is blocked by, but overcomes absolutely the barrier of unintelligence and failure of memory (*dhandhatvāvaraṇa*). Through *samādhi* and the *prajñā-of-meditation*, *Tathatā* completely suppresses the delusion of desire-covetousness (*kāmarāgamoha*) and the delusion of ignoring or disregarding the perfect *dhāraṇīs* of audition and moral cultivation, and realizes itself as the source of all excellent teachings.

Its self-awareness as the independent, self-contained absolute, incapable of appropriation by the divisive concepts of "I" and "mine", is attained in the fourth "land of glowing wisdom" (*Arciṣmatī bhūmi*). Its suppression of the most subtle forms of innate self-belief (*ātmadṛṣṭi*), self-conceit (*ātmamāna*), and self-love (*ātmasneha*), together with any attachment to meditation (*samādhisneha*) or to the Dharma (*Dharmasneha*), and all subliminal residue of them (the *bījas*) is effected through a meditation devoid of all grasping.

Tathatā knows itself concretely as the non-differentiation of *saṃsāra* and *nirvāṇa* in the fifth "land of the mastery of utmost difficulties" (*Sudurjayā bhūmi*). By its opposition to the Hinayāna attachment to *parinirvāṇa*, it totally halts the delusion (actual and potential) of conceiving ideas for the sole purpose of turning away from birth and death and/or for the sole purpose of attaining absolute release. At this stage the human mind is so transformed in innate wisdom, that it is capable of simultaneously perceiving the peculiar characteristics unique to any particular object as well as its fundamental indeterminacy, its absolute Suchness. Any tendency to flee the world of phenomena is obviated by this union of worldly wisdom (*saṃvṛtijñāna*) and fundamental wisdom (*tattvajñāna*) which synthetically perceive all things as the manifest forms of absolute reality. "Because of the necessity of causing these two *jñānas* to be born at the same time and to bear on the same object, this stage is extremely difficult to conquer."[14]

In this fifth *bhūmi*, *Tathatā* not only knows itself as the common essence of phenomenal existence, but simultaneously recognizes the sensible shapes and contours of those multiple existents as its own self-appearances. In the sixth "land of eternal presence"

14. Hsüan Tsang, *Ch'eng Wei-Shih Lun*, p. 709.

(*Abhimukhī bhūmi*), and the following "land of long journeys" (*Dūraṃgamā bhūmi*) it is conscious of transcending the manifold dichotomies of the discriminating intellect, and the particular respective polarities of purity-impurity and birth-destruction.

Up until the sixth *bhūmi*, the various reflections, meditations and contemplations are practised with the aid of images, ideas, conceptions, or notions (*sanimitta*) which the mind holds before itself for its sustained consideration and attention. The problem involved is that the mind instinctively interprets the thing before it as an object distinct from and over against itself as perceiving subject. Even when it is well acquainted with and informed by the truth of mere-consciousness (*vijñaptimātratā*), it is not free from the innate delusion which obscures the essential union of the perception aspect (*darśanabhāga*) with the image or perceived aspect (*nimittabhāga*) of consciousness. Thus, the very reality of mere-consciousness or of *Tathatā* as the genuine nature of all-things-as-consciousness-only is often distortedly retained by the mind as an object or thing transcendent and separate from itself. In the sixth and seventh *bhūmis* this dualism of subject and object is gradually suppressed.

But it is only in the eighth "land of non-agitation" (*Acalā bhūmi*) that a contemplation free of all images (*nirnimitta*) is perfected. Not only does the human mind recognize all forms of phenomenal reality as the transformations and manifestations of absolute consciousness, but through its vital union with it (the *Ālaya*), it is capable of modifying those forms or even of projecting new ones. It is said that the Bodhisattva at this stage can change base metals into gold or silver and can create whole lands and alter vast expanses of space. In this eighth *bhūmi*, *Tathatā* concretely realizes itself "as the supporting basis for the mastery which permits the creation or modification of phenomena, and of lands."[15] As the *Ālayavijñāna*, and through the medium of human consciousness which is no longer deceived by an ignorant conception of otherness in the objects of its perceptions, absolute Suchness knows its own dynamic creativity *vis-à-vis* the ideal forms of its self-manifestation. Since phenomena represent nothing other than the visible shapes and appearances of consciousness, their transmutations

15. Ibid., p. 749.

and novel projections characteristic of the eighth *bhūmi* are merely the conscious self-symbolizations of *Tathatā* as *Ālayavijñāna*. Not only does Suchness perceive itself through the human mind and recognize itself in the diversity of phenomenal existence, but it here concretely knows itself as absolute consciousness and the ideal source of their manifestations.

In the ninth "land of the finest discriminating wisdom" (*Sādhumatī bhūmi*), *Tathatā* is blocked by but overcomes absolutely the innate delusion which consists of the absence of any desire to act for the benefit of others. In its opposition to this form of ignorant self-attachment, *Tathatā* further transforms the human mind with the four unhindered or unlimited powers of interpretation and reasoning (the *pratisaṃvids*) and in so doing reveals itself as the basis and ground of transcendental wisdom. In the *arthapratisaṃvid* it exercises itself as the power to interpret the meaning of the most sublime truths and profound teachings of the *Dharma*. In the *dharmapratisaṃvid* it represents the mastery of explaining the literal significance of all names, sentences, clauses, phrases, words, and syllables. In the *niruktipratisaṃvid*, *Tathatā* manifests the ability of explaining and understanding all languages and any form of verbal expression and vocal sound, while through the *pratibhānapratisaṃvid* it demonstrates an unsurpassed skill in argumentation and discourse, proceeding from a thorough knowledge of the natural qualifications of the sentient beings whom it addresses.

In the final "land of Dharma clouds" (*Dharmameghā bhūmi*), by overcoming any incompletion, *Tathatā* realizes itself as the plenitude of great supernatural powers (the *dhāraṇīs*, *samādhis*, and all meritorious activities) through which it illumines the most profound and subtle mysteries and secrets. Although this tenth *bhūmi* represents the ultimate stage in the mastery of all perfections and the point at which the subliminal traces of innate ignorance have been removed by the transformation of the mind in and through innate wisdom, there yet remains "certain extremely subtle attachments to all known objects." At the moment of *Vajropamasamādhi* (the *samādhi* of diamond-like wisdom) which culminates this stage and initiates the *bhūmi* of perfect Buddhahood, they are absolutely and irrevocably cut off.

THE STAGE OF ULTIMATE REALIZATION

While *aśrayaparāvṛtti* had been generally extended by the *Ch'eng Wei-Shih Lun* to incorporate all the moments of psychic transformation from the earliest stages of the path onwards, there is a definitive, climactic "great transformation" (*vipulaparāvṛtti*) now realized. Alternately referred to as *phalaparipūriparāvṛtti*, it signifies the perfect maturity of "the fruit" of innate Buddhahood, and thus the fifth stage of the holy path, the *niṣṭhāvasthā*, the stage of ultimate realization. The universal equality and profound contemplation wisdoms, initially manifested on the path of insight (*Darśanamārga*), now totally animate and uninterruptedly inform the perceptions of the *manas* and *manovijñāna*. As already noted, they conjointly enable the human mind to know exactly the distinct, particular characteristics of persons and things, and simultaneously to comprehend their fundamental identity, their common reality as the ideal forms of absolute suchness. These two modalities of *Mahābodhi* function whenever human consciousness directs its attention towards any one thing or things; their activity is determined by the particular focus of the phenomenal mind.

However, on this final stage of ultimate realization the Great Mirror Wisdom (*Mahādarśajñāna*), of which the Universal Equality and Profound Contemplation Wisdoms are qualitative manifestations, is actualised. Proper to the *Ālayavijñāna*, the scope of its activity is not bound by the successive, singular regard of the phenomenal consciousness which determines the influence of the *samatājñāna* and the *pratyavekṣaṇājñāna*. While these latter illumine the particular characteristics and general nature of only those objects to which the *manas*, *manovijñāna*, and the sensorial consciousnesses advert, the Great Mirror Wisdom is the light of omniscience, the *sarvākārajñatā*, knowing the precise forms of all things, past, present, and future. By virtue of its innate, universal self-determinations (*bījas*), the *Ālayavijñāna* contains the manifold forms of the phenomenal universe. And as the common ground of every empirical consciousness it receives and retains the creative, residual impressions (the non-universal *bījas*) from every thought, feeling or deed originated as the volitions of those consciousnesses. Yet, its perfect awareness of itself in the totality of these ideal contents is obscured by ignorance, whose seeds (*bījas*) are innate to it, and whose presence is only removed by a similarly innate wisdom, concretely actualized in and through the empirical consciousness. The Great Mirror Wisdom represents the culmination of that process (as demonstrated above), where *Tathatā* knows the exact delineations of all phenomena simultaneously and without hindrance of spatial and temporal distinctions. For, as *Ālayavijñāna* it is the universal storehouse which contains them as its own immanent determinations, its *bījas*. And the Great Mirror Wisdom is the self-luminosity, the perfect self-comprehension of the *Ālaya* in the entirety of those ideal determinations. If the human consciousness in and through the combined Universal Equality and Profound Contemplation Wisdoms recognized the *bījas* in their temporal projections as the phenomenal forms of mere-consciousness (*vijñaptimātratā*), the absolute consciousness (*Ālayavijñāna*) in and through the Great Mirror Wisdom recognizes them in their unmanifest, immediate inherence to itself. For, as the text had noted earlier:

> The eighth consciousness is called *sarvabījaka* or the "seed consciousness", which means that it is endowed or furnished with all the bījas. It is capable of holding firmly and retaining the bījas of all dharmas, without allowing them to be lost. Apart from this consciousness, no other dharma is capable of retaining the bījas of all things.[16]

Thus, while the Universal Equality and Profound Contemplation Wisdoms represent the comprehensive knowledge of each particular thing in its sheer Suchness (*sarvajñatā*) as perceived by the phenomenal consciousness, the Great Mirror Wisdom is omniscience proper, the simultaneous and exhaustively detailed knowledge of all forms (*sarvākārajñāta*), including the Universal Equality, Profound Contemplation, and all other modalities of wisdom itself. It is then as *Mahādarśajñāna*, that *Tathatā* attains its ultimate self-conscious form. In its noetic aspect as *Ālayavijñāna*, *Tathatā* projects the manifold forms of phenomenal existence as the radically ideal manifestations or transformations

16. Ibid., p. 107.

(*pariṇāma*) from within itself. Then, through the medium of human consciousness, grounded upon and animated by it, it perceives and recognizes its own universality as the indeterminate nature, the Suchness, of those self-manifested forms. In this process of comprehensive self-understanding, *Tathatā* realizes itself as perfect wisdom. Since it is to possess itself as its own object by knowing itself as the unconditional nature of all things, its knowledge must be adequate to its content. Through the fivefold stages on the holy path of attainment, from initial faith and simple reflection; the profound meditative realizations of the *nirvedhabhāgīyas*; the incisive conviction of *pudgalaśūnyatā* and *dharmaśūnyatā*; the direct intuition of *nirvikalpakajñāna* and the subsequent *pṛṣṭhalabdhajñāna*, that adequacy is closely approximated in the Universal Equality and Profound Contemplation Wisdoms. Through them, *Tathatā* clearly knows itself in the individual forms of the phenomenal universe. Yet, it is only as the Great Mirror Wisdom that *Tathatā's* knowledge is perfectly adequate to its content. Not only does it represent the mode of formal omniscience (as explained above); it signifies the point at which *Tathatā*, having realized itself as perfect wisdom, *knows* itself as perfect wisdom. Since Absolute Suchness is to know itself as that which it is, it is not enough that it recognizes itself in the mere diversity of physical shapes and material contours. For, in that very recognition it determines itself ever more exactly in the form of the Universal Equality and Profound Contemplation Wisdoms, and its self-knowledge is only complete when it comprehends itself in that form. It does so through the Great Mirror Wisdom.

It must be recalled that according to the *Ch'eng Wei-Shih Lun*, every act of consciousness consists of the object or image aspect (*nimittabhāga*), the perception aspect (*darśanabhāga*), and the self-corroboratory aspect (*svasaṃvittibhāga*) or the awareness of the act of perception itself. In ordinary conscious experience, the *manas* and *manovijñāna* (as the *darśanabhāga*) perceive particular objects (the *nimittabhāga*), and the *Ālayavijñāna* as the ground of the phenomenal consciousness is the reflective awareness of their interaction. As the *svasaṃvittibhāga*, it is consciousness aware of its own activity, and by virtue of which the *Ālaya* is said to store and retain every act of consciousness expressed in bodily movement, speech, and thought. Now in the perfected consciousness of *Mahābodhi*, *Tathatā* knows itself in the multiplicity and variety of phenomenal forms as perceived through human consciousness. It does so as the Universal Equality and Profound Contemplation Wisdoms which thoroughly transform the latter. Thus, the perception aspect (*darśanabhāga*) of *Mahābodhi* is *Tathatā*, as perfect wisdom, recognizing itself as its own object (*nimittabhāga*) in the diversity of material existence. Then, in the Great Mirror Wisdom *Tathatā* realizes its ultimate self-conscious form, since as the *svasaṃvittibhāga* it is absolute wisdom comprehending its own perfection *as* wisdom.

With this conclusion of the analysis of the *Ch'eng Wei-Shih Lun*, it is essential in the following final chapter to summarize the entire development of the concepts of the *Tathāgatagarbha* and *Ālayavijñāna*, and to identify from the preceding and present chapters, the stages of their emergent complementarity.

PART THREE

THE *TATHĀGATAGARBHA-ĀLAYAVIJÑĀNA*: SUMMARY AND COMPARISON

CHAPTER XII

CONCLUSION

THE TATHĀGATAGARBHA IN THE ŚRĪ-MĀLĀ SŪTRA

The present study has sought an understanding of the Mahāyāna Buddhist belief in the inherent potentiality of all animate beings to attain the supreme and perfect enlightenment of Buddhahood. Its principle of exposition has been a detailed analysis of the two concepts through which the Mahāyāna tradition has grounded and sustained that belief. While the *Tathāgatagarbha* or "embryo of the Tathāgata" and the *Ālayavijñāna* or "storehouse consciousness" initially arose as independent theories, it has been shown that their mutual implication and inter-illumination as alternate determinations of *Tathatā* make of each, the necessary complement of the other; together, they define a comprehensive metaphysics of Absolute Suchness and identify the soteriological-epistemological principles consistent with it.

While treating explicitly the *Tathāgatagarbha*, the *Śrī-Mālā Sūtra* anticipated the role of the *Ālayavijñāna* in its conception as absolute consciousness. Having once defined the ontic dimension of the *garbha* as the unborn, imperishable, permanent, steadfast, and eternal ground of phenomenal and absolute reality (*saṃsāra* and *nirvāṇa*), it immediately qualified that status. Its unconditional nature was not to be understood as that of an absolute substantiality, so much as of an absolute subjectivity. The *Tathāgatagarbha* is the support of *saṃsāra* and *nirvāṇa* not as some essential, hypostatic entity, but rather as that which alone possesses an unconditional awareness and consciousness, adequate to the definitive comprehension of phenomenal existence as suffering. Its reactivity to the pain of *saṃsāra* and its simultaneous intentionality toward the emancipation of *nirvāṇa* implicitly identify the *Tathāgatagarbha* not so much as ontic substance, but rather as ontic subject. As such, its generic designation as "embryo" assumes a critical soteriological significance. For, its movement towards *nirvāṇa* is no mere undefined aspiration or indeterminate striving. Rather, it is the generic potentiality of animate beings to attain, not a multiplicity of variant goals, but one and the same "rightly completed enlightenment", the universal awakening of Tathāgatahood. There can be only one ultimate *nirvāṇa*, synonymous with the Absolute Body of the Tathāgata, the *Dharmakāya*, and it is to that end which the *garbha* "matures" all beings.

The *Śrī-Mālā* then, established an equivalence between the *Tathāgatagarbha* and the *Dharmakāya* such that the former is the latter when it has not yet freed itself from the concealment of the defilements. As embryo, the *Tathāgatagarbha* is unconditional awareness of phenomenal existence as suffering, and as realized Absolute Body it is synonymous with the cessation of suffering and is equivalent to the highest nirvāṇa-realm of the Tathāgata. Organically conceived as "embryo", the *Tathāgatagarbha* is the necessary emergence of itself to itself, the inherent process of moving from a latent to an articulate ultimacy, the self-expressive development from potential to actual Tathāgatahood.

But, while all sentient beings may have the potentiality of Buddhahood, may be tacitly considered as already enlightened, through the universal endowment with the *Tathāgatagarbha*, that does not necessarily presume its immediate and total actualization. It admits of varying degrees of self-manifestation within the consciousness of all beings, from those who have scant regard for spiritual values, through the Arhats, Pratyekabuddhas, and the tenfold stages of the Bodhisattva. It is only in the Lord, the Tathāgata, that it becomes what it truly is, that it attains complete self-realization as the Absolute Body (the *Dharmakāya*). In him, the *Tathāgatagarbha* gains an absolute self-confirmatory consciousness of itself as the Great Vehicle (*Mahāyāna*), the One Vehicle (*Ekayāna*). The Buddha is the eye, the perfect knowledge through which the *Tathāgatagarbha* comprehends itself as what it is, as "the Refuge with imperishable nature, permanent, steadfast nature."

The absolute status of the Buddha is a function of his exact and pluperfect knowledge. He alone has achieved an unqualified understanding of all natures, has become omniscient and all-seeing, unrestrained by any faults, liberated from all defilements, and possessed of infinite merit. Since the Buddha represents that stage of the *Tathāgatagarbha*'s perfect self-maturation, wisdom is both the means and end of that self-realization and is the very essence of the *Tathāgatagarbha*. For, inherent to it are the innumerable Buddha natures, the modalities of perfect wisdom and knowledge which progressively disperse "the nescience entrenchment" which, as the fundamental axis of ignorance, is the ground of all primary and secondary defilements. As the obscurative force of the nescience entrenchment is ever more dispersed by the diverse knowledge modes which essentially constitute the Buddha natures, these latter display themselves with greater perspicuity.

By the principle of self-liberation as self-explication, while the defilements of ignorance are eliminated or purified, there is a simultaneous revelation of the virtuous Buddha natures which are the very vehicle of their final and total self-deployment. It is this that constitutes the supreme nirvāṇa-realm of the Tathāgata. The relationship of the Buddha natures to the nescience entrenchment is but an alternate definition of the *Tathāgatagarbha* as the end that is simultaneously its own becoming. For, from the perspective of finality as the Absolute Body (the *Dharmakāya*), the *Tathāgatagarbha* is effect, result, and goal. At the same time, as the processive, self-determined movement towards that actualization it is "embryonic" cause, means, and progression.

Its movement towards itself as goal (and thus, as *Dharmakāya*) is a function of its essential nature as self-explicating knowledge. It is not a self, a sentient being, a soul, or a personality. Rather, the *Tathāgatagarbha* is "embryonic" absolute knowledge. Its essence is to know itself as that which it is, to be aware of itself and to bring itself about. The content of the *garbha's* knowledge is precisely itself as void (*śūnya*) of the extrinsic defilements which nevertheless conceal it, and not void (*aśūnya*) of the inherent Buddha natures. It is this content which must be made manifest; the *garbha's* self-knowledge must be actually adequate to its content. Since the *garbha* is to possess itself as its own object, the known cannot be something parallel to knowledge any more than it can be an external object for knowledge. Knowledge is rather the self-explication of the known content, and the known content is implied knowledge (i.e. the perfect wisdom of the Buddha natures).

When the Buddha natures are fully manifest, the *Tathāgatagarbha* has realized its own plenitude, and is thus referred to as the Absolute Body of omniscience, the *Dharmakāya*. The over-all image projected by the *Śrī-Mālā Sūtra* in describing the relationship of the *Tathāgatagarbha* with the *Dharmakāya* is that of a cycle that presupposes its beginning and reaches its beginning only at its end. Initially posited as an object of faith, the *garbha* is accorded an absolute status as existing without beginning or end; not being born and not dying; not subject to rebirth; but permanent, steadfast, and eternal; the base and support of the intrinsic Buddha natures as well as the adventitious, discrete defilments, and the ground of both *saṃsāra* and *nirvāṇa*. However, its organic designation as "embryo" quickly identified this beginning as the point of departure endowed with the propensity towards its own self-transformation, a process with a most specific teleological direction. For, the self-movement of the Tathāgata-embryo to the Absolute Body is a self-teleological process of inner convergence, where the Absolute Body as *telos* is simply the point of the embryo's fully self-conscious, self-revelation.

In this cycle, if the Tathāgata-embryo is the beginning or cause (*hetu*), then the Absolute Body is essentially result (*phala*), the end where the Tathāgata-embryo becomes what it is in truth. The nature of the embryo is to be actual, that which becomes itself. For if it starts with itself, the *Tathāgatagarbha* reaches its consummation with itself as *Dharmakāya*. Not only is the latter defined by the sūtra with the same attributes as the former, but in fact, is the former when it has not yet freed itself from the adventitious defilements that conceal it, i.e. when it has not yet attained full self-conscious awareness as being intrinsically and always free of those defilements.

Put otherwise, the Absolute Body can be a result (*phala*) only because it is already present from the start in an initial "embryonic" shape or content (the *garbha*). The cyclic transformation then, of the *Tathāgatagarbha* into the *Dharmakāya* is that of an original absolute becoming an articulate absolute, where no new elements are acquired but the latent or inherent ones (i.e. the innumerable Buddha natures) are expressed. The only transition within this sphere of self-exposition for the sake of self-understanding is that from hiddenness to manifestation.

The Tathāgatagarbha in the Ratnagotravibhāga

While the *Śrī-Mālā Sūtra* presented the *Tathāgatagarbha* as the processive absolute which is the very vehicle of its self-manifestation, the self-evolutive potentiality of the embryo to become itself as realized Absolute Body, the *Ratnagotravibhāga* stressed the ontic identity of the two poles. Though linguistically distinct, the *Tathāgatagarbha* and *Dharmakāya* are one and the same reality. What the śāstra examines is the quintessential dimension, the ultimate, ontic nature common to both designations, identifying them as but qualitative modalities of one and the same Reality, absolute Suchness (*Tathatā*). *Samalā Tathatā* designates that aspect of Reality "mingled with defilement" and is the *Ratnagotra's* consistent term for the *Tathāgatagarbha*, while *Nirmalā Tathatā* is its expression for Reality "apart from defilement", and is thus synonymous with the *Dharmakāya*.

The critical axiom that all living beings are possessed of the *Tathāgatagarbha* is grounded on the universality of the *Dharmakāya*, *Tathatā*, and the *Tathāgatagotra*. According to the *Ratnagotra's* hermeneutics, all living beings are penetrated by the Absolute Body of the Buddha by virtue of its universal extension as self-born, omniscient wisdom, pervading all beings equally. Thus, "to attain the *Dharmakāya*" it is necessary first to recognize the wisdom of the Tathāgata as the definitive, constitutive principle of one's own cognitive awareness; it is to fully comprehend the non-differentiation of the Buddha's wisdom and one's own fundamental, noetic substratum. As such, the Buddhist path would be a function of self-transformation through self-recognition. In addition, Absolute Suchness is the unilateral "immaculateness" existing in all beings, their intrinsic, fundamental and ultimate essence.

In its turn, the *Tathāgatagotra* contributed an important soteriological element to the universality of the *Dharmakāya* and *Tathatā*, and as active, causal factor (*hetu*) it reinforced the processive "embryonic" implications of the *Tathāgatagarbha*. As the innate "germinal essence" existing in all beings, it was projected as the imperishable, permanent, unconditional, and supportive ground for the realization of Buddhahood by all classes of persons. As such, it represented the unqualified assurance and validation of a universally attainable supreme enlightenment. Sentient beings could develop into and mature as perfect Buddhas because they have always possessed the innate "germ" (*gotra*) of Buddhahood. Thus, the *Ratnagotravibhāga* posited an equivalence of *Dharmakāya*, *Tathatā* and *gotra* where their inter-illumination and mutual inherence as the threefold nature of the *Tathāgatagarbha* definitively established its status as the self-subsistent, all-pervading, unchangeable, and non-differentiated absolute that is the very vehicle of its own self-manifestation. Absolute Suchness, in its immanent modality as *garbha*, is no statically latent neutrality. Nuanced by its identification with *Dharmakāya* and *gotra*, it is the movement to attain perfect consciousness of itself as the indeterminate, unconditional nature of phenomenal existence.

This subjective dimension of *Tathatā* was suggested by its equivalence with *Dharmakāya* as the Body of omniscient wisdom and with *gotra* as "germinal" absolute knowledge and active intentionality away from saṃsāric suffering towards the liberation of ultimate *nirvāṇa*. But, as "the indiscriminative Innate Mind" its immanent modality within human consciousness was formally determined. Human consciousness was thus clearly identified as the necessary medium through which *Tathatā* realizes its own universality as the indeterminate Suchness of phenomenal existence. Consequently, the *Ratnagotravibhāga* tended to interpret the human intellect as a function of the Innate Mind, and implied that the diverse planes of conceptual awareness were merely the self-reflective moments in which *Tathatā* affirmed itself as the perfectly pure essence, the unconditioned nature of all reality. Such an emphasis upon the primary subjectivity of *Tathatā* as embryonic absolute knowledge or the germinal essence of Buddhahood (i.e. as *garbha* and *gotra*), tended inevitably to minimize the uniqueness of the phenomenal subject. According to the *Ratnagotra* then, the Buddhist transformation process is primarily the emergence of *Tathatā's* perfect self-consciousness, its movement to perfect self-understanding, from hiddenness to manifestation.

While the *Śrī-Mālā Sūtra* identified an inherent, primordial ignorance as the source of all defilements, impeding the perfect self-realization of the *Tathāgatagarbha*, it gave no account or rationale for its ultimate genesis and presence within human consciousness. By contrast, the *Ratnagotravibhāga* examines the nature of ignorance in greater depth. Accordingly, ignorance is said to be the root and source of all subtle tendencies of desire, hatred, and delusion which influence human perception, and when translated into actions of body, speech, or thought become the concrete defilements and thus, the proximate conditions of future rebirth. The critical interpretation of the *Ratnagotra* was that the innate principle of ignorance is not ultimate, but is instead grounded upon and abides within the unconditional, Innate Pure Mind. Ignorance is not any substantial entity, any ultimate element but, as "the irrational action of mind" is itself dependent upon Absolute Suchness, immanently conceived and noetically determined as the Innate Pure Mind. The latter is the necessary condition for the very possibility of ignorance which, while it may be manifested as an unwise discrimination or wrong conception, cannot take place without that fundamental substratum. In its ultimate nature, ignorance is not different from the Innate Mind. If defilements exist, they do so as deluded modes of consciousness, taking their particular appearance as forms (no matter how distorted) of one elemental reality—the Innately Pure Mind.

What the *Ratnagotra* advocated then, for the complete cancellation of ignorance and its consequent defilements is not the conscious resistance to it, but the simple non-apprehension of it. For, ignorance is like all other factors of experience (*dharmas*), devoid of any independent self-subsistent autonomy. Thus, any cognitive activity directed towards it is without factual basis. To regard ignorance as a thing to be opposed and removed is the very attitude that occasions its further retrenchment; it is a serious misperception which, as a form of ignorance, becomes a remedy that strengthens the disease. Since ignorance is synonymous with faulty discrimination, to identify it as the deliberate objective to be overcome by the cultivation of a specific path, is itself a discriminatory and erroneous judgment. It is only with the firm conviction of the unreality of ignorance that it is extracted at its root; through non-apprehension there is no self-contradictory reversion to the principle of ignorance as the vehicle for its own removal. Instead, ignorance is intuitively dispelled through the psychological disarmament of approaching it as it truly is—absolutely empty, "extinct by nature." Consequently, since ignorance is unreal, empty of any substantial referent, the ensuing defilements said to arise from it, are by definition non-essential. When the *Ratnagotra* accepted that the mind is defiled, it did so only as conventional truth, reflecting the empirical presence of greed, hatred, and delusion. In principle, these latter are not ultimate facts, but originated by a series of causes and conditions; as such, they cannot alter the pristine nature of the Innate Mind upon which they ultimately depend.

Within the Buddhist tradition, the *Ratnagotravibhāga* represents a significant movement towards a more positive formulation of Absolute Reality. But while it exercises an explicit censure of the Śūnyavādin tradition, it does so only to amplify the ontological implications of *Śūnyatā* itself. For, the latter is not only the animating principle of an exacting critique upon rational processes, more than just the reflective awareness of the inherent falsities and inner contradictions of the dialectical fluctuations of reason between "is" and "not is". As critical methodology, *Śūnyatā* is the very vehicle of its own manifestation as the non-conceptual, indeterminate, unconditioned Absolute Reality, the highest truth and ultimate nature of things; as such it is a cognate expression, an alternate designation of *Tathatā*. According to the *Ratnagotra*, *Śūnyatā* as logical critique (exercised preeminently in the *Mādhyamika* tradition) lacked sufficient cohesion with *Śūnyatā* as unconditioned, transcendent ground. It, therefore, was as a corrective to what it considered an excessively negative epistemological review, that the *Ratnagotra* advanced its ontology of the *Tathāgatagarbha*. But that it did so as a development upon and integration of the *Śūnyavāda* was clearly obvious from its definition of the *garbha*, or essence of the Buddha, as representing the genuine meaning of *Śūnyatā*. It has been demonstrated that while the *Ratnagotra* speaks of *Śūnyatā* in terms of its doctrine on Absolute Suchness, and while the *Prajñāpāramitā Sūtras* tend to illuminate *Tathatā* through their more specific amplifications on the nature of *Śūnyatā*, both sources understand the two terms as cognate conceptions; as the indeterminate, unconditional reality, they are mutually inclusive, coincidentally inter-reflective.

In fact, the *Ratnagotra* claimed that the different classes of individuals who failed to understand the nature of the *Tathāgatagarbha* simultaneously held mistaken notions concerning the nature of Śūnyatā; to misapprehend the one is to misinterpret the other. On the one hand, ordinary beings assume the uncritical belief in an infinite multiplicity of independent, self-sufficient, mutually exclusive entities; they seize the relative and determinate factors of existence as ultimate and unconditioned. Theirs is the most obvious denial of an undifferentiated, unconditionally real essence, universally common to all phenomena. But the position of the Śrāvakas and Pratyekabuddhas is no more correct. Despite their initial ability to overcome the illusion of the gross substantiality of existent elements, they become trapped by the very categories of their analyses. Reducing phenomena to the major "dharmic" classifications and unilaterally defining them as evanescent, suffering, of no self, and impure, they are unable to escape the implicit realism of those very classifications. They turn the ascriptions of phenomenal conditionality into dogmas of unconditional fact, and focus so intensely upon the discrete components of existence that they never realize the undivided absolute essence, the real nature of things in their Suchness. *Tathatā* is the middle path then (*Madhyamāpratipat*), between the substantive view of phenomena held by ordinary beings and the absolute relativity of phenomena as entertained by Śrāvakas and Pratyekabuddhas.

Then there are those novice Bodhisattvas who tend to substantiate non-substantiality. Some cling to *Śūnyatā* as the medium of liberation, approaching it as the perfect *nirvāṇa*, and thus misapprehend it as an unconditional reality, absolutely transcendent and separate from the realm of conditioned phenomena. The *Ratnagotra* opposed such a dualistic split as completely antithetical to *Śūnyatā* as the principle and ground of comprehensive non-exclusion and universal harmony. It also rejected a similar misrepresentation of *Śūnyatā* as a thing existing outside of, and apart from the five *skandhas* and the entire conditioned world that is coextensive with them. *Śūnyatā* is not some reified object, an extrinsic other, subsisting in a dimension exclusive of form, etc. The *Ratnagotra* insists upon a complete and reciprocal identity in extent and content between emptiness and form; taken as abstract concepts as well as concrete events to which they apply, *Śūnyatā* and *rūpa* are thoroughly coincidental. Therefore, from several different perspectives the *Ratnagotra* resisted all views that either neglect entirely or else significantly misapprehend the true intent of *Śūnyatā* which, as revelatory of the universal, dependent correlativity among phenomena is simultaneously their non-dual, unconditional nature, their indeterminate Suchness.

The positive designations of supreme eternity, bliss, unity, and purity, understood by the śāstra as the antidotal inversions of the error that would attribute "the fourfold non-delusion" (evanescence, suffering, non-egoity, and impurity) to the *Dharmakāya*, are not to be understood as specific attributes, qualifying some quintessential concrete hypostasis. Rather, they refer to the Absolute Suchness of reality whose translogical and indeterminable status was clearly recognized by the *Ratnagotra* as inexplicable, invisible, unutterable, unimaginable, indiscriminative, unthinkable, beyond the *catuṣkoṭi* (being, non-being, being and non-being together, neither being nor non-being) on a plane where analysis based on dualistic views and faulty discriminations is of no value. The four supreme virtues do not compromise this understanding of *Tathatā* as the unqualified Absolute. For, upon examination, they translate as nothing other than *Śūnyatā* as the supreme remedial antidote for the various erroneous views, and as the highest truth, the ultimate essence of things. So then, the perfection of self or supreme unity indicated the absolute reality of phenomenal existence (i.e. *Tathatā*) as the universal non-substantiality of independent, self-subsistent persons and things (i.e. *Śūnyatā*). Likewise, the supreme eternity represented the identity of *saṃsāra* and *nirvāṇa* in a non-substantiality (*Śūnyatā*) that transcends all dichotomic concepts of being and non-being, finite and infinite, permanence and impermanence. The profound cognition of the emptiness of all suffering as extinct by nature (i.e. there is no *duḥkha* in the ultimate sense) accounted for the supreme bliss, while the supreme purity reflected the non-substantiality (*Śūnyatā*) of ignorance and its accompanying defilements and impressions.

The theory of the *Tathāgatagarbha* as formulated by the *Śrī-Mālā Sūtra* and elaborated upon by its principal śāstra, the *Ratnagotravibhāga*, provides a singularly comprehensive interpretation of the Buddhist transformation process and experience of enlightenment. While inconceivable even to the loftiest and purest minds, the *Tathāgatagarbha*, accepted in faith, initiates the self-unfoldment of all the properties and virtues necessary for the removal of ignorance and its obscurative defilements. It does so as embryonic absolute knowledge, explicitated through the practices and observances of the path and the exercise of the perfections of charity, morality, patience, meditation, and exertion. Only thus does it come to the perfect self-revelation in the *Dharmakāya* as actually freed from, because essentially devoid of (*śūnya*) the defilements, and replete with, because intrinsically not devoid of (*aśūnya*) the modalities of omniscient wisdom.

The *Tathāgatagarbha* begins then, as the content of faith and thus, under the form of objectivity as ontic substance; it is *Tathatā* as the pure essence, the fundamental nature, the basic substratum, the unborn, undying, permanent, steadfast, eternal, and ultimate ground of *saṃsāra* and *nirvāṇa*. But the *garbha* must surmount the form of objectivity, must move from the category of ontic substance, through the generic transformation of its inherent nature, to ontic subject, fully self-explicated self-consciousness; as realized *Dharmakāya*, the realm of omniscient wisdom, it is *Tathatā* recognizing itself as pure Suchness in and through all forms of phenomenal reality.

The necessary movement of *Tathatā's* inner convergence upon itself, the stages towards its final and perfect self-comprehension, includes all the teachings and instructions, the prescriptions and praxes embodying the entire *Dharma*. *Tathatā* is the truth which animates and finds self-expression in all the formulations and specifications of the Buddhist Path. As the one vehicle (*ekayāna*), grounding and authenticating the multiple variations of observance and interpretation, *Tathatā*, under its determination as *Tathāgatagarbha*, is the soteriological principle of absolute efficacy. It is the warrant, intrinsic to all sentient beings, for the attainment of the supreme and perfect enlightenment of Buddhahood; thus, its designation as the Great Vehicle (*Mahāyāna*).

If the Doctrine (*Dharma*) is inaugurated as an extraneous code whose faithful adherence promises the emancipation from all sorrow and suffering, it must come to be understood as *Tathatā's* self-objectifying knowledge of itself as the truth of all things. Under the primary axiom of "impermanence, ill, not-self," *Tathatā* manifests an important insight into the conditioned relativity of phenomenal existence; it is a wisdom revealing the nonsubstantiality (*Śūnyatā*) of things, and thus dispelling a form of ignorance that seizes upon the determinate as indeterminate, the relative as absolute. But this dictum itself becomes a perversion, if its truth is constricted into a unilateral literacy, if the world is unqualified as the source of all pain and suffering. Such is an instance where the self-explicating movement of *Tathatā* as embryonic absolute knowledge can be stagnated by its own formulations.

Though necessary to it, these codified moments of its self-reflection must be surmounted and transcended by *Tathatā* if it is to attain that supreme modality in which alone it is able to recognize itself as the Suchness of reality; only as omniscient wisdom does it adequately perceive itself as the ultimate ground and unconditional nature of existent phenomena. The initial truth of "impermanence, ill, and not-self," while revealing the universal relativity of things, must yet annul and transcend itself as incomplete. The Suchness of things may indeed be manifest in this testimony of their interdependent co-origination, their non-substantiality (*Śūnyatā*) as unique, self-subsistent entities, but its revelation is only partial. *Anitya*, *duḥkha*, and *anātman* are propaedeutic and not final; they must yield to the more profound and comprehensive recognition of the absolute quiescence of all things, their original nirvāṇic status as essentially free from the adventitious defilements. Up to that point, *Tathatā's* advance towards total and perfect self-awareness progresses through the innumerable varieties and forms, degrees and levels of self-reflective wisdom constituting the path of the *Dharma*. At each stage, by its efficacy as innate absolute knowledge, it attains a proportionate self-liberation from the obscurative force of ignorance through the instrumentality of its self-formulations. But these latter, while the vehicles of its self-representation, are never (independently) the adequate media for the perfect self-manifestation of *Tathatā*. Instead, they are the necessary moments of self-transcending absolute wisdom as it approaches the goal where the form in which *Tathatā* appears for its own perfect self-consciousness corresponds completely to its essence. Only as omniscient wisdom, unrestricted by the contours and moulds of material existence, does *Tathatā* universally perceive itself as the fundamental and original purity of all things, intrinsically free from the concealing defilements.

Thus it is that the significance of the historical Buddha is as one who has fully awakened to the innate radiance of the Mind (the immanent, noetic determination of *Tathatā*) which he knows to be the essential nature of all sentient beings. While he is recognized as the teacher of the Doctrine, it is as the exemplar and concrete actualization of its truth; it is in him that the essence of omniscience has attained the self-witnessing eye, the unimpeded perception of its absolute freedom from defilements as the pure Suchness of all existence. The Buddha is the historical articulation of the Mind's doctrine concerning its association with, but independence from the covering of the defilements, and the validation of its self-purifying capacity. In the comprehensive theory of the *Tathāgatagarbha* then, the person of the Buddha is subsidiary to the attainment which he represents, viz., the enlightenment of perfect Buddhahood. If in him, Absolute Suchness successfully awakened to itself in an omniscient wisdom as the highest truth of phenomenal reality, its process of self-emergence within the consciousness of his followers is no different than the path it traversed and perfected in him.

However, to argue the thesis of the universal potentiality of Buddhahood entirely from within the dynamics of Absolute Suchness, as the *Ratnagotra* does, is to leave undeveloped the role of the individual human consciousness. Its emphasis upon the primary subjectivity of *Tathatā* as embryonic absolute knowledge or the germinal essence of Buddhahood (i.e. as *garbha* and *gotra*) tended inevitably to minimize the uniqueness of the phenomenal subject. Since the perfect self-awareness of *Tathatā* takes place in and through human consciousness, the *Ratnagotra* failed to adequately explain how finite, particular consciousness functions with, and is transformed into the infinite, universal and absolute consciousness. It neglected to elaborate a generic structure of consciousness that would account for the coherence of such a relationship. While the *Ratnagotra* clearly indicated that the Innate Mind (*Cittaprakṛti*) is the fundamental noetic substratum common to ordinary beings and Buddhas alike, it sustained no detailed analysis of its active interplay with and upon the phenomenal mind. The whole question of how the latter becomes individuated out of, but not separate from that primordial stratum of pure awareness, is not addressed by the śāstra. Its answer and the subsequent question as to how precisely the Innate Mind becomes compromised and defiled as the individual consciousness strays from its identity with it, demands a knowledge of the structural dynamics animating the processes of sensory awareness, intelligible apperception, ideal conceptualization and objective creativity. Together, these represent the essential phases in a coherent morphology of phenomenal consciousness; they are critical mental determinations and as such, must be considered in any discussion of *Tathatā's* self-realization in and through human consciousness. While the *Ratnagotravibhāga* succeeded in establishing the metaphysical context in which to interpret the transformational event of enlightenment, it lacked this adequate psychological detail necessary for the translation of that theory into the practical discipline of the spiritual path. The Vijñānavādin reflection upon the *Ālayavijñāna* provided such a complementarity.

The Laṅkāvatāra Sūtra

The *Laṅkāvatāra Sūtra* effected an explicit union between the *Tathāgatagarbha* and the *Ālayavijñāna*. While the *Ratnagotra* had specified the *garbha* as the immanence of Absolute Suchness within the phenomenal order, the *Laṅkāvatāra* gave it a more exact determination as the grounding principle of human consciousness, through the *Ālayavijñāna*. The latter's ontic status was simultaneously transformed by its union with the *garbha*, from a strictly individual and relative principle of the earlier Vijñānavādin texts, to that of the essentially pure mind. By virtue of its union with the *Ālaya*, the *Tathāgatagarbha* assumed an active causal determination as that from which arises the multiplicity of phenomenal forms.

While the *Ratnagotravibhāga* extended the precise delineations of *Tathatā* as the universal, immaculate essence of phenomenal existence, the *Laṅkāvatāra* explored the manner in which *Tathatā* (noetically conceived as absolute consciousness, i.e. as *Ālayavijñāna*) comes to perfect self-awareness as that comprehensive totality. In doing so, it nuanced the ontological context defined by the śāstra and with which it implicitly agreed, by its focus upon the epistemology proper to that context. This was most apparent in the *Laṅkāvatāra's* references to the three self-natures (*svabhāva*).

Parikalpita or purely imaginary nature, *paratantra* or dependent nature and *parinispanna*, ultimately real nature, all assumed a distinct cognitive expression. Rather than formally indicate the respective level of entitative value or degree of self-being of the particular thing to which each refers, the three categories represented three ways of understanding. In the sūtra, they were not so much states of self-nature, as they were modalities of knowing that nature. The idea was that existence could be understood in three different, characteristic ways, each of which was taken to be the final and true nature of reality by whomever entertained that respective viewpoint.

However, in its focus upon the epistemic process, the *Laṅkāvatāra* tended not to distinguish accurately enough between the activity of discrimination and the content of discrimination. Thus, in the case of *paratantra* there was confusion between the formation of appearances and the "stuff" of which they are formed and upon which the paratantric perception is said to depend. It is not the constitution of formed appearances *per se* (the paratantric activity proper), but their projection as independent, self-subsistent entities of a world, external to and separate from consciousness that is erroneous and imaginary (*parikalpita* proper). *Paratantra* as an ontic reality, a level of dependent self-being (*svabhāva*) was overshadowed by paratantra as a mode of cognition infected by *parikalpita*. This jeopardized the value and significance of phenomenal reality and at times, suggested a nihilistic denial of the human organism and its material environment. Once again, the *Laṅkāvatāra* failed to adequately delineate the ontic structure of the phenomenal psyche from the epistemological processes that define its function. There is a difference between the form of human consciousness and the ignorant activities that characterize it; this distinction is absent in the sūtra.

Even more critical was the direct implication that ignorance is the cause of phenomenal individuation. Thus, it was more than a simple confusion between the structure of consciousness and the deceptive activities that distinguish it. What the *Laṅkāvatāra* ultimately challenged was the very integrity of phenomenal subjectivity. If it was the product of ignorance and the condition for its continued influence, then *nirvāṇa* would in fact imply its abandonment, as the text stated.

It was admitted that a transcendental illusion, the projection of an objective and external world of discrete and independent entities (the principle of "beginningless ignorance"), may indeed distort the interpretation with which the relative consciousness invests that which it apprehends and orders into unified forms of intelligibility. But it was indicated that this interpretative function of false imagination (*parikalpita*) is more formally an epistemological process than an ontic reality; it may be an activity peculiar to relative consciousness, but is not exhaustively definitive of it. The cessation of this deceptive mode of knowing does not necessitate the end of the seven *vijñānas*, as the *Laṅkāvatāra* implied. It was concluded that the problem lay in the sūtra's blurred distinction between ontology and epistemology, between consciousness as a stratum of being and consciousness as an interpretative process.

In general, there is an uneasy integration and amplification of the metaphysics of the *Tathāgatagarbha* into the basic Vijñānavādin psychology of the *Laṅkāvatāra*. While the doctrine of the *garbha* significantly nuanced the ontic status of the *Ālaya* by establishing it as the unconditional absolute, the noetic determination of *Tathatā*, it failed to creatively inform and coherently ground the extensions of that absolute consciousness in the multiple forms of existence. Since phenomenal reality is the self-reflecting image of the *Ālayavijñāna* which, through its identity with the *Tathāgatagarbha*, is the noetic designation of Absolute Suchness, "phenomena" are indeed the manifest "appearances" of *Tathatā*. That reality however was seriously jeopardized by the vague approximation of ontological fact through epistemological statement—the *Laṅkāvatāra's* persistent methodological flaw.

The *Ch'eng Wẹi-Shih Lun* suffers no such confusion, and firmly grounded its pan-consciousness within an ontological framework, consistent with the principles of the *Ratnagotravibhāga*. Unlike the *Laṅkāvatāra*, its references to *parikalpita*, *paratantra*, and *pariniṣpanna* clearly signify the varying degrees of entitative value, the ontic status of that to which they refer. Thus, *parikalpita* represents that level of self-being that is totally null and void, indicating a purely imaginary figment. *Paratantra* designates the mutual interdependence of all phenomena. They reciprocally contribute to and mutually inhere a common identity and that interdependent, correlational totality is ultimately sustained by and dependent upon *pariniṣpanna* as the ultimately real, self-subsistent absolute. As equivalent to genuine Suchness (*Bhūtatathatā*), *pariniṣpanna* is the essential nature of phenomenal existence (i.e. the *paratantra*). It is the self-identical universality, the grounding truth of finite particularity which, through false imagination can be distortedly conceived as a multiplicity of discrete, self-subsistent individualities, and thus be designated, *parikalpita*.

THE CH'ENG WEI-SHIH LUN

The *Ch'eng Wei-Shih Lun* identified the *Ālayavijñāna* as the noetic determination of *Tathatā*, whose essence is to know itself in the universality of its extension as the essential nature (*pariniṣpanna*) of all things, their indeterminate, utter Suchness. The text thus represented a coherent synthesis of the *Ratnagotra's* ontology and the *Laṅkāvatāra's* psychology, clarifying the ambiguity of the one and the contradictions of the other. For, despite its reference to the Innate Pure Mind (*Çittaprakṛti*) as the psychic designation of *Tathatā*, the *Ratnagotra* failed to articulate a sufficiently radical and absolute idealism capable of spanning the gap between phenomenal existence and Absolute Suchness. While the latter was presented as the immaculate essence and the fundamental nature of the former, and while it was said to actualize itself as dynamic wisdom, perceiving itself in the manifold of phenomenal forms, the material density and exteriority of those forms remained unexplained; a distinction lingered between absolute non-substantiality (*Tathatā*) and concrete sensibility (phenomenal existence).

The *Laṅkāvatāra's* union of the *Tathāgatagarbha* (the immanent modality of *Tathatā*) and the *Ālayavijñāna* removed the ambiguity. By virtue of the *Ālaya*, it identified *Tathatā* as the principle of ideal causality. As the fundamenal and absolute consciousness, it is the ideal source of all phenomenal forms. However, the sūtra failed to sustain the ontological value of those forms as the self-manifestations of *Tathatā*, but implicated them instead, as the products of ignorance, thus involving itself in contradiction.

The *Ch'eng Wei-Shih Lun* responded to the *Ratnagotra's* ambiguity and the *Laṅkāvatāra's* contradictions through the central axiom of Yogācāra Buddhism which categorically denies all such dichotomy as matter and spirit, exteriority and interiority, object and subject. There is but one reality: mere-consciousness (*vijñāprimātratā*). Consciousness is the essential nature of phenomena and *Tathatā* is the essential nature of consciousness. Thus, the self-transparency of *Tathatā* in the totality of phenomena is the self-recognition of consciousness in the multiplicity of its forms. For, to say that consciousness is the sole reality, is not to consign material existence to the realm of illusion, but to interpret its sensible shapes and contours as the immanent developments and structured modalities of consciousness itself. Illusion is to imagine the independent self-subsistence of those sensible forms apart from consciousness, when they are instead, the integral patterns of that one reality. Phenomena are forms of consciousness and as such, are real. Their objectivity is only the mode of its appearance (i.e. consciousness). They seem to be "out there" possessing independent self-subsistence; in fact, that is only the way in which the *Ālayavijñāna* projects its contents, its own ideal self-determinations or "universal *bījas*". Since the *Ālaya* is the noetic aspect of *Tathatā*, the latter can know itself as the indeterminate, unconditional nature of all things because they are the radically ideal manifestations or transformations from within itself. The value of the *Ch'eng Wei-Shih Lun* is its articulation of that self-manifesting process, its detailed commentary on the dynamics of the *bījas* as the creative self-particularizations of consciousness.

It had been demonstrated that by virtue of its common or universal *bījas* the *Ālaya* develops into the manifold appearances of the physical universe, while its non-common or non-universal *bījas* account for the unique formations of the individual physical bodies and accompanying sense faculties. Since both types of *bījas* are innate to the *Ālaya*, the forms of human individuality and the empirical universe are the inherent self-determinations of the absolute consciousness. But it was clarified that although the *Ālaya* as the universal grounding consciousness of human individuality innately contains the *bījas* developing into the form of human consciousness, each individual consciousness possesses the freedom to create itself. Within the predetermined forms of *manas*, *manovijñāna*, and the five sensorial consciousnesses, grounded upon the *Ālaya* and supported by the physical body and the larger universe, human subjectivity can transform itself through every activity of body, voice, and mind. These latter are actually volitions, which as modes of consciousness leave their impressions (unique and personal non-universal *bījas*) within the fundamental consciousness of the *Ālaya* to become potential sources of future activities of the same moral category as the activities that originally impressed them.

Thus, the advance of the *Ch'eng Wei-Shih Lun* over the *Laṅkāvatāra* was its validation of the ontic status of the phenomenal universe and of the empirical human consciousness as paratantric realities. They are the radically ideal manifestations or transformations from within the *Ālayavijñāna*, the noetic specification of Absolute Suchness. It is only when they are falsely considered to be self-subsistent particularities, independent of consciousness, that they are designated as mere imaginations (*parikalpita*). Collectively, the forms of the phenomenal universe and of human individuality are the images (*nimitta*) in and through which *Tathatā* appears to and recognizes itself. Since the structure of the phenomenal consciousness evolves from immanent, archetypal self-patternings of the absolute consciousness, and since that phenomenal consciousness exists as the differentiated identity of the absolute consciousness, the perceptions of the phenomenal consciousness are the perceptions of the *Ālaya*. Therefore, the self-perception of the *Ālaya* in the multiplicity of its ideal forms is dependent upon, and at times constricted by, human consciousness whose sevenfold structures are ultimately the self-transformed appearances (*nimitta*) of (the *Ālaya*) itself.

Unlike the *Laṅkāvatāra*, the *Ch'eng Wei-Shih Lun's* detailed epistemological analysis of the problem of ignorance, was firmly grounded in its ontology of consciousness-only (*vijñaptimātratā*) and fully coincident with the principles of the *Ratnagotravibhāga*. Genuine Suchness (*Bhūtatathatā*) is equivalent to the ultimate real, self-subsistent absolute (*pariniṣpanna*) which can know itself as the indeterminate, unconditional nature of all things because they are the radically ideal manifestations or transformations from within itself, noetically conceived as absolute consciousness (*Ālayavijñāna*). The structures of the material universe and of the phenomenal human consciousness meaningfully cohere through the mutual interdependence of various conditioning factors (*pratyayas*), whose ultimate reality are the innate self-determinations (the *bījas*) of the *Ālaya*. The *manas* and *manovijñāna* fail to perceive that their own status is dependently originated and sustained by the universal grounding consciousness of the *Ālayavijñāna*. Their principle of subjectivity while authentic, is conditional and secondary; they are formally *paratantra*. But under the influence of the *manas*' innate *ātmagrāha*, they misrepresent the consciousness upon which they are contingent (the *Ālaya*) as the validation of their own ultimacy and independence; they appropriate it as a function of their own ignorant attachment. Their faulty self-regard spontaneously affects their interpretation of all other persons and things as constituting a world of unrelated egos (*ātmans*) and discrete particularities (*dharmas*). This falsely imagined isolation and self-sufficiency (*parikalpita*) arises from the *manas*' failure to perceive the universal extension of the *Ālayavijñāna* as the grounding principle of *all* phenomena, the thoroughly ideal manifestations and transformations of which, they are. As long as this fundamental misapprehension remains the dominant mental horizon informing all acts of consciousness which prompt physical deeds, produce speech or elicit deliberation and judgment, those acts are rendered impure and defiled.

The Ultimate Status of Ignorance in the Theory of the Tathāgatagarbha-Ālayavijñāna

At this point it is necessary to review the particular interpretation that each of the texts has given to the problem of ignorance, the resolution of which is critical to the integrity of the *Tathāgatagarbha-Ālayavijñāna*. The *Śrī-Mālā Sūtra's* references to "the nescience entrenchment" as the pretemporal, abyssal centre of ignorance were restricted exclusively to the fact of its presence, never to an examination of the how and why of that presence. The sūtra depicted the nescience entrenchment as the fundamental obscurative nexus, the powerful blinding influence which beclouds and ultimately deceives the perceptive faculties and thus spawns all primary and secondary defilements. Despite the sūtra's later assertion that it is subject to the elimination, purification, and extinction by the enlightenment wisdom of the Tathāgata, the status of the nescience entrenchment as the beginningless, originative cause and condition of all defilements rendered that assertion too facile. Ignorance had been accorded such a degree of ultimacy, that the *Śrī-Mālā's* designation of the defilement stores (which were founded upon and arose out of the nescience entrenchment) as adventitious and accidental, lacked conviction. Granted, that "the inconceivable voidness knowledge," the knowledge of the *Tathāgatagarbha* as both *śūnya-aśūnya*, as the wisdom which is capable of uprooting the nescience entrenchment, is an assertion of the latter's conditionality; ignorance is not an absolute state. But still the question persisted, since the knowledge that the *Tathāgatagarbha* is void (*śūnya*) of the defilements that are adventitious does not explain why they are so. While the *Śrī-Mālā* discussed the nescience entrenchment and its accompanying defilements as the inherent epistemic impediment to the self-realization of the *Tathāgatagarbha*, it failed to critically examine the reason and manner of its origination. Its remarks then, on the adventitious nature of ignorance and the defilements remained mostly gratuitous.

In its turn, the *Ratnagotravibhāga* refused to admit the ultimate significance of ignorance. In a way not found in the earlier sūtra, the śāstra clearly demonstrated that ignorance is itself conditioned by its own misperceptions, and that when one correctly understands the compounded nature of things in their universal non-substantiality (*Śūnyatā*) one puts a halt to the cycle of false imaginations upon which ignorance regenerates itself. Having established the unconditional nature of the Innate Mind as the designation for the immanent subjectivity of *Tathatā* in its all-pervasive presence within animate beings, the *Ratna* depicted how ignorance, as the irrational action of the phenomenal mind is grounded upon and thus conditioned by *Cittaprakṛti*. The Innate Pure Mind is the necessary condition for the very possibility of ignorance which, while it may be manifested as an erroneous discrimination or wrong conception, cannot take place without that fundamental substratum. In its ultimate nature, ignorance is not different from the Innate Mind. If defilements exist, they do so as deluded modes of consciousness, assuming their particular appearance as forms (no matter how distorted) of one elemental reality—the Innately Pure Mind. If ignorance is the illusory belief in the reality of separate entities, to regard "the irrational thought" (signifying the principle of ignorance) and its consequent defilements as independent particularities is a perversion as consequential as it is subtle; it is to initiate the path to perfect cognition on a falsely conceived premise which, through self-contradiction, ultimately perpetuates the ignorance that such a path is said to dispel.

Yet, while its analysis was far more profound and insightful than that of the *Śrī-Mālā Sūtra*, the *Ratnagotra's* predominant concern to dispel the principle of ignorance as an ontological reality and to psychologically disarm it through simple non- apprehension, provided no rationale for the incipient origin of empirical greed, hatred, and delusion. To illustrate the metaphysical conditionality of ignorance does not necessarily explain its genesis within human consciousness. The *Ratnagotra* demonstrated the essentially qualified and dependent mode in which ignorance manifests itself without satisfactorily stating why there should be such ignorance in the first place. Its insistence that ignorance "abides in" and is "founded upon" the Innate Pure Mind left open the suggestion that ignorance is in fact posited by *Cittaprakṛti* which would, in fact, be corroborated by the *Ch'eng Wei-Shih Lun* and the *Mahāyānaśraddhotpāda-śāstra*.

Both sources disagree with the *Laṅkāvatāra's* thesis that ignorance is the cause of phenomenal individuation which, in turn, perpetuates it. Having once accorded the *Ālayavijñāna* a degree of entitative value not found in the earlier texts of the Vijñānavādin tradition and thus establishing it as the unconditional absolute, the sūtra shifted the seat of ignorance and its beguiling influence onto the *manas*, *manovijñāna*, and the five sensorial consciousnesses. By its categorical insistence upon the essential purity and non-delusive character of the *Tathāgatagarbha-Ālayavijñāna*, the *Laṅkāvatāra* removed the suggestion of Asaṅga and Vasubandhu that the *Ālaya* represented only an individual and relative principle of finite deluded consciousness. To attribute ignorance to the *Ālayavijñāna* would have implicated it as the seat of delusion and thus involve it in direct self-contradiction as the inherently immaculate Mind. But the sūtra's alternative shift, displacing responsibility for ignorance onto the phenomenal consciousness, threatened the very integrity of human subjectivity and evoked numerous contradictory implications. The source of the

Laṅkāvatāra's dilemma was its failure to maintain an exact distinction between ontology and epistemology, between consciousness as a stratum of being and consciousness as an interpretive process. The sūtra failed to adequately delineate the ontic structure of the phenomenal psyche from the epistemological processes that define its function. While there is a difference between the form of the human consciousness and the ignorant activities that at times may characterize it, this distinction was absent in the *Laṅkāvatāra*. Therefore, unlike the *Ratnagotravibhāga* which clearly understood the metaphysical conditionality of ignorance, the sūtra was incapable of conceiving it as grounded upon and ultimately posited by the *Ālayavijñāna* as an intrinsic, though temporary, stage towards its perfect self-realization.

If the *Ratnagotra* remotely suggested such an interpretation, the *Ch'eng Wei-Shih Lun* and the *Mahāyānaśraddhotpāda-śāstra* clearly advanced it. According to the former, ignorance is inherently associated with, but not exhaustively definitive of human consciousness. *Avidyā* is only an associated mental activity (*caitta*), not the essential nature (*svabhāva*) nor the essential mode of activity (*ākāra*) of either the *manas* or *manovijñāna*. Unlike the *Laṅkāvatāra Sūtra*, the *Ch'eng Wei-Shih Lun* clearly distinguished ignorance as a qualified condition (viz., a *caitta*) rather than the absolute state of the phenomenal consciousness. While in the former scripture, the cognitive processes of the *manas-manovijñāna* are radically compromised as originated by *avidyā*, the latter text preserves their integrity as the innate self-determinations (*bījas*) of the *Ālayavijñāna* through which it perceives itself in the universality of its self-manifested forms. *Manas* is the essential basis and the necessary faculty for the Universal Equality Wisdom, while the *manovijñāna* is the consciousness through which the Profound Contemplation Wisdom functions.

In the *Ch'eng Wei-Shih Lun* the status of ignorance has been clearly altered. Rather than the cause of phenomenal individuation, as stipulated by the *Laṅkāvatāra, avidyā* is sequential to, and a subsidiary mode of human consciousness. Likewise, though the *manas* is originally misled by innate self-delusion, it is not by that fact, itself essentially delusive. It may well be the vehicle through which ignorance is manifested and perpetuated, but it is not its elemental source and productive cause. Just as the structure of the phenomenal human consciousness originates and assumes its sevenfold form from the innate self-determinations (*bījas*) of the absolute consciousness, so too does the ignorance which accompanies it germinally develop from within the very ground of the *Ālayavijñāna*; it does so along with the innate seeds (*bījas*) of wisdom and virtue.

Since it recognizes the essential complementarity of the *Tathāgatagarbha* and the *Ālayavijñāna*, and succinctly recapitulates the ontological perspective of the lengthier *Ratnagotravibhāga*, the *Mahāyānaśraddhotpāda's* further corroboration of the *Ch'eng Wei-Shih Lun's* theory of ignorance should briefly be noted. According to it, all things cohere as one, non-dual world of absolute reality, the *Dharmadhātu*. All distinction between infinite and finite, absolute and conditional, spirit and matter, subject and object, are fundamentally baseless and inapplicable in this realm of interdependent totality where each thing essentially transcends all manner of verbalization, description, and conceptualization. All are equally the forms of the one indeterminate absolute, and equally exist as the appearances of that sheer Suchness. Without the precise detail of the *Ch'eng Wei-Shih Lun*, the *Mahāyānaśraddhotpāda* stipulates that as the absolute consciousness (*Ālayavijñāna*), Suchness embraces all states of existence and creates all states of existence,[1] and that its very essence is self-manifesting wisdom through which it is conscious of itself as the totality of that existence, the *Dharmadhātu*. Following the pattern already identified in the *Śrī-Mālā Sūtra* and the *Ratnagotravibhāga*, the text qualifies an initial impression of *Tathatā* as ontic substance (the eternal, permanent, immutable, pure, and self-sufficient ground of *saṃsāra* and *nirvāṇa*) by illustrating its inherent self-emergence as omniscient wisdom, and thus as ontic subject. Yet, it is in and through phenomenal subjectivity, existing in differentiated identity with it, that *Tathatā* recognizes its plenitude and concretely actualizes itself as "all-embracing knowledge".

While the obstacle to that perfect self-awareness is ignorance,

1. "This Consciousness has two aspects which embrace all states of existence and create all states of existence. They are: (1) the aspect of enlightenment, and (2) the aspect of non-enlightenment." *The Awakening Of Faith, Attributed To Aśvagosha*, trans. Yoshito S. Hakeda (New York: Columbia University Press, 1967), pp. 36-37.

the śāstra avoids the problematic implication of the *Laṅkāvatāra Sūtra* and does not impute human consciousness as the origin and source of that ignorance. Instead, like the *Ch'eng Wei-Shih Lun*, it preserves the integrity of the phenomenal mind as intrinsic to the self-actualization of *Tathatā*. Ignorance is defined rather as the beginningless, yet ultimately terminal coincidence with, and primordial accompaniment of the *Ālayavijñāna* which is itself, essentially pure.[2] Insisting on the primacy of the *Ālaya* as the noetic aspect of *Tathatā*, the text correspondingly stresses the adventitious, dependent nature of ignorance as manifested and grounded upon it.[3] This protogenic status of the *Ālayavijñāna* as the seat of both wisdom and ignorance is existentially reflected within the human mind's initial failure to realize its union with *Tathatā*, but a subsequent belief in it as the essential nature of all things and its own authentic identity. The climax of that belief is the transformation of human consciousness in the omniscient wisdom of Buddhahood. This ultimate dispersal of ignorance is simultaneously the moment of *Tathatā's* concrete and absolute self-awareness as the totality of all things. The point to be emphasized is that ignorance, far from being extraneous to Absolute Suchness, is the necessary condition for its self-explication in and through human consciousness. Implicitly, *Tathatā* is the whole of reality and its essence is to know itself as such not in some vague, abstract conviction but concretely and precisely in every perception of the phenomenal mind. Only through the active process of delineating the emptiness and non-substantiality of apparently discrete, autonomous persons and things, of overcoming the gap between one's self and an illusory world of distinct and mutually exclusive particularities does the implicit wisdom of *Tathatā* determine itself in the explicit emergence of its universality and unity as *Dharmadhātu*.

2. "The Mind, though pure in its self-nature from the beginning, is accompanied by ignorance. Being defiled by ignorance, a defiled (state of) Mind comes into being. But, though defiled, the Mind itself is eternal and immutable. Only the Enlightened Ones are able to understand what this means." Ibid., p. 50.

3. "Grounded on the original enlightenment is non-enlightenment....Ignorance does not exist apart from enlightenment....It may be said that, on the ground of Suchness (i.e. the original enlightenment), ignorance (i.e. non-enlightenment) appears." Ibid., pp. 38, 41 and 56.

The *Mahāyānaśraddhotpāda's* thesis that *Tathatā* beginninglessly integrates ignorance as a phase of its own self-development in wisdom, confirms the *Ch'eng Wei-Shih Lun's* interpretation that ignorance develops from within the very ground of the *Ālayavijñāna* as its own innate self-determinations or *bījas*. These, together with the *bījas* of innate wisdom simultaneously inform human consciousness, grounded as it is upon the *Ālaya*. Therefore, human consciousness is a product neither of ignorance nor of wisdom; its natural condition is the very interplay of their mutual presence. Human consciousness is by nature the processive advance to an ever more perfect *self*-consciousness in which it finally awakens to the plenitude of its identity with *Tathatā*. That the latter, as *Ālayavijñāna*, grounds and posits the phenomenal mind with seeds (*bījas*) of both ignorance and wisdom, defines the mind's active self-emergence as the necessary opposition between the two. Only in the expansive illumination of wisdom, gradually dilating the restrictive vision of ignorance, does human consciousness attain the awareness of its own universality. Only against the fragmented universe of multiple, isolated persons and things projected by *ātmagrāha* and *dharmagrāha*, can the mind begin to comprehend and at last to utterly witness the truth of consciousness-only (*vijñaptimātratā*).

The natural co-existence of ignorance and wisdom is decidedly creative, defining the context and providing the stimulus for the mind's definitive transformation in the fourfold wisdom of *Mahābodhi*. Consciousness is its own becoming, and ignorance is a necessary contributive factor to that self-evolution. Originally posited with it, ignorance is incorporated as a preliminary mode and auxiliary dimension of wisdom's movement towards perfect self-manifestation in and through the phenomenal consciousness. So, far from being the problematic dualism which the obscure ontology of the *Laṅkāvatāra Sūtra* was incapable of avoiding, ignorance, according to the *Mahāyānaśraddhotpāda* and the *Ch'eng Wei-Shih Lun*, is integrated into the essential dynamic through which the mind realizes itself in the omniscience of Buddhahood, and through which *Tathatā* coincidentally knows itself as the unconditional, indeterminate Suchness of reality, the essential nature of all things as mere-consciousness (*Vijñaptimātratathatā*).

The Tathāgatagarbha-Ālayavijñāna and the Hegelian Absolute Spirit

The interpretative principle through which the present study has focused the convergence of the *Tathāgatagarbha* and *Ālayavijñāna* has been the emergence of *Tathatā* from ontic substance to ontic subject. In its immanent modality as *Tathāgatagarbha, Tathatā* is the pure essence; the fundamental nature; the basic substratum; the unborn, undying, permanent, steadfast, eternal and ultimate ground of *saṃsāra* and *nirvāṇa*. But its generic designation as "embryo" qualifies this initial identification as mere substance, and specifies *Tathatā* as a processive absolute, the dynamic movement towards perfect self-awareness of its universal plenitude as the indeterminate, unconditional Suchness of all things. As *Ālayavijñāna*, it assumes a formal subjectivity as the noetic ground of phenomenal human consciousness through which it progressively realizes a concrete self-consciousness as the totality of phenomenal existence.

This principle of active self-emergence from latent, abstract universality to perfect self-explicit awareness of and as that integral wholeness of reality, the processive self-determination of substance to subject, is the very motif animating one of the most influential and comprehensive treatises in Western philosophy. In *The Phenomenology of Spirit*, G.W.F. Hegel details the itinerary through which consciousness journeys to arrive at its fullness as Absolute Spirit, where it knows itself as the whole of existence. Its homologous resonance with the thematic development of the *Tathāgatagarbha-Ālayavijñāna* indicates a convergent understanding of reality from two dominant, culturally distinct traditions of human thought. A brief review of the Hegelian interpretation will sharpen the focus of that convergence and further illumine the Buddhist perspective as set forth in the present study.

According to the *Phenomenology of Spirit*, the Absolute is no mere abstract universality, a bare uniformity, an undifferentiated, unmoved essence. To speak of it simply as "inherent nature", "ultimate being", or "fundamental ground" is to postulate it as some undefined and thus empty substantiality, a blank identity behind the forms and shapes of phenomenal existence. It is instead, the total process of its self-manifestation in and through those phenomena. If the Absolute is Substance, it is as a living Substance or Subject that it assumes its true reality and proper definition. In other words, the Absolute must come to know itself, be fully aware of itself as the totality of existence. It must affirm itself, come to perfect consciousness of itself as that "inherent nature", "ultimate being", and "fundamental ground" if it is to be more than an empty proposition or vague generality. In becoming Subject, the Absolute does not forfeit its status as ontic Substance, but realizes itself as knowledge, the form in which its wholeness as Substance becomes clearly self-explicit. In the concluding pages of the *Phenomenology*, Hegel recapitulates the entire, lengthy analysis of the stages in which the Absolute arrives at perfect knowledge of itself as the totality of all things, as the self-transformation of Substance into Subject:

> But this substance, which is spirit, is the development of itself explicitly to what it is inherently and implicitly; and only as this process of reflecting itself into itself is it essentially and in truth spirit. It is inherently the movement which is the process of knowledge—the transforming of that inherent nature into explicitness, of Substance into Subject, of the object of consciousness into the object of self-consciousness, i.e. into an object that is at the same time transcended....This transforming process is a cycle that returns into itself, a cycle that presupposes its beginning, and reaches its beginning only at the end.... Substance *qua* subject, involves the necessity, at first an *inner* necessity, to set forth in itself what it inherently is, to show itself to be spirit. The completed expression in objective form is—and is only when completed—at the same time the reflexion of substance, the development of it into the self. Consequently, until and unless spirit inherently completes itself, completes itself as a world-spirit, it cannot reach its completion as self-conscious spirit.[4]

Quite simply, the Absolute must become itself, must affirm its universality by recognizing itself as a world, the totality of nature,

4. G.W.F. Hegel, *The Phenomenology of Mind*, trans. J.B. Baillie (New York: Harper & Row, Harper Colophon Books, 1967), p. 801.

and it must do so in the concrete actuality of human consciousness. In other words, reality is a teleological process; and the ideal term presupposes the whole process and gives to it its significance. If the whole process is the self-unfolding of an essence, the actualization of an ideal Absolute, then it is only the term or end of the process that reveals what that Absolute really is—not an abstract substance, but a self-reflecting universe, an Absolute Spirit:

> The truth is the whole. The whole, however is merely the essential nature reaching its completeness through the process of its own development. Of the Absolute it must be said that it is essentially a result, that only at the end is it what it is in very truth; and just in that consists its nature, which is to be actual, subject, or self-becoming, self-development.[5]

Taken literally, many of Hegel's anthropomorphic expressions would easily suggest doctrines of Neoplatonic emanation or Thomistic creation in reference to the material universe, nature. But, within the entire scope of Hegel's philosophy such doctrines are quite foreign. If the Absolute as result of its own self-development is the self-conscious totality, then nature necessarily is the precondition, "the raw material" of that universal consciousness. Logically, the Absolute Spirit as Idea precedes nature, but from the temporal perspective, nature with its manifold shapes and forms is prior to the concrete actualization of that Spirit. As the necessary requisite for the authentic emergence of universal consciousness, nature is spoken of as "the other" of the Absolute as mere Idea and pure abstraction. In nature, the latter is said to assume objective determinate form, to become externality and otherness, to establish itself as its own object. Again, there is no question here of an ontological derivation of nature from the Absolute Idea as efficient cause. The self-objectification of that Idea in nature only specifies the latter as the indispensable proviso for the realization of the goal of the total process of reality, the universe's knowledge of itself in and through human consciousness, the Absolute Idea concretely expressed as self-conscious Absolute Spirit.

The Phenomenology of Spirit details the process by which the

5. Ibid., pp. 81-82.

Absolute Idea reinstates its self-identity in its otherness as nature, in and through the phenomenal mind. In human consciousness, it cancels and supersedes its self-objectification by recognizing itself in the manifold shapes and contours of nature. Behind the apparent immediacy and externality of things, consciousness gradually realizes its own presence and universality. The fixed objectivity of the world is thus annulled and transcended as its elements progressively become the moments in the self-recognition of consciousness. In knowing the world, consciousness knows itself, grasping its own meaning and expanding its own identity as it advances from mere sensation through perception; scientific understanding; social self-consciousness into reason; ethical, moral, and religious consciousness; and finally emerging as absolute knowledge or universal self-reflective Spirit. *The Phenomenology* details the morphogenetic development of consciousness into absolute self-consciousness: a process in which the multiplicity of objects not only defines the authentic identity of consciousness to itself, but the objects are themselves defined as so many moments of consciousness.

The journey which consciousness makes towards its own plenitude is initiated on the level of mere sense-certainty or sensation with a gulf between it (consciousness) and the material world, over against, external to, and independent of it. But this apparent chasm between consciousness and the phenomenal universe quickly collapses as Hegel demonstrates the critical contribution that consciousness makes in the apprehension of any object or thing. To believe that human knowledge is at its richest and fullest simply by opening the senses to the world and receiving whatever impressions come along, prior to any activity of the mind (particularly, conceptual activity) is simply naive and false. Sense-certainty merely establishes that a thing is, not what it is; it is then, the most empty and abstract form of knowledge. To say anything more about the object of sensation is to dissolve it into a series of concepts or universals and to imply intentionality. Since the certainty of what the object is, is no longer sensory at all but is the work of thought, consciousness is seen to contribute directly and crucially to the nature of the sense datum.

In the following stage of perception proper, the object confronting consciousness ceases to be a mere "this" and becomes a "thing," characterized by a number of distinct universals or properties. The thing is identified as the seat or medium of a characteristic pattern of properties which remain constant and self-same. Likewise, the thing is perceived to be exclusive and unitary, i.e. it stands apart from things different in character, and its properties are opposed to various contrary properties. The thing, a grain of salt, is hard and also white, and also crystalline, and also acrid. Taken together, this plurality of properties coalesce to form this one thing; taken separately, they are mutually distinct sense qualities that can be found in any number of other things. What is it then that reconciles the unity and exclusive character of the thing itself (the grain of salt) with the multiplicity of its independent and genuinely universal properties (hardness, whiteness, crystallinity, acridness)? Put otherwise, what is it that simultaneously preserves both the unity of the thing and the distinctness of its qualities? Or again, how is it possible that the thing is essentially one and essentially many, for "the thing contains within it opposite aspects of truth, a truth whose elements are in antithesis to one another"?[6]

As mere perception, consciousness is unable to answer this contradiction and must assume the next stage of its morphogenesis where it becomes understanding which invokes metaphenomenal or unobservable entities to explain sense phenomena. The diversity of aspects or properties of the object or thing is now held to belong to the world of sensory appearance, but to have a backing in a reality or realities which lie behind them at some deeper, inner level. This inner reality or essence is first understood to be a force or power which expands and manifests itself in a multiplicity of aspects. But as Hegel demonstrates, it is only the notion or concept of force, and not its reality, that consciousness posits to explain the multiple universal qualities that constitute the object of its perception. The "forces" are mere mental entities, abstractions which the understanding used to get at reality; they are not themselves real. The same is true of the various natural laws which are only conceptualizations; they are ways of ordering and describing phenomena and are not truly explicit. Like force, law is shown to belong less to things and objects, and more to the under-

6. Ibid., p. 172.

standing which employs them, less to the interior of things than to the understanding conceiving them. It becomes clear that the metaphenomenal or unobservable entities which were said to lie behind and explain the diverse aspects of sense phenomena, are merely products of consciousness functioning as understanding, and that its whole content is purely notional. Consciousness now realizes that the elements of analysis it initially thought it found in the reality analyzed are in fact its own doing. Having begun its attempted explanation of reality by positing forces and laws "out there" behind "the curtain" of sensory appearances, consciousness now discovers itself. Thus, it moves beyond itself as mere understanding and becomes self-consciousness proper:

> Consciousness of an other, of an object in general is indeed itself necessarily self-consciousness, reflectedness into self, consciousness of self in its otherness. The necessary advance from the previous attitudes of consciousness, which found their true content to be a thing, something other than themselves, brings to light this very fact that not merely is consciousness of a thing only possible for a self-consciousness but that this self-consciousness alone is the truth of those attitudes.[7]

According to Hegel, the presence of "the other" is essential to genuine self-consciousness. Developed self-consciousness can arise only when the self recognizes selfhood in itself and others. It must take the form, therefore, of a truly social or "we-consciousness". The fullest self-consciousness is only had in a world of mutually acknowledging, conscious persons, who are conscious also of their mutual acknowledgement. But it begins on a level where this mutual acknowledgement is imperfect, where each one only recognizes his own conscious self and attempts to maintain that self-recognition by negating all other claims to self-consciousness. This earliest stage of social self-consciousness is characterized by the master-slave relationship, where the former arrogates self-consciousness to himself by denying it to the latter who is thus degraded to a thing-like attenuation of life and self-consciousness. The paradox in this is that the master fails to achieve perfect self-consciousness, since the slave in whom he is to find and recognize

7. Ibid., pp. 211-12.

an image of his self has been deprived of that essential character. In addition, the slave actually achieves the more genuine self-consciousness since it is he, not the master, who labours. Through his work, the slave transcends the sheer givenness of matter by transforming it into an image of his thought, and thus attains a more authentic consciousness of self. "By the fact that the form is objectified, it does not become something other than the consciousness moulding the thing through work; for just that form is his pure self-existence, which therein becomes truly realized."[8] Consciousness typified by the slave, in thinking the form which work produces has brought forth a form of self-consciousness all its own, not imposed from what is outside itself. Thus consciousness knows itself as utterly free and independent; it is able to recognize that, while the work forced upon it is not free, the thought which goes into the work is.

Consciousness thus assumes a new form. As the "Stoical Consciousness" it represents that phase of mind that completely withdraws into the universality of thought, admitting nothing to be essential, nothing to be true or good, except insofar as it is acceptable to its own ideas. Having realized a certain independence, consciousness negates the otherness of all external determinations and seeks a greater freedom within itself. It thus quickly passes into skepticism which denies the reality of any influences disturbing to its thought. The skeptical consciousness secures an absolute independence and self-reliance by simply nullifying all fixity and negating the value of everything, but its own thought. But while transcending the contingency of the existent world which surrounds it, this mode of consciousness flounders in the very inessentiality it created through its systematic negation. Likewise, it becomes trapped in self-contradiction between what it says and what it does. It affirms the nullity of seeing, hearing, doing, and yet itself continues to see, hear, and act. It affirms the nullity of all ethical values and purpose, and yet makes them the ruling powers of its own actions.

This implicit self-contradiction of consciousness comes to the fore in what Hegel calls "the Unhappy Consciousness" which, having taken refuge in absolute doubt, now sees that it has no

8. Ibid., p. 239.

one to turn to but itself. But within itself, it is aware of a gulf between a changing, inconsistent, fickle self and a changeless, ideal self. Consciousness thus splits itself into itself and another, and it seeks its meaning in that other, which it itself projects and imaginatively represents as absolute, unchanging, and far removed from its transient world of particularities. Nevertheless, consciousness seeks to be united with this transcendent absolute, and attempts to do so by negating itself, affirming only its own nothingness and the insignificance of its own action. By thus surrendering its own will to the absolute will, consciousness attains to a universality where it can be aware of itself not as a mere, isolated individual, but as inherently the whole of reality.

Whereas formerly in its stoical and skeptical phases, consciousness felt constrained to negate the reality of the world in order to assert its own autonomy, now as reason it has discovered the universality which constitutes the truth of all things. Thus, in getting to the heart of any reality external to it, consciousness will find itself. "The subsistence of the world is taken to mean the actual presence of its own truth; it is certain of finding only itself there. Reason is the conscious certainty of being all reality."[9] Consciousness is convinced that reality is rational and that, therefore, in discovering reality, consciousness will discover reason, itself as reason.

With this certainty, consciousness once again turns to the world of phenomena where it acutely observes things in the attempt to find itself, and thus recognize its own contribution to the determinateness and concreteness of reality. But moving from the description and explanation of organic and inorganic nature through the logical laws of thought, the principles of empirical psychology, and the pseudo-sciences of physiognomy and phrenology, consciousness as observant reason fails to find an adequate reflection of its own rationality. Consciousness cannot find its universality in the mere givenness and immediacy of physical and biological reality. Thus it considers the practical activity of individual self-conscious reason. How does self-conscious reason reveal its universality to itself in its activity?

In mere hedonism the only universality that is obvious is the

9. Ibid., p. 273.

crass universality of reference to the individual self: everything and everyone exists only for the pleasure of the individual. Obviously, in this pursuit of one's own satisfaction to the indifference of everyone else, the universality shared by all men as self-conscious beings is totally disregarded. Just as dis-satisfactory is the sentimental universalism of ethical demand where the individual seeks to impose the dictates of his own heart as the universal good for all. But these supposedly impersonal and universal laws are in fact distressingly personal and particular and often in direct conflict with the ethical feelings of other hearts. Thus, sentiment is not a framework which can contain the universality proper to self-conscious reason.

What is necessary is to find a principle of human activity that is universally applicable to all men and recognized as such. It is not that self-consciousness should universalize its moral demands, but that it itself become universal. If law is to be truly law, eternally valid, it is to be rooted in the will of all. It cannot be a mere maxim or idea or feeling which ought to be a law; it simply is and has validity in itself. Such laws have an inherent rightness of their own and need no validation from logical reasoning. Their source is Universal Spirit, and in following them rational consciousness transcends it own individuality and becomes one with Absolute Spirit. Human consciousness, in recognizing the unilateral demands of these universal laws, realizes itself as the self-consciousness and existing actuality of the ethical absolute substance that is their source:

> Since, however, this existing law is absolutely valid, the obedience given by self-consciousness is not service rendered to a master, whose orders are mere caprice and in which it does not recognize its own nature. On the contrary, the laws are thoughts of its own absolute consciousness, thoughts which are its own immediate possession....The ethical self-consciousness is directly at one with the essential reality, in virtue of the universality of its own self...
>
> That the right is there for me just as it stands—this places me within the substance of ethical reality: and in this way that substance is the essence of self-consciousness. But self-conscious-

ness, again, is *its* actualization and its existence, its self, and its will.[10]

Therefore, the universal dimension of the human spirit is not attained simply by generalizing what is essentially individual (which rational consciousness has been doing), but by turning to the subjective universal which is spirit. And this spirit is the ultimate ground of moral behaviour, the ethical substance, recognized by all men when they are conscious of a moral demand which is not of their own doing. It finds concrete expression and actuality first in the unreflective ethical life of the community regulated by traditions and customs that are accepted in their givenness, rather than questioned and rationally examined. This results in a tragic conflict between the human and divine laws whose dictates are mutually contradictory and doom the individual to profound guilt by forcing him to choose the one and thus violate the other. At this level, human beings have nothing to say as to what the laws are, but where only an impersonal, alien "ethical substance" dictates what is to be done. Thus, it is not enough that men unreflectively recognize the demands of the ethical substance, but that they be rationally formulated in laws which would define all individuals universally.

But when this is done at the next stage of consciousness where all individuals assume the juridical status of "persons", each equal to the others, each accorded rights by the law, the universality that is established is extrinsic: it is imposed on all from without. Each and all are what they are and who they are only by being legislated as such by law. Nothing of the inner essence of personhood is recognized, only the impersonal personhood decreed by the law. Thus self-consciousness is split between a private and a public self and world, and it is the responsibility of each individual to give to himself a form of universality which is more than that of mere equality with everyone else. It attempts to do so in the form of "culture", but this only perpetuates the dichotomy between the individual spirit and the cultural norms to which it must conform despite itself. This results in a revolution against the tyranny of culture and the absolute emancipation from all social

10. Ibid., pp. 451-53.

and supernatural ties. The problem is that the demand for universal freedom often results in a cold, doctrinaire insistence whose end is violence, chaos, and death. On the one hand, freedom is meaningless unless each, single individual is free. But on the other hand, if it is not expressed in the concrete political order, freedom remains mere abstraction. All too often, the process of actualizing that latter order severely compromises the former. This failure to reconcile the demands of individual and universal freedom forces consciousness to assume another form, that of the authentically moral spirit which simultaneously enjoys the individuality and the universality of moral reason, i.e. an individual reason whose grounds are universal.

Consciousness once again turns to acknowledge those inherent moral demands, those universal ethical laws which are its own immediate possession as one with the absolute. In the community regulated by unreflective custom and tradition, as well as that which explicitly legislated personhood on a universal basis, what ultimately determined human individuality came from outside itself. In the consequent rebellion against all cultural constraint, consciousness simply went farther afield and only now returns to itself and the innate categorical imperative which it shares equally with all men and which thus reconciles its activity as an isolated individual with the moral activity of all others. In the form of conscience, the universally recognized "duty" of the categorical imperative attains a necessary concreteness; not only is there a knowledge of what is to be done, but a capacity to will the doing. The individual recognizes that the limitations of morality on its freedom are self-imposed limitations, and what impels it to act, is its own conviction.

But as he has done throughout the *Phenomenology*, Hegel demonstrates the inability of this mode of conscientious consciousness to perfectly harmonize individuality and universality. For if its actions are ultimately based on personal conviction, then there is no universally valid judgment regarding the morality of its actions; conscience makes anything right and cannot be questioned. Personal conviction is not necessarily synonymous with the truth. It is all too easy to rationalize one's actions and to ignore the fact that what one considers a good, might be an injustice in the eyes of others. The universality of conscience then is only a universality of form, not content. Whatever one conscientiously holds as right is respected as right for him, but it need not coincide with what another holds as right for himself, and which he in turn expects all others to recognize as right for him. Objective consciousness thus ceases to have any significance, where that matters is each one's consciousness of himself.

Another aberration of conscientious consciousness is "the beautiful soul", the conscience which refuses all activity for fear of committing a wrong and thus of sullying its purity. Prizing its own internal innocence, it proceeds to judge all others who commit themselves to decision and action, not realizing that its own judgment is as much a commitment and an act as those which it condemns. Putting excessive negative weight on deeds, this mode of consciousness completely fails to understand that deeds, even evil ones, are not irreparable; healing through forgiveness is as yet foreign to its thought. Yet it is only the forgiving consciousness that is able to transcend the isolated singularity of the individual conscience following its own convictions, and "the beautiful soul" trapped in its own inactivity and critical judgments upon those who do act.

The most concrete manifestation of universal spirit up to this point is the reconciliation of men with each other. By dissolving the tension between action and judgment, the forgiving consciousness fosters mutual tolerance and indulgence among individuals who thus constitute the only authentically concrete universal self, the community. Consciousness here emerges as spirit (not yet Absolute), since as loving forgiveness it breaks down the barriers between persons and "overcomes the otherness of the other". In this reconciling activity, human individuality is lifted to its divine, universal dimension:

> The reconciling affirmation, the "yes" with which both egos desist from their existence in opposition, is the existence of the ego expanded into a duality, an ego which remains therein one and identical with itself, and possesses the certainty of itself in its complete relinquishment and its opposite: it is God appearing in the midst of those who know themselves in the form of pure knowledge.[11]

11. Ibid., p. 679.

Having realized its own universal subjectivity, consciousness as spirit now seeks in religion, the form that will perfectly correspond to its universal essence and will enable it to see itself as it is. Since the *Phenomenology* had already established that all consciousness is self-consciousness, the progressive spiritualization of the God of whom man is conscious is concomitant with a progressive recognition of the spirituality of human consciousness. It must suffice to say that all forms of religious consciousness reviewed by Hegel prior to Christianity proved inadequate. They represented to themselves either a god or gods not recognizable as spirit (as in the religion of nature), or else gods who, while having some of the attributes of spirit, were not present in their man-made representations (as in the religion of art).

It is the Christian doctrine of the Incarnation that reveals to human consciousness that to be totally human is to be divine. Christ is at once "absolute" and human, who reveals to man the utmost in human potentialities. He is God Who is self-conscious spirit and man who is conscious of himself as divine. In Christ, the Absolute Substance becomes concretely self-conscious, and an externalized, individual self-consciousness becomes concretely universal. This twofold movement is expressed determinately in the death of the God-man. What dies on the one hand is the particularity of the singular individual which passes over into, and is resurrected within the divine essence. On the other hand, but in the very same process, it is the Divine Being that dies in its empty abstraction as a blank identity and undefined substantiality, and its self-actualization as Subject. This divine death is,

> ... in point of fact, the loss of the Substance and of its objective existence over against consciousness. But at the same time, it is the pure subjectivity of Substance, the pure certainty of itself, which it lacked when it was object or immediacy, or pure essential Being. This knowledge is thus spiritualization, whereby Substance becomes Subject, by which its abstraction and lifelessness have expired, and Substance therefore has become real, simple, and universal self-consciousness. In this way then, Spirit is Spirit knowing its own self.[12]

12. Ibid., p. 782.

In the Incarnation and death of Christ then, the divine nature is the same as what the human nature is, and the process of man's becoming universal spirit and God's becoming concretely Subject is one and the same. In the self-consciousness of Christ, God is known as self-consciousness and is immediately present to self-consciousness, for He is that self-consciousness itself.[13]

However, if Christian religious consciousness only knows God as knowing Himself in Christ, if the self-consciousness which knows God is only the self-consciousness of Christ as individual, then the identity of Christian God-consciousness and Christian self-consciousness is not yet explicit. The self of which the individual Christ is conscious must be universalized, must be the self of the entire Christian community. The divine absolute Substance that became Subject in the self-consciousness of Christ, must extend and confirm that Subjectivity in the life of the community. For, "its truth consists not merely in being the substance or the inherent reality of the religious communion; ... but in becoming concrete actual self, reflecting itself into self, and being *Subject*. This, then, is the process which Spirit realizes in its communion; this is its *life*."[14]

But so long as the religious consciousness continues to represent Christ to itself as independent, objective self-consciousness instead of appropriating that consciousness as its own authentic reality, it is not yet totally conscious of its own fullness. In being conscious of God as absolute self-consciousness, religious consciousness conceives of Him as another, external to it, and does not identify itself with the God of which it is conscious. While it may feel and speak of a union with Him, it is merely implicit; God is still "presented to", and not yet the very self of human consciousness. In its awareness of God, religious consciousness is aware of itself as being in some way universalized in order to correspond to its object, but it does not fully comprehend that the consciousness of God and the consciousness of itself are one and the same.

Thus far, the various stages through which consciousness has evolved from mere sense certainty have revealed themselves to be the forms in which consciousness, in knowing what is other than

13. See Ibid., pp. 759-60.
14. Ibid., p. 764.

itself, actually comes to know itself. Gradually, the distinction between its objects and itself has been overcome, such that the appearance of reality and the consciousness of it are one and the same process. Thus, when individual consciousness has as its object universal, absolute Being it ceases to be merely finite and particular; in conceiving infinite reality, that which has no limits, human consciousness (free of the representational forms of its religious modality) transcends its own singularity, and itself has no limits. Coincidentally, in being thus conceived, absolute reality renounces the rigidity of its abstract universality and attains, in and through human consciousness, a definite and concrete self-awareness. In this final stage of consciousness, mere universality and mere particularity are self-transcendent in the complementarity of one and the same moment of self-consciousness: to be fully conscious of oneself is to be conscious of the Absolute which realizes a genuine self-awareness in and through that very consciousness.

This dynamic union of finite and infinite self-consciousness represents the completed self-actualization of Substance as Subject, the self-evolution of spirit as Absolute. Hegel's prefatory definition of true reality as the process of its own becoming, the whole reaching its completeness through its own development, of reinstating its self-identity in and from its other, has been exemplified in detail. Absolute Spirit is the active process of its self-emergence from the bare uniformity of an undifferentiated, abstract essence or substantiality into the subjectivity of individual consciousness which initially regards the whole of existence as separate from and objective to itself. Yet, through the reflective process outlined above, consciousness supersedes that distinction, recognizing its own central contribution to the being of the objects it perceives. Its conception of them is the very vehicle of their self-manifestation. For the true being of an object is its being conceived, since apart from being conceived it is not an object. Therefore, the split between self and world, consciousness and content, subject and substance is not invidious, but is itself the very manner in which Spirit realizes itself as totality and thus, as Absolute. By themselves, neither consciousness nor phenomena constitute Absolute Spirit. But taken as an integral whole, the distinction between them ceases to be one of antithetic poles, and becomes instead the distinction between transitional steps or complementary moments of one and the same dynamic process of self-realization.

A key passage from its preface broadly summarizes the *Phenomenology's* exhaustively detailed analysis of Spirit's self-movement from Substance to Subject. As the former, it is the initial abstract essence of all things. As the latter, it is the conscious self-explication of that original unity. In and through human consciousness it is aware of the diversity and multiplicity of forms which specify its universality, the awareness of which (in and through that same consciousness) negates the apparent opposition of those forms and preserves them as differences-in-identity. Spirit is Absolute only upon its return to itself in and through human consciousness from its self-estranged manifestation, its "otherness" of the phenomenal world. This self-evolution of Spirit takes place within the closed circuit of totality to totality. It is the movement of an original absolute becoming self-explicit, where the only transition is from the inarticulate immediacy of substance to the perfect subjectivity of a comprehensive self-consciousness:

> The living substance, further, is that being which is truly subject, or, what is the same thing, is truly realized and actual solely in the process of positing itself, or in mediating with its own self its transitions from one state or position to the opposite. As subject it is pure and simple negativity, and just on that account a process of splitting up what is simple and undifferentiated, a process of duplicating and setting factors in opposition, which (process) in turn is the negation of this indifferent diversity and of the opposition of factors it entails. True reality is merely this process of reinstating self-identity, of reflecting into its own self in and from its other, and is not an original and primal unity as such, not an immediate unity as such. It is the process of its own becoming, the circle which presupposes its end as its purpose, and has its end for its beginning; it becomes concrete and actual only by being carried out, and by the end it involves.[15]

Several points of convergence between the Buddhist conception of the *Tathāgatagarbha-Ālayavijñāna* and the Hegelian Absolute

15. Ibid., pp. 80-81.

Spirit thus emerge under the common principle of the self-evolution of Substance to Subject. Both share a common interpretation of reality as a generic process of self-transformation, the conscious disclosure of itself to itself as integral totality. *Tathatā's* movement to know itself as the indeterminate Suchness of all things (discussed in terms of either the *Tathāgatagarbha's* self-maturation as *Dharmakāya,* or the *Ālayavijñāna's* self-luminosity as *Mahābodhi*) is paralleled by the movement of Hegelian consciousness towards its universality as self-reflective Spirit. Both assume a more specific common focus and denote a self-teleology of inner convergence. On the one hand, *Dharmakāya* (or *Mahābodhi*) as *telos* is simply the point of the *Tathāgatagarbha's* fully self-conscious, self-revelation. Similarly on the other hand, the Hegelian Absolute Spirit represents the self-consummation of consciousness, knowing itself through its various phases (from mere sensation to absolute philosophical knowledge) to be the whole of reality. In both the Buddhist and Hegelian systems therefore, the Absolute is the very process that culminates in itself as result: a process of self-exposition, leading to perfect self-understanding.

That the Buddhist and Hegelian Absolute is its own becoming, both means and end of its self-actualization, stems from a further point of convergence between the two. For both, the essence of Reality is knowledge: the inherent self-activity which modifies it from mere substance to subject, and defines both the process and the goal as self-consciousness. The latter corresponds to the notion of subject, and that which the self-consciousness is about corresponds to the notion of substance. Thus, the *Tathāgatagarbha-Ālayavijñāna* represents the self-conscious activity of *Tathatā*, its subjective modality, confirming itself in its plenitude as the universal essence, the indeterminate Suchness of all things. Its self-comprehension is possible since the totality of phenomena are in fact, the radically ideal manifestations or transformations of consciousness, the essential nature of which is itself (i.e., *Tathatā*); the self-transparency of Suchness as the whole of reality is the self-recognition of consciousness in the multiplicity of its forms.

Similarly, the Hegelian Absolute is hardly expressed by mere propositions that simply proclaim it to be "the Eternal", "Being", "Universal Essence", etc. While such substantive propositions or first principles may be true, they are blank expressions incapable of expressing what is implied in them. The Absolute must ratify itself as such through a process of self-development in which it becomes objective to itself. The Absolute is a living, spiritual reality which can exist only in the vivid consciousness and affirmation of itself, and which can only rise to such active self-consciousness by being first embodied in a long series of distinct and opposed forms, in all of which it comes to see itself. That it does so in and through human consciousness demonstrates a further coincidence between the Buddhist and Hegelian systems.

Both posit a dynamic union of infinite and finite consciousness in which the latter is transformed and perfected in the self-realization of the former of which it (finite consciousness) is the very vehicle. Without the phenomenal mind, the subjectivity of the Absolute would be mere abstraction. Thus, in itself *Tathatā* may be spoken of as *Pariniṣpanna,* the ultimately real, self-subsistent Absolute. But without human consciousness (*paratantra*), it would be incapable of transcending that category of bare substance to attain a concrete self-awareness as that Absolute. Since that stage simultaneously represents the formal liberation of the human mind from all trace of ignorance and its definitive maturation in the perfect wisdom of Buddhahood, finite and infinite consciousness are generically united in one and the same process of self-realization; *Mahābodhi* signifies the climactic threshold not of the *Ālayavijñāna* alone, but in organic collaboration with *manas*, *manovijñāna* and the sensorial consciousnesses.

Even less pronounced is the distinction between finite and infinite consciousness in Hegel's *Phenomenology* whose definition of the latter emerges only through an exact and sustained focus upon the former. The continuity of consciousness from mere sensation to absolute knowing, where each stage is preserved in the subsequent stage and is not only a means to, but a part of the ultimate totality, invalidates any rigorous separation into finite and infinite. The dynamic of the end, viz., universal self-reflective Spirit, is present in the dynamic of the process in which consciousness at each level, confronted by what is other than itself, comes to recognize itself. Where the activity of self-consciousness pervades and determines the entire process, the distinction between finite and infinite consciousness is without significance; both are phases in

Reality's knowledge of itself, and the human mind is the actual locus of their integration and its realization.

A final point of convergence between the Buddhist theory of the *Tathāgatagarbha-Ālayavijñāna* and the Hegelian *Phenomenology of Spirit* lies in their similar accommodation of the obstacles which impede the consummation of *Mahābodhi* and absolute knowledge, respectively. As a critical development of the present study has revealed, ignorance, far from being extraneous to Absolute Suchness, is the necessary condition for its self-explication in and through human consciousness. Implicitly, *Tathatā* is the whole of reality and its essence is to know itself as such not in some vague, abstract conviction but concretely and precisely in every perception of the phenomenal mind. Only through the active process of delineating the emptiness and non-substantiality of apparently discrete, autonomous persons and things, of overcoming the gap between one's self and an illusory world of distinct and mutually exclusive particularities, does the implicit wisdom of *Tathatā* determine itself in the explicit emergence of its universality and unity as *Dharmadhātu*.

The Buddhist thesis that the Absolute beginninglessly integrates ignorance as a phase of its own self-development in wisdom, finds resonance in the Hegelian notion that the self-consciousness of Absolute Spirit is a result of the subjugation of otherness, in the sense of having the latter as a necessary condition. Without a beginning in sense, the activities of consciousness would have nothing to sublimate, unify and universalize, and hence could not *be* at all. Without the particularity of feeling and impulse to control and organize, consciousness would never move from mere sense certainty through perception and understanding to self-consciousness and reason. Absolute Spirit emerges only in and through the active process of transcending the determinate fixity of objects in space and time, by revealing the ideal laws and patterns of their universality. Finally, the richness of content that defines Absolute Spirit as self-conscious Totality is not the result of dissipating and absorbing all specificity and distinction into a blank, undifferentiated identity. The Hegelian Absolute exists not despite nor at the cost of phenomenal multiplicity; they are instead, its very manifestation, its differentiated identity, that of which it is conscious in knowing itself.

Differences between the Buddhist and Hegelian perspectives undoubtedly exist regarding the value of the temporal process and its implied social transformations for the self-realization of the Absolute, as well as the determinative role of conceptual elaboration and/or intuitive insight for the attainment of that realization in and through human consciousness. But such discrepancies, among others, are not within the scope of the present study.

The emergent complementarity of the *Tathāgatagarbha* and *Ālayavijñāna* as sustaining a comprehensive and coherent metaphysics of Absolute Suchness has been the controlling thesis and unique contribution of the present study. The noetic character and processive dimension of that metaphysics had been formulated in the principle of the Absolute's self-determination from Substance to Subject. As such, its resonance with Hegel's *Phenomenology of Spirit* had been noted. The importance of that corollary lies not merely in its indications for future dialogue between Buddhist thought and Western philosophy on the relationship between the Absolute and phenomenal orders, facilitated by a common focus on human consciousness as their mutual coincidence. It has likewise confirmed the value of this study whose demonstrated convergence of two principal notions within the Buddhist tradition has delineated the psychometaphysical orientation out of, and upon which that dialogue may proceed.

Appendix 1

NUMERICAL LISTINGS FROM THE *ŚRĪ-MĀLĀ SŪTRA* AND THE *RATNAGOTRAVIBHĀGA*

The Ten Vows of Queen Śrī-Mālā

The first five vows adhere to the ethics of the Hīnayāna, i.e., entertaining no thought of violating morality; of disrespect towards the teachers; of anger and ill-will towards any beings; of jealousy towards others, and of covetousness. The second group of five generally constitutes the Mahāyāna ethical code, i.e., non-accumulation of wealth for private use; seeking the benefit and conversion of all beings; the liberation of all beings from all suffering; the non-toleration of sinful occupations and violations of the Doctrine and Discipline (*dharma-vinaya*); and finally, the vow never to forget the Illustrious Doctrine for even a single moment.

The Four Confidences of the Buddha as recorded by the Śrī-Mālā Sūtra

The confidence that he is fully enlightened about all natures; the confidence in knowing the destruction of all defiling fluxes; the confidence that he explains exactly and definitely the obstructive conditions; and the confidence in the correctness of his path of salvation for realizing all success.

The Ten Powers of the Buddha as recorded by the Śrī-Mālā Sūtra

The discernment of the possible; knowledge of every direction of the path; knowledge of the various realms of the world; knowledge of the diversity of faiths; knowledge of the addictions and merits of others; recognition of the auspicious and inauspicious force of karma; knowledge of defilement and purification, of meditation and equipoises; knowledge of the many modes of his former lives; the attainment of the perfectly clear divine eye; and the attainment of the destruction of all defilements.

The Eighteen Exclusive Buddha Natures (the Buddha Eye) as recorded by the Śrī-mālā Sūtra

Unhindered knowledge of the past; of the future; of the present; all his acts of body; of speech; of mind are preceded with knowledge and attended with knowledge; there is no loss of longing; of striving; of mindfulness; of samādhi; of insight; of liberation; he has no faltering; no harsh note; no forgetting; no unequipoised thought; no unpremeditated indifference; and no idea of multiplicity.

The Eight Qualities of Buddhahood as recorded by the Ratnagotravibhāga

Immutability (*asaṃskṛtatva*); freedom from any effort (*anābhogatā*); enlightenment not dependent on others (*aparapratyayābhisaṃbodhi*); wisdom (*jñāna*); compassion (*karuṇā*); supernatural power (*śakti*); fulfilment of self-benefit (*svārthasaṃpad*); and fulfilment of benefit for others (*parārthasaṃpad*).

The Eight Qualities of the Dharma as recorded by the Ratnagotravibhāga

Unthinkability (*acintyatva*); non-duality (*advayatā*); non-discriminativeness (*nirvikalpatā*); purity (*śuddhi*); being manifest (*abhivyaktikaraṇa*); hostility against obstacles (*pratipakṣata*); deliverance from passions (*virāga*); and cause of deliverance (*virāgahetu*).

The Thirteen Factors Defining the Bodhisattva Path as recorded by the Abhisamayālaṅkāra

The six dharmas conducive to spiritual achievement (i.e., the four aids to penetration, the path of vision, the path of development); the production of the antidotes; the forsaking of detrimental states; the state of being able to overlook the difference between those two (i.e., between antidotes and harmful states); wisdom together with compassion; the virtues of a Bodhisattva which are not shared with the Disciples; the successive actions for the welfare of others; and the action of the cognition which works without any effort for the welfare of others; and the action of the cognition which works without any effort for the welfare of beings.

The Ten Perspectives through which the Ratnagotravibhāga analyses Tathatā

Its own nature (*svabhāva*); its cause (*hetu*); the result of its purification (*phala*); its function (*karman*) towards that purification; its union (*yoga*); its manifestation (*vṛtti*); the various states of its manifestation (*avasthāprabheda*); its all-pervasiveness (*sarvatraga*); its unchangeability (*avikāra*) through various states; and its non-differentiation (*abheda*).

The Eight Virtuous Roots (Kuśala-Mūla) of the Bodhisattva as recorded by the Ratnagotravibhāga

Non-satisfaction in searching for accumulation of merits; acceptance of existence through origination by their own will; earnest wish to meet with the Buddhas; unweariness towards the perfect maturity of living beings; efforts for the perfect apprehension of the sublime Doctrine; endeavour after works to be done for living beings; non-abandonment of propensity of desire for phenomena; and non-reluctance from fetters of the highest virtues.

The Four Dhyānas as recorded by the Ratnagotravibhāga

Dwelling with thoughts applied, and discursive, born of detachment, full of rapture and ease; without thoughts applied and discursive, born of concentration, full of rapture and ease; through distaste for rapture (dwelling) even-mindedly, mindful and clearly conscious, and with ease; forsaking ease, experiencing neither pleasure nor pain with utter purity of even-mindedness and mindfulness.

The Five Supernatural Faculties (Indriyas) as recorded by the Ratnagotravibhāga

Faith; vigor; mindfulness; concentration; and wisdom.

The Thirty-Two Buddha-guṇāh as recorded by the Ratnagotravibhāga include: The ten powers (balānvita)

The power of knowing about the proper and improper place; of knowing about the results of former actions; of knowing about the faculties; about the component elements; about the various faiths of the people; of knowing about the path; about purity and impurity in contemplation; about the memory of previous abodes; of knowing about the divine eyes; and of knowing about quiescence (how to destroy evil influences).

The four forms of intrepidity or the four confidences (caturvaiśāradyaprāpta)

In his perfect Enlightenment of all the elements, the Buddha knows and causes others to know all things cognizable in all their forms; in rejecting all obstacles, he destroys everything that is to be rejected and causes others to reject them; in preaching the path, he serves and lets others serve in the method to be practised; in acquirnig the extinction, he attains and causes others to attain the highest and purest state.

The eighteen exclusive properties (Āvenikadharmas)

With Buddha there is no error; no rough speech; no loss of memory; no distraction of mind; no pluralistic conception; he is not indifferent; not without consideration; he knows no deprivation of zeal; no deprivation of energy; no deprivation of his memory; no deprivation of the transcendental intellect; no deprivation of liberation; no deprivation of the intuition of this liberation; his actions of body, speech, and mind are preceded by wisdom; his intuition acts unimpededly in the past, future, and present.

The Fourteen Mahāvastu as recorded by the Ratnagotravibhāga

The various previous births of the Buddha; the birth in the Tuṣita-heaven; the descent from it; the entrance into the womb; the birth in this world (as Gotama); the skilfulness in various arts and works; pleasureable entertainments among ladies in the harem; the renouncement of the world; practice of asceticism; passage to the excellent seat of Enlightenment; the conquest over the army of evil demons; the acquisition of Enlightenment; setting into motion the wheel of the Doctrine; and the departure into Nirvāṇa.

Appendix 2

NUMERICAL LISTINGS FROM THE *CH'ENG WEI-SHIH LUN*

The Ten Śastra-Masters of the Vijñanavadin Tradition

Bandhuśrī, a contemporary of Vasubandhu.
Citrabhānu, a contemporary of Vasubandhu.
Gunamati (420-500 A.D.).
Sthiramati (470-550 A.D.).
Nanda (450-530 A.D.).
Śuddhacandra, a contemporary of Sthiramati.
Dharmapala (530-561 A.D.), whose interpretation of Vasubandhu was the one generally accepted by Hsüan Tsang.
Viśesamitra, a disciple of Dharmapala.
Jinaputra, a disciple of Dharmapala.
Jñānacandra, a disciple of Dharmapala.

The Ten Categories of the Ch'eng Wei-Shih Lun's Analysis of Parikalpita, Paratantra, and Parinişpanna

The unconditioned non-active dharmas with particular attention to the infinity of space (*ākāśa*), discrimination-annihilation (*pratisāmkhya-nirodha*), and non-discrimination-annihilation (*apratisāmkhyanirodha*). *The seven aspects of Bhūtatathatā*, consisting of the *Tathatā* of transmigration; of the two realities; of mere-consciousness; of the real nature of suffering; of wrong conduct; of untainted purity; and of right conduct.
The six dharmas-matter; sensation; conception; predisposition; consciousness; and the unconditioned non-active dharmas.
The five objects—appearance; name; discrimination; right knowledge; Suchness.
The four realities (*tattvas*)—empirical truth; reasoned conclusion; the four Noble Truths; and *Bhūtatathatā*.

The four Noble Truths.
The objects of the three liberations—liberation through emptiness, through the absence of desires and aspirations, and through the absence of characteristics.
The two truths—mundane truth and ultimate, supramundane truth.
The two wisdoms of the Pṛthagjanas and of the Aryas.
The two modes of existence—existence as designation and real existence.

THE TEN FUNDAMENTAL VEXING PASSIONS (MULAKLEŚAS)

Covetousness (*rāga*); anger (*pratigha*); delusion (*moha*); conceit (*māna*); doubt (*vicikitsā*); and erroneous views (*kudṛṣṭi*) which include: the notion of "I and mine" (*satkāyadṛṣṭi*); one-sided extreme views (eternalism and nihilism) (*antagrāhadṛṣṭi*); false views (*mithyādṛṣṭi*); the consideration of certain erroneous views as excellent (*dṛṣiparāmarśa*); the consideration of certain practices and exercises as excellent (*śīdavrataparāmarśa*).
Though one hundred twenty eight *kleśas* can be enumerated, they are all included in these fundamental six.

THE TWENTY SECONDARY VEXING PASSIONS (UPAKLEŚAS)

Fury (*krodha*), a form of anger; enmity (*upanāha*), a form of anger; hypocrisy or concealment (*mrakṣa*), a form of delusion and covetousness; vexation (*pradāśa*), a form of anger; envy (*īrṣyā*), a form of anger; parsimony (*mātsarya*), a form of covetousness; deception (*sāṭhya*), a form of covetousness and delusion; duplicity (*māyā*), a form of covetousness; harmfulness (*vihiṃsā*) a form of anger; pride (mada), a form of covetousness; shamelessness (*āhrīkya*); non-integrity (*anapatrāpya*); restlessness (*auddhatya*); torpidmindedness (*styāna*); unbelief (*āśraddhya*); indolence (*kausīdya*); idleness or nęgligence (*pramāda*); forgetfulness (*musitasmrtitā*); distraction (*vikṣepa*); and non-discernment (*asaṃprajanya*). It is said that though there may be many more *upakleśas*, essentially they are all included in these twenty.

The Barriers of Ignorance (Jñeyāvaraṇas) Peculiar to Each of the Ten Bhūmis

The barrier constituted by the nature of the ordinary unenlightened person (*pṛthagjanatvāvaraṇa*) is, along with the kleśāvaraṇa, a barrier of ignorance (*jñeyāvaraṇa*) which arises through speculation and discrimination. It is an obstacle to the first bhūmi.

The barrier of perverse conduct (*mithyāpratipattyāvaraṇa*) is a barrier of innate ignorance impeding the entry to the second bhūmi.

The barrier of unintelligence and failure of memory (*dhandhatvāvaraṇa*) obscures the samādhis and dhāranīs of the third bhūmi.

The barrier of ignorance comprising the erroneous "I and mine" notion (*sūkṣmakleśasamudācārāvaraṇa*) hampers the attainment of the fourth bhūmi.

The ignorant attachment to parinirvāṇa (*hīnayānaparinirvāṇāvaraṇa*) impedes the wisdom of non-differentiation of the fifth bhūmi.

The barrier of clinging to ideas of purity and impurity as ultimately real (*sthūlanimittasamudācārāvaraṇa*) hampers the wisdom of the sixth bhūmi.

The ignorance positing an ultimate beginning (birth) and/or ultimate end (destruction) (*sūkṣmanimittasamudācārāvaraṇa*) opposes the contemplation of the seventh bhūmi.

The innate ignorance that prevents a non-conceptual contemplation, free of all notions and characteristics from functioning effortlessly and spontaneously in the eighth bhūmi (*nirnimittābhisaṃskārāvaraṇa*).

The ignorant attachment to one's own self-cultivation with no desire for the welfare of others (*parahita-caryā-akāmanā-āvaraṇa*) blocks the development of the four unhindered powers of interpretation and reasoning characteristic of the ninth bhūmi.

The ignorance preventing the complete mastery of all the dhāraṇīs, samādhis, meritorious activities and supernatural powers (*dharmeṣuvaśitāpratilambhāvaraṇa*) prolongs an extremely subtle attachment to all known objects. It is cut off on entrance into the tenth bhūmi.

The Five Stages of the Holy Path of Attainment

The stage of moral provisioning (*saṃbhārāvasthā*); the stage of intensified effort (*prayogāvasthā*); the stage of unimpeded penetrating understanding (*prativedhāvasthā*); the stage of exercising cultivation (*bhāvanāvasthā*); and the stage of final attainment or ultimate realization (*niṣṭhāvasthā*).

The Nirvedhabhāgīyas (Factors Leading to True and Pure Intelligence)

The meditation known as "illumination-attainment" (*ālokalabdha-samādhi*) which enables one to attain the state of "heat" or "warmth" (*uṣmagatāvastha*) is the "forerunner of the fire which illumines and warms the pure path."

The meditation known as "increasing illumination" (*ālokavṛddhi-samādhi*) which leads to the highest acme of reflection through the continual increase of illumination, and is thus called "the state of culmination" (*mūrdhāvastha*).

The meditation known as "spontaneous recognition" (*yin-shun*) which is the state in which there is recognition or admission (*kṣānti*) of the emptiness of subject and object.

The meditation of uninterrupted continuity (*ānantaryasamādhi*) which realizes the state of "the first worldly truth" (*laukikāgra-dharma*) confirming the realization of the former state.

SELECTED BIBLIOGRAPHY

PRIMARY SOURCES: ORIGINAL SANSKRIT AND CHINESE TEXTS

Chatterjee, A.K., ed. *Readings on Yogācāra Buddhism*. Banaras: Banaras Hindu University, 1971.

Hsüan Tsang. *Ch'eng Wei-Shih Lun*. Edited and translated by Wei Tat. Hong Kong: Ch'eng Wei-Shih Lun Publication Committee, 1973.

Johnston, E.H., ed. *Ratnagotara-vibhāga-mahāyānottaratantra-śāstra*. Patna, 1950.

Nāgārjuna. *Mūlamadhyamikakārikā*. Edited and translated by Kenneth K. Inada. Tokyo: Hokuseido Press, 1970.

Vaidya, P.L., ed. *Saddharmalaṅkāvatārasūtram*. Darbhanga: The Mithila Institute, 1963.

Vasubandhu. "Vijñaptimātratāsiddhi-Triṃśikā" in *Ch'eng Wei-Shih Lun*, pp. CXI-CXXI. Edited and translated by Wei Tat. Hong Kong: Ch'eng Wei-Shih Lun Publication Committee, 1973.

PRIMARY SOURCES: WESTERN TRANSLATIONS

Blofeld, John., trans. *The Zen Teaching of Huang Po on the Transmission of Mind*. New York: Grove Press, 1958.

Buddhaghosa, Bhadantācariya. *The Path of Purification*. Translated by Bhikkhu Nyāṇamoli. 2nd ed. Colombo: A. Semage, 1964.

Bu-ston. *History of Buddhism*. Translated by E. Obermiller. Heidelberg: Materialien zur Kunde des Buddhismus, 1931.

Conze, Edward., trans. *Abhisamayālaṅkāra*. Rome: Instituto Italiano Per Il Medio Ed Estremo Oriente, 1954.

——. *Buddhist Wisdom Books: The Diamond Sūtra and The Heart Sūtra*. London: George Allen & Unwin, Ltd., 1958; reprint ed., New York: Harper & Row, 1972.

——. *The Large Sūtra on Perfect Wisdom*. Berkeley: The University of California Press, 1975.

——. *The Perfection of Wisdom in Eight Thousand Lines and its Verse Summary*. Bolinas: Four Seasons Foundation, 1973.

Dogen. "Shōbōgenzo Buddha Nature." Translated by Norman Waddell and Abe Masao. *The Eastern Buddhist* 2 (1975): 94-112.

Hakeda, Yoshito S., trans. *The Awakening of Faith*. New York: Columbia University Press, 1967.

——. *Kukai: Major Works, Translated, with an Account of His Life and a Study of His Thought*. New York: Columbia University Press, 1972.

Hegel, G.W.F. *The Phenomenology of Mind*. Translated by J.B. Baillie. London: Macmillan Co., 1910; reprint ed., New York: Harper & Row, 1967.

Lamotte, Etienne, trans. *L'Enseignement de Vimalakīrti*. Louvain: Publications Universitaires, 1962.

——. *Saṃdhinirmocana Sūtra*. Paris: Bureaux Du Recueil, Louvain, Librairie D'Amérique et D'Orient, 1935.

——. *Le Traité de La Grande Vertu de Sagesse de Nāgārjuna*. Louvain: Bureaux du Muséon, 1949.

Luk, Charles., trans. *The Śūraṅgama Sūtra*. London: Rider & Co., 1966.

——. *The Vimalakīrti Nirdeśa Sūtra*. Berkeley: Shambhala, 1972.

Poussin, Louis, de La Vallée., trans. *L'Abhidharmakośa De Vasubandhu*. 6 vols. Paris: Paul Geuthner; Louvain, J.B. Istas, 1923-1931.

——. *Vijñaptimātratāsiddhi*: *La Siddhi de Hiuan-Tsang*. Paris: Librairie Orientaliste Paul Geuthner, 1928.

Śāntideva. *Bodhicaryāvatāra*. Translated by Marion L. Matcs. London: Macmillan Co., 1970.

———. *Śiksha-Samuccaya*. Translated by Cecil Bendall and W.H.D. Rouse. Delhi: Motilal Banarsidass, 1971.

Soothill, W.E., trans. *The Lotus of the Wonderful Law*. Oxford: Clarendon Press, 1930.

Stcherbatsky, F. Th., trans. *Madhyānta-Vibhaṅga*. Soviet Indology Series, No. 5; reprint ed., Calcutta: Indian Studies, 1971.

———. "A short Treatise of Logic by Dharmakirti with its commentary by Dharmottara," in *Buddhist Logic*, Vol. 2, pp. 1-253. Leningrad: Academy of Sciences of the U.S.S.R., 1930; reprint ed., New York: Dover Publications, 1962.

Suzuki, Daisetz Teitaro, trans. *The Laṅkāvatāra Sūtra*. London: Routledge & Kegan Paul, 1932.

Takasaki, Jikido, trans. *A Study on the Ratnagotravibhāga*. Rome: Instituto Italiano per il Medio ed Estremo Oriente, 1966.

Tucci, Giuseppe., ed. and trans. *Minor Buddhist Texts, Part One*. Rome: Instituto Italiano Per il Medio ed Estremo Oriente, 1956.

Arahant Upatissa. *The Path of Freedom*. Translated by N.R.M. Ehara, Soma Thera and Kheminda Thera. Ceylon: D. Weerasuria, 1961.

Vasubandhu. *Wei Shih Er Shih Lun*. Translated by Clarence H. Hamilton. New Haven: American Oriental Society, 1938.

Wayman, Alex, and Wayman, Hideko., trans. *The Lion's Roar of Queen Śrīmālā*. New York: Columbia University Press, 1974.

Yampolsky, Philip, B., trans. *The Platform Sūtra of the Sixth Patriarch*. New York: Columbia University Press, 1967.

Secondary Sources: Books

Berry, Thomas. *Buddhism*. New York: Thomas Y. Crowell Co., 1975.

Bharati, Agehananda. *The Tantric Tradition*. New York: Doubleday, 1965.

Chang, Garma, C.C. *The Buddhist Teaching of Totality*. University Park: Pennsylvania State University Press, 1971.

Chatterjee, Ashok Kumar. *The Yogācāra Idealism*. 2nd ed. Delhi: Motilal Banarsidass, 1975.

Ch'en, Kenneth. *Buddhism in China*. Princeton: Princeton University Press, 1964.

Conze, Edward. *Buddhist Thought in India*. London: George Allen & Unwin, 1962; reprint ed., Ann Arbor: The University of Michigan Press, Ann Arbor Paperbacks, 1967.

———. *The Prajñāpāramitā Literature*. The Hague: Mouton & Co., 1966.

Dasgupta, Surendranath. "Philosophy of the *Laṅkāvatāra*." In *Buddhistic Studies*, pp. 859-876. Edited by B.C. Law. Calcutta, 1932.

De Bary, William Theodore., ed. The *Buddhistic Tradition*. New York: Random House, Vintage Books, 1972.

Dumoulin, Heinrich. *A History of Zen Buddhism*. New York:

Random House, 1963; reprint ed., Boston: Beacon Press, 1969.

———. *Zen Enlightenment*. New York: John Weatherhill, 1979.

Goddard, Dwight. *Self-Realization of Noble Wisdom: a Version Based on Dr. Suzuki's Translation of the Laṅkāvatāra Sūtra*. Thetford, 1932.

Govinda, Lama Anagarika. *The Psychological Attitude of Early Buddhist Philosophy*. London: Rider & Co., 1961.

Guenther, Herbert V. *Buddhist Philosophy in Theory and Practice*. Boulder: Shambhala, 1967.

———. *Tibetan Buddhism Without Mystification*. Leiden: E.J. Brill, 1966.

Hsiang-Kuang, Chou. *The History of Chinese Buddhism*. Allahabad: Indo-Chinese Literature Publications, 1956.

Jayatilleke, K.N. *Early Buddhist Theory of Knowledge*. London: George Allen & Unwin, 1963.

Keith, A. Berriedale. *Buddhist Philosophy in India and Ceylon*. Varanasi: The Chowkhamba Sanskrit Studies, 1963.

Kim, Hee-Jin. *Dogen Kigen-Mystical Realist*. Tucson: The University of Arizona Press, 1975.

Lancaster, Lewis, ed. *Prajñāpāramitā and Related Systems*. Berkeley Buddhist Studies Series, no. 1 Berkeley: University of California and the Institute of Buddhist Studies, 1977.

Lévi Sylvain. *Matériaux Pour L'Étude Du Système Vijñaptimātra*. Paris: Librairie Ancienne Honoré Champion, 1932.

Mookerjee, S. *The Omniscient as the Founder of a Religion*. Nava-Nalanda: Mahavihara Research Publication, 2.

Murti, T.R.V. *The Central Philosophy of Buddhism*. 2nd ed. London: George Allen & Unwin, 1970.

Ramanan, K. Venkata. *Nāgārjuna's Philosophy*. Rutland: Charles E. Tuttle Co., 1966; reprint ed. Delhi: Motilal Banarsidass, 1975.

Robinson, Richard H. *Early Mādhyamika in India and China*. Medison: The University of Wisconsin Press, 1967.

Ruegg, David Seyfort. *La Théorie Du Tathāgatagarbha et Du Gotra*. Paris: Ecole Francaise D'Extreme-Orient, 1969.

Sangharakshita, Bhikshu. *A Survey of Buddhism*. 5th ed. Boulder: Shambala, 1980.

Sarathchandra, R. *Buddhist Psychology of Perception*. Colombo, 1958.

Stcherbatsky, F. Th. *Buddhist Logic*. 2 vols. Leningrad: Academy of Sciences of the U.S.S.R., 1930; reprint ed., New York: Dover Publications, 1962.

———. *The Central Conception of Buddhism (and the Meaning of the Word "Dharma")*. Calcutta: Susil Gupta, 1956.

Streng, Frederick J. *Emptiness, A Study in Religious Meaning*. Nashville: Abingdon Press, 1967.

Suzuki, Daisetz Teitaro. *Studies in the Laṅkāvatāra Sūtra*. London: 1930; reprint ed., London: Routledge & Keagan Paul, 1957.

Takakusu, Junjiro. *The Essentials of Buddhist Philosophy*. 3rd ed. Edited by Wing-Tsit Chen and Charles A. Moore. Honolulu: Office Appliance Co., Ltd., 1956.

Thomas, Edward J. *The History of Buddhist Thought*. New York: Barnes & Noble, 1951.

Verdu, Alfonso. *Dialectical Aspects in Buddhist Thought*. International Studies, East Asian Series, no. 8. University of Kansas: Centre for East Asian Studies, 1974.

Waddell, L. Austine. *Tibetan Buddhism*. New York: Dover Publications, 1972.

Zurcher, E. *The Buddhist Conquest of China*. Leiden: E.J. Brill, 1959.

Secondary Sources: Articles

Conze, Edward. "The Mahāyāna Treatment of the Viparyāsas." Oriens Extremus 9 (1962): 34-46.

———. "The Ontology of the Prajñāpāramitā." *Philosophy East and West* 2 (1953): 117-130.

Demieville, Paul. "Sur l'authenticité du Ta Tch'ing K'i Sin Louen." *Bulletin de la Maison Franco-Japonaise*, no. 2, 2 (1929): 1-78.

Dutt, N. "Tathāgatagarbha." *Indian Historical Quarterly* 33 (1957): 26-39.

Frauwallner, V.E. "Amalavijñānam und Ālayavijñānam." *Beitrage zur Indischen Philologie und Altertumskunde* (Festschrift W. Schubring, Hamburg, 1951): 148ff.

Hamilton, Clarence Herbert. "Hsüan Chuang and the Wei Shih Philosophy." *Journal of the American Oriental Society* 51 (1931): 291-308.

Jaini, P. "The Sautrāntika theory of Bīja." *Bulletin of the School of Oriental (and African) Studies* 22 (1959): 236-249.

———. "Theory of Viprayuktasaṃskāras." *Bulletin of the School of Oriental (and African) Studies* 22 (1959): 537.

Kunst, MM.A. "The Principle of the Excluded Middle in Buddhism." *Rocznik Orientalistyczny* 21 (1957): 141-147.

Liebenthal, V.W. "New Light on the 'Awakening of Faith'." *T'oung Pao* 46 (1958): 155-216.

Masson-Oursel, Paul. "Tathāgatagarbha et Ālayavijñāna." *Journal* Asiatique 210 (1927): 295-302.

Nakamura, H. "Buddhist Logic Expounded by Means of Symbolic Logic." *Indogaku Bukkyogaku Kenkyu*, no. 7, 1 (1958): 1ff.

———. "Critical Survey of Mahāyāna and Esoteric Buddhism." *Acta Asiatica* 6 (1964): 70.

———. "Critical Survey of Mahāyāna and Esoteric Buddhism." *Acta Asiatica* 7 (1964): 49ff. & 63ff.

Obermiller, E. "A Study of the Twenty Aspects of Śūnyatā." *Indian Historical Quarterly* 9 (1933): 170 ff.

———. "The Term 'Śūnyatā' and its Different Interpretations." *Journal of the Greater India Society* 1 (1934): 105ff.

Poussin, Louis de La Vallée. "Notes sur l'Ālayavijñāna." *Mélanges Chinois et Bouddhiques* 3 (1934-1935): 151, 166-167; 5 (1937): 231ff.

———. "Reflexions sur le Mādhyamika." *Mélanges Chinois et Bouddhiques* 2 (1933): 40.

Ruegg, David Seyfort. "On the dGe lugs pa Theory of the Tathāgatagarbha." *Pratidānam* (Mélanges F.B.J. Kuiper, La Haye, 1968): 500-509.

Shively, D. "Buddhahood for the Non-Sentient." *Harvard Journal of Asiatic Studies* 20 (1957): 135-161.

Solomon, E.A. "Problems of Omniscience." *ALB* 26 (1962): 36 ff.

Tamaki, Kōshirō. "The Development of the Thought of Tathāgatagarbha From India to China." *Journal of Indian and Buddhist Studies*, no. 1, 9 (1961): 378-386.

Tucci, Giuseppe. "Notes on *Laṅkāvatāra*." *Indian Historical Quarterly*, no. 4, 4 (1928): 630-636.

Unno, T. "The Buddhatā theory of Fa-tsang." *Transactions International Conference of Orientalists in Japan* 8 (1963): 34-41.

Vidyabhushan, Satis Chandra. "An Analysis of the *Laṅkāvatāra Sūtra*." *Journal of the Royal Asiatic Society of Bengal* 1 (1906): 159-164.

———. "Notes on the Laṅkāvatāra Sūtra." *Journal of the Royal Asiatic Society* (1905): 831-837.

INDEX

BUDDHIST TRADITION SERIES

General Editor: ERNST STEINKELLNER
Joint General Editor: ALEXANDER VON ROSPATT
Founder Editor: Late ALEX WAYMAN
ISBN: 978-81-208-0287-2

1 Indian Buddhism—*Hajime Nakamura*
2 Nagarjuniana—*Chr. Lindtner*
3 Chinese Monks in India—*Latika Lahiri*
4 Buddhism in Central Asia—*B.N. Puri*
5 Dharmakīrti's Theory of Hetu-Centricity of Anumāna—*M. R. Chinchore*
6 The Legend of King Aśoka—*John S. Strong*
7 Buddhist Insight—*George R. Elder*
8 Buddhism Transformed—*Richard Gombrich* and *Gananath Obeyesekere*
9 The Buddhist Tantras—*Alex Wayman*
10 The Lion's Roar of Queen Śrīmālā —*Alex Wayman* and *Hideko Wayman*
11 The Buddha Nature—*Brian E. Brown*
12 Evolution of Stupas in Burma —*Sujata Soni*
13 Buddhist Parables—*E. W. Burlingame*
14 The Debate of King Milinda —*Bhikkhu Pesala*
15 The Chinese Madhyama Āgama and the Pāli Majjhima Nikāya—*Bhikṣu Thich Minh Chau*
16 Sudden and Gradual—*Peter N. Gregory*
17 Yoga of the Guhyasamājatantra—*Alex Wayman*
18 The Enlightenment of Vairocana —*Alex Wayman* and *R. Tajima*
19 A History of Indian Buddhism—Tr. *Hirakawa Akira*, Ed. *Paul Groner*
20 Introduction to the Buddhist Tantric Systems—*F.D. Lessing* and *Alex Wayman*
21 Anāgatavaṃsa Desanā—Tr. *Udaya Meddegama*, Ed. *John Clifford Holt*
22 Chinnamastā—*Elisabeth Anne Benard*
23 On Voidness—*Fernando Tola* and *Carmen Dragonetti*
24 Nāgārjuna's Refutation of Logic (Nyāya) Vaidalyaprakaraṇa—*Fernando Tola* and *Carmen Dragonetti*
25 The Buddhist Art of Nāgārjunakoṇḍa —*Elizabeth Rosen Stone*
26 Discipline—*John C. Holt*
27 Philosophy and its Development in the Nikāyas and Abhidhamma —*Fumimaro Watanabe*
28 Untying the Knots in Buddhism —*Alex Wayman*
29 Early Buddhist Theory of Knowledge —*K. N. Jayatilleke*
30 Calming the Mind and Discerning the Real—Tr. *Alex Wayman*
31 A Comparative Study of the Prātimokṣa—*W. Pachow*
32 The Rise of Esoteric Buddhism in the Tibet—*Eva M. Dargyay*
33-35 Saṃyuktābhidharmahṛdaya (3 Parts) —*Bart Dessein*
36 A Millennium of Buddhist Logic —*Alex Wayman*
37 The Buddhist Pilgrimage—*Duncan Forbes*
38 Chanting the Names of Mañjuśrī —*Alex Wayman*
39 The Literature of the Personalists of Early Buddhism—*Bhikshu Thich Thien Chau*
40 The Laṅkāvatāra Sūtra—*D.T. Suzuki*
41 Studies in the Laṅkāvatāra Sūtra —*D.T. Suzuki*
42 The Vimalakīrti Sūtra—*Burton Watson*
43 The Gāndhārī Dharmapada—*John Brough*
44 Imaging Wisdom—*Jacob N. Kinnard*
45 Pain and Its Ending—*Carol S. Anderson*
46 Apparitions of the Self—*Janet Gyatso*
47-49 Rules for Nuns according to the Dharma-guptakavinaya (3 Parts) —*Ann Heirman*
50 The Chinese Hevajratantra—*Ch. Willemen*
51 The Historical Buddha—*H. W. Schumann*
52 Dana—*Ellison Banks Findly*
53 Hermeneutics & Tradition in the *Saṃdhinirmocana-sūtra*—*John Powers*
54 Skillful Means—*John W. Schroeder*
55 The Two Truths in Chinese Buddhism —*Chang-Qing Shih*
56 The Bodhisattva Path—*Jan Nattier*
57 Becoming the Buddha—*Donald K. Swearer*
58 Approaching the Land of Bliss —*Richard K. Payne* & *Kenneth K. Tanaka*
59 Indian Monastic Buddhism: Collected papers on Textual, Inscriptional and Archaeological Evidence— *Gregory Schopen*